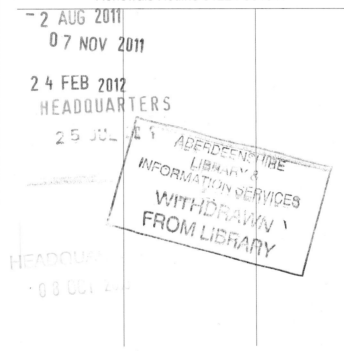

MAGPIES, SQUIRRELS & THIEVES

MAGPIES, SQUIRRELS & THIEVES

HOW THE VICTORIANS COLLECTED THE WORLD

JACQUELINE YALLOP

Atlantic Books
London

First published in Great Britain in 2011 by Atlantic Books, an imprint of
Atlantic Books Ltd.

Copyright © 2011 by Jacqueline Yallop

10 9 8 7 6 5 4 3 2 1

A CIP catalogue record for this book is available from the British Library.

ISBN: 978 1 84354 750 1

Printed in Great Britain by the MPG Books Group

Atlantic Books
An imprint of Atlantic Books Ltd
Ormond House
26–27 Boswell Street
London
WC1N 3JZ
www.atlantic-books.co.uk

'Things' were, of course, the sum of the world.

Henry James, *The Spoils of Poynton*, 1897

Contents

Pride, Passion and Loss: Collecting for Love
JOSEPH MAYER

Fashion, Fine Dining and Forgeries: Dealing in Society
MURRAY MARKS

Collecting the Empire: In Pursuit of the Exotic
STEPHEN WOOTTON BUSHELL

List of Illustrations

1. The South Court at the South Kensington Museum. *Illustrated London News* (6 December 1862). © Illustrated London News Ltd/Mary Evans.

2. Portrait of John Charles Robinson by J. J. Napier. © National Portrait Gallery, London.

3. Robinson's collection at Newton Manor. © Ashmolean Museum, University of Oxford.

4. Portrait of Charlotte Schreiber by George Frederic Watts. From Charlotte Schreiber's *Journals: confidences of a collector of ceramics and antiques throughout Britain, France, Holland, Belgium, Spain, Portugal, Turkey, Austria and Germany from the year 1869–1885* (1911).

5. Portrait of Charles Schreiber by George Frederic Watts. From Charlotte Schreiber's *Journals: confidences of a collector of ceramics and antiques throughout Britain, France, Holland, Belgium, Spain, Portugal, Turkey, Austria and Germany from the year 1869–1885* (1911).

6. Gourd-shaped bottle. Courtesy of Sotheby's Picture Library.

7. Portrait of Dante Gabriel Rossetti and Theodore Watts-Dunton by Henry Treffry Dunn. © National Portrait Gallery, London.

8. The Peacock Room. Freer Gallery of Art, Smithsonian Institution, Washington, D.C. Gift of Charles Lang Freer, F1904.61.

MAGPIES, SQUIRRELS & THIEVES

Preface

oday we are accustomed to the mechanisms that allow collectors to build a collection: auctions and antique dealers, car-boot sales and internet trading sites. We expect to have public collections in town and city museums, even if we rarely visit them. The motivations that drive collectors have frequently been examined by psychologists and psychoanalysts, and this has given us some understanding of why collecting is such a popular activity and how it can become so obsessive. What I want to do with this book is to take a step back, to a period during the nineteenth century when many of the aspects of collecting which we now take for granted were being newly explored, when collectors were emerging into the public eye and when the hunt for objects was at its most inventive and eccentric. The thrills and perils of Victorian collecting will, in some respects, appear very familiar; it was the collectors of the nineteenth century who laid the foundations for later collectors and many of their networks remain. In other ways, however, we will discover outlooks and experiences very different from those which collectors might expect today. Victorian collecting had a character of its own, and it is this robust and intrepid spirit of adventure that I hope to convey.

There was no single archetypal Victorian collector: individual tastes meant that one collection was very different from another. Some collections were ordered, scholarly or scientific; others were quirky, highly personal narratives. Changes in fashions, attitudes and economic climate also influenced the objects people chose to collect. This book presents the stories of five collectors to give some sense of this diversity and of the ways in which collecting evolved through the nineteenth century. It also uses these individual stories to explore more general issues about collecting. What is a 'collection'? What kind of cultural, social and political factors influence the life of a collection? What drives the collector? What is the relationship between the private collector and the public museum?

Each of my five collectors left lively archives, letters or journals which document their collecting and each has a fascinating story to tell. Between them, they turned their attention to all kinds of art and historical objects. John Charles Robinson was an influential curator at the South Kensington Museum, which would be renamed the Victoria and Albert Museum in 1899, becoming one of the most famous public collections in the world. He collected both for the museum and for himself, indulging a taste for significant, and often expensive, pieces of art and becoming a specialist in the Italian Renaissance. Lady Charlotte Schreiber, the widow of a steel magnate and an intrepid traveller, sought out china and playing cards, fans and glass in showrooms and junkshops across Europe. Murray Marks, a dealer as well as a collector, used his connections in Holland to exploit the fashion for blue-and-white ceramics and his friendship with the Pre-Raphaelites to create elaborate domestic interiors. Liverpool jeweller Joseph Mayer had a taste for Roman remains, Egyptian antiquities, coins, Anglo-Saxon archaeology and quirky objects from history. Stephen Wootton Bushell was sent to China as doctor to the British delegation and ended up becoming a pioneering expert on Chinese art.

The five individual stories offer a portrait of the collector, from the eccentric and obsessive to the scholarly and the professional. Together, they also show us how art-collecting changed during the Victorian period, moving away from the great pictures and sculpture that had fascinated the wealthy in the eighteenth century towards smaller, more varied decorative objects. Science and natural history collections, which were equally popular and active at this time, could not be covered within the scope of the book, but it is worth bearing in mind that this created yet another growing community of collectors, working alongside – and occasionally overlapping – with art collectors. For those whose tastes lay towards stuffed animals, geological specimens or mechanical instruments, there was a correspondingly influential and flourishing network of organizations, museums and collectors to feed their enthusiasm.

None of my five collectors is well known. Even John Charles Robinson has been little studied; in comparison to his colleague at the South Kensington Museum, Henry Cole, his work has been overlooked. Only some of the objects from their collections were important and valuable; some were just as much a demonstration of individual taste or little more than a frivolous purchase. None of the collections survives intact to be seen now. But each one was significant in its own time; some were even famed. And, taken together, these five histories give an insight into a Victorian phenomenon that went much further than just a handful of extraordinary lives, revealing a passion for collecting that helped shape how we see the nineteenth century and the legacy it has bequeathed to us today.

Catching
the Collecting Bug

CHAPTER ONE

Exhibition Road, London, 1862

It was a hot June day in 1862. South Kensington was bustle and dust and noise, as it had been for months. Horses, carriages and omnibuses moved slowly in the packed streets. On Exhibition Road, on a site that would, in twenty years' time, become home to the terracotta columns of the Natural History Museum, two great glass domes shone in the sun. They formed the extravagant centrepiece of the London International Exhibition of Industry and Art, an enormous fair of artworks and manufactures from across the world in the tradition of the 1851 Great Exhibition. Visitors queued at the entrances, eager to see what was on show, crowds inside pushed their way through the glittering displays and Victorian London was, once again, in thrall to the excitement of spectacle.

Sponsored by the Society for the Encouragement of Arts, Manufactures and Commerce, the new exhibition boasted 28,000 exhibitors from thirty-six countries. The specially erected building, designed by government engineer and architect Captain Francis Fowke, covered 23 acres of land, with two huge wings set aside for large-scale agricultural equipment and machinery, including a cotton mill and maritime engines, and a façade almost 1,200 feet long, of high arched windows, corner pavilions, columns and flags. At a cost of almost half a million pounds, the exhibition was intended to dazzle and impress even those who had visited the Crystal Palace extravaganza a decade earlier, and the two crystal domes of Fowke's design, each 260 feet high and 160 feet in diameter, were then the largest domes in the world, wider than (although not quite as high as) both St Paul's in London and St Peter's in Rome.

Not everyone liked the building. The popular press seemed to think the vast domes resembled nothing so much as colossal overturned soup bowls; *Building News* joined other national papers in describing it as 'one of the ugliest public buildings that was ever raised'.[1] But the exhibition inside was very much an attraction. In the six months of its life, between 1 May and 1 November 1862, over 6 million visitors paid between a shilling and a pound, depending on the day, to see new inventions, industrial machinery, home wares, works of art and the occasional splendid folly, such as the huge pillar of gold sent from the Australian gold rush. Not to be put off by a touch of architectural vulgarity, the London crowds flocked to the display galleries where bootmakers rubbed shoulders with baronets; young designers sketched ideas; whiskered manufacturers confided trade secrets; pickpockets, no doubt, flourished, and everyone had a good time.

The taste for this kind of event was by now well established; most visitors already knew how to negotiate the vast spaces and overwhelming displays. They liked the bewildering array of exhibits, the crowded corridors and the chance to see and be seen. Not only the 1851 Great Exhibition, but other international exhibitions such as the 1855 Paris Exhibition and, closer to home, the 1857 Art Treasures Exhibition in Manchester, had accustomed the Victorians to the idea of huge and eclectic displays, sparkling showcases for the most beautiful, the most efficient and the most innovative. Even those who had never before visited such an exhibition would have read about them in the newspapers, and seen all kinds of prints and photographs of what they had been missing. This new event filled the front pages of the press: the *Illustrated London News* was just one of the papers to issue a special event supplement, and to use its editorials to update readers with news of the exhibition's progress. Visitors came to the International Exhibition at South Kensington expecting to be amazed and entertained by the practical, the pioneering and the extraordinary.

The objects brought together under Fowke's clumsy crystal domes included everything from a working forge to sewing machines, from slates and rock salt to the Brazilian 'Star of the South' diamond. The exhibition was a symbol of mid-Victorian aspiration, manufacturing success and consumer confidence. It was a message to the world about the ambition of Britain and its Empire. But to the millions of visitors that pushed through the crowded galleries, it was also, quite simply, a chance to admire and desire beautiful and unusual things. It evoked, on an enormous scale, the Victorian idea of the collection and what it might mean to bring things together, to compare them, to own and value them, to present them in public with pride.

It was not only the brightly painted and lavishly ornamented arcades of the International Exhibition that hummed with activity. On the other side of Exhibition Road, more objects and more collections were attracting public interest. The new South Kensington Museum, which had been emerging since 1857 in a mish-mash of temporary buildings, was also noisy and crowded. The recently opened permanent galleries of the North and South Courts – also designed by Francis Fowke – more than rivalled the glamour and glitter across the road. Here, too, there was a glass roof to let in light and air. Boldly painted walls in deep blood-red and purple grey prepared the eye for corridors packed with elaborate highly coloured arrays of patterned wallpapers, mosaics, friezes and stained glass. Here, too, visitors clustered close together around cases of fascinating and attractive things, preening, laughing and flirting, enjoying the buzz. Voices, and the chink of fine china, drifted from the mock-Tudor refreshment rooms where colourful flocks of women took afternoon tea; in the new display spaces collectors, connoisseurs and the simply curious marvelled at some of the world's finest art objects brought together for the delight of the public.

This was the 'Special Exhibition of Works of Art of the Medieval, Renaissance, and more Recent Periods, on loan at the South Kensington Museum', a complementary – or perhaps rival – attraction to the more manufacturing-based displays across the road. The catalogue played down the ambition of the exhibition, describing it simply as 'fine works of bygone periods', which had been made possible with 'the assistance of noblemen and gentlemen, eminent for their knowledge of art'.[2] In fact, the displays featured some of the rarest and most beautiful objects ever set before the British general public, over 9,000 works of art from over 500 of the country's richest and most influential owners, from the Queen, aristocracy and the Church, to London livery companies, municipal corporations and public schools. These were private treasures, not normally on open display, brought together for the first and only time – a triumph of negotiation and diplomacy.

The exhibition covered over 500 years of art production, and included all kinds of media, from painting, ceramic and glass, to metal, ivory and textiles. Objects were organized in the catalogue into forty categories, which more or less corresponded to the layout of the galleries. There was no chronological arrangement to the displays, which were bewildering in their haphazard glamour and sheer abundance. Beginning with sculptures in marble and terracotta, the exhibition moved on to nearly 300 carvings in ivory, bronzes, furniture, Anglo-Saxon metalwork, enamels, jewellery and glass, textiles and illuminated manuscripts. There was a Sèvres porcelain vase in the form of a ship painted with cupids and flowers; a Limoges enamel casket, one of the many enamels on display from the collection of the Duke of Hamilton; a silver-gilt handbell which 'doubtless' came from the chamber of Mary Queen of Scots; and a modest pair of Plymouth porcelain salt cellars, in the form of shells, belonging to the Right Honourable William Gladstone MP.

Contributors had loaned not only individual objects but sometimes entire collections, often with ancient family roots. This was particularly true in the case of bookbindings, portrait miniatures, jewellery and cameos, the popular mainstays of country-house collections: 'The Devonshire Gems', for example, assembled in the eighteenth century by William Cavendish, 3rd Duke of Devonshire, was displayed in its entirety, apart from eighty-eight of the cameos which had already been committed to the International Exhibition. So extensive and unique was the collection, and so difficult to assess in the short period of time that had been given over to organizing the exhibition, that the catalogue was forced to confine itself to listing just a few 'of the finest gems'.

The show was designed to delight and amaze, without reference to the grind of manufacture and industrial production that was the backbone of the displays at the International Exhibition. Its emphasis was on the romantic and the historic, and it focused public attention on the beauty of medieval and Renaissance objects for the first time, introducing unknown styles and techniques. The press marvelled at a display that was 'unequalled in the world' and 'rich beyond all compute and precedent', and the chance to see rare works of art drew visitors from across the country.[3] But this was not just a splendid art exhibition: with objects from over 500 collectors, each of whom was named on labels and in the catalogue, the resplendent galleries were specifically designed to bear witness to the richness and variety of British collecting. The packed cases clearly showed how deeply embedded was the idea of the collection, both in national institutions like the monarchy and in the private lives of many of the country's wealthiest and most influential men and women. And over a million visitors – more than a third of the population of London – came to the new museum to see the displays, suggesting how great was the public appetite for the beautiful and quirky, and how widespread the curiosity about, and commitment to, collecting.

Making all this possible was one man – John Charles Robinson. Robinson was a collector himself, a connoisseur, but he was also Librarian-Curator at the South Kensington Museum where he had responsibility for buying objects, researching the collections and, as the exhibition triumphantly demonstrated, creating public displays. Crucial to all of this activity, for Robinson, was nurturing a community of collectors, creating an intimate mutual relationship between individuals and the museum that would benefit everyone. And at the heart of this community, he put himself. He knew all the most active and influential collectors, dealers and scholars; he made some of the most glamorous and talked-about transactions. It was Robinson's influential network of contacts that turned the Special Exhibition from a modest display of private loans to the stunning art show that greeted the South Kensington visitors.

Robinson was a founder member of the Fine Arts Club, a London-based club of wealthy collectors. In 1858, he wrote to his superiors at South Kensington to suggest that he and his collecting colleagues should organize a small and select display of historical art, as an adjunct to the forthcoming International Exhibition. It would provide something extra, he suggested, for those whose tastes inclined towards older and more refined pieces than would be included in the trade-based displays at the International Exhibition; it would recognize that the public's interest in all kinds of art had been stimulated by events like the Manchester Art Treasures Exhibition in the previous year, when over a million visitors, from royalty to cotton-mill workers, had clamoured to see everything from sculpture and armour to photographic montages and Limoges enamels. Permission for the loan show was given, but there were plenty of sceptics who were quick to dismiss the proposal, and members of the press warned that Robinson's enterprise would be 'overshadowed by its imposing and all-absorbing neighbour, and. . . be recognized only by the connoisseur'.[4]

Robinson, however, had other ideas. Through the Fine Arts Club, he formed a committee of seventy of the nation's most influential collectors, including the aristocracy and clergy, eight Members of Parliament and Sir Charles Eastlake, President of the Royal Academy and Director of the National Gallery. Between them, these men knew almost every collector in the land. Robinson's exhibition became a rallying point, a prestigious and glamorous event that celebrated collecting. 'Private cabinets were thrown open with an alacrity which showed that the only offence to be feared was not rifling them enough. . .' marvelled the *Quarterly Review*. 'The great floodgate was opened.'[5] Over the coming months, more and more treasures were pledged to the exhibition until the organizers were swamped by both the sheer volume of objects they were being offered and the practical demands of getting everything safely to the London galleries.

When the exhibition finally opened its doors, it was something of a triumph, a tribute to Robinson's unrivalled network and what the international press called his 'incessant activity'.[6] Probably no one else could have made it happen. It clearly showed the value of bringing works of art together for comparison, and it began to inspire a new taste for the medieval and the Renaissance, then obscure periods that had received little critical attention. Robinson's scholarly catalogue, too, was recognized by specialists as 'a work of the highest importance'.[7] But perhaps more than anything else, the exhibition signalled to the world the extent of Victorian collecting. For the first time, it offered a glimpse of just how many collectors there might be. It gave a sense of the shared and irrepressible enthusiasm that brought together so many of the country's men and women, and it revealed the range and magnificence of the objects they collected. It brought into the open a fascination with things that was shaping people's homes, forging municipal and national identities, and putting the collector at the heart of an increasingly commodified world.

CHAPTER TWO

The Useful and the Beautiful

*I*n all kinds of ways, the buzz of activity at South Kensington during 1862 was a legacy of the enormously successful 1851 Great Exhibition, a monumental enterprise that had as much influence on political, economic and social life as it did on art, science and technology. Like the 1862 International Exhibition, the earlier event was organized by the Society for the Encouragement of Arts, Manufactures and Commerce, which had been established in 1754 to support activities as diverse as spinning, carpet manufacture, tree-planting and painting. It soon became known informally as the Society of Arts (finally to become the Royal Society of Arts in 1908) and by the 1760s it was holding regular exhibitions, both of contemporary art and industrial innovations. But these were relatively modest affairs and there was little British precedent for such a huge and ambitious undertaking as the Great Exhibition. What is now commonly recognized as a landmark of Victorian achievement was a courageous experiment, and almost didn't take place at all.

The exhibition was intended to restore the fortunes of British trade and manufacturing, by showing off British endeavour, bringing together the best of the world's products as an inspiration to business and providing models for the future. A 'Select Committee on Arts and their connection with Manufactures' reported to the government as early as 1835 that both manufacturers and the public needed educating in matters of art and design. Pandering to a public appetite for novelty, and with an eye on keeping production costs to a minimum, British design standards were falling. Skills were dwindling and foreign competitors were flourishing. In the shops and department stores increasingly powerful middle-class consumers were flexing their spending muscles in unexpected directions, choosing goods from rival countries – tableware and furniture from France, Italian ornaments, and even glassware or jewellery imported from America. They were displaying what the government regarded as dubious taste; turning up their noses at traditional British wares and instead filling their drawing rooms with showy conversation-pieces that more obviously displayed their wealth and status. In the face of such competition, British manufacturers were suffering and the economy was faltering. What was needed was a showcase where examples of the best design could be displayed; where diligent manufacturers and aspiring young designers could come and study; where they could learn new skills and be inspired by new patterns.

In the course of the planning process leading up to 1851, however, and in response to the need to raise money and support for the project, the organizers attempted to head off public criticism by accommodating, wherever they could, all kinds of aspirations for the event. The apparently simple original plan – to raise the standards of British industrial design – was reshaped to take account of a range of other preoccupations and priorities. Local committees were established to help source objects and raise awareness and funds, but these often had their own agendas, from Chartism to women's rights. While on a national level it became clear that, to survive, the exhibition would need to reflect, among other things, the enthusiasm of the Prime Minister, Lord John Russell, for celebrating commercial liberalism and free trade; the desire of the influential East India Company to show off the Empire's raw materials; the Church's concern with illustrating divine benevolence; and the conviction of the liberal middle classes that the show should assert the British political and social model to the rest of the world. Not surprisingly, these pressures took their toll. The original intentions faded in the face of so many demands and the clear purpose of the exhibition faltered. The final display, while spectacular, was confused and often discordant, and the 'meaning' of the exhibition was further addled by the enormous variety of interpretations offered by the press and visiting public. No one could quite agree, it seemed, exactly what they were looking at.

Yet, despite these problems, the idea of the exhibition caught the popular imagination, both at home and abroad. Enough of the original focus on manufacture and trade remained to inspire generations of industrial spectacles across the world over the course of the century, while in the immediate aftermath it spurred the French into organizing a World Exhibition of their own, with an understandable emphasis on restoring French manufacturing and design to pre-eminence. The French, in fact, had already hosted an Industrial Exhibition in 1844 and had a tradition of official exhibitions of art and industry stretching back to the late eighteenth century. The London show, however, had been on a different scale, forcing organizers across the English Channel to redouble their efforts in response. The subsequent 1855 Paris Exhibition was even larger and more elaborate than the Great Exhibition had been, although it was significantly less successful financially (leaving a crippling shortfall of over 8 million francs) and visitor numbers were comparatively low. It succeeded in inflaming old Gallo-British rivalries even further, however, and driving home the idea that British design was still lagging behind its European counterpart. In London, there seemed nothing for it but to stage yet another event, bigger and better than any that had preceded it, demonstrating beyond doubt the technological progress that the British were making across the world. So work began on the 1862 International Exhibition and, despite financial setbacks, conflict in Italy and America which threatened to derail foreign loans, and the untimely death of Prince Albert in December 1861, just months before the scheduled opening, the show managed, in scale at least, to eclipse all others.

But the International Exhibition was not the only legacy of 1851 at South Kensington. Surplus funds from the Great Exhibition (around £180,000) were set aside to improve standards of science and art education, and parcels of land were bought around the district for a number of educational and cultural projects. One of these was the new museum, which had been in a temporary home at Marlborough House on Pall Mall, and which also inherited large numbers of objects from the Great Exhibition. Just as significantly, the museum's first Director, Henry Cole, had been a key organizer of both the 1851 and 1862 extravaganzas, and brought with him a commitment to the original Great Exhibition principles of improving standards in manufacturing, raising the quality of industrial design and educating public taste through the display of objects. Perhaps the greatest legacy of the 1851 exhibition, however, was the least tangible one: a growing sense that collecting and display was a serious, public affair. Coverage in the press, political debate and drawing-room gossip began to discuss, appraise and compare works of art, and in the wake of this enormous attention there was an increasing appreciation that objects could have profound personal and social meanings.

The Great Exhibition offered the most visible, spectacular evidence of a fascination with collecting that had been growing since the beginning of the century. It showed just how many issues might be inherent in the apparently simple idea of making a collection. And, as a result of this, there was increasingly open and varied debate about what kind of role art might have in public life, about the purpose of design, and about thorny questions of taste, patronage, ownership and education. This was a period when even many of the defining terms we take for granted today were new and the distinctions between them ambiguous: what, exactly, was a 'public' collection? What was a work of 'decorative' or 'applied' art? How could you define the difference between an amateur, a connoisseur and a professional? What was a curator's role?

Many of these questions would take decades to resolve; some are still being debated today. But what was immediately clear was that there was more interest than ever in what collecting might mean, and how collections might best be achieved. By the middle of the century, debates that had been rumbling for years, and which were implicit in the collecting activities of Robinson's influential colleagues and the wealthy members of the Fine Arts Club, were being aired ever more frequently in public. It was increasingly evident that collecting could not be seen as a private interest detached from events going on around it; it was part of a wider conversation inextricably linked to political ideology and social change. Robinson's 1862 loan exhibition came, in many ways, at the perfect time. It made collecting visible, topical and desirable at the moment when the discussions inspired by the Great Exhibition were reaching maturity.

Appointing Henry Cole as Director of the South Kensington Museum signalled the government's desire to continue with the work they had begun at the Great Exhibition. Intimately involved

19

with both the 1851 event and the 1862 International Exhibition, and publicly espousing the values behind them, Cole was an enthusiastic advocate for the campaign to improve standards and educate public taste. He would use the objects on display at the museum to show people what they could and could not like; what they did and did not want to buy. He would change habits and restore manufacturing fortunes. He would, he boasted, 'make the public hunger after the objects... then they [will] go to the shops and say, "We do not like this or that; we have seen something prettier at the Museum"; and the shop-keeper, who knows his own interest, repeats that to the manufacturer and the manufacturer, instigated by that demand, produces the article.'[1]

Even by Victorian standards, Cole was fiercely energetic, an apparently unstoppable force of opinions and activity. By the end of his life, in 1882, he was an institution, known as 'Old King Cole', but both his stubborn, temperamental approach and his reforming zeal tended to arouse admiration and antipathy in equal measure: 'His action has often been harshly criticized,' began his obituary in *The Times*. 'His untiring energy and perseverance have frequently made him enemies.'[2] He was a career civil servant; having joined the Public Record Office in 1823 at the age of fifteen, he was the author of a series of pamphlets advocating reform of the public record system. He wrote for a range of newspapers and journals and in 1840 won a prize for developing a workable Penny Postage plan. By the time he turned his attention to art and manufacturing, around 1845, he was already an experienced and confident administrator. He immediately began to assist the Society of Arts on a series of exhibitions to stimulate industry and invention, finally securing his place, according to his obituary, as 'the leading spirit and prime mover' of the reform impulses which led to the Great Exhibition.[3]

Following this success, Cole was invited in 1852 to reorganize the government Schools of Design. These had been established in twenty cities from 1837, one of the earliest indications of the government's commitment to design reform. Created by the Board of Trade, they were supposed to promote an establishment consensus on art and good taste, improving education and training new designers in approved styles and techniques. In practice, however, many of the Schools had concentrated as much on academic art as on industrial design and during the 1840s a series of internal battles raged over exactly what should be taught. Cole aimed to give the system a new sense of direction and control, and put the focus firmly back on to 'useful' skills. As the first step, he put the Schools under the control of a new Department of Practical Art, soon renamed the Department of Science and Art, a subdivision of the Board of Trade. He appointed himself Superintendent, and made clear his intention to direct things with a firm hand: the new department was to be managed from South Kensington, with his protégés slotted into key roles.

The new museum was part of the same package. It was seen as another weapon in the battle for design reform, working alongside the Schools but with a more public emphasis. It fell under the same umbrella at the Department of Science and Art, which meant there was no independent board of Trustees to distract or hinder Cole. It could build on the impetus that had been created by the two industrial exhibitions, giving a more permanent face to government policy and taking its place without restrictions as the flagship of a wider movement for improving practical education nationwide. The galleries were intended to be just as instructional as any school, driving home messages about art and its role in national life. Cole glowed with the righteousness of educational principles: in a rallying speech, he laid out his aim to 'woo the ignorant' and ensure objects at the museum were 'talked about and lectured upon' until no one could be left in any doubt about what constituted good taste.[4] No longer would the manufacturing and shopping public make bad choices: they had someone to guide them. The South Kensington Museum would be useful, practical and modern, displaying things that could be copied, redesigned and mass-produced, providing clear information about process and construction, and lucid explanations of design principles. It could show reproductions, if that's what it took to make a point. It would show art with a purpose; art which could, with Victorian skill and confidence, be made to shape the future.

As the museum's leading curator, Robinson worked closely with Cole in acquiring objects and arranging them for display. He supported the general principles of education at the museum but he did not fully share Cole's views about the importance of manufacture and the best ways to instruct and influence the public. His real interest was in beautiful and historical things, and he was convinced that he knew better than Henry Cole how to find, treasure and display them. His relationship with his employer was edgy and barbed, liable to erupt in furious explosions. Both men were obstinate, confident and opinionated, and their ambitions collided too frequently for comfortable coexistence. Robinson was not above claiming, in public, that Cole did not know very much about art; Cole struggled to assert his authority over his excitable curator. Inevitably, in time, the friction between them would rub bare uncontainable feelings of anger, disappointment and betrayal. Within a few years, working relations would sour beyond the point of no return. But for now Robinson bided his time. It was with the two contrasting displays either side of Exhibition Road that he made his case.

In many ways, the two men and their exhibitions represented opposing sides in the debate about the value of art that had been raging for over a century, but into which the Victorians had entered with particular gusto. Did art need to have a function or purpose, or could it exist for its own sake? How did one attach value to an object – because it was useful or because it was beautiful? Did art have to be linked to social and moral responsibility, or was it autonomous, following its own rules? Such questions had been exercising educated minds since Edmund Burke's influential *Philosophical Enquiry into the Origin of Our Ideas of the Sublime and Beautiful*, published in 1757, and the emergence of the Romantic movement's preoccupation with personal creativity and emotional and artistic truth at the end of the eighteenth century. Proposals to create a national gallery of art at the beginning of the nineteenth century had reinvigorated the debate, in and out of Parliament, setting the case for historic art against modern examples, and looking at ways of organizing displays to best make them meaningful. An exhibition of 'Ancient and Medieval Art' held by the Society of Arts in London in 1850 and the Art Treasures Exhibition in Manchester seven years later both linked the viewing of works of art to a useful purpose: 'To the Artist and Manufacturer, an opportunity is afforded of comparing the handiwork of ancient times with the productions of our own skill and ingenuity,' explained the 1850 catalogue, 'to the Amateur, means are supplied of correcting the taste and refining the judgement'.[5]

By the middle of the nineteenth century, the discussion was by no means confined to the intellectual elite. Most of those in the public eye, as well as those writing in the popular press, had an opinion. Nor was this a distinctly British trend: across Europe, museums, galleries and governments were discussing what kind of art to collect, and how to show it. Many successful mid-century Victorians considered the fine arts to be some kind of adjunct to the real business of mechanical invention and production, where value was attached to accuracy and originality. Others maintained that art could not be conflated with commerce and that its value was as much emotional as practical. Writers like Tennyson, the poet laureate, and painters like William Holman Hunt preferred their art with a moral message; advocates of the Arts and Crafts movement emphasized the utility and social community of craftsmanship; on the other side, critics like Walter Pater argued vehemently that formal, aesthetic qualities should take precedence over moral or narrative content. In 1857, the critic and writer John Ruskin launched a scathing attack on the South Kensington Museum because, in his opinion, 'fragments of really true and precious art are buried and polluted amidst a mass of loathsome modern mechanisms, fineries and fatuity'; ten years later, Matthew Arnold's influential series of articles, 'Culture and Anarchy', appeared in the *Cornhill Magazine*, exploring 'what culture really is, what good it can do, what is our own special need of it' and discussing the role of art in a rapidly changing world.[6] It was not a debate that was going to be resolved in the galleries of the South Kensington Museum: at the end of the nineteenth century, it was still a matter of intense argument as the Aesthetic movement and Oscar Wilde made an ostentatious case for 'Art for Art's Sake'. But many of the museum visitors would have been well versed in the discussion, and would have recognized in Robinson's loan exhibition an unexpected contrast to Henry Cole's usual principles of display. Robinson's emphasis on beauty and on collecting for pleasure set the display well apart from the paean to commercial progress that was Henry Cole's International Exhibition.

Robinson was clear on the point: for all Cole's hectoring, what visitors really wanted to see – what a museum was about – was the exhibition of the most exquisite and refined objects. 'What', he asked an audience at one of his lectures, 'is there to trust to but the silent refining influence of the monuments of Art themselves?'[7] Not lectures and labels, not modern mass-produced pieces straight from the production line, but the 'monuments' most able to assert their 'silent refining influence' – the medieval silverware, the exotic oriental screens, the jewelled Renaissance chalices. Robinson was a connoisseur: his enthusiasm for collecting went hand-in-hand with an appreciation of the beautiful. And, as the

THE USEFUL AND THE BEAUTIFUL

Victorians continued to debate the ways in which art might influence their lives, more and more people were making their allegiances evident by also choosing to collect, making space for objects in their homes because they liked them there and because the desire for lovely things seemed irrepressible.

CHAPTER THREE

A Public Duty and a Private Preoccupation

The mid-Victorian period saw a boom in collecting. Explorers and adventurers to new and distant lands brought back plants, seeds and shells, pinned butterflies, bright beetles and stuffed animals to fill the gardens and display cases of the natural history collector. Enthusiasts dug for fossils, dinosaur bones and geological specimens, while archaeologists unearthed beads, weapons and brooches to fill shelves and cabinets. Art collecting moved away from the country homes of the rich into the fashionable townhouses of the increasingly confident and wealthy middle classes, and in turn attention moved from Old Master paintings and sculptures to more domestic works in materials such as ceramic or glass. A trend for highly decorated parlours, stuffed with all kinds of pictures, statues and objects, became endemic: showing off a collection of curios sent out messages about social status, and helped the owner appear educated and cultured.

Collecting had long been part of the upper-class way of British life. Most of the country's leading families boasted a collection of art and sculpture, jewellery or elite porcelain such as Meissen or Sèvres. The tradition of the Grand Tour had been flourishing since the middle of the seventeenth century, serving not only as a cultural education and a rite of passage but also as an opportunity to add to the family's collection by buying up works of art to ship home. Collecting was considered a fit occupation for a gentleman, drawing on the habits of European royalty and the erudite tradition of the *Wunderkammer*, or cabinet of curiosities, which had emerged among the wealthy during the Renaissance. The custom for collecting was inextricably linked to power, prestige and riches: during the sixteenth century, the Holy Roman Emperor Rudolph II, for example, was an obsessive collector of paintings, and the seventeenth-century Archduke Leopold Wilhelm of Austria employed the Flemish painter David Teniers the Younger to care for a hugely expensive collection which boasted everything from works by Italian masters to Cromwellian souvenirs of the English Civil War. The fortunes of the royal and aristocratic houses of Europe were clearly reflected in the ebb and flow of their collections, which were regularly sold, moved or broken up as the result of marriage and war, gambling debts and revolution. The Orléans Collection of over 500 paintings was assembled at the beginning of the eighteenth century by the French prince Philippe II, Duke of Orléans and nephew of Louis XIV. Its core, however, already dated back to the 1600s when Swedish troops sacked Munich and Prague during the Thirty Years War, looting masses of objects including the Habsburg collections of Rudolph II and Emperor Charles V from Prague Castle. These were added to by Queen Christina of Sweden, with a particular focus on Renaissance and Roman art, before being sold off at her death in 1689 to cover her debts. When he bought the collection, Philippe II added to it extensively, investing in a range of prestigious works from all over Europe including many of the key pieces accumulated by Charles I of England, another avid collector. The collection was celebrated as one of the gems of European culture, housed in the magnificent Palais Royal in Paris, and asserting the power and splendour of the French monarchy.

When Philippe died in 1723, his pious son Louis inherited the collection. But his tastes were not the same as his father's, and he was alarmed by the subject matter of some of the paintings. In a fit of religious zeal, he attacked several of the most famous works with a knife, slashing Correggio's *Leda and the Swan* which depicted an erotic scene from Greek mythology, and ordering three more of Correggio's works to be cut up in the presence of his personal chaplain. The collection survived, but neither Louis nor his son, Louis Philippe, had the will or money to be active in their collecting, and at the end of the eighteenth century the pieces were put up for sale in a desperate attempt to pay off enormous debts. It was the complex political pressures and the financial uncertainty of the French Revolution which finally decided the fate of the collection, however. Extravagant displays of personal wealth and royal power were out of fashion, a liability, and in 1793, just as Louis Philippe was arrested at the height of the Reign of Terror, almost 200 paintings were shipped over to London's salerooms. In the months prior to his execution at the guillotine in November, negotiations were finalized for selling the rest of the collection, mainly Italian and French paintings, to a Brussels banker.

During the mid-seventeenth century and in the period following the French Revolution, political upheaval and changes in European social order saw many collections from the Continent, such as the Orléans collection, dispersed, relocated or re-formed. By contrast, in England the nineteenth century started with considerable security among the landed classes, with the aristocracy generally thriving and their collections benefiting from the distress of their European counterparts. But this gradually changed. In August 1848, *The Times* reported on the sale of the collection at Stowe, the home of the 2nd Duke of Buckingham and the first of numerous country-house sales that would have been unimaginable a couple of decades earlier. It was, the report explained, 'a spectacle of painfully interesting and gravely historical import . . . an ancient family ruined, their palace marked for destruction, and its contents scattered to the four winds of heaven'.[1] The auction was the first symptom of a lingering malaise among country estates that was to last throughout the century, and to bring more and more art treasures on to the open market. A changing economic climate favoured industry rather than land as a way of making money, and old families feeling the pinch often turned to the sale of at least part of their collections as a way of boosting funds.

In 1882, the Settled Land Act brought things to a head. The old system of entailment had prevented the sale of land and collections, keeping them intact. Property passed from generation to generation through the eldest son (or, in the event of there being no son, via another male relative). Under the rights of primogeniture, he held a lifetime's interest in the land, house and contents: he was not free to sell or divide anything. With the new Act, this age-old arrangement was overturned. Restrictions on the sale of property were lifted and the tenant for life was given much stronger powers for dealing with his inheritance. Suddenly, family collections could be viewed as marketable commodities, and so converted into cash – and treasures from the most venerable and celebrated collections soon came under the hammer. In 1882, immediately after the Act was passed, the Duke of Hamilton sold most of the contents of his South Lanarkshire palace for almost £400,000 (the equivalent today of over £30 million); two years later, at Blenheim Palace, the Duke of Marlborough was given leave to dispose of some of his family's collections in a series of sales. The 18,000 volumes of 'The Sunderland Library' raised

£60,000, and over the following years a collection of enamels and some of the palace's major works of art, including Raphael's *Madonna degli Ansidei*, were also sold.

The collectors who took advantage of these misfortunes were often members of the newly influential middle classes. After a series of complicated financial manoeuvres, much of the Orléans collection finally found a home in Britain when it was bought in 1798 by a consortium consisting of Francis Egerton, 3rd Duke of Bridgewater, a coal and canal magnate; his nephew Earl Gower; and the Duke of Carlisle. But, in a reflection of changing fortunes and tastes, it was to be broken up yet further. Only 94 of the 305 paintings were retained for the family galleries. The rest were sold on again, raising over £42,000 to cover expenses, finding their way into the hands of a range of buyers that included four painters, four MPs, six dealers, two bankers and six gentleman amateurs.[2] While the sale of the collection into the hands of the Duke of Bridgewater seemed at first to reinforce the impression of ownership by the aristocracy, it was the Duke's new wealth from manufacturing and trade, rather than ancient land rights, that made the deal possible. And the sales which followed showed even more clearly how the finest objects were moving out of the hands of the European elite into the homes of the middle classes – bankers and MPs, as well as those dealers who were making a profitable profession out of what had once been a royal diversion. Collections that had been as much a display of power and influence as cultural appreciation were being broken up and abridged. The very nature of collecting itself was beginning to be transformed.

On the death of the Duke of Bridgewater in 1803, his collection was put on semi-public exhibition in Westminster, open on Wednesday afternoons to those who wrote requesting a ticket, or to artists recommended by the Royal Academy. This was a further demonstration that the idea of the inaccessible, aristocratic treasure house was beginning to disappear. Increasingly, private collections were getting a public airing, some being bequeathed to national or regional galleries but many more occupying a grey area by allowing restricted access to a vetted group of visitors. It was a long way from full public access: the Bridgewater collection was exhibited grandly in Cleveland House with a staff of twelve luxuriously liveried attendants, giving an impression not unlike a private palace. But it offered the aspiring middle classes, in particular, new opportunities for viewing and it was an indication of changing perceptions of the role of collecting and collectors. Collecting was no longer the preserve of the very rich; objects that had once been in the collections of royalty were now finding their way into much more modest houses and on to sightseeing itineraries. The changing face of European society was being reflected in increasingly widespread opportunities to collect.

Paintings and sculpture, however, still demanded plenty of wall and floor space, and investing in Old Masters required a particular kind of education. In addition, around the middle of the century, there was a dramatic rise in the prices of the kinds of works collectors had traditionally sought. New directions had to be explored. More and more, the emerging middle-class collectors took an interest in different kinds of pieces, particularly those they could pick up at reasonably limited expense, such as old English glass or pewter, decorations for the home – including mirrors, vases and textiles – and objects which might prove to be a shrewd speculation, like Staffordshire ware or silver. Although one or two earlier collectors had been interested in these areas – most notably, perhaps, the eighteenth-century historian and politician Horace Walpole – they had, until now, been largely neglected. By the middle of the century, however, this was changing and several large-scale, highly public sales helped cement the idea that collecting had moved away from its traditional preoccupation with expensive masterpieces and was becoming accessible, educational and profitable. In particular, in 1855, Christie's in London undertook the sale of the collection of Ralph Bernal, who had died a year earlier. Bernal epitomized the new type of collecting. He was educated and cultured, but as a barrister and MP he was firmly middle class. His apparently mystical ability to hunt out treasure from ordinary bric-a-brac shops earned him the epithet 'lynx-eyed' in *The Connoisseur*, an illustrated magazine. And the £20,000 he had invested in his collection was turned into nearly £71,000 at the Christie's sale which lasted thirty-two days and was an extravaganza of the metalwork, ceramics, glass and miniatures that were beginning to fascinate collectors.[3]

The impulses that were evident in Britain were repeated across Europe as the political and social fabric was rethreaded. Shops and dealers sprang up in major urban centres to cater for the increasing number of collectors seeking out treasure. They were not just the aristocratic sons of the ruling European classes, professional artists or dilettantes; they were merchants and bankers, clergy, military officers, wives and mothers. There was a revolution in attitudes, suggesting everything was within reach, for more or less everybody. What made English collectors unique, however, was their taste for showing things off in their homes: 'They like to *live* surrounded by their pictures and antiquities,' marvelled Gustav Waagen, art historian and director of the Kaiser-Friedrich Museum (later the Bode Museum) in Berlin, something that was 'virtually unknown elsewhere in Europe'.[4]

This intimate relationship between a collector and his things intrigued the public. As more and more homes began to display the spoils of private collecting, so the press began to carry detailed coverage of major sales and to record the growing numbers of people seduced by the idea of the collection. After the Bernal auction, *Punch* noted that the country had been gripped by 'Collection Mania', an 'enormous quantity of money' changing hands and stimulating 'the ambition of great numbers of

"Collectors" all over the country'.[5] In 1856, Henry Cole came to the conclusion that 'the taste for collecting' was now 'almost universal', and, by the end of the 1860s, *The Graphic*, an illustrated political journal, was able to go a step further by claiming that 'this is the collecting age'.[6] During the 1870s, *Punch* embellished the simple reporting of sales, featuring a number of cartoons of dishevelled and obsessive collectors which developed the idea of 'mania'. From enthusiastic shoppers to expert connoisseurs, the collecting habit was becoming entrenched in the homes of the Victorian middle classes.

Collecting was by no means confined to the home, however. Alongside the growing number of private collectors was a developing habit of public collecting. The new galleries at South Kensington were part of an emerging network of museums across the country. Inextricably associated with education and enlightenment, with order and stability and self-improvement, these offered a perfect outlet for both civic pride and visible philanthropy. Many wealthy and influential Victorians saw it as nothing less than a public duty to provide spacious, airy galleries where people could learn about art and science, and to construct imposing and stately buildings that reflected the confidence and affluence of their communities. Public collecting was active and fashionable.

Establishing a museum sent a clear message about the aspirations of a town, and the apparent generosity and far-sightedness of its leading inhabitants. Those with an eye for boosting local dignity and their own reputations found museums an effective way of securing positive publicity and public support: in Sunderland, the Museum and Library, opened in 1879 by US President Ulysses S. Grant, was largely the work of Robert Cameron, a Member of Parliament, Justice of the Peace and temperance campaigner; in Exeter, it was two MPs, Sir Stafford

Northcote of Pynes and Richard Sommers Gard, who proposed and developed the plans for the city's Albert Memorial Museum. All over the country, those with an interest in municipal matters and affairs of state began to look at ways of developing and displaying public collections that would entertain and inform, and before long a web of museums started to grow across industrial towns and expanding cities, offering more and more people the opportunity to see precious and fascinating things.

Despite their sudden high profile, the emerging museums did not appear completely out of the blue. Many were an extension of local associations such as Mechanics' Institutes and Literary and Philosophical Societies, established early in the century to encourage and facilitate the research, discussion and display of disciplines as diverse as geology, anatomy and phrenology, ship-building, mine engineering, painting and foreign languages. Mechanics' Institutes varied according to local traditions but, although they ostensibly catered for the working classes, many soon became a means for aspirational white-collar workers to advance themselves while also acting as meeting places for the middle class: the *Manchester Guardian* claimed in 1849 that of the thirty-two Mechanics' Institutes in Lancashire and Cheshire only four had any working-class support.[7] One of the results of this membership profile was an increasing number of exhibitions. No longer confined to providing practical instruction for workers, a number of committees turned their attention to the arts. In 1839, Leeds Mechanics' Institute organized an exhibition of 'arts and manufactures', while in 1848 Huddersfield described its effort as 'a polytechnic exhibition on a small scale . . . of pictures and other works of Art and objects of curiosity and interest'.[8] Perhaps the most actively enthusiastic of the Institutes was Manchester's, which organized five exhibitions, the first from December 1837 to February 1838, and the last finishing in the spring of 1845. These eclectic displays included everything from models of steam engines, ships and public buildings, to paintings, phrenology and geological specimens but the first exhibition was typical in also featuring over 400 examples 'of beautiful manufactures and of Superior workmanship in the Arts'.

By the 1830s and 1840s, most industrial centres, many smaller towns and even some rural villages had a Mechanics' Institute, generally offering a range of lectures, exhibitions, libraries and specialist classes. The network flourished so rapidly that by 1850 there were over 700 Institutes, boasting more than half a million members.[9] Alongside them, many larger cities also had established Literary and Philosophical Societies, often with roots in the eighteenth century. Combining elements of the academic society and the gentleman's club, they mainly drew their members from among the educated and the influential. But they were not divorced from practical progress and by the 1830s many had evolved into hybrids representing utilitarian, even industrial, interests, while retaining an air of genteel debate. They produced further opportunities for provincial displays, and some even formed collections, often based on a core of natural history objects, with rooms set aside to show everything from prints and paintings to stuffed birds: Newcastle Lit and Phil, for example, opened a special 'Museum Room' in 1826 to display the collection of books, manuscripts, prints and natural history specimens which had originally formed the private museum of Marmaduke Tunstall at his home at Wycliffe Hall near Bernard Castle in County Durham, and which the Society had purchased in 1822.

The newly developing museums fitted comfortably into this tradition of public learning and debate and increasingly took the next steps in creating and caring for collections. They were part of a general movement towards improving education in general, and art education in particular, with a focus on allowing ordinary people access to extraordinary things. In 1835, when he was asked by the Government Select Committee how to improve the knowledge of art among the general public, Gustav Waagen replied that better public understanding depended on 'accessible collect-ions. . . giving people the opportunity of seeing the most beautiful objects'.[10] By the mid-century, John Ruskin was again making a public case for places where visitors could experience the finest works of art. 'Art', he asserted in his 1859 lecture 'The Two Paths', 'is always helpful and beneficent to mankind, full of comfort, strength and salvation' and his writing indicated a growing and ambitious realization that public access to art could be linked to an improved understanding of everything from social structures to economics, as well as engendering better skills, work habits, personal conduct and even morals. 'A museum,' Ruskin claimed, 'is. . . primarily a place of education. . . teaching people what they do not know. . . teaching them to behave as they do not behave.'[11]

In 1845, a Museums Act was passed by Parliament, allowing borough councils to raise up to a halfpenny on the rates to go towards funding these emerging museums. This was followed five years later by a Public Libraries and Museums Act. Some towns acted promptly: Warrington opened a rates-funded museum in 1848, and the town council in Colchester agreed in April 1846 to provide a place 'for the deposit of articles of antiquity or curiosity', although it was not until 1860 that a building was finally opened to the public.[12] By the middle of the 1880s, Exeter, Nottingham, Bristol, Liverpool, Wolverhampton, Birmingham, Sheffield, Aberdeen, Leeds, Sunderland and Preston had all taken up the challenge, and so important did a museum become to municipal identity that there was fierce competition to see who would be quickest to create the biggest and best. As museums came to be seen as a symbol of modernity and sophistication, no town of any size wanted to be left behind, and the press fuelled the competition, reporting on efforts nationwide and judging one achievement against another. In 1878, the citizens of Nottingham must have glowed with delight at praise from the *Magazine of Art*:

J. C. Robinson's native town had, it suggested, 'at a single stride, outstripped all the towns in the U-K- in the race to provide themselves with local museums'.[13]

The new museums were, as we have seen at South Kensington, a way of making concrete philosophical discussions about art and culture. Throughout Europe, there was a drive to develop museums, as politicians, reformers and critics each attempted to prove their point. In Germany, especially, there was a concerted campaign to establish collections in the major cities. For Gustav Waagen, this was 'to advance the spiritual education of the nation through the experience of beauty', but for many of his colleagues the emphasis was on education: 'systematically arranged collections should be for the instruction of the *Volk* and the advancement of scholarly work', maintained Hermann Grimm, another high-profile German art historian.[14] In France, still rebuilding after the Revolution at the end of the eighteenth century, the focus was also on creating resources for public instruction, and during the 1860s the displays at the Louvre were redesigned to accommodate increased labelling, explanatory materials and guidebooks, further emphasizing its distance from the exclusive habits of its royal past.

This didactic impulse was part of the ongoing desire to make art generally more accessible, and to include all classes in a richer cultural life. A state museum opened in Berlin, for example, as early as 1830, with the intention of creating an opportunity for 'the general public' to experience art 'without regard to social status or education'.[15] But this kind of rhetoric tended to mask other, more complex, underlying factors. In Britain, the impulse to educate the masses, and to use museums as a tool for education, was, as Ruskin had asserted, also about changing behaviour. As early as 1834, a government select committee established to investigate 'vices of intoxication among the labouring classes' recommended museums as one solution to public drunkenness.

And in the wake of the 1832 Representation of the People Act, commonly known as the Reform Act – with the 1867 Reform Act further extending the franchise to the urban working class – establishment discomfort about the widening of the right to vote provided another impetus to develop museums. If people were going to be allowed to vote, then they needed to be instructed in the 'right' things, and the choice and arrangement of collections provided one way of moulding attitudes. The emerging museums grew out of a desire for moral authority and universal order as much as from pedagogic fervour or a commitment to beauty. They were a way of organizing people, enforcing norms of behaviour and driving home approved messages.

By the Victorian mid-century, there was a growing middle-class fear that increasing leisure time would, undirected, encourage the working classes to crime. In 1860, the opening of Manchester's free libraries, for example, was heralded by *Chambers Journal* as an effective solution for preventing unrest: 'As it is almost certain that the progress of civilization will produce more and more leisure to the human race,' it explained, 'it becomes a subject of the first importance to provide means for occupying that leisure in moral and intellectual progress.'[16] Museums fitted the bill as neatly as libraries. In his 1862 manifesto for a national museum of natural history, Robert Owen, industrialist and reformer, argued that the development of more museums could effectively counter revolutionary impulses, while the opening of the Nottingham Museum in 1872 was lauded for its wholesome and regulatory effect. It was, claimed *The Builder*, 'an important addition to the educational and refining influences... by the means by which those who labour may be lifted upward and at least deprived of their present excuse for merely sensual enjoyments', a respectable alternative to 'the gin-palace and drinking-saloon... in which elevation, not degradation, shall result'.[17]

38

The philanthropic impulse to provide for 'those who labour' was always complicated. It tended to submerge questions about power and status, and to fudge issues of common access and exclusivity. This was particularly true of the creation of smaller collections by well-meaning individuals which occupied a grey area between the public and private. They were often established specifically with public access in mind. Visitors – in particular, the working classes – were given generous admittance and were often allowed a much more intimate relationship to the objects than in the larger museums. But the objects still belonged to the private collector and, harking back to the *Wunderkammer* tradition of the past, the rooms of marvels were clearly stamped with his character. Although some of these collections in time became the foundation of more genuinely public museums, at the outset they showed how private and public collecting were still in the process of divergence during the nineteenth century, leaving plenty of room for confusion.

In many cases, these collections existed entirely for their benefit to the visitor: the collector's pleasure was in the wider good the objects bestowed, rather than in the objects themselves. An interesting example of this was John Ruskin's experimental collection which he installed in a small cottage museum in Sheffield in 1875. He chose Sheffield as the archetypal industrial city, with a tradition of craftsmanship but with many poor working-class citizens who might benefit from education and cultural enlightenment. Always vociferous in public debates about art, Ruskin's views often seemed inconsistent: as a collector and critic he espoused the spiritual value of beautiful works, championing the paintings of J. M. W. Turner, for example, but as a social reformer he also firmly believed in the more utilitarian processes of copying, drawing and close observation as a way of improving the life and work of the country's artisans. He intended the Sheffield museum to be the first of a series of similar teaching collections nationwide (the others never materialized), offering carefully chosen works for study, from prints, drawings and paintings to mineral specimens and coins. Ruskin oversaw the way in which things were displayed with a clear view to making the works as approachable as possible. Visitors were allowed to draw from, or handle, artefacts and the curator was requested by Ruskin to 'put everything away but what people can see clearly'.[18] Admission was free and, in an attempt to make the collection of genuine use to the working men of the city, the building was open until 9 at night and, unusually, from 2 until 6 on Sunday afternoons, as well as by appointment.

The model worked. Entries in the visitor book show that around two-thirds of the visitors were local, representing almost every district in Sheffield including those deep in the heart of the industrial centre and East End where the metal trades and heavy industries were concentrated. Several visitors became regular, suggesting a programme of study, and several identified themselves as 'art metal worker'. There was also a stream of female visitors from a range of social classes, from Lady Cunliffe-Owen and her daughter to the illiterate Mary Newbold of Spital Hill and Mrs Hobson of Pitsmoor, who both signed with crosses alongside the curator's entry of their name.

The pattern was repeated across the country. The tension between genuinely egalitarian public opening and inherent systemic inequalities may have remained, but museums proved enormously popular on a practical level. Whatever their philosophical basis, a trip to the local museum became fashionable for people from all walks of life. Museums were pleasant places to be, and the collections offered a novel brand of entertainment. The crowds poured in. In Sunderland, loan exhibitions proved so popular that the North Eastern Railway Company laid on special trains, while the original museum building was deemed inadequate for the volume of visitors just fifteen years after its opening in

1879. In Sheffield, a letter to the local paper complained of 'an invasion of Sheffield roughs of both sexes last Sunday pm. . . some hundreds of the worst played at gymnastics over the seats, and afterwards, with girls at their sides, made a promenade of the galleries'. An exhibition in Nottingham in 1872, 'showing the application of fine art to industry', attracted over 2,500 visitors a week, amounting to a total of over 760,000; more than 100,000 visitors admired a special display in Halifax, and the national journals published regular pieces about exhibitions which 'have attracted much attention on the part of the public having been inspected by tens of thousands'.[19]

Behind every public museum project were the private scholars and collectors who made things happen. The money from the Museums Acts could only be used for buying a site or constructing a building – not for acquiring objects for a collection – and so inevitably the creation and expansion of the new museums throughout the Victorian period was as much a personal as a municipal achievement. In a few cases, as at Ruskin's Sheffield museum, individual benefactors were to the fore, but more frequently private collectors simply made small cumulative contributions to activity in their towns or cities. They were the lifeblood of the system, lending, giving and bequeathing objects, volunteering their knowledge and expertise, and bringing their experienced eye to bear on acquisitions and displays. Just as Robinson had brought together an army of collectors for his 1862 exhibition at South Kensington, so museums up and down the country were turning to individuals to fill the cases. And just as Robinson was overwhelmed by eager contributors, so most local museums found collectors were only too willing to have their names attached to such a respectable municipal venture.

Unfortunately, this enthusiasm frequently gave an impression of amateurism and muddle. Even though many museums established specialist loan committees to seek out and woo significant local collectors, most found it hard to turn down objects that they were offered on a more ad hoc basis. Not surprisingly, this tended to result in a diverse, and frequently bizarre, mixture of exhibits which often appeared even more confused as a consequence of poor presentation and interpretation. In 1874, a Royal Commission found that 'the only label attached to nine specimens out of ten is "presented by Mr. or Mrs. So-and-so," the objects of the presentation having been either to cherish a glow of self-satisfaction in the bosom of the donor, or to get rid under the semblance of doing a good action of rubbish that had once been prized, but latterly had stood in the way'.[20] Bursting with everything from butterflies and minerals to celebrity memorabilia and poorly executed watercolours, these museums were public testimony to the pervasiveness and irresistibility of collecting – but they also demonstrated the need for studious, focused and devoted collectors who could create something lasting and meaningful.

This was where the bigger London institutions, the national collections, might have stepped in. Although the provinces were generally new to the idea of museums, public collections in the capital had a longer history. Sir John Soane bequeathed his collection of antiquities, sculpture, furniture and paintings to the public in the early nineteenth century, and in 1838 the National Gallery was opened in Trafalgar Square. By the middle of the nineteenth century, the original collections of books, antiquities and natural history that had been brought together to found the British Museum in 1753 had been expanded to include ethnographic artefacts, Asian treasures, classical sculpture and key pieces such as the Rosetta Stone, engraved with the three scripts of ancient Egypt and brought back from Alexandria by British troops in 1801. In addition, several high-profile private institutions allowed at least some kind of public access: the independent Royal

Academy had held influential summer exhibitions since its formation by George III in 1768, while the British Institution, founded by art connoisseurs and private subscribers in 1805, held a series of loan exhibitions at its premises on Pall Mall, a popular society haunt. Throughout the century, the Society for the Encouragement of Arts, Manufactures and Commerce had, as we have seen, been drawing the crowds to its series of exuberant trade shows.

In many cases, however, the visitor and would-be collector found much less encouragement in London than elsewhere in the country. Exhibitions at the Royal Academy and the British Institution were, in reality, rather closed affairs, partly because there was an entrance fee and partly because they were entangled with the tradition of gentleman's clubs and the artistic elite. They were extremely popular among certain sections of society but they did little to promote the idea of genuinely public access to art, nor did they necessarily suggest that collecting could be an egalitarian activity. The British Institution was governed by the interests of the aristocratic community that had made up its management since it was founded by the Marquess of Stafford; the Royal Academy was as much a stronghold for establishment artists as it had been when it was launched by successful painters like Sir Joshua Reynolds in the 1760s. The membership of these influential art organizations seemed to have evolved little from the days of clubs like the Society of Dilettanti, formed around 1732 with a select membership of the noble and the fashionable: according to Horace Walpole, 'the nominal qualification is having been in Italy, and the real one, being drunk'.[21] Even the growth of private commercial galleries in the 1870s and 1880s did little to alter the situation. With the most valuable markets in mind, most of them concentrated on an upper-class clientele and actively promoted the exclusive feel of the Royal Academy: the Grosvenor Gallery was established in the art marketplace of

Bond Street in 1877, for example, but its founder Sir Coutts Lindsay set it apart by nurturing an aristocratic air and a commitment to showing works from private collections. 'The whole has the affect of a private salon, richly and harmoniously furnished,' noted one visitor, while another enthused at how quickly the Grosvenor's series of exhibitions and private viewings had become another stop on the ritualized merry-go-round of elite London social life: 'Sunday afternoon parties at the Grosvenor Gallery, by personal invitation only, were some of the high points of the season.'[22]

The National Gallery did have a commitment to free opening and its site on Trafalgar Square had been chosen, in principle at least, because it was accessible on foot from the poor streets of the East End. In 1822, Sir Robert Peel talked optimistically about the beneficial reward to society of bringing the rich and poor together in forming a national collection of art. But in general it remained the private preserve of connoisseurs until the 1860s and 1870s, operating on a modest scale, and functioning more or less as a sub-department of the British Museum – it was only after 1856 that the gallery became independent. Acute lack of space meant that many of the pictures were not displayed at all, or were shuttled around London: the bequest in 1856 of over 1,000 paintings by J. M. W. Turner, for example, had to be moved to South Kensington. Confusion and disagreement between the gallery's trustees also led to periods of almost complete paralysis in terms of developing the collection. Some advocated following the German model being developed in Berlin by Gustav Waagen, buying works to show the progression of art through history, while others, including members of the Royal Academy, argued that acquisitions should be confined to important works in styles derived from the classical and Renaissance periods. The result was that between 1847 and 1850 no acquisitions were made at all, even though London salerooms were awash with affordable masterpieces. In the light of such confusion and missed opportunities, there was an ongoing, very public campaign for the complete reorganization of the collections. The press carried frequent letters about the issue and a public commission in 1857 further aired discontent: in his evidence, John Ruskin complained of the 'continual change of temper and tone of thought' occasioned by the existing arrangements of the works.[23]

The British Museum was equally disordered and ill-managed. Until the beginning of the nineteenth century, entrance was only permitted after applying to the chief officer of the museum for a signed ticket. It could take months for this to come through, after which the visitor was hurried around the galleries on a rushed guided tour. From 1810, matters improved, but the museum was still only open between 10 a.m. and 4 p.m. on three days a week, to those deemed to be 'of decent appearance'. Daunted by conservative church opposition and suffering from lack of funds and staff, it was the last to offer Sunday opening, while concerns about the hazards of gas lighting meant that evening opening was also severely restricted. As a result, the collections were all but inaccessible to the working classes. In *Little Dorrit* (1855–7), Charles Dickens associates a 'Sunday evening in London, gloomy, close, and stale' with the museum's dark, locked rooms:

Everything was bolted and barred that could by possibility furnish relief to an overworked people. No pictures, no unfamiliar animals, no rare plants or flowers, no natural or artificial wonders of the ancient worlds – all taboo. . . Nothing to see but streets, streets, streets.[24]

But it was not only the process of getting into the galleries that frustrated visitors. Once inside, the displays themselves retained an air of muddled academia that made it very difficult to understand or appreciate the collections. In 1860, *Chambers Journal* suggested that the British Museum was too 'cribbed, cabined and confined' to do any justice to the objects and that it was in danger of degenerating into 'a gigantic curiosity shop'. Two years later, *The London Review* described the exhibits as 'so crowded together as to be rendered almost useless'.[25] Between 1850 and 1860, a number of parliamentary inquiries and Royal Commissions discussed everything from space in the galleries to conservation requirements, but popular support for the museum was low, and its galleries seemed to present a sad comparison to the lively display spaces of fashionable events like the Great Exhibition.

With public discontent in the national institutions running high, the relationship between the growing network of regional museums and their larger London counterparts was a complex one. Many of the new museums were fiercely provincial, and unwilling to associate themselves too closely with what they regarded as the failing examples in the capital. Cities and towns outside London were eager to prove they had their own vibrant identities, and events such as the Mechanics' Institutes exhibitions or, on a larger scale, the 1857 Art Treasures Exhibition in Manchester had already provided an important means of doing this. The museums were a novel, potent means of displaying provincial progress and pride. They were an indication of how well the outlying towns and cities were doing, showing off the wealth of key benefactors while also displaying the cultural and educational credentials of the populace more widely. The collections were often local or regional in nature, and the displays were clearly regarded with a certain sense of ownership by visitors. The trades, materials and styles on display were familiar, and the names of local collectors were attached to most of the objects.

This powerful sense of provincialism was tempered, however, by the importance of loans from the national collections, especially from the South Kensington Museum. These loan exhibitions were seen by the government as complementary to the regional Schools of Design, and as part of the crusade to raise manufacturing standards. They were also crucial in establishing many regional museums, enabling cities to develop audiences for displays and create support for a more permanent local collection. Between 1854 and 1870, loans from South Kensington were made fourteen times to Sheffield, ten times to Birmingham, eight times to Liverpool and Nottingham and seven times to Leeds. At the Mechanics' Institute in Manchester in 1845, the display included 'textile fabrics, bronze, iron and other metal castings, porcelain, and earthenware' and drew visitors from across the city before everything was packed up and moved on to Glasgow.[26]

Victorian advances in transport made such peripatetic exhibitions increasingly possible. As the speed and efficiency of the rail system effectively shrank distance, moving objects around the country seemed as simple as it was desirable. There was no longer any reason for everything to be centred on the national institutions in London, or on London audiences. Displays, and the expertise behind them, could be shared because the railways ran quickly and efficiently, changing perceptions of what was achievable. The magnificence of Robinson's loan exhibition at South Kensington was possible because it had already been demonstrated that substantial collections could be brought together temporarily, and then dispersed, without much fuss. The travelling exhibitions proved just how many visitors could be reached and how popular collecting was becoming nationwide. They also emphasized how modern technologies were altering the very nature of collecting, opening up new possibilities and inextricably linking the collection to travel and discovery. Small local displays were giving way to ambitious exhibitions that drew crowds from a distance; museums aspired to become municipal models for the masses rather than elite palace playgrounds of the rich. And the collector was evolving from the gentleman amateur in his isolated study into the scholar with links across regions and even nations. Times were changing, and the role of the collector was inevitably changing too.

Making Museums: Collecting as a Career

JOHN CHARLES ROBINSON

CHAPTER FOUR

On the Banks of the Seine

*D*rawing was John Charles Robinson's escape. In the long days of childhood he would idle around the country lanes near his home in Nottingham, sketching and scribbling, dreaming of what might be. He was not close to his siblings; his father, a printer and auctioneer, was sternly preoccupied with business, and he was largely raised by his grandfather, who was a bookseller. Robinson spent hours by himself. Physically slight and unremarkable, with a sharp mouth and a high, pale forehead, he was little noticed as he sat practising his skills of composition, perspective and shading. But he did not mind this. He preferred his art to anything and was happy to be left alone. He rapidly developed a self-assurance bordering on arrogance and, as his drawing skills developed, so did his confidence. He compared his work to that of others around him, and he became convinced that he had talent. He began to imagine a future for himself as an artist or an architect, leading a life of creativity and inspiration. His ambition began to shine bright and hard.

Robinson knew he could expect little financial support from his family. Moreover, he had few contacts and sparse knowledge of the world of art. The small-scale auctions run by his father were the closest he had come to the international world of the artist. But his early confidence was unshakeable and, soon after leaving school, he began work in an architect's office. Life behind the drawing board was not quite as he had imagined, however. Studying the style of the nineteenth-century Gothic revival, he was, for a while, inspired by the ideals of craftsmanship and the elegance of Gothic decoration, but the day-to-day routine of a small-scale architect seemed largely mechanical and tedious. Robinson was convinced he could do better. And in 1843, at the age of nineteen, he was accepted into a major artists' teaching atelier in Paris. Taking a big step towards creative and personal independence, Robinson turned his back on his life in Nottingham to begin again.

There was no better place than Paris to learn an artist's trade – up in Montmartre, the crowded narrow streets were teeming with painters and sculptors and poets. Robinson worked with two of the city's leading ateliers. Under the guidance of Michel Martin Drolling, professor at the Ecole Nationale Supérieure des Beaux-Arts, he studied bright, theatrical scenes from the Bible or from history; with Henri Lehmann, a young German-born draughts-man only ten years older than himself, the emphasis was on graceful portraits and nude studies. Robinson studied hard. He drew from the classics or from copies of masterpieces, worked from plaster casts of sculptures, painted in parks and in the open country and made life drawings. He was robustly confident in his own talents. Every week there was a competition among Drolling's students, who were then arranged around the studio in order of merit. In 1845, Robinson wrote proudly to a friend: 'I am now the "premier dessinateur" in the atelier. There are several who have drawn consistently for four or five years whilst I have drawn little more than 8 or 9 months and have already got top of the list.'[1] Robinson may have been exaggerating the speed of his achievements – he had been in Paris, although not at the same atelier, almost two years – but it was clear that he had an eye for perspective, form and colour, and was, as with all things he was to undertake, conscientious and determined. He may have looked boyish and angelic, lightweight even, but he fully believed in his own talent to succeed.

Robinson's practical Paris education was indeed a success. He would work as an artist for the rest of his life, exhibiting several times at the Royal Academy and regularly selling his work. Prints of two of his landscapes can still be seen in the collection at the Tate Gallery. But it was another aspect of his time in the French capital that was to have most influence on the rest of his life – and on the future of British collecting. Robinson's study at the ateliers finished every day at midday, leaving afternoons free. And not far from his lodgings were the high-ceilinged galleries and wide courtyards of the Palais du Louvre. It was there that Robinson discovered for the first time the bold, flourishing masterpieces of the Italian Renaissance, da Vinci's *Mona Lisa*; Raphael's angels and demons; Titian's elegiac nudes; bronzes, busts and sculptures by Michelangelo. For a young man from the Midlands, ideal- istic and lonely, slightly homesick and desperate to succeed, these works of art were both overwhelming and seductive. Robinson developed an interest in the Renaissance that would endure for the rest of his life. The history and beauty of the masterpieces of the past permeated deep into his understanding until he felt the physical tingle of them in the cool breath of the galleries, the magnificent colours and full forms imprinting themselves unforgettably on his mind's eye.

Robinson spent as many hours with the dead artists of the

Louvre as with the living ones of Montmartre, and it was there, rather than in his studio, that he metamorphosed from a gauche young man into an erudite connoisseur. With its history as a royal palace, the Louvre was spectacular and ornate. The building had dominated the centre of Paris since the twelfth century, developing from a fortress to a sumptuous expression of imperial power. In 1674, the French king, Louis XIV, moved the permanent court to Versailles, and by the end of the seventeenth century the Louvre buildings were starting a new life as home to a gallery of antique sculpture as well as the Académie Française, the Académie des Inscriptions et Belles Lettres and the Académie Royale de Peinture et de Sculpture, the last of which launched a series of popular annual exhibitions, or salons. Visitors came from the French political and academic elite, and the activities within the Louvre were held up as a shining example of the nation's cultural pre-eminence and prestige. But the hierarchical structures of the Académies, as well as the yearly salons, clearly promoted the established interests of the ruling minority and the Louvre remained closed to all but a handful of visitors.

A century later, however, the French Revolution changed the old systems of power and reinvented its strongholds. The emphasis now at the Louvre was on creating a national collection that belonged to the people and an institution that was open to everyone. Masterpieces 'which were previously visible to only a privileged few... will henceforth afford pleasure to all: statues, paintings and books are charged with the sweat of the people: the property of the people will be returned to them,' asserted Abbé Grégoire, one of the most influential Republican leaders.[2] The Louvre began a long period of development as a genuinely public site, opening in 1793 as the Musée Central des Arts, displaying paintings which had been confiscated from royal and aristocratic families, including the *Mona Lisa*. Admission was free, and large amounts of state money and energy were devoted to building collections that would be esteemed throughout France and beyond.

In practice, it was not always easy for the newly empowered citizens to view their artistic heritage: at the beginning of its life, the museum was only open to the public at weekends, and artists were always given priority over ordinary visitors. But gradually more of the building was opened as the French collections expanded, and extensions were also added to create more gallery space. The Louvre was as important to the Republic as a symbol of state power as it had been to the monarchy as a royal palace. Its public collections signified national unity and the regeneration of the people, while the display of the nation's new-found artistic wealth was also a means of displaying the political success of the new government; it was hoped that the galleries would forge a visible link between the care and display of respected works of art and the perception of responsible Republican rule. Between 1794 and 1813, treaties with Italy as well as the spoils of Napoleonic conquests swelled the collections: three huge convoys of marbles and paintings from Rome, central Italy and Venice were sent to Paris, with the arrival of the last, in July 1798, prompting a spectacular celebratory festival. Throughout the period, ongoing confiscations from aristocratic families further swelled the Louvre's acquisitions. After Napoleon's defeat at Waterloo in 1815, some of the works looted from Germany, the Netherlands, Austria, Italy and Spain were, grudgingly, returned. For the next couple of decades, until 1830, the unsettled politics around the brief restoration of the monarchy also meant that attention drifted from the Louvre, funding faltered and the galleries were neglected. But this still left plenty to see. By the time of Robinson's visits during the early 1840s, the displays included Egyptian antiquities, ancient bronzes, medieval decorative arts,

Etruscan vases, rooms devoted to 'modern' sculpture and a gallery of Spanish art.

Robinson was fortunate to be in Paris at the beginning of a period of active expansion of the Louvre collections. From 1848, in particular, with the birth of the Second Republic, the government invested heavily in the building and the collections, allocating two million francs for repair work. And as the French economy grew during the middle of the century, so too did the number of works on display: over 20,000 works were added between 1852 and 1870. But even in the years before this, it was a unique resource for a young artist. The Revolution and its aftermath had made it possible to view, in one place, a range of artworks from many periods and in many styles arranged specifically to instruct students like Robinson. The emphasis was on works that could be usefully copied, and on hanging pictures chronologically and by national schools of artists (with French painting given pride of place) to explore the historical evolution of style and technique, 'a character of order, instruction and classification', as one of the early museum directors explained.[3] This was a relatively untried way of displaying works, with only a handful of German galleries experimenting with similar principles; the National Gallery, in contrast, modelled its displays on the domestic traditions of private country-house collections.

In Britain, art was crammed into rooms from floor to ceiling and displays were arranged according to the aesthetic judgements of the organizers, the size and shape of works – or just to accommodate the space. It was unlikely Robinson could have profited from the type of education he received in France. 'Nothing has so much retarded the advance of art,' suggested John Ruskin, 'as our miserable habit of mixing the works of every master and every century... Few minds are strong enough first to abstract and then to generalise the characters of paintings hung at random.'⁴ Moreover, British royal and aristocratic collections were still fiercely private, and Robinson's routine of drawing and studying from private collections could not have been easily achieved: 'The country was indeed rich in works of art, richer perhaps than any other,' Robinson admitted, 'but these treasures were the possessions of private individuals, scattered broadcast in a thousand places and town and country houses, for the most part hidden treasures, often unappreciated by their possessors even, and but casually revealed to the world at large.'⁵ Even aside from such scattered country-house collections, there was very little for the student. Sweden had had a national gallery of art since 1794; in Amsterdam the Rijksmuseum opened in 1808; and in Madrid the Prado was founded eight years later. London's National Gallery, in contrast, was in its infancy. It did not move into its permanent building until the late 1830s and even then, as we have seen, its development was unsteady; its slowly expanding collections remained a matter of debate and disagreement. In addition, the French Revolution, the turbulence of the Napoleonic Wars and the violence and revolt across Europe in 1848 were fresh in the Victorian imagination. The tendency to public access and universality that was evident in France was in stark contrast to something of a backlash among the English establishment. Haunted by the prospect of unrest and revolution spreading to Britain from the Continent – and further stoked by the progress of the working-class Chartist movement during the mid-century – the British ruling classes tended to tighten their grip on power. This showed itself in a variety of ways, from increasing restrictions on women to a greater emphasis on the doctrines of the established Church. It also meant that, while government select committees and initiatives like the Schools of Design voiced the ideals of greater public access to art, in reality those who owned or controlled most of the works were more interested in closing ranks against the perceived threat of the masses. The French model of universal access, born out of the principles of the First Republic, was still some way off across the Channel.

The only real British alternative lay with a number of exhibition societies that flourished in the second half of the century. While these did not show historic masterpieces, they did offer support to many artists considered too progressive to please the conservative members of the Royal Academy, and they welcomed visitors who wanted to view new work in a sympathetic environment. Many of these societies had open membership and modest subscription rates: the Society for the Encouragement of the Fine Arts founded in 1858 held lectures and debates and organized visits to private galleries for an annual subscription of £1.1s. Several specialized in encouraging artists who worked outside the oil painting tradition favoured by the Royal Academy – these included the Photographic Salon which met at the Dudley Gallery Art Society in Piccadilly and the Bookplate Society based at the nearby John Baillie's Gallery – while others provided studios, study rooms and drawing classes, or even allocated grants to young artists. But such opportunities were limited. The exhibition societies were largely confined to the capital and were without real influence or prestige. Perhaps more significantly, their open membership policy and resistance to selection meant that the quality of exhibits could be poor. Displays frequently failed to inspire the serious student, and Robinson would have stood little chance of seeing many significant works of art at first hand.

In France, it was the Louvre's Italian Renaissance master-pieces that most captivated Robinson's interest. He learned quickly and before long he was an expert. Eventually, he studied other periods and schools of art – he particularly came to value the workmanship of the medieval craftsman and to admire the detail of eighteenth-century composition – but his first love was for the extravagance of the Renaissance. It was never to leave him. Inevitably, when his years at the Paris ateliers were over, he brought it with him back to England. In time, this enthusiasm would influence his work at the South Kensington Museum, and have an impact on the type of collections he developed there. But there was more to Paris than the Louvre, and alongside Robinson's education in the public galleries he threw himself into the more informal training of the private collector. The lure of the hidden and the mysterious took him deep into the network of backstreets as well as into the smarter districts of the 7th *arondissement* where the curiosity shops were clustered. He became known to a number of successful and influential dealers, noting a preference for Monsieur Delange on the Quai Voltaire, opposite the Louvre and the Tuileries Gardens; he regularly bought the more reasonably priced wares of Mister Evans, who owned the next-door shop; and he was a frequent visitor to the small but packed showroom of Monsieur Couvreur, on the rue Notre Dame des Victoires, in the criss-cross of streets around the fashionable Opéra.

By 1846, hopeful visits to the most promising dealers had already become an integral part of Robinson's life. A young man of twenty-two, he was collecting in earnest, haggling over the spoils of war and revolution, travelling to Orléans and Tours as well as keeping an eye on bargains to be had in Paris. For the next sixty years, his letters, diaries and published articles, and even his account books and official museum minutes, would show a man completely captivated by the idea of collecting. In Paris, the opportunity to visit several thriving and inspiring collections rooted in private connoisseurship provided a touchstone for what he might go on to achieve, proving what could be done with dedication and commitment. Perhaps most important of these was the collection of Alexandre Du Sommerard in the atmospheric medieval Hôtel de Cluny. Open to the public on Sundays from 1832, the elaborate rooms drew on the influence of the *Wunderkammer*, evoking the cluttered, treasure-trove effect of the impassioned collector and drawing crowds as large as those at the Louvre.

By the time of Robinson's visits, the state had taken over the collection, arranging the pieces more systematically and allowing more frequent public access from 1844. The Musée de Cluny was already making news among English politicians and commentators as a resource for educating taste and encouraging the skills of artisans and manufacturers, being held up as a model for British projects like the Schools of Design. Robinson had probably heard of the collection in this light. But it was also a scholarly celebration of collecting the medieval and Renaissance decorative arts. Du Sommerard published a highly illustrated, five-volume catalogue (1838–46) with an emphasis on the pieces as 'strange and rare history' instead of as evidence of design standards, and it was this sense of the more idealistic possibilities of collecting that Robinson seems to have found most inspiring.[6] Du Sommerard had a dull day job in the French Audit Office, but his heart was in collecting and for an impressionable young visitor like Robinson this enthusiasm was in itself exhilarating.

Robinson was already finding his way into the circle of collectors. A recommendation from a fellow connoisseur would have granted him access, via three flights of steep stairs, to the tiny apartment of Charles Sauvageot, in rue du Faubourg-Poissonière in an outlying district of northern Paris. Sauvageot lived completely surrounded by his things. 'The objects were so crowded that I tucked in my sleeves from fear,' wrote another English visitor, clearly afraid of accidental breakage. 'It is evident that he buys articles from real love of the beautiful.'[7] Sauvageot, like Du Sommerard, had a 'normal' career, working at the Customs office, and his rooms were small and cramped. He had little money, but he was an indefatigable scavenger, alert to the possibilities for acquiring unusual and valuable works in the long aftermath of the Revolution. His collection showed that with patience and spirit it was possible to achieve a great deal. Robinson took such models to heart. He became acutely aware of the variety and beauty of the objects on offer. He developed a taste for Limoges enamels and an enduring fascination with textiles. He bought sixteenth- and seventeenth-century silks, with their colours still bold, an ornamental carpet and a magnificent altar cover. He became voracious in his collecting, developing a sense of urgency and competitiveness that was to last a lifetime. But late in 1846, after a period of intense collecting, Robinson's money finally ran out. He was forced to return home to Nottingham in the middle of an English winter, complaining in his diary that the city was 'desolate'.[8]

Back in Nottingham, Robinson missed desperately the romance of Paris and the thrill of making contacts there. He continued to paint, but could not find a way of supporting himself as an artist. For a while, his life seemed dull and miserable. His years in France had made an enormous impact on him, inspiring his collecting and offering glimpses of what could be. Short of money and lonely, these possibilities suddenly seemed all too distant. But Robinson was lucky. On 1 June 1847, he was appointed to work at the Nottingham School of Art, before moving just two months later to a post as Assistant Master at the government School of Design in Hanley, where he doubled his salary to one hundred pounds a year. At first glance, teaching drawing skills in the industrial smog of the Midlands potteries was not a glamorous job. But one of Robinson's first tasks was to return to France, to report on the state of pottery and design, and on the teaching of art. He was delighted to be back in Paris, and he was convinced that he had found a quick route to promotion. He was confident that, with his inside knowledge, his report would get him noticed, releasing him from the stagnancy of his provincial backwater and into a more vibrant life in London. In the meantime, he could stroll again by the Seine and rummage in junkshops.

For the next few years, before starting at the South Kensington Museum in 1853, Robinson travelled as much as his job would allow – for work, for pleasure and to make himself an expert. In 1851, he discovered the pleasures of Italy, and found for the first time a beauty and romance to challenge anything he had seen in France. Apart from the 'curse' of mosquitoes, which he bemoaned in his letters, there was nothing to upset his enthusiasm. He was overwhelmed by the spectacular sculpture and the magnificent architecture of cities like Verona and Padua; in Florence the glories were so numerous that Robinson was 'too excited to go to bed'; and then there was Venice. 'I have just got in from a moonlight sail through Venice,' he wrote to a friend. 'The moon is at the full – brilliant – pouring down floods of light through a deep blue endless sky, such as *you* have never seen and never will til you come to Italy – Imagine, but you can't imagine! – and I am too stupid to describe and no I can't, I can't begin, what an ass I am.'[9]

Robinson was inspired by Italian architecture and art, by the landscape, the language and the culture. He felt he had found a spiritual home, one which was to influence his collecting for the rest of his life. For several months during the summer of 1851, he went from city to city, from Milan to Brescia, Verona to Padua, Ferrara to Bologna. Italy was beginning to occupy a particular place in the Victorian imagination, and Robinson was at the heart of this impulse to celebrate, and romanticize, what could be experienced there. Since the eighteenth century, the British elite had shown a fascination with Italy and its art: half of the paintings sold for more than £40 at London auctions between 1711 and 1760 were by Italian masters, and the Italian towns were well-established highlights of the Grand Tour. Canaletto's idealized paintings of Venice, showing aristocratic palaces alongside pristine canals, were hugely fashionable in eighteenth-century Britain. But travellers like Robinson were beginning to look beyond the well-trodden paths to the Grand Masters. In 1851, the same year as Robinson's journey, John Ruskin published the first volume of *The Stones of Venice*, an influential book-length essay which held up Italian Gothic architecture, and the communities of craftsmanship from which it emerged, as a model for cultural and social reform. Ruskin's campaign to save neglected and shabby Italian buildings, including St Mark's Cathedral in Venice, took on the vehemence of a crusade, and he arranged for paintings, photographs and plaster casts to be taken of what he considered the most threatened architectural features. Works like *The Stones of Venice*, and the earlier *Seven Lamps of Architecture* (1849), inspired the Victorian public to look at Italy in a new light, not just as the fashionable birthplace of Dante or a place of restless politics and retarded modernity, but as a medieval and Renaissance treasure.

This was something Robinson was delighted to discover first-hand. But collecting in Italy during the middle of the century was not easy. Transport was unreliable, treasure-hunting was notoriously hit-and-miss, and armed scuffles were not at all uncommon. Since the defeat of Napoleon in 1815, the movement towards unification of the Italian states had gathered pace. The years 1848 and 1849, just before Robinson's visit, marked the high point of revolutionary idealism with popular support from all classes: from Sicily in the south to Venice and Lombardy in the north, people took to the streets against both native rulers and the Austrian Habsburgs. Though the insurgency collapsed in the summer of 1849, through a combination of dynastic rivalry, foreign invasion and the withdrawal of key support from papal and Neapolitan forces, the movement rumbled on uncertainly and a series of internecine conflicts broke out, especially in the central Italian states. For travellers this could be disruptive and even dangerous: 'We are expecting a battle every hour, and however exciting and romantic it might be, it would not be pleasant to be rolled amongst the debacle of a beaten army and a panic-stricken population,' Robinson wrote during an eventful journey from Florence.[10]

But there were advantages to such upheaval. Collecting in Italy had rarely been so rewarding. As the old structures of power were challenged, objects from both the aristocracy and the Church found their way on to the open market and into the hands of collectors. Charles Eastlake, the first Director of the National Gallery (1855–65), was just one of those who were drawn to the treasures made newly available by the troubled political climate. He made a series of collecting trips to Italy throughout the 1850s and 1860s; his acquisitions included Fra Angelico's *Adoration of the Magi* and thirty other paintings from the Lombardi-Baldi collection in Florence in 1857. Whatever the risks, the allure of Italy, it seems, was too great to resist.

Despite his eventful holidays, and his preoccupation with collecting, Robinson's day job continued to go well. He was, as he had foreseen, creating an immediate impression at the School of Design and, by 1852, after just over five years, he had been promoted to Teachers' Training Master. His timing could not have been better. It was the same year that Henry Cole began to reorganize and reinvigorate the government design programme, and Robinson soon came to Cole's notice, partly for his practical work, and partly because he put himself in Cole's way by sending him, with characteristic confidence, a series of suggestions for improving the Schools. Less than a year later, in September 1853, Robinson was in London, at the heart of things, in a new position at the South Kensington Museum. It seemed like the perfect job. He could bring to bear all the art knowledge he had gleaned, he would have public money to spend and he could immerse himself in collecting. What began as a temporary post was confirmed as permanent on 8 July 1854, and Robinson took his place in the ranks of professional collectors.

CHAPTER FIVE

The Battle of South Kensington

W ithin two years of starting work in London, John Charles Robinson was sitting at his desk, watching the tree tops scraping a bare spring sky. It was early March 1855 at the end of a particularly cold fortnight. Frosts had set hard in the city parks, making them shine white through the smoke-thick air, and the pavement corners were slippery with ice. From the window of his office in Marlborough House, on London's Pall Mall, Robinson could see uniformed doormen stamping their feet to keep the chill from their bones. A discreet notice at the end of the closely raked gravel path tried to entice the public into the warmth to see the displays of 'manufactures', all that yet existed of what would eventually become the splendour of the Victoria and Albert Museum. Visitors made their way steadily into the striking red-brick building and up the marble stairs to peer into the heavy glass cases that lined the rooms inside. In the dignified Georgian townhouse which Sir Christopher Wren had designed for the first Duke of Marlborough and his wife Sarah, porcelain, glass and metalwork were displayed on the first floor; plaster casts were pushed into chimney niches, paintings hung high from the elegant coving and Indian textiles draped over couches. There was plenty to admire.

Robinson watched the visitors arrive. On Mondays, Tuesdays and Saturdays, entrance was free, but the rooms were enormously crowded; on the remaining weekdays, an entrance fee of 6d ensured more space for those who wanted to study quietly. From an average of a thousand visitors a day on free days, attendance on paying days fell to fewer than eighty, but still annual visitor figures for the mid-1850s hovered around the 100,000 mark. During the same period, at the much larger and more established British Museum, figures were sliding rapidly from a peak of over 2 million in the year of the 1851 Great Exhibition to around 300,000. The ideal of public access that had been heralded by the Crystal Palace event seemed to have dissolved and the grand galleries of the British Museum were once again viewed by many as the exclusive haunt of scholars and the wealthy. The six rooms at Marlborough House, in contrast, appealed to the middle classes and the temporary displays were a lively source of entertainment for everyone from serious students to families.

For Robinson, this popularity was a matter of pride. When the Marlborough House rooms were first opened in 1852, Henry Cole had featured an exhibition of 'False Principles in Design', popularly nicknamed the Chamber of Horrors, a practical demonstration of how not to do things that was supposed to stand as a warning to British buyers and manufacturers: 'a gloomy chamber hung round with frightful objects in curtains, carpets, clothes, lamps and whatnot', wrote one reviewer, a mess of decorative excess and offending aesthetics.[1] By showing people how terrible the worst objects could be, this brash display was supposed to elevate public taste and put the moral case for design reform. It was a clear indication of what Cole thought the museum was about. But in his short time in post, Robinson had set to work rearranging the galleries, reorganizing the showcases, making the exhibitions more varied and, quite deliberately, changing the emphasis of the museum from Cole's focus on educating artisans to his own vision of providing a more general public with the chance to admire the old, rare and beautiful. He was not without sympathy for Cole's general principles of education, but he wanted visitors to use works from history for 'the gradual and progressive cultivation of the judgement, until it assumes almost the readiness and certainty of intuitive conviction'. In his view, the Chamber of Horrors had no part in a museum: 'the object of the Museum is to illustrate the history, theory and practical application of decorative art,' he claimed, making sure that alongside 'objects of utility' there were also 'works avowedly decorative'.[2] He wanted to show the best – and not the worst – drawing visitors with the expectation of delight rather than from disgust or curiosity.

It was the beginning of a battle of philosophies that would divide Cole and Robinson throughout their work at the museum, and would finally highlight the gap between the museum's rhetoric about collecting, and what it collected in practice. Henry Cole displayed occasional enthusiasm for antiquarian objects and pieces of fine art, and he showed characteristic energy in acquiring some of these works for the museum. But, for him, they were always a means to an end. His acquisitions were always made with a view to the larger cause of design reform, and the museum displays were always created with an eye on education. Robinson delighted in beauty and craftsmanship – at heart he was a connoisseur. He wanted the museum to be more than a training ground; he hoped to create a collection that aimed to foster aesthetic appreciation rather than to deliver design rules.

Robinson argued that the museum he had in mind would serve not only the art student or the general public, but also 'the collector, whose pursuit it is... clearly a national duty to countenance and encourage'.[3] For Robinson and his friends, collecting needed to be at the heart of things. There was a sense in which it was much more than an individual preoccupation – it was 'a national duty'. As we have seen, museums all over the country were emphasizing their public value; there is no doubt that Henry Cole viewed South Kensington as a national crusade. But Robinson was suggesting that it was not only beautiful objects themselves that were important, but also the very 'pursuit' of collecting them. Tracking down objects, studying them, comparing and treasuring them was much more, for Robinson, than an enjoyable habit. It was at the root of the emerging museums network; it was the underlying mechanism that made everything else possible. In statements like this, Robinson was able to give his ransacking of European salerooms a gloss that highlighted its public benefit. But more than that, he was staking a claim for each and every collector, putting their activity into a wider context that gave them influence within the political, economic and social manoeuvring that was striving to make Victorian Britain great.

As Robinson watched the visitors come to Marlborough House, there was also some sadness. He could feel how things were changing. Just south of Hyde Park on quiet rural land, Henry Cole was working on his site for a grand project – the building of a permanent museum. He had the support of Prince Albert, who was hopeful that the new building in South Kensington would be the catalyst for the utopian Royal vision of a magnificent 'Albertopolis', a series of striking buildings amid landscaped parkland, drawing together London's learned and artistic societies. So enthusiastic was the Prince, in fact, and so keen to play his part, that he had begun to design the new museum himself. And with his energy and influence, added to Cole's determination, things had progressed quickly. Plans had been drawn up and measurements taken. In just a few more weeks, building would begin.

But Robinson was fond of the rooms at Marlborough House and did not want to relocate, particularly not to the backwater that was South Kensington. 'Everyone predicts ill luck to the move to Kensington on the score of distance,' he grumbled in a letter to Cole, pointing out what the popular press had already highlighted: that the new site was unfamiliar, isolated, difficult to access and little more than 'wilds and swamps'.[4] What's more, Cole's plans were so vast and disparate that it was not at all clear how it would all fit together. There were proposals for a Patent Museum and for manufacturing displays but also for an exhibition of exotic foods like French snails and Chinese birds' nests, and of animal products, including a case showing silkworms at work. There was to be a huge plaster cast of Michelangelo's *David* and an extraordinary range of objects that apparently could not find a home elsewhere. There was even to be space on the second floor for fish hatcheries, with the runs of salmon and trout announced in the newspapers. The proposed museum seemed a curious mix of the fairground atmosphere of the International Exhibitions and the old-fashioned jumble of curiosities that had inspired the *Wunderkammer*. It lacked a sense of historical progress and threatened to confuse, and overwhelm, the visitor. Once Cole's Chamber of Horrors had been put away, the rooms at Marlborough House were well focused, with planned collections and organized displays. For a museum of its time, it was remarkably clear-sighted. It demonstrated the growing sense of professionalism among curators and rigorous principles of scholarship. Much of this was Robinson's work. He liked the intimacy and coherence of Marlborough House, and was sure that the new museum would be a disaster, nothing better than a 'motley, medley chaos. . . assimilated in an illogical and bewildering manner'.[5]

Entangled with Robinson's discontent about the new museum

was a lingering feeling that at the same time his own role was being overlooked and undervalued. He was travelling extensively to seek out objects: in 1854 alone, he had acquired over 1,400 new pieces. He was writing and lecturing vigorously on the collections; he was making contacts. Delighted by the growing number of visitors, he was constantly refining the rapidly expanding displays, and he was bombarding the board with requests for money to make acquisitions. He had taken responsibility for most of the collections, added a couple of titles to his role and had brought some of Europe's finest objects to the rooms in Marlborough House. His work with the Fine Arts Club and networks of private collectors also allowed him to see the wider influence of his activity. His buying on behalf of the museum was changing the market, pushing up prices rapidly. During the museum's five years at Marlborough House, the value of its collections rose so much that Robinson was able to report happily that he had 'speedily doubled or trebled' the original investments. There was also, however, a downside to this, as the competitive Robinson was quick to recognize. As the market boomed, the museum needed to keep pace, he said, with 'a host of wealthy amateurs, who, unfettered by the delays and difficulties impeding all governmental action. . . step in, and, by the power of ready money, triumphantly beat out of the field the unlucky curators of our public collections'.[6] It was clear that the mutual, and complex, relationship between the museum and the private collector, and the markets they shared, was developing quickly. And in this cut-and-thrust environment Robinson felt that his collecting skills were needed more than ever.

Since he was of such benefit to the museum, Robinson could see no reason why his salary, at least, should not be raised in recognition of his contribution. At the beginning of March 1855, he wrote to Henry Cole to ask for more money. Acknowledging his young curator's energy and enthusiasm, Cole agreed promptly to the pay rise. But he just as promptly regretted it because, less than six months later, Robinson was writing again to demand another raise.[7] The collections were continuing to thrive under his hand and his devotion to them was evident. His every thought was about the objects he might bring to Marlborough House and improvements he might make to the displays. He had completed two scholarly catalogues, 'with critical or theoretic illustrations for the information of the student' and more and more visitors were coming to see what was being achieved.[8] He believed he had a convincing case for promotion and, with a successful precedent behind him, Robinson was confident. He could not see how Cole could fail to reward him again.

But weeks passed, the builders moved on to the site in South Kensington and still there was no official answer to Robinson's request. Slowly the iron frame of the new museum grew into the London landscape, the grass around became muddy with the tramp of workers' boots, and still Robinson waited. He was angry and puzzled. He wondered if Cole and the museum board had somehow overlooked his request in the flurry of activity caused by the building project. But when he tried to raise the matter again, he received only awkward and evasive answers. He was convinced that Cole could do more and he grew increasingly frustrated and cross. Worse still, he could not bring himself to admit the heart of the matter. It was true that he was indispensable to the growing museum. It was clear that it needed his scholarship. He may well have deserved better remuneration for the work he was doing. But more immediately apparent than any of these arguments – to Robinson and to his disapproving bank manager – was that he was in desperate need of the extra money for which he was asking.

Robinson had never lived cheaply. He aspired to keep a household that suited his sense of refinement and announced his success. On accepting the job in London, he had taken on both a substantial and elegant townhouse in York Place, Portman Square, along with the requisite number of servants, and a wife. Marian Elizabeth Newton, the daughter of a successful Norwich tradesman, was quiet and undemanding. As far as we know, she did not share Robinson's taste for stalking antiques shops and dealers in search of costly pieces of bric-a-brac, nor his habit of spending money on European travel. But nevertheless, with a household to support, Robinson's costs escalated and, within a few years of marriage, the first of seven children arrived. Robinson's expenses were rising along with his sense of frustration. It was not just that he felt he deserved more money; he *needed* more money.

For a young man establishing a family and a professional career, it was not unusual to find daily expenses running over budget. But Robinson's collecting could be seen as something of an extravagance and, in the mid-century, this kind of excess was subject to a raft of moral judgements that, if turned in Robinson's direction, could have threatened his future. Profligacy, bankruptcy, financial disaster and the lack of good moral character they suggested fascinated Victorian writers such as Charles Dickens and Wilkie Collins, who kept the spectre of 'living beyond one's means' firmly in the public eye. The plot of Dickens's *Little Dorrit*, published between 1855 and 1857, at the same time as Robinson was making his overtures to the museum authorities, highlights the shame, personal decline and poverty that accompany bankruptcy, while almost a decade later, in *Our Mutual Friend* (1864–5), the contrast between the simple living of the impoverished Mortimer Lightwood and the glittering, unpaid-for interiors of the Lammle household has a clear moral message: 'how often have I pointed out to you that it's the moral influence is the important thing?' asks Lightwood's friend Eugene Wrayburn.[9] Too overt a display of possessions was not only an indication of suspect taste, but also of dubious character. The glut of objects on show in the Lammle household acts to conceal both their lamentable financial situation and their sinister intentions:

The handsome fittings and furnishings of the house in Sackville Street were piled thick and high over the skeleton up-stairs, and if it ever whispered from under its upholstery 'Here I am in the closet!' it was to very few ears. . .[10]

Robinson needed to take care that his collecting did not come to be seen as simply an expression of wanton spending and lack of moral fibre. Nor would he have wanted to get caught up in the Lammle fashion for objects merely as display. To maintain his course towards serious, meaningful collecting, it was imperative that he steady his financial situation.

Disappointed with Cole and obstructed by the board, Robinson continued to wait. If he could not succeed in increasing his regular salary, then the obvious next step was to sell some of his collection to supplement what he earned. But such a move was not to be taken lightly. Souvenirs of his youth in Paris; bargains from French and Italian junkshops; finely framed paintings and mirrors; jewel-coloured tapestries – they all meant something special to him. In the spring of 1855, Robinson was still, at thirty-one, a young collector. In time, he would become accustomed to the idea of changing his collection, of selling on some pieces to buy others, of investing for profit. His own preferences would evolve as his knowledge increased. At this stage, he found such a prospect difficult to contemplate. It seemed like a betrayal of the idea of the collection that he was still building. Daunted by such a step, nothing much happened.

The weeks and months passed, and no letter came to signal an upturn in Robinson's fortunes. The final touches were put to the building at South Kensington, and articles quickly appeared in the press to mock it. Reporters marvelled at its ugliness and its spirit of utilitarianism. Prince Albert's giant structure, clad in iron and looking like a cross between a beached ship and an oversized oil drum, was ridiculed as 'a threefold monster boiler'.[11] And the name stuck. Robinson shuttled backwards and forwards between Marlborough House and the new South Kensington site, 'The Brompton Boilers'. He moved objects and arranged displays. With the criticism of the Prince's design ringing in his ears, he battled with the weaknesses of the clumsy architecture: leaking roofs and poor drainage; galleries that baked in summer and were brittle with winter cold. Hastily, he had to move the plaster casts from their planned home upstairs as the floors groaned and buckled under the weight. But in June 1857, despite all the doubts and disturbances, he stood proudly at the opening of the new museum, holding himself tall and straight for the curious eyes of the press and public, stupefied for a moment by the enormity of what had been achieved and feeling his future unfolding before him.

The opening of the new buildings at last prompted the cheque-writing hands of the board into action, and Robinson settled into his new professional home with a slightly improved salary of £450 a year, the dual responsibility of Librarian-Curator and an assistant. This was a comfortable living: probationary police officers were paid only £10 a year, a chaplain could expect a salary of around £30 and a letter sorter at the General Post Office earned £90 a year, about the same as a senior teacher, although solicitors and barristers could expect to earn as much as £1,800 a year by this time. But in the context of Robinson's professional colleagues, the pay rise was minimal, far from the £600 a year, plus accommodation, enjoyed by the curators at the British Museum or the £750 salary granted to the Keeper of the National Gallery.[12] Moreover, it still did not pay the bills. There was no choice: some of Robinson's collection would have to be sold.

I have not found a record of exactly what Robinson chose to part with at this time. Certainly, the core of his collection remained intact, but even so the process was a wrench. Characteristically, he took refuge from the distress of the sale, and the frustrations of life at the museum, in the showrooms of Europe's antique dealers. The museum may have been unwilling to raise his salary substantially, but it was prepared to fund continuing research trips abroad. Robinson undertook a series of yearly expeditions, each lasting several months, and each yielding 'an infinity of treasures. . . at fractional prices'. In the summer of 1857, just after the museum opening, Robinson took off to Dresden and Vienna. By the summer of 1859, he was back in Italy on the trail of 'cartloads of majolica ware, innumerable cassoni, terra–cottas, and bronzes'. He was in the mood for aggressive collecting. The spoils of Italian cultural life 'must be diligently fought for', he asserted, throwing himself wholeheartedly into the crusade to find new objects and writing home enthusiastically that 'Florence has not had such a raking out as this within the memory of man'.[13]

Robinson relished the independence of collecting on the move. His days took on the rhythms common to collectors across the Continent: bursts of enthusiastic buying, long hours of frustrated travelling and the enduring desire to discover more and better things. If there were gaps in his knowledge, he plugged them with scholarly reading and conversation, so that he could hunt out and identify the best objects. Alongside his study of sculpture, he launched into the appreciation of bookbinding and manuscripts, textiles, metalwork, furniture and jewellery. He travelled quickly and bought extensively. He felt liberated again. He could ignore the irritations of the museum, and what he viewed as Henry Cole's attempts to limit him.

But such freedom was not to last. Robinson, with his nose on the trail of prestigious collections, perhaps misread the mood back at South Kensington. The museum, installed in its new site, was becoming more professional, and Henry Cole, free of the burden of the building project, was turning his attention to improving administration; there was a growing realisation that the museum should provide a model of what could be done, a blueprint for budding municipal projects up and down the country, and, indeed, across the world. In the years after the opening of the South Kensington Museum, a number of institutions were established along similar lines, with an emphasis on educating and developing public taste, raising the quality of manufactures and providing a showcase for craftsmanship. In Vienna, the Museum of Applied Arts opened in 1864, and in Berlin and Hamburg, two large and ambitious museums began assertively collecting the decorative arts during the 1860s with such success that by 1878 *The Athenaeum* was proud to announce that 'Art and Industrial Museums, humble copies of our own parent establishment in South Kensington, continue to spring up all over Germany'.[14] And it was perhaps in the USA that the specific example provided by South Kensington was most admired and emulated. *Harper's New Monthly Magazine* claimed that the founding of museums in Cincinnati, Chicago, Philadelphia and Boston was in direct and admiring imitation of the London model and hoped that this new generation of public institutions would be as successful as South Kensington in 'widening waves of taste and love of beauty through the country'.[15] Meanwhile, the *New York Herald* looked forward to the opening of the Metropolitan Museum of Art in early 1872 by explaining that it would be modelled on 'the splendid South Kensington Gardens London [sic], which is probably the most perfect thing of the kind in the world. . . a great work in behalf of civilization and education'.[16]

In the light of such praise, Cole was no doubt aware that others were scrutinizing his models of curating and display. With the management of the British Museum and the National Gallery drawing such frequent criticism, he may well have seen a further chance to impress. Public discussion of the National Gallery had singled out the museum at South Kensington – as well as his leadership – for commendation: 'We cannot refrain from bearing testimony to the ability, knowledge, and devotion displayed by Mr Cole in the management of the Kensington Museum,' suggested an article in *Quarterly Review*. 'The varied and admirably arranged collections exhibited there now form one of the most useful and interesting exhibitions of the metropolis, and are a convincing proof of what may be accomplished in a short space of time by well-directed and unfettered energy.'[17] With such approval from the critics, and as the museum matured, Cole turned his attention more and more to securing its administration. Creative collecting and active educating needed reinforcing with clear and accountable day-to-day systems. This meant the careful management of staff and finances – and it meant keeping a close rein on Robinson.

In Rome in 1859, Robinson sat down to write again to the museum from the cramped cold of his winter lodgings. This letter was swiftly scribbled, the tone urgent and sure. Robinson had his mind firmly on collecting and not on museum administration. He wanted to buy fifteen key pieces from the collection of Giampietro Campana who had spent years leading archaeological expeditions and bringing together Etruscan, Roman and Greek art, as well as Renaissance masterpieces. Campana was well connected – he was adviser to the Grand Duke of Saxe-Weimar, and his wife's family was related to Napoleon III. He was also responsible for the papal Monte di Pietà, a system offering financial loans. It worked almost like a pawn shop: wealthy patrons contributed to a central fund, without the expectation that their money would be returned. Those needing a loan could apply to the fund, exchanging an object of value for ready cash. In 1857, however, Campana was arrested for using the Monte di Pietà to finance his own collecting. He was stripped of his collection and imprisoned. Almost immediately a scramble began across Europe to take advantage of his disgrace. Collectors poured into Rome, and Robinson was just one of the international connoisseurs negotiating for the best pieces as they came on sale. Campana's magnificent collection finally raised about £207,000, the largest amount ever realized, to that date, for a single collection.

Robinson also wanted over half of the collection (almost seventy pieces) which had belonged to Campana's agent, who had also found the Monte di Pietà funds a useful way of supporting his personal collecting and who had been caught up in Campana's downfall. He believed he had negotiated a fair price. He wrote to the museum and made the case for the purchase plainly, requesting that the money be sent without delay so that he would not have to risk fending off rival collectors. But again, Robinson had to wait and, when an answer finally came, it infuriated him: there would be no funds forthcoming, he was told, and he was to make no immediate purchases. The Campana treasures went elsewhere – many were bought by Stepan Gedeonov on behalf of the Imperial Hermitage in St Petersburg and by Napoleon III for the French collections – and Robinson had no choice but to return to London empty-handed.

It is easy to imagine the gloom of the journey. It was a wet spring and tensions were running high among the various Italian factions vying for power as unification loomed. Roads were frequently blockaded and travellers stopped and searched. Progress was slow. And all Robinson had to think about as he waited at barriers was the humiliation and disappointment of having his advice spurned by the museum. He was not a man to doubt himself and he could see no satisfactory reason why his acquisitions should have been blocked. The museum was clearly mistaken and short-sighted in its refusal to buy the Italian works.

He felt that his ambition for the collections was being wasted, and his vision for their future distorted. He was burning with a sense of injustice and grievance that was to smoulder inside him for a very long time. And on his return to South Kensington in the autumn of 1859 there was a furious row.

Both Robinson and Henry Cole, it seems, were tired of playing cat and mouse with each other. Their rumbling complaints and accusations cracked open in a series of irate exchanges. Robinson bemoaned the uncertainty of his position, his poor salary and the lack of trust the museum appeared to have in his judgement. Belligerent and cantankerous, he stamped and puffed and hollered. In return, Cole, who was more than able to hold his own in an argument, prodded away at Robinson's administrative shortcomings. He demanded to know why Robinson was not keeping any record of his movements and transactions and why his official diary was little better than blank.

Robinson's old-fashioned, self-reliant way of collecting was finally colliding with Cole's administrative priorities and the growing sense of the curator as a public servant instead of a free-wheeling connoisseur. Robinson's habits of collecting for the museum were much the same as the habits of a gentleman collector spending his own money. He believed that the justification for buying the best things was self-evident, and he could not understand the need to constrict or explain his activities by means of record-keeping. There was a sense in which he saw himself as some kind of crusader, travelling Europe to liberate the most beautiful treasures, like those of Campana's collection, and bringing them back to safety. The spheres of private and public collecting were intimately entangled during the Victorian period, more so than ever before or since: the collection being developed at South Kensington was so much a part of Robinson's character and had his identity so clearly written into it that it was difficult to see any distinction between his personal choices and those he was making on behalf of the nation. He took advantage of the ambiguities of a role that was still evolving, letting his personal collecting priorities drive what existed of a public policy.

Cole's accusations only acted to entrench Robinson yet further in his ways, and to reignite the continuing battle over the philosophical basis for the collections. The two men seemed to be moving ever further apart. Robinson complained that the office accommodation was cramped and uncomfortable, moaning that 'we are all packed close as pigs' in the square rooms. But alongside his physical discomfort he also started to complain about the 'ceaseless tramp' of visitors to the popular new galleries.[18] It seemed as though the practicalities of open public access were beginning to grate on Robinson's sensibilities. His discontent with Cole's mish-mash of modern collections at South Kensington was becoming identified with a wider disillusion with the way the museum was developing. Robinson's interests remained with Europe's elite collectors, and, as his contacts grew among the members of the Fine Arts Club and his own collecting became increasingly expensive and erudite, he was perhaps beginning to feel superior to the populist approach at South Kensington. His sense of what was right for the museum was constantly being offended: in 1861, funds for Robinson to take another planned trip to Italy to study Renaissance sculpture were diverted instead for Cole to go to the International Exhibition in Florence to buy objects for the less refined museum displays, including food and animal products as well as examples of contemporary design. Cole's new attack about record-keeping only added to Robinson's feeling that policy was heading in the wrong direction. He was desperate to prove that Cole was wrong – and that he was right.

It was a relief, in the end, to close the 1862 exhibition and to be able to walk through the galleries again in the heavy quiet, with the visitors gone and the noise of activity in the rest of the museum somehow distant and without meaning. Robinson could take a moment now to breathe deeply in the calm, catching the scent of the past. The exhibition had proved a success, and had reasserted his position as the champion of the rare and the beautiful. It had boosted the collections: many of the lenders had been persuaded to donate their objects permanently to the museum. And it had cemented Robinson's role at the heart of the Fine Arts Club, and at the heart of British collecting.

Robinson had founded the Fine Arts Club just six years earlier in 1856, dedicating it to helping collections grow and improve, and to finding the best objects. The Club, which was later rechristened the Burlington Fine Arts Club, began quietly enough with evening receptions in Marlborough House, 'frequently', as Robinson boasted, 'of the most elaborate and costly character': fine wines and fine food shared among those who enjoyed talking about art.[19] But it soon became extremely popular and membership had to be limited to two hundred, to make it manageable.

The club's membership was erudite and varied, drawn from all kinds of professional backgrounds and crossing political affiliations. There were practising artists such as John Henderson, a gifted amateur painter and archaeologist, and Baron Carlo Marochetti, a sculptor. There were wealthy establishment figures such as Sir Henry Thompson, surgeon to the Queen. Politicians included Lord Overstone, a celebrated banker and High Sheriff of Warwickshire, and Alexander Beresford Hope, a vehement opponent of the 1867 Reform Bill which aimed to extend the vote to the urban working class. There were also, inevitably, representatives of the English aristocracy, such as the Duke of Hamilton and Sir William Holburne, whose renowned collection was displayed in his fashionable Bath townhouse. And there were members who were very much engaged in the debates about public education and access to art. Meetings were attended by both Charles Eastlake, director of the National Gallery, and John

Ruskin. The membership also included the Liberal politician William Gladstone, who was to serve the first of his four terms as Prime Minister from 1868, and who managed to persuade Parliament to pass the Education Act of 1870, to establish public school boards. In a departure from the usual model of the gentleman's club, women, too, were invited and by 1867 there were eight female members.

The club's mixed membership no doubt led to some lengthy discussions, but the emphasis was firmly on collecting, rather than politics, and members clearly relished the chance to meet, if only to keep an eye on what others were doing. It was an indication of the power of the collecting impulse that the club managed to draw together such a disparate crowd with one common aim. It was also a testament to Robinson's diplomatic skills, and it demonstrated just how confident he was – as a curator from an ordinary background – mixing in such circles. Under Robinson's guidance, meetings flourished and when the museum became established in South Kensington, so too did the Fine Arts Club. But in time meetings were also held increasingly in private houses. This clearly allowed members to show off their collections to each other, but it might also have signalled a growing closing of ranks, and a desire to create a more elite atmosphere. The election of members by invitation created a structure for excluding more modest collectors; the membership limit of two hundred could be seen in this light as a matter of policy as well as practicality, ensuring the club was reserved for a comfortable coterie of learned friends. Collecting at this level was still entangled with the traditions of social class, and many members of the Fine Arts Club were no doubt keen to differentiate their activity from populist spectacles like the Great Exhibition. Robinson himself was certainly alert to such distinctions: the 1851 event at Crystal Palace was, he recognized, 'the apotheosis of commerce and the shopkeeper. The aristocratic and cultured classes had comparatively little sympathy with the great exhibition, and had little or nothing to do with it', whereas the Fine Arts Club 'comprised every connoisseur of note in the country'.[20]

Despite some of the club members' more liberal credentials, it was this atmosphere of exclusivity and culture for the privileged few that became an issue in the wake of the 1862 exhibition. Cole found he was having to fend off assaults from the press and Parliament who accused the museum of forgetting its original educational purpose. The splendour and refinement of the 1862 show – displaying, perhaps too clearly, the obvious wealth of those who organized it – reinforced the impression that the museum had abandoned its roots in favour of a more glamorous and elegant existence. Despite all of Cole's hard work on the core principles of design education, many visitors were getting the impression that the South Kensington galleries were straying away from sound and useful practice. During one debate, MPs harangued Cole by name and claimed the museum was no longer fulfilling its express original purpose of providing examples for education and training and had become instead 'nothing but a great toyshop for the amusement of the residents in the west-end'.[21]

Although Cole vociferously defended the museum against such criticism, there was no disputing the fact that the evidence looked damning. Students themselves, at design schools both in London and the provinces, complained continually that the museum was letting them down and that the collections were inaccessible and of little use to their studies. A written statement from the students at the London School of Design in 1864 declared the displays of 'limited utility' and one Lambeth student claimed that the museum 'might as well be in the moon' for any use it was to him.[22] Cole was under increasing pressure to justify the amounts that had been spent – mostly by Robinson – on paintings and other objects which were of only slight relevance to design education: 'What use to the practical workmen of the present day is the reliquary purchased recently... in Paris for the enormous sum of £2,142?' demanded *Art Journal*.[23] And indeed, when the accounts were finally examined, it was found that most of the public money given to the museum by the government in the decade since its opening had been used for non-educational purposes: to fund the increasingly complicated administration, to develop and maintain the growing complex of buildings, to finance travel abroad and to buy expensive works of art for the collections, in line with Robinson's private tastes. Visitor numbers continued to be healthy: figures hovered around 40,000 to 50,000 a month, for admission on free days, with as many people coming after work during evening opening as during the day.[24] But the purpose of the museum seemed, especially to those who were funding it, to be increasingly opaque and confused.

Cole could not shake off the feeling that much of the criticism was Robinson's fault. During the grey, smoggy days of January and February 1863, the mood at the museum became fierce and gladiatorial. Cole found a host of accusations to level at Robinson, complaining in particular about his unremitting insolence. Once again, he ripped into the state of Robinson's record-keeping. This time, however, he had a new complaint. Cole suspected something other than just administrative incompetence. Robinson was not simply forgetting to record his movements and to write up his sales – he was apparently being purposely secretive. He was, Cole believed, ensuring that the museum could not trace his movements nor piece together his activities. With the wet sleet falling thickly on to the glass roofs of the new galleries, melting into the courtyards in heavy streams and stifling the rattle of the world beyond, Cole finally voiced the accusation that had been gnawing within him for so long: was Robinson collecting for the museum, or for himself?

Robinson did not respond. It was clear that the line between his public and private collecting was becoming increasingly blurred, and that his enthusiasm for collecting was apt to override all other concerns, but in reply he simply repeated his own grievances: he complained again about the trouble he had getting his purchases sanctioned, about the heating of the cranky building and about the poor lighting in the galleries. Cole's question remained unanswered and, as the cold days dragged on, so too did the series of bitter exchanges. Cole could not break down Robinson's cantankerous self-confidence; Robinson continued to make it clear that he regarded much of the museum's achievement as his own work. Inevitably, the dispute leeched into the wider workings of the museum, drawing the staff and authorities into the venomous quarrel. During March 1863, Robinson bombarded two of the museum board members, Lord Granville and Lord Lowe, with a series of letters. In reply, the board registered its strong disapproval of Robinson's ragged financial paperwork and bristled at the news that he had made purchases in Italy without waiting for permission, taking the decisions on behalf of the museum 'on his own responsibility'. It noted that Robinson's accounting from the 1862 loan exhibition was 'loose and unsatisfactory' and in desperation withheld the cash gratuity Robinson was due as a reward for his hard work.[25]

The unending squabbles took their toll on Robinson's health. He suffered from almost permanent indigestion, headaches stopped him working and he found he was getting unusually confused by even quite simple tasks. But he would not give up the fight. His tone was confrontational, contemptuous and bitter. His irresistible ambition for the collections was at the heart of his continuing complaints, but his subject matter, more often than not, was Henry Cole. He continued to send a string of disparaging notes to individual board members, damning Cole's 'administrative talents and practical energy' with faint praise and openly challenging his superior: 'his specific knowledge of Art', he wrote on one occasion, 'is in my opinion not equal to the actual work of forming and technically directing a public Collection of such a varied and comprehensive nature'. As if that was not condemnation enough, more was in store. Cole was, Robinson claimed, unfit to make decisions or negotiate deals on the museum's behalf: 'Unfortunately, Mr Cole's selections were rarely either timely or judicious, made on the spur of the moment by accident or momentary impulse,' he alleged.[26]

Robinson's accusations were not without precedent elsewhere. In November 1853, William Gladstone, as Chancellor of the Exchequer, had bought sixty-four German paintings for the National Gallery. By the summer of 1854, William Dyce, an established artist and previously the head of the government School of Design in London, had looked at the paintings and found that most of them were of low quality. Only seventeen were worth keeping for the national collection. On this occasion, it was the gallery, rather than Gladstone, that attracted criticism: the incident was used as further evidence that the trustees were failing and that public money was being ill-spent. By directing a similar attack at Henry Cole – perhaps with the Gladstone incident firmly in mind – Robinson was reminding the board members that they were likely to be held to account if Cole's alleged incompetence came to light. He was clearly hoping to use the board's discomfort for his own ends. His concern for the use of public funds seems ironic, given his habitual free-spending on the museum's behalf, and it was more likely that he was hoping for a fundamental change in leadership that would allow him to take charge, or at least rid him of an irritant.

As spring arrived in South Kensington, the leaves splitting green on the trees and the rotten mud in the streets beginning to harden, the internecine war at the museum was at its most vicious. Cole was at his wits' end with his subordinate's defiance, and Lord Lowe, on behalf of the board, proclaimed angrily that Robinson's letters must stop. Robinson, however, remained in rebellious mood and, when the museum failed to allocate him one of four new purpose-built staff residences, he took it as the final slight. By Easter, as a flush of warm weather blew into the city, things were at boiling point.

It was just before the Easter of 1863 that Henry Cole asked to see Robinson. Cole had had enough of his irritating curator and had decided to act: 'never keep a man who is dissatisfied, he is mischievous. . . this would perhaps apply to J.C.R.', he admitted to his diary.[27] He told Robinson that he would have to leave his post as curator. The museum was changing; it needed a new staff structure, and Robinson was being offered the role of salaried consultant or 'Art Referee', without control of the collections but still with a remit to give advice on purchases. Robinson was taken by surprise. At first, he was convinced that he would find a way to overturn the decision against him – and get rid of Cole in the process. But in the end there was nothing to be done. The board told him firmly that 'he must submit or go' and for a while – and against his natural instincts – Robinson chose submission.[28] But he was uncomfortable in his new role and his wounded pride blistered. He soon found there were to be three art referees, and he was not even destined to be the most senior of them: that role was to be filled by an old friend of Cole's from the Schools of Design, Richard Redgrave. Pushed further down the hierarchy, Robinson felt that his vision was being purposely slighted.

Beyond the museum, Robinson's expertise was already being missed and his demotion noted with alarm. His fellow collectors knew all too well that they were determining the shape of the national collection at South Kensington just as much as the utilitarian creed of Cole and the board, and Robinson's network soon began to rumble with the discontent of losing their linchpin. At the Fine Arts Club, influential members were dismayed to find that their interests were being sidelined and the discussion at meetings regularly slipped away from the objects on display to an animated discussion of Robinson's fate. A stinging piece in the influential *Art Journal* publicly voiced the growing dissatisfaction. In an opinionated article that was read by all the most important collectors, dealers and curators, the magazine took a snipe at Cole's leadership and lauded Robinson. 'It is to his [Robinson's] indefatigable industry, no less than to his sound and matured knowledge, that we are mainly indebted for the value of the Museum,' *Art Journal* announced. The article made its loyalties plain and recognized, too, where the real power lay – not with the museum or with its administrators, but with individual collectors up and down the country. Collectors mattered, and Robinson, it claimed, 'has the confidence of every collector in the kingdom'. As the journal warmed to its subject, its attack on Cole became increasingly spiteful. Cole's abilities, it noted scathingly, were 'not at all equal' to Robinson's scholarly connoisseurship and it was with distinct pleasure that it offered a final, damning judgement: 'it is not pleasant for a colonel to know that a corporal he commands is a better soldier than himself'.[29]

With the backing of his collectors, and in defiance of his real lack of influence, Robinson harried and annoyed the museum staff and directors, and Cole, of course, in particular. For four years, he goaded and bothered and griped. Minutes of the museum board meetings noted, wearily, that Robinson still needed constantly reminding of the limits of his duties, but, even in the face of persistent reprimands, he still could not believe that he would not make progress.[30] He continually tried to conjure up authority for himself, anxious to make it appear that he retained the vestiges of power. Even in the face of a Select Committee of the House of Commons in 1867, he raged against Cole's commitment to purchasing examples of con-temporary design for the museum, arguing fearlessly and proudly that the works he had been buying were 'vastly more important'.[31] It became clear to Cole that even at arm's length Robinson was making a nuisance of himself. He decided to act before he was undermined by Robinson's constant sniping and the distressing criticism from his allies. He looked around for something – anything – that would give him the excuse he needed to make the final break. And in his neat piles of paperwork and closely written documents, he found it.

It was Christmas 1867. The windows of the small stores along the Brompton Road, a short stroll from the South Kensington site – including the premises of the rapidly expanding Harrods – were bright with gifts and treats and lights. Delivery boys pushed their barrows and carts anxiously through the traffic as the ladies of the fashionable middle classes, bobbing within the frames of their wide crinolines, shopped diligently and, if they could, stylishly. Robinson's seven children were no doubt light-headed with the excitement, with the promise of change from their strict routine, with the soft smells drifting through from the kitchen and with the thought of puddings and sweets and oranges.

Alone in the museum, Henry Cole was reading a museum staffing report written two years earlier for the Treasury. The language was formal and elaborate, the tone sombre. There was nothing festive about it. But contained within the convoluted sentences was the ammunition he needed to rid himself of Robinson for good. The report proposed saving money by reducing the museum staff to its general administrators. Specialist expertise, it suggested, could be bought in temporarily, as and when it was needed. The idea of art referees drawing a salary for consultancy work was, perhaps unsurprisingly, highlighted as uneconomic. A committee, drafted in to look at the implications of restructuring, agreed. Two days before Christmas, on 23 December 1867, Robinson's post was abolished. 'Request that Mr

Robinson's superannuation may date from 1 April 1868. He is to have notice from 1 January,' noted the official memo blandly.[32] Robinson's life was about to change irrevocably. As he celebrated the close of the year at home with his family, the unaccustomed lightness and gaiety of the season lifted, for a moment, his disappointment and frustration. But there was no escaping the bleak realization that his tenure at South Kensington was over. On 10 January 1868, the board wrote to Robinson again, reaffirming their decision, and he was forced to accept that things were really at an end. He would have to leave.

Working out his notice was frustrating and painful. His fifteen years as a curator had shaped him. He had started as an eager and knowledgeable young man, ambitious to succeed in London, but naïve and obscure. He was leaving as an established connoisseur and scholar, respected at home and abroad, and with a reputation for clever and imaginative collecting. He had become integral to the growth of the South Kensington Museum from a few borrowed rooms in Marlborough House to an important international collection in purpose-built galleries. He had developed the first British collection of medieval and Renaissance decorative art and, in doing so, helped create a whole new field for British collectors. His spiky relationship with Henry Cole and his bitter exchanges with the board had sharpened his determination and clarified his sense of purpose. His self-belief had swelled and his confidence matured. Now everything was crumbling.

Suspicions and accusations that had been grumbling poisonously in the background for months, and even years, came bubbling to the fore now that it was certain that Robinson was leaving. There were plenty of disgruntled colleagues willing to step forward to tell tales. Robinson was not an easy man to work with and he was not afraid to offend those he regarded simply as clerks, bureaucrats and charlatans. Now, with his power draining from him, he found he was prey to the spite of gossip and unconstrained resentment. And the museum authorities, thoroughly weary of Robinson's defiance, seemed eager to make it clear just how right they were in dismissing him. Cole's long-held allegation that Robinson had been using his position at the museum to make money as a dealer – that he had been buying and selling on his own behalf when he was travelling on museum business – resurfaced with unpleasant vigour: 'An Art Referee has not considered himself precluded when abroad from purchasing objects of art for friends,' noted the board brusquely in early January.[33] Robinson responded to the allegation with his usual energy. He may have been out of favour, but he remained defiant. As far as he was concerned, his name was being slandered and his work belittled. So furious did he become that the board backtracked, perhaps unwilling to get too embroiled when it was only a matter of weeks until they were free of Robinson's bickering: 'It is not intended to cast any imputation or reflection on your honour and fidelity as a public servant,' the museum reassured Robinson on the 20th.[34] But it was a small victory, and a chilly valediction. By the spring of 1868, Robinson was gone.

Cole and Robinson seemed to enshrine two possible futures for the museum at South Kensington, with Cole's breadth of activity and administrative professionalism standing in contrast to Robinson as the scholar and collector. Cole was committed to the principles of public service and was eager to explore all kinds of different projects from inventing commercial Christmas cards to mounting international trade fairs; Robinson could not be shaken from his independent habits and was happiest at the heart of his collection. But the sense of the two philosophies being completely irreconcilable was largely illusory. Across Britain and Europe, at other museums, the same principles were being debated and the same changes were being worked through as the ideas and practice of curating collections evolved. It was largely as a result of the clash of two belligerent and opinionated men that the process at South Kensington was so painful.

A few miles away at the British Museum, another collector, Augustus Wollaston Franks, was making his own personal mark, creating an environment of professionalism and scholarship that evolved a little more peaceably than at South Kensington. He joined the staff at the British Museum in 1851 (two years before Robinson first took up his post at Marlborough House), with responsibility for developing the neglected collections of British objects, and he remained at the museum for almost half a century, until his death in 1897. Determined and strong-willed, and occasionally temperamental, he completely changed the collecting policy and departmental structure. He made significant personal contributions to the collections, and oversaw the growth of the British galleries from 154 feet of wall cases and a handful of table cases to 2,250 feet of wall cases, 90 table cases and 31 upright cases. He is regarded by many as the founder of the modern British Museum.

Educated at Eton and Trinity College, Cambridge (where he spent much of his time collecting and pursuing his own architecture and archaeology projects), Franks was keen from the outset to develop an intellectual environment at the British Museum. His sympathies lay with the scholar: he would countenance general visitors to the museum if he had to, but he outlawed children, who could, he was sure, 'derive no benefit from seeing the collections'.[35] He became an expert on a range of subjects from Japanese flint instruments and Anglo-Saxon ivories to Indian sculpture and English ceramics. He wrote original and learned articles (though he did not publish very much), kept up an energetic correspondence with other collectors and travelled widely, becoming an important member of an international group of scholars who met throughout Europe to discuss anthropology and archaeology. Like Robinson, he combined a commitment to public collections with a private collecting habit. Alongside his curatorial work, he amassed an encyclopaedic personal collection, some of which was left to the British Museum in a vast bequest that included 3,300 finger rings, over 500 pieces of high-quality European porcelain, 1,500 netsuke (miniature Japanese sculptures), 30,000 bookplates and other pieces of jewellery. 'Collecting,' he admitted, 'is a hereditary disease, and I fear incurable.'[36]

Franks' drive to collect – for himself, his friends and colleagues and his museum – meant that his activities often occupied the grey area of confusion between the public and private. Like Robinson, the strength of his personality seemed to be the cohesive force that often made sense of what and how he collected, although to modern eyes the failure to delineate between his personal and public roles can seem strange. Objects came and went freely between his own collection and the museum displays. In 1885, for example, Franks was cataloguing a 'painted figure of a bald person' brought from Japan for the British Museum, when he decided to swap it for a better one of his own: 'in place of this, removed by me from the collection, has been substituted a much finer wooden figure', he noted. Between 1864 and 1883, when Franks was looking after part of the British Museum's collections in a store in Victoria Street, Westminster, he explained that 'I paid myself the clerk or secretary who worked at it with me', rather than burdening the museum with extra costs.[37] There is no doubt that he saw little difference between the different aspects of his collecting; to him, the priority was to amass the finest things, however that might happen. To Franks' advantage was that he was a more conscientious administrator than Robinson and so his decisions and acquisitions were better documented.

On his arrival at the British Museum, Franks, like Robinson, soon began to reshape the collections. The British Museum had been dominated by the library departments, with the Director also being Librarian, and it was objects from the classical world that mostly filled the galleries. Almost single-handedly, Franks created collections from other countries and other periods that established whole new areas of interest: instead of classical pottery, he bought Japanese porcelain; he introduced English pre-historic material; and he invested in Chinese bronzes and objects from European archaeological excavations. Just as Robinson was challenging Cole's vision for South Kensington, so Franks was circumventing the traditions and bureaucracy in Bloomsbury to achieve what he wanted.

Unlike Robinson, however, Franks was also a skilled politician. After some initial sparring about the direction in which he seemed to be steering the museum, those above and around him came to respect and support his work. He was friendly with many of the museum's trustees. Coming from a distinguished aristocratic and banking family, the grandson of a baronet and cousin to the Earl of Harewood, and being a man of considerable fortune (although it is unclear exactly where this came from), Franks was also in the enviable position of being able to sweeten his politicking with generous, practical gestures. He gave over 7,000 objects to the museum during the time he was a curator there. With this kind of incentive, it is perhaps no surprise that his work was so widely admired by those above him in the hierarchy, nor that, unlike Robinson's superiors, they never cast doubt on whether public money was being siphoned off to feed Franks' personal collecting habits. No matter how he disguised it, Robinson could not escape the fact of his humble provincial origins. The leeway Franks was given, in contrast, was a reflection of his upper-class background and the consequent, instinctive, assumption that he could be trusted. It appeared to be taken for granted that Franks should be allowed to collect, obsessively, and that in the end the British Museum would benefit; there seemed to be little need to bother Franks with discussions about a conflict of interest.

Franks became a mainstay of Victorian collecting, the epitome of the scholar-collector. And the work he undertook to move the British Museum towards a more scholarly, collections-based approach was not unlike Robinson's crusade at South Kensington. For Robinson, however, it was the nature of the collections at South Kensington – as well as his clash with Henry Cole – that meant progress was particularly tortuous. South Kensington embodied a new and largely untried idea of a museum that might collect neither antiquities nor paintings, but something from the vast number of objects that fell somewhere beyond and between such categories. It is little surprise that the politics were complicated and fiery, nor that the identity of the collection was sometimes vague and confusing. The work both Robinson and Franks were doing, however, showed the increasing importance and influence of professional collectors. Working with large sums of public money, among a community that stretched across Europe, these new collector-curators were very much at the heart of things, forging a new vision for collecting that would last for generations.

CHAPTER SIX

The Tricks of the Trade

*D*espite Robinson's spirited defence, and the board's retraction, the notion that he had, for some while, been combining his work for the South Kensington Museum with work for private collectors proved hard to shake. There were plenty of people who marvelled at his ability to run his smart household on a curator's salary alone, and the conspicuous blanks in his museum diaries, especially when travelling abroad, were commonly held to conceal all kinds of private transactions. The belief that he had been using his knowledge and contacts as a collector to make money from dealing was widespread – and the idea stuck because there was truth in it. Travelling for the museum across Europe, Robinson was ideally placed to know where and when pieces were coming on to the market. From his discussions at the Fine Arts Club, he also knew exactly what people were collecting, and which works they were eager to acquire. It was not difficult to put the two together for profit. Robinson was a collector who revelled in the thrill of collecting, the sport of it, the hunting out and tracking down, the negotiations, intrigues and manoeuvrings; he also had a voracious appetite for acquisition. Funding this was desperately expensive. Adding to his museum salary seemed to make sense, either by buying directly for friends or by speculating on pieces that he knew he could sell on himself for a reasonable profit at auction.

Robinson bought and sold furiously. It was not necessarily unusual at this time for the distinction between collector and dealer to appear hazy. Dealers could end up amassing far more stock than they could sell, and so metamorphosed into collectors; the lively and extensive interaction between collectors meant that it was common for prized objects to change hands between them. But Robinson's official status at the South Kensington Museum made his situation sensitive; his foray into dealing, especially while on official trips abroad, was a disquieting complication of his role as a public servant with responsibility for public money. On top of this, there was also a lingering sense among some collectors that collecting and dealing should remain separate.

When Augustus Franks applied to join the British Museum in 1851, there was much discussion among his family as to whether a gentleman of his standing should be considering paid work. He had a ready entrée into high society and the reputation of being a keen member of his prestigious gentleman's club, the Athenaeum. He was certainly wealthy enough to be dismissive of the salary on offer, regarding it as pocket money. In these circumstances, the idea of a 'job' was distinctly uncomfortable. In the end, however, Franks managed to construct a philosophical basis for his work that satisfied his family's sensitivities, while allowing him to continue professional collecting: he positioned himself very clearly as a public servant, in the same way as other gentlemen of means in the Foreign Office, Parliament or the Church. He accepted a paid role at the museum, but also managed to keep himself apart from the usual administrators and workers. He made frequent purchases from his own money that he then donated to the museum, amounting to a value of around £50,000 (which would correspond to as much as £2 million today). This alone set him apart, reinforcing the impression that he was a gentleman of rank.

Robinson, it was clear, was treading a tricky path. Dealers were men of trade, while collectors were gentlemen. It would not do for the two to be confused. Austen Henry Layard, a diplomat, MP and archaeological pioneer, as well as a trustee of the National Gallery, voiced the concerns of the establishment. Robinson, he snorted, was 'bumptious and odious... the more I hear of Mr Robinson the less I like him. He is nothing but a dealer – up to every trick of the trade.'[1] Layard was, like Robinson, a collector. He was an excellent draughtsman and a scholarly historian and writer, specializing in European art. The two men's interests intersected particularly in their enthusiasm for Italy – where Layard was born and where he was to retire in the 1880s to write on Italian art and to develop his collection. They should, perhaps, have been friends. But Layard's assessment of Robinson, and his easy dismissal of dealers in general, was a clear indication that in many minds there remained a gulf between collecting and dealing. To be 'nothing but a dealer', Layard implied, was to be nothing much at all.

Robinson may well have harboured similar reservations himself. He was now a man with excellent social connections, a reputation for scholarship and a first-rate collection, and he was surely loath to sully any of these with the suggestion of commercial coarseness. But in 1868, with his tenure at the museum now at an end, he needed funds more than ever. He put fifty-six paintings and seventy-one Old Master drawings into a sale in Paris in May, but still money was tight. He could not afford to ignore the potential for using his knowledge to make a living. Moreover, he was distinguished, energetic and, at forty-three, still young. He was well equipped to deal with the demands of a new challenge, and well placed for forging a new career. If he was obliged to reinvent himself, what could be better than becoming a helping hand for other collectors, an expert friend, a seeker out of bargains and a stalwart at the sales? He would, at least, be free from the restrictions of public administration and accountability.

In 1871, Robinson was put forward for the directorship of the National Gallery, but when this fell through it seemed certain that his formal connection with British museums was over. His new life trading objects had begun in earnest. Nevertheless, it was likely that Robinson regarded himself as a successful collector, rather than as an outright dealer. He never owned a shop and he only worked with a range of refined, high-quality objects. But in practice the outcome was the same: collecting was making a profit, and Robinson's new career flourished rapidly. In 1873, just five years after leaving the South Kensington Museum, he had made enough money to begin looking around at suitable properties to supplement his London townhouse at York Place in Portman Square. He chose Newton Manor, near Swanage in Dorset, a secluded seventeenth-century house with walls of local Purbeck limestone, nestling among tall elms that creaked in summer winds.

When Robinson first discovered the old manor house, it had been used for years as a farm store and was putrid, neglected and shabby. Nonetheless, he was immediately taken with it and quickly set to work clearing the mess of low agricultural buildings and lean-tos from the back, and emptying the rooms of their animal inhabitants. 'Bats, rats and mice occupied the bedrooms, a colony of owls was established in one of the stone chimneys, and a swarm of bees was installed. . . at the other end of the roof,' he noted delightedly in a pamphlet of his reminiscences. Even better, 'we possess a private breed of spiders, fine, big, long-legged creatures, as active as race horses. One of their amiable customs is to drop down on the shoulders of our lady guests at dinner time.'[2] Robinson improved land on the estate, building new roads and planting trees, and discovered an interest in horticulture. He took to spending time outdoors and became fond of the many fine views stretching away across England's south coast.

There was just one disappointment – the house lacked a ghost. It certainly looked as though it should be haunted but, no matter how hard Robinson listened out for tell-tale bumps and moans, the ghosts failed to appear. To make matters worse, the little cottage at the edge of the estate, which had traditionally been used as the dower house, was notoriously haunted. Robinson could not suppress his envy: 'my house has not got a ghost whilst the cottage rejoices in the possession of a first-rate one,' he complained.[3] Despite this cause for regret, however, Robinson was in his element at Newton. He would be intense and emotional to the end of his days – without his 'extreme enthusiasm', noted his wife patiently, he would be a lesser man, a 'Samson with shorn locks' – but Newton Manor provided a sanctuary from the worst of life's irritations.[4] The angry days at South Kensington seemed to have passed.

Newton Manor was also the perfect location for an intimate, informal showroom. Robinson was keen to maintain the distinction between what he was doing and the tradition of the shopkeeping dealers pressed into Europe's major cities. Here he could create an environment that established him as the country gentleman. He could fill the house with his collection in the tradition of the aristocratic elite and create tasteful, elegant displays that had the illusion of being completely divorced from the financial realities of trade. Over the years, Robinson made a small fortune out of his knowledge of the art markets, but he spent much of it making Newton Manor beautiful. The house and its grounds became an extension of his collection. The garden was filled with Venetian sculpture, columns and fountains, including a life-size statue of Sylvanus, a muscular Roman woodland god, which puzzled and apparently alarmed locals passing by on the road. The dining room was hung with sixteenth-century Spanish panelling, Italian fireplaces and heavy carved wooden doors which gave it the sombre magnificence of an ancient ancestral home. Seventeenth-century suits of armour stood guard in the corridors; Roman busts gazed out across the estate and all kinds of fine paintings lined the walls of the old house, including a full-scale portrait of a nameless *Dutch Gentleman*. At Newton Manor, Robinson displayed his learning and scholarship, his eye for grace and refinement, his collector's instincts and his exquisite taste – everything his clients wanted in someone buying and selling works on their behalf. But Newton Manor had the added advantage of conveniently obscuring the fact that Robinson was a first-rate dealer and not a very wealthy private collector. In the simple solid walls of an old manor, Robinson set up a complicated illusion, a house of mirrors, the perfect salve for Victorian anxieties about class and the changing world of trade.

The genteel lifestyle at Newton Manor was as important to the way Robinson saw himself as to how he wanted others to see him. He bemoaned the break-up of the English country-house collections of the past and there is little doubt that he admired the tradition of collecting that had its roots in the aristocracy. As a dealer, he drew on his conservative credentials to emphasize the discretion and sheer class of the service he was offering. He tried to tempt even the most wary of men with his promise of prudent and tactful dealing, and he was able to count society heavy-weights such as William Gladstone, who somehow found time to be a ceramics collector, among his most honoured customers. Gladstone, who was Chancellor of the Exchequer at the time, sent Robinson a speculative £2 in 1869 for the purchase of 'an interesting piece of Italian ware' and, suitably reassured by the return on his investment, continued to patronize Robinson from time to time.[5]

Not all of Robinson's clients were society figures, but they were all influential or wealthy, or both. Nearly six hundred works, including some by renowned artists such as Michelangelo and Raphael, passed through his hands to John Malcolm, the 14th Laird of Poltalloch, in Argyll, Scotland, who inherited three houses in 1857. He traded energetically for Robert Napier from Dunbartonshire, who had made a fortune patenting a new naval engineering method, and for Sir Francis Cook, a textile trader, who was left more than £2 million by his father. Abroad, he worked for influential collectors such as Wilhelm von Bode, the creator of the Kaiser-Friedrich Museum who shared Robinson's taste for the Italian Renaissance, and the art historian Stephan Bourgeois. He even managed to establish himself as a royal dealer, cultivating the business of the Kaiserin Victoria, more familiarly known as Princess Vicky, the Empress of Germany, eldest daughter of Queen Victoria and wife of the German Emperor Frederick III. Shrewdly recognizing the value of such exclusive clients, Robinson seemed content to use high-profile royal transactions as a loss leader: he sold the Princess a still life of *Dead Game and Fruit* by Frans Snyders in 1877 for nothing more than the price he had paid for it, generously adding a complementary new frame, and during their long association as dealer and client he carefully adhered to a non-profit policy. He even presented a number of valuable works as gifts to celebrate the silver wedding anniversary of Vicky's marriage to the Kaiser in 1883, including a *Sketch of Hampstead Heath* by Constable and Reynolds' *A Portrait of a Child with Doll.*

Princess Vicky was a collector, from a family of collectors. Her father, Prince Albert, had thrown himself enthusiastically into raising the quality and reputation of the arts; the Royal Collection expanded in all areas under her mother's rule. Together, Victoria and Albert commissioned artists for all occasions, treated themselves and each other to sculpture for Christmas or birthdays, shopped excitedly for decorative pieces to furnish their houses at Osborne House and Balmoral, and began to encourage scholars to publish about the Royal Collection, which was begun by Charles I. Growing up with this enthusiasm, and with unrivalled access to great works of art, Vicky was knowledgeable, cultured and sophisticated, if rather conventional in her tastes. During years of political machination in Germany, and three bitter wars of German unification during the 1860s and 1870s, the Princess's love of fine things had been a comfort and an inspiration. And the environment Robinson created at Newton Manor clearly offered her a retreat: *The Times* noted that she visited there with her four daughters.[6]

Such a royal visit was a great achievement for Robinson. It linked him to collecting in the very highest circles and was a clear indication that his activities as a dealer had been accepted. He seemed to be offering a certain type of wealthy Victorian collector just the kind of refined and discreet personal service they demanded. And, in return, they seemed content to reward him with a great deal of money. Details of Robinson's account books reveal the considerable profit he made on reselling works to his elite network of collectors: he bought a Dutch painting of A *Lady at a Harpsichord* at a sale in May 1877 for £88, and sold it two months later for £320. Similarly, a Rubens portrait bought for £90 was sold a few weeks later for £300; a painting described simply in his notes as 'Venus and Cupid' and acquired for just £5 was marked up to £375; and a *Rainbow Landscape*, again by an unknown artist, secured Robinson well over £500 profit. As his client list grew, and as he counted more and more obsessive collectors among his customers, Robinson was making transactions with impressive ease. He was working in London, travelling to Europe, entertaining at Newton Manor, networking through his cluster of clubs and societies, and making deals at every turn. He never tired of the adventure of finding the right object for the right client and, during a typical three-month period of the 1870s, he made almost 800 sales of paintings alone, as well as the unrecorded business in his other diverse interests such as Old Master drawings, sculptured bronzes, oriental ceramics and glassware.[7]

Robinson's energy and success as a dealer can be seen as a blueprint for other internationally renowned dealing careers at the end of the nineteenth and beginning of the twentieth century. Those that followed adopted Robinson's enthusiasm for mixing in influential circles, and combining erudition with a sharp business sense. Joseph Duveen, for example, one of the most well known and influential of British art dealers, began work in his father's business in 1886 and made a fortune by selling works to wealthy Americans and trading on the idea that owning pieces of art was a way to acquire social standing. Like Robinson, he had an eye for the art of the Renaissance and he too moved easily in the company of royalty and millionaires. He was also, like Robinson, confident, ambitious and single-minded. Before the First World War, he established a virtual monopoly on the trade in Old Masters and his talent for salesmanship allowed him to deal on an unprecedented scale. With his success assured, he donated money and paintings to many British galleries and funded the building of the Duveen gallery at the British Museum to house the Elgin Marbles. He was finally knighted for his philanthropy in 1919.

But Duveen was not alone. The growing number of collectors throughout the Victorian period meant a corresponding growth in the number of dealers who, in turn, created the kind of active, profitable market that later allowed men like Duveen to make a fortune. By the last decades of the nineteenth century, the advertising pages of the daily papers teemed with colourful advertisements for dealers and their showrooms. Businesses such as Gladwell Brothers offered everything from 'new and

MAGPIES, SQUIRRELS AND THIEVES

choice etchings' to cornices and console tables; the family firm of William Dyer boosted trade as picture restorers by selling a few works on the side, while higher-class dealers such as Agnew's were responding to the growing market for Old Masters and eighteenth-century portraiture. Others were following more closely in Robinson's careful footsteps, negotiating the tricky boundaries between trade and social prestige: in the 1880s, for example, Marcus Huish combined his occupation as a barrister and a role as director of the Fine Arts Society with a profitable career in art dealing.[8] In the late 1860s and early 1870s, Robinson was at the vanguard of this new profession. He was one of the first to take on the demands of dealing alongside his own collecting. Cloaked in the disguise of the gentlemanly amateur, he was forging new possibilities as a commercially minded professional, and in the process altering perceptions both of collectors and the markets in which they moved.

The contradictions of Robinson's career at the South Kensington Museum were not entirely confined to the past, however. He could not shake off his attachment to the South Kensington collections, nor the idea that he should continue to play a part in shaping them. In 1873, little more than five years after Robinson's ignominious dismissal, Henry Cole retired from his post as Director, worn out by battles with the government and half a century of life as a civil servant. He was replaced by Philip Cunliffe-Owen, who had been primed by Cole as his successor: after a number of posts in the Science and Art Department, he was officially made Cole's deputy in 1860, taking particular responsibility for the British contributions to the International Exhibitions which took place all over Europe during the 1870s. He was efficient and shrewd, and praised by *The Times* for being 'robust and capable of much hard work... the capable man of business'.[9] More significantly, he had no axe to grind with

Robinson. His work on the International Exhibitions had kept him largely out of Robinson's way, and he had spent so much time travelling that he had been able to maintain a healthy distance from the worst of the squabbles. Besides, he made no claims to be an expert on objects or collecting and so did not see Robinson as any kind of direct threat to his authority. He was content to be an organizer and, when he succeeded Cole as Director, he was happy to focus on administration. He was a man, noted *The Times*, of 'little expert knowledge, [who]. . . had little to do with the actual purchases of objects'.[10]

With Cole out of the way, Robinson launched something of a charm offensive. He kept an eye out at sales for lots that might tempt the museum and began offering some of his own pieces on loan in the hope that they might prove indispensable. He moved quickly and confidently. By 1879, over 300 of Robinson's objects were on display as loans, but with a view to a sale, including a stunning twelfth-century Flemish standing cross with a base inlaid with crystal; an elaborately decorated dress sword; a set of eighteenth-century Italian clerical vestments; strings of jewels, silver chalices, old Venetian glass, blue-and-white china, bronzes, wood carvings, ivories and books. The objects were magnificent and conspicuous and they filled gaps in the existing collections. But Cunliffe-Owen was wary about directing public money towards Robinson without being sure it was to the museum's advantage, and he drew on support and expertise from other national institutions to bolster his position. The pieces were scrupulously inspected by Franks at the British Museum, who found them 'remarkable for the taste displayed in collecting them', and by the painter Edward J. Poynter, a member of the Royal Academy who was, at the time, Principal of the National Art Training School and who was later to become Director of the National Gallery. He too approved, writing to Cunliffe-Owen that 'ALL the specimens appear to me to be admirably chosen for their artistic value.'[11] With the government establishment in accord, Robinson found his objects once again taking pride of place in the South Kensington galleries.

To consolidate the impression that he was still invaluable, Robinson offered the pieces as part of a deal which, he assured Cunliffe-Owen, would be 'as advantageous as possible to you'. There would be no haggling over price: Robinson was prepared to offer the museum a bargain, selling the whole lot at a rate 'very much smaller' than the market value.[12] This still amounted to the not inconsiderable sum of £6,800, and the museum, perhaps unsure about exactly how generous Robinson was inclined to be towards an institution that had sacked him, called on Poynter and Franks again for advice. When both advisers approved the price as being 'very moderate', however, the deal was made.[13] It was a marked divergence from Cole's desire to concentrate on modern manufactures, a very obvious demonstration that after his retirement in 1873 the museum moved more rapidly to adopt a policy that owed much to Robinson's early collecting. The idea of making contemporary acquisitions was gradually abandoned, so much so that by 1880 the displays of modern manufactures that had been at the heart of the original museum were moved from the main building to an outpost in Bethnal Green. In their place, Cole's successors concentrated their efforts on creating a vibrant visual encyclopedia of connoisseurship. Potential acquisitions were no longer assessed on whether they could be used to improve public taste or as models for students but instead, as Poynter said, 'for their artistic value'.

A decade after he had been dismissed by Cole from the South Kensington Museum, it was as if Robinson had never left. The eagerness and zeal of youth was quickly rekindled, and once again he was undertaking lengthy journeys to Europe to buy on behalf of the museum, sending back extravagant deliveries of packing cases which piled up awkwardly in the corridors 'awaiting instructions' on his return: in January 1882 alone, he sent the museum twenty-nine cases of miscellaneous objects from Italy, as well as seventeen cases of marbles and bronzes.[14] Once again, Robinson was apt to commit sums for acquisitions with little regard for the due forms of process or finance. In January 1881, during a huge snowstorm that brought much of London to a standstill, Robinson, undeterred by the weather, acquired two Florentine inlaid marble tables at a sale at Christie's. They were rare and lovely, but expensive. Robinson bid for them without a second thought, and wrote unrepentantly to Cunliffe-Owen that 'there was no time to tell you about them and I am aware that your funds for purchase for this year are exhausted – However, I considered them so important that I determined to purchase them.'[15]

By 1881, Robinson was writing to the amenable Cunliffe-Owen to explain that recent months had 'quite revived the old habits. . . In short almost without intending it, I have found myself doing just the same kind of work as before.'[16] A year later, he was plainly preening himself in front of the museum board, making sure that everyone knew to whom credit was due for years of success. 'May I be allowed to remind your Lordship,' he wrote to Earl Spenser, 'that it is to my having assumed personal responsibility. . . and to having risked my own pecuniary resources on occasions that the Nation owes a large proportion of the great monuments of art which form the pride and glory of the Museum. . . The building of the South Kensington Collection has been mainly my work.'[17] Henry Cole, who would be dead within a few weeks, had little chance to set the record straight.[18] Robinson was displaying a talent for rewriting the past to fit the way he saw things, and he seemed to be reinstating himself with ease into the museum's history books. Better still, as a recognized dealer and an independent man, he was vigorously running a double life, combining public and private business without fear of reprimand,

and keeping himself determinedly unfettered. He refused to accept a salary from the museum, maintaining a discreet distance from its committee of art referees, and choosing for himself whether to be in London, at Newton Manor or travelling in Europe. He was making all his own decisions about the buying and selling of objects. He was earning substantial sums of money from private clients, and winning priceless prestige for his work at the museum. It was the best of both worlds.

Robinson was astute enough to recognize the value of his work with museums to his broader activity as a dealer: the National Gallery, Birmingham Museum, Dublin Museum and the Bowes Museum at Barnard Castle all benefited from both his connoisseurship and his commitment to supplying pieces for public display at little or no profit. Occasionally, he even offered works as donations: in April 1877, for example, he bought El Greco's *Christ Driving out the Moneylenders from the Temple* for £25. 20s. 0d from a sale at Christie's and later presented it to the National Gallery. At South Kensington, this policy was mingled with a lingering sense of responsibility. He often sold objects to the collections there at cost price, and was flexible about payment so that the museum could stagger instalments to suit its budgets. He offered only what he considered the finest pieces, worthy of a place in the galleries, and he was happy to take back works that the staff rejected. When he returned from a trip to Italy in early 1881, he brought with him a wealth of objects wheedled out of churches, palaces and private collections, allowing the museum to make a choice depending on what could be afforded. 'I want it to be thoroughly understood', he said reassuringly to Cunliffe-Owen, 'that I have bought these things entirely on my own account, to please myself, and that I have not the slightest desire to *urge* them on the Museum.'[19] Nevertheless, in the end, Robinson made a very satisfactory transaction, selling a range of pieces from a 1560 sundial from the Pitti Palace in Florence, priced at £8, to a sixteenth-century wooden coat rail, at 8 shillings.

As ever, Robinson's relationship with the museum was complicated. In everything he did, there was ambition and pride, but there was also an unshakeable, altruistic belief in the importance of the collection and its value to generations of visitors. Robinson was delighted to be back at the centre of things because he believed so fervently in what he was doing – and that he was the best man to do it. He trusted his own judgement absolutely and he had faith in his ability to use his talents for the future glory of South Kensington. He boasted an imposing knowledge of European art, and was certain he could find the most important pieces; he understood the markets, and was confident of getting the best deals. He saw himself as a champion for collectors and what they could achieve.

Yet Robinson spent the best part of the late 1880s and 1890s in a very public, and damaging, crusade to highlight the faults at South Kensington, complaining that his own heyday of astute and visionary collecting had been replaced by a 'mechanical system, carried out by mere laymen, superabundant clerks, secretaries and shopkeepers'.[20] He could not free himself of the idea that he should have influence over the beloved collection; even as an established dealer, leading a life quite separate from the museum and more than twenty years after he had been sacked, his relationship with the objects at South Kensington remained intimate and highly personal, his desire for control absolute. He typified the ambiguous unresolved distinction of the time between public and private collecting; in turn, this confusion helped fuel a character that was naturally difficult and contradictory. He even stood before a government select committee in July 1893 to reiterate the litany of complaints that had started life in his battles with Henry Cole. His old habits died hard. He did not seem to be able to shake off his discontent with those whose views failed to match his own, and he was openly critical of the museum that had first nurtured his talents.

But, as a collector, Robinson's energy and expertise, confidence and commitment could not be faulted. His ongoing dedication to collecting – no matter on whose behalf – could never be doubted. And, in many ways, his stubborn insistence on publicly raising issues about South Kensington and its collecting policy was good for collectors. His constant letters of complaint to *The Times*, his frequent articles and his impassioned contributions to public discussions continued to cement the idea that it was, as he had once claimed, a 'national duty' to encourage good collecting and the systems that made it possible. He clearly raised the profile of collecting in general, pushing it into public notice alongside other political and economic matters. His vociferous criticisms helped ensure that the debate about what and how to collect remained lively in the public eye for the rest of the century.

CHAPTER SEVEN

Changing Times

Robinson's collecting continued to focus on the expensive and the rare. As his wealth grew, so did the amounts he invested. He assembled a collection of nearly 300 rare Renaissance portrait and commemorative medals cast in copper, tin, gold or silver; he developed a substantial collection of paintings by major British artists including Constable, Gainsborough, J. S. Cotman, Girtin, Landseer and Turner; he took to buying Louis XVI clocks, Japanese lacquerware and jewellery. His expenditure was so large that, despite his dealing success and a rash of sales in his final years, Robinson had little over £500 in his account at the London, County and Westminster Bank at his death in 1913.[1] It was a collection to impress, a lifetime's work and a testament to his knowledge and energy. In recognition, he was acquiring a number of titles: Fellow of the Society of Antiquaries, Curator of the Royal Society of Painters and Etchers, honorary member of the Academies of Art in Rome, Florence, Bologna, Antwerp, Madrid and Lisbon, and Knight Commander of the Order of Isabella in Spain and Portugal. Then, in 1882, at the age of fifty-eight, Robinson received the acknowledgement he had always felt he deserved for his role at the forefront of British collecting: he was appointed Surveyor of the Queen's Pictures.[2]

By the time Robinson was appointed as Surveyor, the Queen was sixty-three years old, and had been widowed for over twenty years. Art had been something she had shared with her husband and, without him at her side, her enthusiasm for collecting waned. During the 1870s and 1880s, when she finally resumed public and political life long after Albert's death, she found affairs of state sat too heavily to allow for personal pleasures: she was travelling extensively on a tiring succession of engagements in an attempt to suppress a growing republican voice and she had little free time to think about buying or commissioning works, even had she wanted to. Without special attention, the collection became little more than a passive receptacle for randomly acquired pieces. It became increasingly muddled and disordered, separate from the life of the sovereign and no longer an integral part of royal affairs. And for Victoria, there was something more: a lingering sense of loss that was made particularly poignant by the paintings and sculptures she had enjoyed in happier times. The collection acted as a reminder of life as it had once been and as a memorial to Albert's taste. The Surveyor was expected to maintain the status quo and to content himself with the minor administration associated with keeping the collection in reasonable shape. He was expected to make periodic reports and deal with any gifts from grateful subjects. He was not required to create opportunities for either acquisition or public exhibition. There was not a lot to do. It was the prestige of the role that was important, embedding its holder firmly in the ranks of the elite establishment – and it was this that Robinson cherished. Finally, in 1887, at the Queen's Jubilee, he was knighted, confirmation of the distance he had travelled from his days as an impoverished art student.

As a collector, however, it was important for Robinson that his objects, too, were given official recognition, and as the century drew to a close he began to make numerous overtures to public collections to secure the future of his pieces. He demonstrated a special fondness for the Whitworth Institute in Manchester, which had been established with the fortune left by Sir Joseph Whitworth, a manufacturer of machine tools. The Institute was in the process of developing an art gallery under the governorship of William Agnew, a fellow London art dealer. Robinson knew Agnew well, and was happy to 'show any assistance in my power' to make the new Whitworth scheme a success.[3] At first this remained a vague commitment, but the Manchester board was determined to keep him to his word and was soon negotiating to buy 1,000 items from Robinson's magnificent collection of textiles, even luring him into 'coming from my own home to personally arrange the specimens'.[4] The pieces had to be teased out of Robinson, who had a collector's reluctance to relinquish them, but the sale was finally settled in 1891. For the modest sum of £3,570, he delivered a collection of European ecclesiastical textiles from the sixteenth, seventeenth and eighteenth centuries, vestments from the celebration of High Mass, rare altar tapestries and a handful of British embroideries of exquisite workmanship and design.[5]

Apparently undeterred by the fact that until recently he had been openly and vehemently critical of the work of the South Kensington Museum, Robinson also approached the curators there, confident that he had long ago earned the right to a permanent welcome. Rather remarkably, he was greeted with patient goodwill. The latest in the long line of Henry Cole's successors, Caspar Purdon Clarke, was, perhaps fortunately, known 'for geniality and good fellowship. . . a well-liked man both by his subordinates and the general public'.[6] Perhaps he saw Robinson as little more than an eccentric old duffer, an occasional thorn in the side; or perhaps he was clear-sighted enough to see beyond any personal difficulties with Robinson to the prized pieces the museum was being offered. Whatever the reasons for his tolerance, he listened enthusiastically to Robinson's proposals, and, although he politely turned down the full extent of the collection Robinson had hoped to deposit, he happily agreed to take a smaller selection for display in 1901. In the end, this amounted to seventy-three choice objects, including a miniature Spanish prayer book, set with rubies, which had belonged to Charles V; another Charles V jewel, the 'Bezaar stone', set in gold, and presented to the king by Hernan Cortes, the 'conqueror of Mexico'; a fourteenth-century Hungarian reliquary cross; and the walking staff which had once belonged to Sir Nicholas Bacon, Lord Keeper of the Great Seal to Elizabeth I.

But even as the pieces were being prepared for display, as a permanent recognition of Robinson's achievements as a collector, it was becoming clear that times were changing. The works were being assessed and arranged by the museum's Assistant Director, Arthur Banks Skinner, who had climbed through the ranks during his twenty years at South Kensington. Robinson had written the display labels to accompany the pieces, presumably because he believed that he was best placed to explain them to the public. Skinner, however, whose 'knowledge of works of art was singularly wide and accurate' and who 'enjoyed the confidence and esteem of many foreign collectors and heads of museums', had his reservations.[7] 'These descriptions were prepared by him, and in my opinion are open to considerable doubt,' he explained to Purdon Clarke, before asking incredulously, 'Do you wish them to go out as they are?'[8] Purdon Clarke, ever the diplomat, proposed a compromise. He suggested that the labels remained unedited, but that it was made abundantly clear that they were Robinson's own idiosyncratic work, and not a reflection of the museum's scholarship.

It was a small but significant exchange between the new generation of professionals at South Kensington. By the end of the nineteenth century, men like Arthur Banks Skinner were taking the haphazard knowledge of the hosts of Victorian collectors and connoisseurs and beginning to formalize it into the discipline that we now know as art history. This movement had begun in earnest in the 1850s with what was later referred to as the Vienna School of Art History. In 1852, Rudolph Eitelberger was appointed to the world's first chair of the history of art at the University of Vienna, and a succession of scholars there followed in his footsteps, trying to find ways to make the appreciation of art more objective. This meant taking into account historical sources and adopting a more factually based approach to the examination of artistic achievement. To some extent, this academic work was consolidating the more practical efforts of curators like Gustav Waagen. Alongside his publications, Waagen's displays at the Kaiser-Friedrich Museum in the 1830s and 1840s presented objects within their chronological and social contexts, supported by explanatory labels and catalogues. This allowed visitors to get a sense of how one artist's work related to another's, and how practice had evolved across time and in different places. Waagen also advocated re-creating a sense of the original spaces in which the works of art would have been displayed, 'to lessen as much as possible the contrast which must necessarily exist between works of Art in their original site, and in their position in a museum. . . to realise in some degree the impression produced by a temple, a church, a palace or a cabinet'.[9]

By the mid-nineteenth century, as had been seen at the Louvre, other European curators were also beginning to experiment with presenting art in 'schools', grouping works together to explore similarities in technique, style or subject matter, and to demonstrate ways in which artists influenced each other. During the 1880s and 1890s, the principles of this art historical approach were further developed by Heinrich Wölfflin, a Swiss scholar and critic. While teaching in Basel, Berlin and Munich, he formulated pairs of opposing ideas – such as whether a work demonstrated a 'linear' or a 'painterly' approach – to underpin the study of art.

It was not until well into the twentieth century that the academic discipline of art history became fully established, but British curators in the nineteenth century were certainly aware of what was being accomplished by their European counterparts. From the 1850s, articles and pamphlets discussed the arrangement of picture galleries in particular, trying to define the ideal display system. The debate was focused around the National Gallery: the shortcomings of the existing gallery had prompted numerous calls for something completely new, on a different site, and this in turn acted as the catalyst for a wider discussion about different ways of displaying and interpreting the works inside the proposed new building. Waagen himself contributed to the debate, outlining his ideas in a lengthy article in the *Art Journal* in 1853 and including a model classification for presenting paintings within a public museum. Robinson, Ruskin and Eastlake were just some of the others to enter the fray in a process that seemed to typify the Victorian enthusiasm for inquiries, reports, articles and counter-articles, protests, statements and official proceedings.

In the end, the plans for a new National Gallery fizzled out into a modest extension of seven rooms on the existing site and the display principles remained inconsistent. But the idea that art history was a serious area for study continued to flourish and the new breed of scholars, as Skinner demonstrated, became increasingly confident in its challenge to the accepted wisdom of the past. As Skinner's incredulous note suggested, Robinson was no longer, in other people's eyes, at the vanguard of scholarship; he was simply a respectable veteran collector, part of a generation that was being left behind as knowledge about art continued to evolve. He was a Victorian in the dawning years of a new century and a different age.

* * *

Robinson's collections fared little better in creating a lasting impression for posterity. In the early 1890s, at the same time as he was agreeing terms with the Whitworth, he was putting works into four different sales at Christie's with a view to improving his finances. Three hundred and seventy-five oil paintings, thirty-five prints, forty-one Old Master drawings and a hundred and sixty-eight pieces of decorative art went under the auctioneer's hammer at these sales alone, allowing him to meet the not inconsiderable expenses of his lifestyle. With the death of Queen Victoria in January 1901, however, Robinson lost the position of Surveyor in a sudden change of royal politics that came as 'a most painful surprise'.[10] Suddenly, the pressures on his purse grew even more acute and in April 1902 Robinson parted with a significant portion of his collection of sculpture and ceramics at Christie's, quickly followed in two more sales by the majority of his Old Master drawings. In contrast to his reputation for slapdash administration at the museum, these personal pieces were carefully recorded; Robinson noted the source of each of the works, how and when he had bought them, and what he knew about their earlier provenance. In May, over 450 drawings, attributed to the principal artists of the Italian, Dutch, French, German and Spanish schools, were announced in the auctioneer's catalogue as the 'valuable collection. . . formed by a well-known amateur over the last 40 years', and Robinson watched with mingled pride and regret as other collectors clamoured to acquire what he had taken so long to amass.[11] His collection was being irretrievably scattered. After a lifetime's accumulation came months of determined dispersal. There was plenty left – Newton Manor was still a treasure trove – but the sales set a tone of closure, the sad parting of a collector with the objects he prized.

Robinson's collection did not survive him. After his death at the age of eighty-eight in April 1913, the rest of the works were gradually sold on. By September, many of the drawings were being put up for sale, and by February 1914 the Robinson name was appearing regularly at Sotheby's. With an eye perhaps on this kind of insecurity, Robinson had left a number of financial gifts in his will, primarily to organizations that encouraged collectors and artists and preserved their work for the future. The Burlington Fine Arts Club, not surprisingly, was top of the list, but there were also legacies to Dorset County Museum, the National Art Collections Fund, the Royal Society of Painters and Etchers, the Society of Antiquaries and the Society for the Protection of Ancient Buildings.[12] Through the work of these kinds of institutions, Robinson knew, arts scholarship would continue to progress and flourish, collectors would meet like-minded colleagues, and the best objects would be admired, studied and displayed.

The South Kensington Museum had changed greatly since Robinson's years as a curator, becoming known as the Victoria and Albert Museum from 1899 and unveiling a massive new building and a grand stone façade ten years later. Nonetheless, Robinson left to the collections there a parcel of his own etchings, which he selected just weeks before his death. He wished to be remembered, it seems, not just as a collector and dealer, a learned middleman, but as a peer of the painters, sculptors and craftsmen whom he so much respected. The etchings, however, were not enough to accord Robinson a lasting presence in the museum. The opening of the new building in June 1909 – almost fifty years after Robinson had scurried across from Marlborough House to see the first work begin on the site – was seen by staff as an opportunity for rearranging the collections and asserting their modern relevance. There was even a backlash against what was seen as the excesses of Victorian taste: the art critic of the *Daily Telegraph* noted that the practical new building was so plain that it gave 'the general impression... of some immense, finely-appointed modern hospital' and until the outbreak of the First

World War there was a controversial campaign to remove the most highly decorative elements of the original building because they 'belonged to a bygone age'.[13] Robinson was increasingly out of fashion and his etchings out of place in a collection which was once again reinventing itself for new generations.

Robinson's long life straddled the Victorian age and his biography as a collector reflects the changes of his time. In the complicated twists and turns of his career – as private connoisseur, professional curator and successful dealer – we begin to see the complexities of the Victorian relationship to the collection, the achievements and disappointments, the shifts and disputes and contradictions. In the fate of Robinson's beloved things, we also glimpse a motif which will be repeated at the heart of these collecting stories – a collection does not last. Tastes change, financial and family concerns intervene; what seems to one collector like a logical arrangement of lovely pieces often looks to the next generation like a hotchpotch of odd personal trinkets. Individual objects survive through history, often gathering meaning and value; the collection is ephemeral. It acquires life and meaning from the collector who makes it. It is a very personal treasure.

Ransacking and Revolution: The European Crusade

CHARLOTTE SCHREIBER

CHAPTER EIGHT

Mrs Schreiber's Big Red Bag

It was a long and tedious journey to Paris. Charlotte Schreiber and her husband Charles were woken in time to join the noisy huddle of travellers at the inn in the centre of Bordeaux, all clamouring in the cold dawn for a place on the omnibus to the capital. They had arrived from Spain the previous day by train, reaching Bordeaux in the middle of the night, but there was no chance of taking a break. Paris was emerging from the Franco-Prussian War and was in the middle of an armed uprising which was to become known as the Paris Commune. Transport to and from the city was unpredictable: railway bridges had been destroyed or cut off, trains halted, roads blocked by barricades, and horses, carriages and carts caught up in the confusion. Places on the omnibuses that were still making the journey to the city were at a premium. In the courtyard of the inn, the mood was hectic and slightly aggressive; the driver was surly and blatantly profiteering. But as a seasoned and level-headed traveller, Charlotte conducted her negotiations amicably and in impeccable French. She was a wealthy woman, and offered to pay handsomely for places in the coach for herself, her maid and her husband. She was polite and unruffled. She agreed a price for three seats on the fourteen-seat omnibus, and, with her appetite sharpened by the brisk May air, she set her mind to breakfast.

The problem came with the bag – not with the usual cases and hat boxes that could be piled on to the roof and tied on to the railings for safety, but with the floppy, soft red velvet bag that the Schreibers insisted on carrying between them. The driver would not take it inside, and they would not relinquish it to the roof. It was a stalemate. And since it was a stalemate of a particularly French kind, quiet and smoky and stubborn, there was little the middle-aged English couple could do to press their point. Just over an hour later, the omnibus pulled slowly out of Bordeaux, the horses steaming in the early-morning air, and Charlotte and Charles Schreiber were left behind – with their bag – in the chilly shadows of the city's medieval streets.

Since there were no more omnibuses and no trains, the Schreibers ended up riding to Paris in a farm cart with a horse Charlotte described in her journal as 'sturdy' and a 'loquacious' driver.[1] They rattled slowly through the French countryside, bumping along rutted roads, with no shelter from the wind and occasional spitting rain, and the incessant chatter of the driver drumming in their ears. It was a long and uncomfortable journey, but they had their red bag safe in the cart between them, and that was the main thing.

The bag itself was not, on the whole, remarkable. It was roomy and practical, and slightly patched. What was special was what was in it. By May 1871, when the Schreibers were making their steady progress towards the outskirts of the French capital, they had been on the road already (not to mention the seas, the railways and the back alleys) for almost a year. Throughout their journey, Charlotte had maintained her lifetime's habit of keeping a daily journal, recording the trials of collecting on the move and giving us a colourful picture of what it took to be a collector. They had trekked through the South of France before attempting the 'wretchedly bad' crossing of the Pyrenees, where the roads were no better than 'ill-ploughed fields' and progress was only made by taking pickaxes to the wheels and whips to the horses.[2]

In Spain, hardly pausing for breath, they moved down through Gerona and Barcelona to Seville (with Charles suffering from headaches, a sore throat and inflammation of the eyes) and then on to Cadiz before crossing to Gibraltar. When their train ground to a halt in front of a broken railway bridge between Valencia and Cordoba, during a thunderstorm, Charles, along with other passengers, stepped in to help as the carriages were uncoupled and then pulled, one by one, across the ravine. At another unsound and unfinished railway bridge, they were transferred from their train to 'a sort of temporary contrivance' which shunted them across 'very slowly' with the men still at work around and below them.[3] They had endured a twenty-six-hour journey between Granada and Madrid, having stayed up all night in advance to savour Granada's fabled nightlife. They had toiled on foot through Northern Spain and back into France during an unseasonable spring heatwave, carrying their big red bag between them, and stopping at shabby inns whose owners displayed a distrust of such odd English visitors. They had even spent one memorable night in Valladolid in the omnibus on which they had arrived in the city, much to the dismay of the driver who simply unharnessed his team of horses and pushed the carriage into the inn yard. The Schreibers were woken the next morning, early, by the stamping of mules, the neighing of horses, a cacophony of cocks and hens and 'the tinkling of a bell on a very playful, restless goat'.[4]

Every moment of that year, every bright day in a pale Spanish town, every dusty evening in a Mediterranean port, every rain-sodden afternoon in a small, damp French village, had been filled with the unrelenting, resolute and entirely absorbing hunt for things. And the spoils of the hunt – a delicate fan of exotic birds' feathers, a perfect silver serving jug, pieces of fine china carefully wrapped in paper, unusual figurines and a bright enamel – were safely stowed away in Charlotte's big red bag. So intense and energetic was Charlotte's search, so absorbing and dogged, that, when the farm cart finally trundled into the outskirts of Paris, the Schreibers were in for a shock. With her eyes fixed on the details of fine china, larger events in Europe had largely passed Charlotte by. The Franco-Prussian War, which had devastated Northern France and Germany for over a year, had registered simply as an inconvenience, prompting her to note blandly in her journal that Calais 'looked sad and chastened' and Paris was 'impassable'.[5] None of this had really mattered, as long as the search was not interrupted. But now the Schreibers were thrown into a city in turmoil.

After the French defeat by the Prussians in the autumn of 1870, Paris had failed to accept the surrender offered by the rest of France. The victorious Prussian army had laid siege to the city with over a quarter of a million troops, and throughout the winter months Paris had defiantly starved. When the national government finally tried to enforce a truce in the spring, the workers and people of Paris, inspired by the ideal of '*la république démocratique et sociale*', had declared the city a separate commune. From March until May 1871, while the Schreibers had been further south, the revolutionary citizens had built over 600 defensive barricades. This time, however, it was not the Prussian army but the French army which marched on the capital. It arrived just a fortnight ahead of the Schreibers, overwhelming the revolutionaries in a series of violent, hand-to-hand street battles. Charlotte, her husband and her maid finally arrived on 1 June. Three days earlier, the revolutionaries had taken their last stand at the end of a week which saw as many as 30,000 casualties. Riding expectantly into Paris, what Charlotte discovered was not the lively cultural capital she so much admired, with its network of dealers and showrooms and junkshops, but instead what she described forlornly as a 'City of the Dead'.

Charlotte found Paris ravaged, and its people demoralized. No corner was untouched by the ferocious fighting of the past weeks. There was, she wrote in her journal, 'no life or animation; scarce anyone in the streets. . . the Tuileries and other public buildings still smoking; the Vendôme Column lying in pieces on the ground'. She was shocked and bewildered, moved to tears by the destruction, but still undeterred by smoking ruins and bodies half-hidden in the rubble. She managed to secure a small apartment – with 'a sort of cupboard' for the maid – in a building where workmen were bricking up the ground floors against the threat of arson. During the last days of the Commune, the Palais de Tuileries and the Hôtel de Ville had been burned down and rumours were rife that working-class women – *les pétroleuses* – were stalking Paris with bottles full of petroleum or paraffin, ready to start fires through unprotected cellar windows. In fact, *les pétroleuses* turned out to be mythical, a construct of fear and suspicion, but at the time they were considered a formidable threat. The sale of flammable liquids was banned for several months, and as far as Charlotte was concerned, her lodgings could be burned to the ground at any moment in an act of revolutionary spite. There is no doubt that she was frightened and overwhelmed by the situation she and her party had wandered into blindly. Perhaps because of this, she set her mind even more firmly on collecting. Within minutes of arriving in Paris, she went out into the ruins to try to discover what had become of her trusted dealers and whether there were any bargains to be had.

It took time to establish exactly what had happened. Entire streetscapes had been altered, first by the building of the huge barricades and then by their destruction and the hand-to-hand fighting. Houses and shops were burned out and deserted, and many Parisians were sheltering in cellars or attics, afraid to venture on to the streets for bread, far less to talk about antiques with English travellers. Eventually, though, through perseverance and with the aid of a few substantial banknotes, Charlotte began to get a trickle of information. And the news was not good. Two of her oldest and most trustworthy dealers, Mme Caillot and Mme Oppenheim, had, Charlotte noted sadly, 'both died of fright'. Nothing was left of their stock, which had been burned or looted. For another of Charlotte's contacts, 'poor old Fournier', the fear and confusion had proved too great: he had reportedly gone mad, and could not be found. The only dealer Charlotte could locate was Mme Flaudin, and the next morning she set out early for the small dark shop which she had visited many times before on happier occasions. Remarkably, it was open and largely unscathed by the fighting. Mme Flaudin was waiting with a jug of hot coffee and a table covered in things she hoped would tempt her intrepid customer. But even in the aftermath of revolution, Charlotte would not be rushed. She took her time browsing, and carefully examined any of the objects that caught her eye. She asked questions, and bartered fiercely. She was in her element; she had found what she was looking for, a surviving Paris dealer, and, better still, a dealer with things worth buying. Not even her walk back through the bloody wreckage of the city could blunt her joy at unearthing some decent china, a 'matching old maroon Chelsea set'.[6]

Rescued from the rubble of Paris, Charlotte's set of china was tenderly wrapped and given a temporary home in the big red bag. Produced in the eighteenth century by a factory founded around 1740 in the rapidly expanding but still rural town on the outskirts of London, Chelsea china was regarded as the very finest of English porcelain. Its famous claret-red tableware, daintily decorated with gilded borders and golden curlicues, was prized above everything. It had been popular since the day it was made and so demanded high prices, finding its way into the homes of the very wealthy. Charlotte admired the deep tones and fine shapes of the china, and was shrewd enough to recognize that what she was offered in Mme Flaudin's was a bargain. The Chelsea set was to become one of her treasured pieces. Fittingly for such a glamorous refugee of the Paris violence, it was to end up in the refined cabinets at South Kensington, part of the huge collection that Charlotte donated to the museum – one of the finest, most detailed and most interesting collections of English china ever amassed.

A couple of weeks before arriving in Paris, Charlotte Schreiber celebrated her fifty-ninth birthday. It was a day like any other, spent hunting for collectables with her husband. Good wishes had been sent from some of her children in the letters which straggled into foreign post offices in the days running up to the occasion, but 19 May 1871 was passed quietly in Tangiers. The most special and welcome thing about the day was the quality of the Victoria Hotel, chosen by chance rather than as a birthday treat, but worth noting in Charlotte's journal as 'clean and comfortable, unlike any since leaving England'.[7]

Charlotte looked like any other elderly traveller, taking in the fabled and relaxed culture of the North African port. She was slightly plump and matronly; she was not, and had never been, particularly beautiful, and she dressed sedately and neatly in sombre colours, even in the African heat. Perhaps her one concession to vanity was that her grey hair was dyed. This was not an easy thing to achieve in the midst of so much travelling, and Charlotte may well have resorted to using Condy's Fluid, a mixture of the mineral pyrolusite (largely magnesium dioxide) with potassium hydroxide that had been patented in the mid-nineteenth century and which could be conveniently carried as a disinfectant as well as being used to colour hair. Even with

Condy's Fluid, however, the process was not straightforward and would have given Charlotte's maid a great deal of work: each hair had to be dyed individually. In addition, it was something that would have had to be done discreetly. While it became very popular for Victorian women to dye their hair, and magazines were awash with advertisements for products, it was not quite accepted as thoroughly respectable, especially among the middle and upper classes. 'Above all dyes will be renounced', proclaimed Baroness Staffe authoritatively, in a French etiquette manual that was influential enough to be translated into English towards the end of the century. 'The natural colour of the hair will be kept and grey hair itself will not be powdered... At this cost the hair will remain abundant and vigorous, even in those of advanced age, and will allow of being prettily and gracefully dressed.'[8]

Even with the fashionable rebelliousness of dyed hair, Charlotte did not look like a woman whose name was becoming known across Europe. She looked ordinary; a woman of her class and time. And even she, as she admitted in her journal, was surprised at the way things were unfolding. She had not expected to be ransacking foreign lands for china. She had not planned to spend her days hurrying from one dealer to the next, excited by rumours of the rare and beautiful, exhausted and exhilarated by the chase. There was little in her earlier life to suggest that she was to become such a dedicated and inventive collector, and she was almost fifty when the obsession overwhelmed her. Her enthusiasm for collecting came late, and apparently out of the blue.

But, while there may have been few clues in Charlotte's first fifty years to suggest she would become such a significant and respected collector, the energy, determination and curiosity that characterized her collecting were clearly evident in the range of activities to which she dedicated herself as a younger woman. She was born in 1812 with a title, Lady Charlotte Elizabeth Bertie, the daughter of Albemarle Bertie, the 9th Earl of Lindsey, an army general and an MP. She was the first of three children, but her father was already sixty-eight years old when Charlotte was born, and he died just six years later. By the time Charlotte was nine, her mother had married again and her new husband, the Reverend Peter Pegus, had moved into the family home at Uffington House in Lincolnshire; a year later, Charlotte began the journal which she was to keep candidly and faithfully until she was seventy-nine years old and almost completely blind.

Charlotte hated her new stepfather. Pegus was a bully and a drunk who was once so desperate for beer that he downed a mug of lamp oil instead. Unpredictable and violent, he was quick to flare into a rage; passionate about the most trivial of domestic habits, on one occasion he sacked the entire household of servants on the spot. Family life was stormy and miserable, and Charlotte was lonely. The house at Uffington was isolated and there were no suitable friends for Charlotte nearby. Her eldest brother suffered from what would now be regarded as a mental disability; her younger brother was baffled by her bookish tastes; and she was never close to her mother, who sank into decline after her second marriage. Charlotte spent hours alone in the garden, particularly among the avenue of lime trees, and she immersed herself in her studies. She was serious, literary and fiercely bright. She worked with her brothers' tutor whenever she could (falling in love with him at the same time) and studied hard outside the hours officially allocated to her schooling, rising each morning to begin work by four, setting herself strict routines, devouring the books in the library and reciting poetry in her garden walks. She taught herself a variety of languages, including Arabic, Hebrew and Persian; she worked diligently at her mathematics; she practised her drawing skills until she became an accomplished draughtswoman; she played piano and harp, she read Chaucer and Ariosto for pleasure – and she played a mean game of billiards.[9]

By the time she was sixteen, Charlotte had a reputation for learning and culture. She followed contemporary affairs closely from the newspapers and her journal was full of her thoughts on politics. In contrast, she found the demands of fashionable society – the dress fittings and the long afternoons, the predictable parties and the 'gazing at each other in listless indolence' – tedious and unsatisfying, preferring the company of scholars to the chatter of female acquaintances.[10] This may have done little to impress the pleasure-loving young men of the Regency, but her title, and a not insignificant personal fortune, more than made up for her unfortunately thorough education. She was something of a catch, and society was not slow in conjuring up all kinds of potential matches for her. Terrified of being trapped in a miserable alliance to satisfy her family's ambition, however, she refused a marriage arranged by her mother in 1832 to the sixty-seven-year-old Robert Plumer Ward, a politician and novelist who was already twice widowed, and instead enjoyed a brief, but chaste, flirtation with the future Prime Minister Benjamin Disraeli.

Disraeli was handsome and dashing, described by Charlotte's cousin as 'wearing waistcoats of the most gorgeous colours and the most fantastic patterns... velvet pantaloons and shoes adorned with red rosettes... his black hair pomatumed and elaborately curled and his person redolent with perfume'.[11] Not yet elected to even the most minor of political offices, he was instead writing novels which Charlotte admired, and he took her to a series of fashionable concerts and bought her flowers. He even wrote enthusiastically to his sister about her fortune. But the relationship came to nothing (Disraeli later married one of Charlotte's closest friends), and in April 1833 Charlotte left Uffington for London.

Almost immediately upon her arrival in the capital, at the age of twenty-one, she met the forty-eight-year-old Welsh ironmaster and MP Josiah John Guest, known simply as John. Already a widow, John Guest was a handsome, curly-haired, practical man who, like Charlotte, was a rather diffident outsider amidst the glamour of London society. After a whirlwind romance, Guest walked with Charlotte in Kensington Gardens on 12 July 1833 and proposed to her. Charlotte accepted.

Most of Charlotte's family seem to have been pleased to be rid of her to a wealthy man. Although he was in trade, they could console themselves with the knowledge that it was no ordinary trade – the rail tracks made at Guest's factory in the Welsh town of Merthyr Tydfil were to criss-cross the globe, opening up lands from Russia to India. They celebrated at Uffington with a ball and an ox roast. Her stepfather Pegus, however, was horrified. He objected vociferously to the marriage and continued to detest his new son-in-law, even calling him out for a duel on one occasion, which, Charlotte duly noted, 'is too absurd an idea'.[12] He was habitually rude and dismissive of Charlotte's new husband, and he was not alone. London society in general was offended at the thought of a daughter of the aristocracy marrying a man whose hands were dirtied by the dust of the factory; a man descended from farmers and coal miners and who worshipped in the dissenting chapels that challenged the established hierarchy of the English Church. The new couple were ostracized: they were not invited to the events that mattered, and Charlotte's drawing room was distinctly quiet during the usual visiting hours.

Charlotte was naturally emotional and prone to sentimental tears, but she wasted few of them on the newlyweds' situation. Relishing the thought of a different life, she was untroubled by the opinions of the social elite. She believed in her husband, and in herself, and she believed that marriage to an active, industrious and political man would, in the end, open more interesting and challenging doors than the ones that were being closed to her. In August 1833, after a honeymoon tour of Sussex, Charlotte accompanied her husband for the first time to his ironworks in

Dowlais, in South Wales, where it was evident that London sensibilities were not shared by John Guest's friends and workers. Charlotte described with great delight the couple's arrival in Cardiff, which was celebrated by 'a volley canon, fired in grand style'. Furthermore, 'a triumphal procession and an illumination were planned' to greet them, intended on such a grand scale that 'no less than from 15 to 20 thousand people would probably have collected on the occasion'.[13]

The thought of such a reception horrified Guest, however, who, despite his public role, was a shy man; he had experienced a similar event before, during which a boy had been killed in the press of the crowd. But he did not want to seem ungrateful or heavy-handed in putting an end to the celebrations. In a pattern that was to be often repeated during their twenty years of marriage, John Guest turned to his wife for advice, and they decided to order a prompt dinner at a local inn, allowing them to press on to Dowlais and arrive a day earlier than expected, so that, diplomatically, 'the complimentary machinations for the following day might be eluded without being rejected'. In compensation, John and Charlotte gave out celebratory beer to over 4,000 people at the ironworks a couple of days later and 'they gave us some discharges of canon in return'.[14]

Charlotte's married life was extraordinarily active and successful. She embraced the Victorian ideal of the wife and mother, following her husband's political and industrial interests with pride and giving birth to ten children in the space of thirteen years. She also took her responsibilities for the Dowlais workers' welfare to heart, developing housing and recreational projects and working hard to introduce a fresh water system. She was particularly keen that all the children should have the benefit of a good and useful education, and she founded six schools, raising large amounts of money for their upkeep by private subscription. So important did she become to the success of the ironworks, and the lives of the people who worked there, that a friend noted that in many respects she was more influential than her husband: 'for in all that he was deficient she excelled, and while we credit him with founding the greatest ironworks in the world, and giving sustenance and substantial comfort to twenty thousand souls, it is chiefly to her influence we must look for all that was done in the way of moral and mental elevation'.[15]

In order to better accommodate their rapidly expanding family, Charlotte also set her mind to improving their home. In August 1835, she gave birth to Ivor Bertie Guest, a son and heir, and with the dynasty secure, she encouraged Guest in 1846 to buy Canford Manor in Dorset, a convenient distance from business both in London and Wales. The manor of Canford Magna had history. It dated back to Saxon times and had been an important base for the Earls of Salisbury. It had also been the home of William Ponsonby, the brother of Byron's lover Lady Caroline Lamb. It boasted extensive rolling parkland, dropping down to the River Stour, shaded woodland paths and neatly kept formal gardens, but the house itself was unremarkable, a muddled conglomeration of earlier buildings and practical extensions to the original medieval manor. Charlotte thought it dull and was immediately determined to make some alterations; to stamp her character on the place.

The Guests commissioned the architect Sir Charles Barry (who was, at the same time, rebuilding the Palace of Westminster with Augustus Pugin) to improve and expand Canford. Together, they created a fairytale, battlemented neo-Gothic house, complete with towers and turrets and a spectacular garden pavilion that housed twenty-six ancient Assyrian sculptures, including two colossi, one with two human heads and a lion's body, the other in the form of a bull. Charlotte worked closely with Barry, enjoying the challenge of learning about architecture and undertaking extensive discussions with the skilled stonemasons, carpenters and designers on site. John Guest, too, took a close interest in the house but he had less time to spend in Dorset and his role was primarily to pay the bills: the improvements became so costly that he became known locally as 'paying Guest'.[16]

So much was being achieved in the valleys of South Wales; so spectacular was the Canford house becoming and so influential was John Guest proving in public life that news could not fail to reach fashionable London society of Charlotte's increasing wealth and influence. What had amounted to social ostracism came to be conveniently forgotten, and during the 1840s and 1850s showers of invitations duly arrived from those eager to make the family's acquaintance. Along with her commitments in Wales and Dorset, Charlotte became famed as one of London's most entertaining and gracious hostesses. Before long, there were splendid dinners at the Guests' London house in Spring Gardens, Westminster, with the children playing on the back stairs, the table laden with veal cutlets, woodcock pie and boars' head, and leading statesmen such as Sir Robert Peel and the Duke of Wellington discussing politics in the parlour.

Nevertheless, Charlotte's life was not confined to entertaining, society events, philanthropic projects and running a family. Even with the interest of rebuilding Canford, and the challenge of keeping ten children healthy and occupied, she wanted more. She saw her marriage as a professional, as well as a personal, partnership and was eager to take an active role in the development of the ironworks. Just as she had been willing to challenge Victorian convention in marrying Guest, so she was determined not to be confined by the usual nineteenth-century restrictions on a woman's role. The day after she first arrived at Dowlais with her new husband, she insisted on seeing the furnaces and the forges, and after dinner she walked back to the works to watch the iron being cast. She was soon able to take an informed view of the processes and before long she was translating technical documents into French, to better disseminate developments in the industry, and was writing pamphlets on ironworking techniques and improvements. The prospect of entrepreneurial business excited her, not so much for the wealth and prestige which accompanied it, but because it offered a means of reaching and understanding people and cultures across the world. During her husband's frequent absences, she was in sole charge of the expanding Dowlais empire and she entertained streams of influential visitors: iron masters from France, Germany, Holland, Italy and Poland, the Nawab of Oudh from India and Russia's Grand Duke Constantine. Charlotte believed fervently in the value of what was being achieved at Dowlais and, when John's work as a politician and industrialist was recognized in 1838 with a baronetcy, she thought he deserved more: 'I consider it a paltry distinction and was much averse to his taking it... I shall not rest till I see something of more value bestowed upon him.'[17]

Alongside her husband's industrial interests, Charlotte also became increasingly involved in the political issues closest to him: free trade, the abolition of slavery and the reform of the Church. The curiosity she had shown for political discussion as a teenager flourished into an active engagement that even took her on to the streets. She canvassed openly on Guest's behalf, and was frequently to be found sneaking into large and unruly public meetings in Merthyr market to hear him speak. She was a practical, informed and unflappable spouse for a politician attempting to push through liberal reforms in what could be stormy times: when the works and house were threatened by Chartist riots during the autumn of 1839, Charlotte made composed plans for 'the case of a siege' and arranged for the children to be sent away to safety, noting in her journal only that since there were 'from fifty to a hundred special constables all in the house. . . the succession of suppers and tea-drinkings that went on amongst all that entered was really a curious thing'.[18]

Remarkably Charlotte also found time – in the midst of political riots, the children's scarlet fever scares and entertaining high society – to continue with her studies. She began to teach herself Welsh within weeks of her marriage, and took on what proved to be the eight-year task of translating eleven medieval tales collectively called *The Mabinogion*, providing extensive scholarly notes to explain the stories and their contexts. The Mabinogion myths were at the heart of Welsh folklore and are some of the greatest tales of Celtic literature, set in a bizarre and magical landscape, part Wales and part mysterious underworld, populated by giants, enchanted horses and magnificent heroes. They introduced figures like King Arthur and Merlin into European storytelling, and they brought together some of the most influential myths of the oral tradition. Welsh scholars knew of the stories and William Owen Pughe, a Welsh teacher, antiquarian and writer of grammars, had left an unfinished translation at his death in 1835; but no English speaker had thought them worth much trouble.

Charlotte took a different view. She valued *The Mabinogion* as more than an obscure element of Welsh tradition or a personal academic challenge. It was a way of understanding and popularizing the culture which she had embraced so enthusiastically. It was a means of sharing the stories with her own children, and of exploring the magical cultural landscape which was too often obscured by the noise and dirt and fire-blowing furnaces of the Dowlais ironworks. It was a labour of love. But unexpectedly, when it was published in several beautifully produced volumes between 1838 and 1849, it also became something of a publishing sensation. Charlotte's translation, which remained the standard for almost a century, made the tales famous: they became popular and fashionable almost immediately, not just in England and Wales, but also across Europe and America.

With both industrial wealth and a family background in the English gentry and aristocracy, Charlotte was perfectly placed to become a collector. Her interest in ceramics and smaller decorative objects such as fans and playing cards placed her at the forefront of the changing fashions in collecting, moving on from paintings and sculpture to more portable and domestic pieces. She was clever and studious, and in many ways she inherited her interests from the long line of gentlemanly amateurs who had gone before her. But her collecting was in no way inevitable. She might have continued as an industrialist and a reformer, and been remembered as a mother, a scholar and a pioneering translator.

There were a few signs in her early life that suggested Charlotte might be destined to become a collector. When she was nineteen years old, her mother gave her a feathered fan which she treasured, not only as a gift, but as a work of art and a cultural artefact, reading more into the fan's construction and design than might most young women of the period. She was also a close friend of her cousin, Austen Henry Layard, the man who would later dismiss J. C. Robinson as 'nothing but a dealer' and who was related to Charlotte on her mother's side. She was a keen supporter of Layard's pioneering archaeology while he, only six years her junior, came to rely on her as a patron. There has been some suggestion that the two were lovers, but any romantic relationship between them was certainly conducted with the utmost discretion and no evidence has been found to support the rumours of the time. There is, however, little doubt that at least some of Layard's enthusiasm for the idea of adventurous collecting had rubbed off on his cousin: he gave Charlotte numerous pieces from his excavations, and in time, as we have seen, she made over a building at Canford, known as 'the Nineveh Porch', to show off his finds.

This included a relief taken from the throne room of the Assyrian king Ashurnasirpal II (883–859 BC) and brought back from the ancient city of Nimrud in northern Mesopotamia (now Iraq), which Layard began excavating in 1845. The relief, among the first Assyrian pieces to be seen in Britain, was rediscovered at Canford in 1992 and sold two years later at Christie's for £7.7 million, by far the highest price ever paid for an antiquity and a pleasant windfall for the boarding school that now occupies the Canford buildings.

Without a change in circumstances, however, the early feathered fan might have remained nothing more than a treasured gift and Charlotte might well have remained a passive bystander to Layard's own collecting. Her future as a collector depended on a combination of events in the early 1850s which altered her personal and professional circumstances, and introduced her to the temptation of rare and beautiful objects. The first of these was the Great Exhibition in Joseph Paxton's magnificent Crystal Palace in 1851. As members of the social elite, the Guests were invited to the official opening of the exhibition on 1 May; they spent the previous day researching the best places to sit so that when the pageant began they would have an unobstructed view of the Queen and her entourage.

But Charlotte was not just there to see and be seen. When the pomp was over, she made return visits and, along with more than six million other visitors, she was fascinated and delighted by the display of objects from around the world. The examples of manufactures absorbed her; the details of international trade and commerce intrigued her; and the models of technological innovation excited her. Taking her place in the crowds, she enjoyed the sheer exuberant spectacle: the circus, tightrope walkers, dog shows, pigeon shows and flower shows, the life-size reproductions of dinosaurs, the replica lead mine, and the fountains in the park with over 12,000 individual jets of water. But what was to change her life were the packed and dazzling displays of furniture, textiles and china, jewellery and silver, glass and sculpture, paintings, carvings and antiquities from ancient civilizations. It was a treasure trove. Charlotte had never before seen so many beautiful and fascinating things gathered together, the past and the present – as well as glimpses of what was to come – so jumbled and interweaved. For a woman devoted to learning, there was much to study. For a woman with a sharp eye for detail and value, there was much to admire. And for a woman with wealth, there were many opportunities to buy. Charlotte did not become a collector overnight as a result of visiting the Great Exhibition, but it gave her a sense of what might be possible.

One of the reasons Charlotte could not, or would not, indulge any enthusiasm that had been sparked by her visits to the Crystal Palace was that by 1851 John Guest was seriously ill. Her visits to the Great Exhibition were overshadowed by her concern for his deteriorating health, and by November, with her husband often feverish and incoherent, Charlotte was doing everything for the business. He could not travel, nor attend meetings, nor even sign letters or cheques. Doctors tried a variety of treatments but were, on the whole, baffled and pessimistic. There were periods when Guest had the energy to make short journeys and entertain, but these became shorter and fewer. Charlotte could do nothing but take on the burden of the business and hope.

Guest's illness dragged on another year, coming and going, but in November 1852, after a sharp turn for the worse, he finally died. It was the end of a marriage, an unusually intense and equal business partnership, and of Charlotte's direct influence in political circles. It was also an enormous personal loss. Charlotte was, for many weeks, inconsolable. Two months after the funeral, when she visited Canford for the first time since her husband's death, she tried to describe her intense sorrow: 'When we stopped at the door, I got out silently, and leaving them all went straight to the

Library, where luckily there was a light. A slight veil had been thrown over his bust, which at once I removed and then I flung my arms around it, and remained clasping it for some minutes, kissing the cold lips – not colder than his own when I kissed them last – and shedding torrents of passionate tears. And this cold marble is now all that is left me!'[19]

However, it was not John Guest's death which affected Charlotte's future as a collector so much as her remarriage. John's death inevitably involved much change, but as executor to his will, and a trustee of the estate, Charlotte continued to be heavily involved with the day-to-day running of the Dowlais works, much as she had been in the past. She continued to take charge of the business, struggling to make the works profitable in a changing economic and industrial climate, and negotiating a resolution to a strike among the workers in South Wales in 1853 – a fraught affair that turned her hair white. But she was hardly out of her heavy widow's weeds when she caused another scandal with her blatant disregard for Victorian proprieties. In 1855, at the age of forty-three, Charlotte married again. This time she chose 'Charley' – Colonel Charles Schreiber – a handsome soldier from a military German family, not yet thirty years old, a classical scholar and a fellow of Trinity College Cambridge. Respectable enough, perhaps, but he was also the tutor who had first come to Canford to school Charlotte's oldest son Ivor just twenty-four days after John's death. Her friends and acquaintances, and even her daughters, were shocked and horrified. It was not only that Charlotte had been so recently widowed, and that Schreiber was so much her junior, but Charles's role as a family servant put the relationship beyond the pale.

Once again, Charlotte was challenging Victorian convention, but she did not seem to care if her choice of husband was regarded as unfortunate. She did not worry that many considered that she had demeaned and disgraced herself, nor that her daughters were horrified by the thought of having Charles Schreiber as a stepfather. And she was quite relieved when Pegus disowned her. Her love affair reinvigorated her. She was ready for a new challenge. Under the terms of John Guest's will, a second marriage meant she had to relinquish the running of the ironworks to the other trustees. It also left her substantially less buoyant financially, and she immediately had to forgo luxuries like ponies and a carriage of her own. But she was content to sacrifice material comfort. Charles Schreiber's modest nature, good humour and energetic mind delighted her, and it was with growing excitement that they made plans together.

The marriage, in April 1855, was a quiet affair. This time, there was no cannon salute or triumphal procession. And the first few years of Charlotte's new life were unsettled and sometimes sorrowful. By 1856, the newlyweds were overspent by £6,000, and money was a worry. Schreiber's personal wealth was negligible – or he would never have been forced to take on the role of tutor. The youngest of Charlotte's children by Guest was still only eleven years old, and the financial demands of raising her family were not inconsiderable. It was ten years before the Schreibers' affairs settled down and money pressures eased, with three daughters safely and successfully married. In addition, Charlotte was having to labour, for a second time, to edge back into polite society, being seen riding out in Rotten Row and attending Court. But her progress was slow and frustrating, and it was hard not to look back at the glittering social events she had been hosting just a few years earlier. Worst of all, however, were the disappointment and agony of three miscarriages, the last of which marked the end of the Schreibers' hopes to have children together, followed by the death, in 1862, of Charlotte's son Augustus at the age of just twenty-one.

It was not until all this upheaval and grief passed, almost ten years after Charlotte's second marriage, that she could begin to look around and think what she might like to do with her new life. And it was now that she found herself increasingly attracted to the idea of collecting. Things from her past, like the feathered fan, provided a catalyst for new areas of study. The people around her, particularly her husband and her cousin, tempted her with the idea of travel and adventure. The allure of beautiful and curious objects held out a romantic promise that seemed suddenly irresistible. Charlotte did not fall into collecting; she made a conscious decision that it was how she wanted to spend the rest of her life. By the mid-1860s, she had devoted herself to the idea, one which took her far from Dowlais and its furnaces, and which would beguile and consume her for the next forty years. She confided every high and low of her collecting, every expectant journey and successful transaction, to her numerous volumes of journals, kept in her elegant handwriting. Sometimes these are pithy notes relating little more than travel schedules, objects and prices, but more often the entries run away with colourful descriptions of journeys, people and places, glowing with delight in what she is doing and giving a real taste of what it was like to be a traveller at this time. Her journals take us to the heart of the day-to-day life of the Victorian collector. They reveal Charlotte's dedication, scholarship and courage; they give a lively sense of an all-consuming desire to collect, and they show just what it took to manoeuvre successfully in the cut-throat world of nineteenth-century collecting.

CHAPTER NINE

Pushing and Panting and Pinching their Way

$\mathscr{I}$t was spring 1873 and the collecting season had begun in
earnest. Fine weather and easier travelling conditions had
coaxed collectors out of their drawing rooms and into the streets.
Dealers, too, were restocking their shelves and refilling their
displays. The Schreibers were far from alone as they made their
way through the now familiar towns of Holland and Belgium.
Speed and stamina were everything: on 8 April, after a half-past-
five start on a misty morning, they squeezed in visits to Gouda,
Utrecht and Rotterdam, before reaching The Hague in the
evening in violent rain and with Charles, perhaps unsurprisingly,
feeling 'ill and tired'. Nevertheless, their efforts proved to be in
vain. There was nothing in any of the shops worth the trouble of
the journey, and the Schreibers' big red bag remained empty. It
was not that dealers were struggling to find new objects, nor that
the usual supply routes from impoverished gentry and declining
European aristocrats were drying up. It was that they were being
outmanoeuvred by the competition. Exasperated, disappointed
and defeated, Charlotte confided to her journal: 'we find everywhere

that Duveen of Hull has been there before us making wonderful purchases.'[1]

Rivalry between collectors throughout Europe was fierce. When J. C. Robinson was sitting in Rome in 1859, waiting for the South Kensington Museum's reply to his request to buy works from the Campana collection, it was the manoeuvrings of other collectors that most concerned him. During the 1860s and 1870s, an increasingly sophisticated European travel network was making it possible to cover ground reasonably quickly, cheaply and easily. By 1860, there were nearly 800 miles of railway in Britain for every million people, amounting to almost 10,000 miles of track. In France and Germany, railway development emerged more slowly during the early part of the century, but a boom in construction meant that by 1880 France had caught up with Britain and boasted some 15,000 miles of track, while Germany's political unification in 1871 was facilitated by almost 20,000 miles of railway that joined the major states in a public system of *Länderbahnen*.[2] In addition, the increasing number of museums emerging across Europe, and the growing state investment in collections, meant that men such as Robinson, Franks and Eastlake were travelling and collecting with the wealth and power of national institutions behind them. If and when they could disentangle themselves from government bureaucracy, they could often beat private collectors – who had fewer resources – to the spoils.

Clubs and galleries and organizations brought collectors together across Britain and Europe, but collecting in the mid-nineteenth century was as much about competition as about cooperation. As an expression of state prestige on a national level, museums were anxious to lead the way for their country – or indeed within their country. J. C. Robinson always asserted that there was no conflict between his collecting at South Kensington and the medieval and Renaissance treasures being accumulated at the British Museum by Augustus Franks, but there was little doubt that the two men were at times competing for the best pieces. In 1855, it was the rivalry between the two institutions which put a stop to the idea of acquiring the Bernal collection in its entirety for one or the other. Instead, the grant had to be shared. Robinson at once recognized what this meant: 'the state virtually committed itself to the formation of two concurrent new undertakings of the same character. . . with little co-operation betwixt the managers of the separate establishments, if not indeed with tacit rivalry betwixt them.' Fortunately, he and Franks came to an understanding for dividing the Bernal spoils, but the rivalry went further than just the two principal collectors. Henry Cole had a distinctly predatory attitude towards the British Museum: in 1852, he proposed bringing 'the overflowings of the Brit Mus' to South Kensington, and after the Bernal sale he was delighted to hear Antonio Panizzi, who was soon to be appointed Principal Librarian of the British Museum, suggest that 'the whole shd be handed over [to South Kensington] & even Franks with them'.[3]

By 1859, Cole was talking to Panizzi about taking long-term loans from the British Museum, which would in effect strip the Great Russell Street galleries of their entire medieval collections. After Henry Cole's retirement, the rivalry continued but it was the British Museum that appeared now to have the upper hand: a Select Committee investigating the relationship between the two museums in 1873 proposed that the South Kensington Museum should be subsumed into its older rival. The autonomy of South Kensington was, for a while, under real threat, but the move was fiercely opposed by staff there, and by the mid-1870s it had been agreed that the two museums should continue to coexist. As the collections at South Kensington turned their attention even more from manufactures and towards precious objects, however, there were inevitably areas in which interests clashed.

* * *

Among individual collectors, the instinct to be first was compelling. Despite constant weariness and not infrequent ill-health, the Schreibers took night trains and battled with omnibuses when easier options were available, not just to reduce costs, but also because they needed to pounce quickly on objects. In many cases, they were successful: in March 1874, for example, they 'espied a printed Battersea box, very handsome' in an auction in Brussels, and stepped in to buy it before it was offered to the gathered dealers, 'coming away well pleased with our bargain'.[4] They took the competition seriously, and had the advantage over many collectors in that they travelled almost everywhere together. This meant that, when one of them, as was not unusual, felt too tired or sick to be out of their hotel, the other could continue the constant round of shopping that marked their days. In Duveen, however, as Charlotte's journal suggests, the Schreibers felt they had found their match.

In 1873, when Charlotte was writing, Joseph Joel Duveen was thirty years old, energetic, astute and beginning to establish a dealership that, in the hands of his successors, would influence the markets for generations to come. It was his son, also Joseph, who would in time become one of the wealthiest and most prominent dealers ever known, shipping paintings across the Atlantic to the American millionaires of the early twentieth century and funding celebrated extensions to the British Museum and the Tate Gallery. In the early 1870s, however, all this was just beginning. Joseph Joel, sent by his Dutch family to launch an import business in Hull specializing in Delft porcelain, was still in the throes of establishing himself as a dealer, drawing on his connections across Europe and familiarizing himself with the machinations of the market.

Duveen had learned his lessons as an apprentice in an ordinary porcelain merchant in Hull. The shop he joined as a young man was not doing well. European suppliers were pulling out of deals, apparently without explanation; objects which were expected from Europe would fail to arrive and then turn up days or weeks later in competitors' showrooms. Somehow, information was leaking out, making the business increasingly vulnerable. And so the young Duveen took himself off early one weekday to the town's busy docks and watched as shipments were loaded and unloaded in the morning half-light. He stood amongst the soot and the salt and the baffling noise, watching as papers were signed and consignments counted; and, against the cranking of the machinery, the dull hooting of the ships and the shouting of dockers on the wharf, he listened. Gradually, things became clear. He heard details of the shop's transactions – its trade secrets – flung from one part of the dockside to another. He saw confidential lists sold on. He heard new, rival, deals struck. By the end of the morning, he knew exactly how information was escaping, who was betraying the company, and just how important it was to know exactly what was going on, all the time, everywhere.

Duveen immediately booked himself a berth on a fishing boat to Holland so that he could visit personally the company's old suppliers and win back lost business. He was handsomely rewarded for his initiative: within a year, his salary was raised by his grateful employers from fifteen shillings to fifteen pounds a week, making him the highest-paid employee in the Hull import business. But this was not enough. It was not money that drove Duveen's ambitions – it was the thrill of competition. He soon began trading for himself, setting up a company with a colleague called Barney Barnett and using what he had learned in the commotion of Hull docks to make it thrive. With a network of friends and family acting as informants across Europe, he would pursue the whisper of a deal quickly and decisively, making the gathering of information as critical to his activity as the amassing of objects. He was, as Charlotte found out, first off the mark and first to the spoils. He had a superb memory for people, places and, above all, things, and, while at home his wife Rosetta was busy raising fifteen children and his brother Henry was establishing family showrooms in Boston and New York, Joseph Joel was slipping quietly from one European town to the next, following his precious tip-offs and outstripping competitors.

It was his connections in Holland that were most active and effective, and it was here in the spring of 1873 that Duveen first heard rumours of some valuable pieces of china. It was not quite clear what the pieces were, only that they were old and rare and in pristine condition. Duveen did not need to know more: immediately, he set off to buy them. But the journey was far from straightforward. Duveen's informant had been travelling through small, remote villages, making inquiries about anything local families might be willing to sell, and the pieces that had come to light were in an old house in a tiny hamlet deep in the Dutch countryside, miles from the railway or a town of any size. The only means of travel was by heavy carriage on the country tracks that wound their way slowly through woods and farmland. It was a long and tedious journey. Duveen spent hours rattling past isolated settlements, the carriage wheels dragging through the mud of the lanes. There were no inns to provide refreshment and nothing to see but flat fields stretching out bare to the horizon. It was with enormous relief that, finally, he caught sight of the roofs of the houses in the village where he was heading and knew that his journey was nearly over. He would negotiate quickly, clinch the sale and return to civilization as soon as he could.

But just as the tired horses were pulling the final half-mile, Duveen spotted a fast-moving fly coming towards him from the village. With just two large wheels and a cabin for the passenger, the fly was lighter and quicker than a normal carriage and could cover the uneven ground at greater speed. It was not the kind of vehicle Duveen expected to see in such an out-of-the-way place and he was puzzled. Perhaps he even had an inkling that, for once, he had been outdone. Because as the fly came rumbling towards him, he saw Charlotte Schreiber, bumping along with the quick jolting rhythm, a large red bag safely snuggled in her lap. As he was to tell amused listeners for many years to come, it soon became all too clear that he had been defeated: Charlotte 'had snatched the prize, which she was carrying off with her'; and Duveen was left to face the monotonous return journey in the knowledge that his efforts had been thoroughly wasted.[5]

There is no exact record of what Charlotte managed to snatch from under Duveen's nose – he remembered it only, rather vaguely, as being 'objets d'art'. I find it surprising that Charlotte herself does not mention the victory in her journal, but she was probably unaware that Duveen was behind her and, with her new objects to savour, failed to notice him rattling past in his carriage. If so, it seems a shame. Such a triumph would surely have been sweet to her and would have reassured her that she was winning a place among the competitive community of collectors. There can be little doubt that the story added to Charlotte's reputation among her rivals scouring Europe for the best pieces. The very fact that Duveen dined out on the tale, passing it on with admiration as proof of her ability to outwit the opposition, shows just how seriously she was regarded by her colleagues, and how widely her name was becoming known.

From the very beginning of her collecting career, however, Charlotte was at a disadvantage: she was a woman pursuing a distinctly male occupation. Most of the collectors and dealers were men, with easy access to learned societies, social clubs and the male hierarchies of the museums. Despite her obvious enthusiasm and knowledge, and even with her husband at her side, Charlotte sometimes found relations with the more misogynistic of European shopkeepers difficult. Among her family and friends, too, her collecting was regarded by many as a bizarre idiosyncrasy that distracted from her role as wife and mother and prevented her from attending to the essential demands of running a household. For the Victorian middle and upper classes, the home was a sanctuary from the uncertain social and economic forces of the world beyond, a still point in the changing, and increasingly commercial, environment of modern life. The royal couple of Queen Victoria and Prince Albert with their obvious devotion to each other and their children, and a public domestic life built round a clear sense of duty, offered an embodiment of respectability to which those below them could aspire. Within this ideal, the woman's place was to anchor the home and provide a safe private space that would reassure and fortify her husband, however buffeted he was by public life.

This was not Charlotte's way. Her collecting was not confined to Europe – she spent weeks and months tracking down objects in Britain, too – but it always required travel, and most of her attention. Her son, Montague Guest, remembered that she would 'come back, after weeks on the Continent to Langham House, where she lived, rich with the fruits of her expeditions', and, once reinstalled, she would spend a great deal of time and energy sorting, cleaning, assessing and cataloguing what she had acquired.[6] In the eyes of conventional upper- and middle-class Victorians, these were not the actions of a sane and proper woman; instead, such behaviour suggested neglect of her family and household, and a disregard for her social position. For nineteenth-century women of the middle and upper classes, some knowledge of art, and the formation of an artistic taste, might be valued as a fashionable accomplishment, but it was expected to remain an amateur hobby. Engaging with dealers while researching and financing a substantial collection was unusual, and, in devoting herself to her collecting, Charlotte was openly flouting convention.

Such expectations did not mean women were prevented entirely from collecting, but they certainly restricted the aspirations of most female collectors. The growing enthusiasm for natural history and science collections, for example, threw up few successful female role models. The celebrated Mary Anning was a skilled fossil hunter, palaeontologist and dealer in Lyme Regis during the 1820s and 1830s, but not only was she a woman, she was also a poor woman from a working-class, dissenting family. Despite being well known in geological circles, and winning a certain degree of respect from many of her male colleagues, she remained an outsider and was never given full credit for her contributions to a scientific community that was dominated by wealthy Anglican gentlemen. Similarly, with the development of disciplines such as botany and zoology over the course of the nineteenth century, many women found themselves increasingly excluded and marginalized, forced to study, collect and draw informally, as amateurs based at home, rather than being included in the developing hierarchies of professionalized practice.

Women also often found themselves excluded from areas such as painting, sculpture and antiques, which were all very much embedded in a male tradition that had, for generations, governed the stately homes, scholarly clubs and even schools, where the habit of collecting often began. Women were not admitted to the Society of Antiquaries until 1920, and of the two nineteenth-century archaeological clubs only one, the Royal Archaeological Institute of Great Britain, was open to women. Despite a petition to admit women in 1859, the august schools of the Royal Academy did not allow female members until 1922 (even though two women had been founder members in 1768); women students were admitted from 1861, but only under restrictive rules that insisted on their drawing from draped models. Similarly, the Royal College of Art shunted its women students into a special 'Female School' where life drawing classes featured a series of well-clothed dummies. It was not until the end of the century that many conservative societies began to extend membership to include women: the Royal Society of Painters in Water-colours, for example, did not give full membership rights to women until 1890.

The Fine Arts Club, as I have already mentioned, allowed women to attend meetings from the mid-century, but, even then, it did so rather grudgingly. For the first year after its foundation, female connoisseurs were only afforded honorary instead of full membership and of the 201 members only eight were female. Charles Schreiber joined the club early in its life in 1858, and was an active contributor, exhibiting his first objects there in 1863 and organizing a display of porcelain, lacquer and jewellery for fellow members at the Schreibers' home in April 1866. Charlotte was encouraging and often attended meetings, as well as hosting those that were held at her house, but she never became a member, perhaps because even she felt uncomfortable in an environment that so closely resembled a gentleman's club. While the example of pioneers like Mary Anning suggests that class was one of the factors determining the degree to which women were allowed to participate in a scholarly community, it was clear that even for Charlotte Schreiber, with an impeccable family background, the right upbringing and a place in elite social circles, it was far from easy to earn the respect of male peers or to take advantage of the opportunities offered to male collectors.

Such restrictions inevitably influenced the type of objects Victorian women tended to collect. Instead of ancient classical artefacts and Old Masters, their attention often turned to things that did not appear inappropriately scholarly or assertive, or which many of their male counterparts regarded as trivial. This was not necessarily a mark of defeat. Charlotte was typical in exploiting the lack of interest of most male collectors in objects such as playing cards, fans and especially ceramics, not only creating for herself a new and defined area of expertise but also allowing her to take shrewd advantage of less volatile, and less expensive, markets. Many male dealers knew little or nothing about these less traditionally popular types of object: 'ignorance was the prevailing characteristic,' explained Charlotte's son in introducing her journal. 'Nobody wanted Old Sheffield Plate, Pinchbeck, old English jewellery, needlework pictures, old English glass, pewter, Staffordshire ware, excluding Wedgwood, old steel, brass etc. . . my mother was able to pick up the finest specimens of china and other such articles for quite a moderate outlay.'[7]

The enthusiasm for 'specimens of china', especially porcelain, among female collectors was particularly pronounced. England's Queen Mary II had collected oriental porcelain in the seventeenth century, helping to make the craze for Japanese china fashionable and respectable. In his *History of England*, Macaulay looked back scathingly at the way the fashion had taken off, dominating many women's lives: 'In a few years almost every great house in the kingdom contained a museum of these grotesque baubles. . . a fine lady valued her mottled green pottery quite as much as she valued her monkey and much more than she valued her husband.'[8] At first, only noblewomen and women of the gentry could afford to follow in Queen Mary's footsteps but despite, or perhaps because of, this the fashion flourished. In the first half of the seventeenth century, imports of Japanese ceramics peaked while cheaper, less ornamental pieces from China began to flood into the European market, making it easier for less wealthy collectors to join the fray.

There are many reasons why women took to collecting china, and particularly porcelain. Not only were ceramics enormously fashionable, but such a collection was associated with wealth and power and so was also extremely prestigious – owning even a few pieces could go a long way towards boosting social standing. The growing popularity of domestic rituals around tea-drinking also gave women the opportunity to take a more visible role in polite gatherings. Their tea sets placed them at the heart of a new kind of social event, taking control of the occasion and using their china to orchestrate it. For many, however, the attraction of china was much more straightforward: seventeenth- and eighteenth-century women were seduced by the bright colours, the extravagant decoration and the sheer sense of luxury of their porcelain treasures.

By the nineteenth century, this tradition meant that there was a great choice of secondhand 'old' china for collectors, alongside new china being produced or imported to meet the demands of the market, and the growing sense that china had a history started to change the way in which it was perceived. It was no longer viewed as simply decorative and fashionable – it began to acquire the status of art. When public museums like the South Kensington Museum, and popular exhibitions like the 1857 Manchester Art Treasures Exhibition, included ceramics in their displays, this consolidated the idea that ceramics had artistic merit, and might be worth collecting. The 1860s and 1870s witnessed the publication of a variety of books and pamphlets offering histories of English and Continental ware, as well as enticing the collector with hints on which pieces to look out for, which shops and dealers offered the best bargains and which were the most profitable hunting grounds. Charlotte and Charles Schreiber, beginning their collecting around 1865, were at the vanguard of this Victorian chinamania. They made the most of the fact that knowledge was not yet quite widespread nor the market entirely prepared for the onslaught of collectors. They also set an example for those who came after them with their energetic and skilful ceramic collecting, remaining somewhat critical of those who were ignorantly swept along by what Charlotte called the 'ridiculous rage' for china.

Increasingly, the wealthy and influential housewives of the middle classes began to collect ceramics, even if modestly. Some men, too, developed a taste for ceramic collecting, but this was more unusual. China came to be seen as so much a female speciality that a man's enthusiasm for ceramics was often regarded as evidence of effeminacy. Charles Lamb, the English essayist of the late-eighteenth and early-nineteenth centuries, was one of the small number of men who admitted to a fascination with ceramics, and in an essay on 'Old China' he openly admitted that this was not an entirely masculine predilection: 'I have an almost feminine partiality for old china,' he confessed.[9] In contrast, for women, a small collection of china was considered a proper and reputable outlet for their energies. An enthusiasm for china collecting could be roundly approved by the male establishment: it was useful enough for the tea table and pretty enough to keep a woman amused. It accorded neatly with Victorian ideals about the woman's role in the home, and a few nice pieces of china or a handful of tasteful 'objets d'art' reflected well on the standing of the household. Surveying the various types of possible collections, one commentator noted condescendingly: 'CHINA. This is a hobby that ladies should cultivate. . . Women, as a rule, have little taste for collecting books, prints or pictures, but it is a fact that they evince quite an attachment to their ordinary china service.'[10]

But it was not simply that china was viewed as an appropriate distraction for women, particularly those of the upper classes; it was also usually regarded as personal – instead of family – property. Unlike jewels, classical antiquities or paintings, which would usually pass from father to son, pieces of china were rarely subject to the strict rules of primogeniture inheritance and could often pass quietly from mother to daughter, or from sister to niece. This had the advantage of potentially circumventing the restrictions on female ownership. Unmarried women, though often marooned in a social no man's land, at least had the privilege of owning their possessions. Married women, in contrast, handed over the rights of ownership to their husbands. If they became collectors, by law they could not own any of the objects they collected, nor choose to whom they left them after their deaths. It was not until 1870 that the government passed the Married Women's Property Act, which allowed women to own possessions they had acquired after their marriages, and it was another twelve years before the same right was extended to objects owned before marriage. Until these laws came into force, a woman's possessions, like herself, were considered to be simply an extension of her husband's property. A few pieces of china, however, were frequently considered to be unworthy of much attention; husbands often allowed their wives to dispose of such a collection as they wished. Bequeathed through the generations in this way, the best or favourite pieces could become heirlooms down the female line.

Collecting was what the Schreibers did together, and they worked side by side in every aspect of creating and developing their collection. But other women were not so fortunate as to have a family which sympathized with the all-consuming urge to collect. Many Victorian men believed that their wives, mothers and daughters would be unable to control themselves if they became too involved with the stimulating world of 'things'. They feared that such obsession would lead to personal instability, the breakdown of domestic order and even sexual licentiousness. During the Great Exhibition of 1851, *Punch* highlighted a variety of dangerous impulses that might be prompted by the glittering displays. In one cartoon, middle-class ladies are shown resisting police eviction from the Crystal Palace at closing time with a defiant, even violent, show of solidarity, opposing 'civil power at the point of a parasol'. In another, 'The Awful Result of Giving A Season Ticket to Your Wife' is a neglected and empty house. Worse still, in another cartoon, flocks of women are depicted relishing the highly physical, sexually charged atmosphere of the Exhibition as they 'push, and pant, and pinch their way amongst each other' to see the famous and fabulous Koh-i-Noor diamond.[11]

Over twenty years later, the idea that collecting was somehow at odds with healthy female instincts still lingered. A *Punch* cartoon of 1874 shows a dishevelled middle-class mother bemoaning the breakage of a valued vase. Her oldest daughter tries to comfort her as five younger siblings look on, but a family is apparently no consolation: 'You child! You're not unique!! There are six of you – a complete set!' wails the mother disconsolately.[12] The message was clear: left to their own devices, women could not be trusted to bring self-control and dignity to the collecting and display of lovely objects.

This discomfort with display and a woman's part in it revealed all kinds of Victorian anxieties. During the eighteenth century, the capitalist spirit was frequently seen as a positive attribute which could keep in check other more unruly and immoral inclinations, and act as a counterweight to undesirable behaviour. By the middle of the nineteenth century, however, attitudes towards conspicuous consumption had become much more ambivalent. Despite the growth of a commodity culture, the development of department stores, extravagant shopping habits and spectacular one-off events like the International Exhibitions, the Victorians' response to the objects with which they liked to surround themselves was complex. The activity of creating wealth had acquired overtones of coarseness and taint, and the realities of commercial enterprise needed, at least in public, to be separated from the higher moral priorities of family and social or religious responsibility. The display of too many objects within the home ran the risk of being perceived as exhibitionism, which in turn could be linked to degenerate and even immoral behaviour. Women, in particular, who exhibited too openly a preference for 'things', for shopping and luxury and spending, could be portrayed as artificial and untrustworthy, and even sexually promiscuous.

In the light of these attitudes, it is perhaps no surprise that female collectors were often reticent about their activity and, officially at least, appeared to be thin on the ground: of the 131 ceramics collectors recorded in 1851 by Joseph Marryat, the first writer in English to address the history of ceramics, only twelve were women. Even though these numbers rose to thirty-three by the late 1860s, female collectors still represented only a fraction of the total.[13] But for all the reasons we have seen, collecting was, in fact, not unusual among women. On the other hand, it *was* unusual for women to be high-profile collectors like Charlotte Schreiber and it was also rare for them to make large bequests to public museums to cement their place in collecting history. (It is perhaps revealing that, while Charlotte's name is associated with the collection of English ceramics now at the Victoria and Albert Museum, it was Charles Schreiber who first proposed a permanent public home for it.) Nonetheless, collecting was a popular female pastime. It tended, however, to be a more private pleasure than it was among men, and it was often linked to the home education of children, particularly girls. It was often viewed as a welcome means of self-expression, rather than an historic investment, and it tended to be an aesthetic as much as a scholarly pursuit: Charlotte Schreiber's collection is unique among Victorian women's collections in the range, quality and extent of the documentation that she maintained.

With few opportunities to join the male-dominated art and collectors' clubs, those women who did enjoy collecting had to find more informal ways to meet to discuss their enthusiasm, exchange information and arrange for the buying and selling of objects. Compared to male networks, the female equivalents were small and distinctly less powerful, but nonetheless they brought like-minded collectors together to share ideas. Charlotte's journals are littered with references to helping out her sister collectors. In November 1869, for example, she spent 'two very pleasant hours' with Mrs Haliburton, a widowed china collector who became a regular visitor and correspondent, and in June 1884 she called on

Lady Camden, in Eaton Square, to discuss china. By the 1870s, Charlotte was already being recognized as an expert and she was able to use her unusual level of access to the male worlds of curating and dealing to act on behalf of her female friends both at home and abroad. In October 1873, while in Rotterdam, she called at Boor's Bazaar 'to execute a commission for Mrs Haliburton', and a few months later she took a ceramic mould to elicit an opinion from Augustus Franks at the British Museum on behalf of a friend, Dorothy Neville, another active collector.

Charlotte's women friends clearly recognized that she had battled her way into the male bastions of the collecting world. Her collecting was undertaken on a different scale from almost any other woman of her time, and this was what set her apart. She herself often refers to her collecting in her journals as 'work', an indication of just how serious and consuming a matter she considered it. And the male establishment certainly did not view her collecting simply as a genteel lady's hobby. Augustus Franks was a close friend and collecting confidant. The two shared regular discussions about their objects, and frequently bought and sold pieces between themselves. Franks was, according to Charlotte's son Montague, 'a constant visitor at her house'. When she was abroad, Charlotte mixed as an equal with museum professionals: in Tarragona in 1870, the director of the museum took time to show her personally 'all over the antiquities collected there', and in November 1874 she was shown around the Utrecht Museum by its founder, Monsieur Van Huckelm, 'a most well-informed and agreeable man... making this collection... quite wonderful'.[14] In the 1870s, when the china craze was at its height, the London dealers Mortlocks, based in Oxford Street, even relied on Charlotte as a 'runner', asking her to use her European connections to purchase blue-and-white ceramics on their behalf. Mortlock openly admitted 'that nearly all he knew about China he learned from her', something which, as Charlotte's son

163

acknowledged, was 'a marvellous tribute indeed, from the professional to the amateur'.[15] In spite of being a woman, Charlotte was respected, and even feted, as a collector. So completely did she challenge the conventions of what female collectors could achieve that few of her companions, male or female, could boast such success. Few kept up such an energetic life of travelling, research and bartering; few made so many confident and profitable deals; and few demonstrated such commitment to collecting as a way of life.

CHAPTER TEN

The Gourd-shaped Bottle

*C*harlotte and Charles Schreiber made twenty-three foreign trips between 1869 and 1882, spending around half of each year, and sometimes more, travelling in Europe. This had the advantage of being cheaper than maintaining an appropriately large and fashionable household in England, and they were eager to see the sights in the towns and cities they visited. But the driving force by far was their collecting. Prices abroad tended to be more reasonable, even for British wares, and Charlotte's journals reveal how the Schreibers sought out shops and dealers, private collectors and museums, in a constant rush to view, compare, buy and sell objects. Whatever the length and tribulations of a journey, it was usually just a matter of minutes before Charlotte was out into the streets of a new destination, continuing her search: in August 1869, for example, she bemoans arriving so late in Gouda that they were 'barely in time to save daylight to ransack the old dealers' stock'; on 8 March 1872, they disembarked from the night train in Amsterdam and immediately 'took a carriage and went straight to Van Houtum's to see what he might have'.[1] The Schreibers continued their collecting at a similarly frantic pace during the months back in England, but the attention given to the European crusade in Charlotte's journals indicates just how absorbing and exciting it was to be collecting abroad at this time.

As we have seen, Europe was ready for collectors. Thanks to the French Revolution, the Napoleonic Wars, the Franco-Prussian War, the revolutions and political instability that accompanied nationalist movements in Italy, Germany, Denmark, Hungary and Poland; changes to the old structures of royalty, nobility and the church; growing urbanization; shifting patterns of wealth; fashionable commercialism and economic fluctuation, there had never been a better time to be collecting. In Holland, the Schreibers hoped to pick up the distinctive blue-and-white ceramics of seventeenth- and eighteenth-century delftware, or even 'original' blue-and-white that had been imported from China. Such pieces had been popular as domestic furnishings in the seventeenth century but had since dropped out of fashion and been relegated to back rooms and store cupboards, junkshops, auctions and markets. In Dresden, the Schreibers were on the trail of more ceramics, in particular from the renowned Meissen works, but they were also offered ecclesiastical relics and the entire interior decoration of a local church. In Belgium, they were shown choice examples of oriental china, imported from Japan, Chelsea ware that had made its way from Britain, and an ornamental metal picture frame that had once graced the palace of Louis XIII of France. All over Europe, objects that had been hidden away in homes, castles and churches were coming on to the open market, while new and expanding trade routes were moving objects across the Continent, and even the world.

The Schreibers travelled from north to south, taking advantage of a changing Europe. But for all the riches to be had elsewhere, it was in France that the network for collectors offered most. As Robinson had discovered as a student in Paris during the 1840s, by the middle of the century, the French had already discovered a widespread interest in collecting. In Germany, in contrast, undisturbed collections of treasures from the Middle Ages and Renaissance continued to languish quietly in the houses of the nobility. But in France, in the aftermath of the Revolution, greater instability created a much more vigorous marketplace in which similarly impressive objects changed hands frequently. 'The French Revolution,' according to writer and critic Jules Janin, 'began to break everything, to destroy books, to cut paintings in pieces. . . to melt gold and silver. . . to sell – at auction even – the marbles of tombs.' This, however, was not the end of the story. What was cast out was usually immediately rescued, Janin went on to explain, by 'a whole army of antiquarians. . . whose life and fortune are spent in collecting these scarce remains, in saving from oblivion these precious remembrances'.[2] Medieval and Renaissance art works could be picked up cheaply in junkshops and market stalls – everything from sixteenth-century furniture to prints by Dürer or Rembrandt, from armour and ceramics to marriage caskets. Across France, church silver pulled from the altars now appeared in auction rooms, and family collections were broken up and sold. Within a generation, a treasure trove of previously hidden, often completely unknown, objects became available: silver and tableware that had belonged to princes and nobles; paintings, tapestries and jewellery; precious religious objects and even entire walls, altarpieces and massive doorways torn from churches, private chapels and monasteries. Some of Europe's most beautiful and valuable pieces were now appearing for sale to anyone who could afford them.

By the 1850s, when the fashion for the leftovers of the French *ancien régime* had really taken off, Paris was the heart of the collectors' circuit. Calling at a renowned dealers in Utrecht in 1869, Charlotte found there was 'absolutely nothing' because 'he had 84 cases packed up for Paris', and visits to the curiosity shops of Alicante in March 1870 were equally unsuccessful because 'the best things' were all kept back to be sold to the French capital.[3] The violence of the Commune in 1871 interrupted Paris's pre-eminence but the setback was temporary. By May 1872, Charlotte was noting that 'all the great English dealers' were again gathering at the Paris sales, and not long afterwards she was delighted to be finding so many promising shops. 'We enjoyed our *chasse* very much,' she observed.[4]

The Schreibers' peripatetic lifestyle was not always so enjoyable, however. Charlotte's journals include plenty of accounts of days when nothing was bought. The couple were sometimes ill, and frequently tired. The stock of worthwhile objects was often exhausted and dealers could be obstructive, rude or even mad. Disappointment was commonplace.

The story of Charlotte's gourd-shaped bottle at first appeared to be one such disappointment. It was February 1873 and, unusually, Charles was alone on a short trip to dealers in Holland, leaving his wife at home. We know very little about Charles as a partner in the couple's collecting. Charlotte's journals provide her point of view, and, although she sometimes records her husband's opinion – referring to him always as C. S. – we learn little of his character. We discover most about his often precarious state of health, the apparently constant headaches, sore throats, inflamed eyes, undefined pains and exhaustion that may have been symptoms of an underlying and untreated condition. He was clearly as enthusiastic about collecting as his wife, however, and it may even have been his encouragement which first inspired Charlotte's interest. Beyond this, it is difficult to be sure of the nature of his contribution.

As a scholar, it is likely that he shared in the research that made their collecting of such value, but he never published anything. The impressive catalogue of the collection of English ceramics at the Victoria and Albert was written after his death and bears his wife's name. Like Charlotte, he clearly had an interest in politics and was elected MP for Cheltenham in 1865, but he lost the seat three years later and did not stand again until 1880, when he became MP for Poole without distinguishing himself on any particular political issue. Apart from his parliamentary role, he did not work. Charlotte herself suggests that he was often at a loose end: after a visit to the 1857 Art Treasures Exhibition in Manchester, she noted: 'Having no profession, no pursuit at this particular moment, I cannot describe how pleased I was to see how heartily he threw himself into the spirit of all around him.'[5] I could find no other contemporary accounts of him and in his portrait he appears unremarkable, even insipid. It is only from his anecdotal role in incidents from Charlotte's collecting life, such as the story of the gourd-shaped bottle, that we get any sense of his perspicacity, dedication and skill as a collector.

The trouble with Charles Schreiber's Dutch trip was that he had bought too many things. His boxes and cases were full and heavy. Although he had already made arrangements to send as much as he could back to England, without Charlotte and her big red bag, he found he could not carry all the remaining purchases alone. Worse still, he found himself amongst the plinths and shelves of a cluttered showroom in Rotterdam known as Kryser's, and he wanted to buy more: a large Wedgwood bowl and cover, which had been partly decorated in Amsterdam in 1808, and a strange bottle, also apparently Wedgwood, but shaped like a gourd and decorated with a painted landscape bright with flowers. Charles clearly felt he had to have both pieces, even at the risk of leaving things behind, and so he negotiated with Kryser. But when it came to finding space for them in his already overstrained luggage, he realized that he had overreached himself. All he could do was ask Kryser to put the purchases to one side so that he could collect them on a future visit. It was not the ideal solution, because they were two of the finest pieces he had managed to unearth during the trip, but he knew that he and Charlotte would be back in Rotterdam before the spring was out.

In the end, it was not until the beginning of April that the Schreibers managed to return. It was a few days before Easter, and in the warmer weather it was a pleasure to stroll together around the busy port and into the labyrinth of lanes behind. The town gardens were beginning to blossom, there was more life in the streets, and it was easy to spend the spring hours idling in front of shop windows. Doors were thrown open to the street, and the alluring treasure in the dark interiors twinkled in the spring sunlight. The Schreibers were not here to dawdle, however; their minds were fixed on retrieving their treasure from Kryser's. But, when they reached the shop, Kryser pretended that he had never seen either of them before, even though they had both shopped there on many previous occasions. Worse still, he denied all knowledge of the sale a few months earlier.

Puzzled and annoyed, the Schreibers clattered up the wooden steps to the top rooms of Kryser's shop and there found the bowl and bottle. Kryser's memory, however, still refused to be jogged. He was adamant that no previous transaction had ever taken place. The negotiation had to begin again. Finally, a sale was agreed. The Schreibers paid a sovereign, again, for the bottle, and carried it off with them at last. Back at the hotel, their purchases safely carried between them, it was the bottle that took pride of place. Charlotte did not know exactly what it was but she was sure it was uncommon and of the best quality. Perhaps it was Delft china, or perhaps something even rarer. Whatever it was, she was certain they had a bargain. Only a few days later, however, she was upset by a very different valuation. She was in The Hague, hosting a tea party for some friends, fellow travellers from England and old Dutch acquaintances. Charlotte proudly showed off her newly acquired bottle and it elicited a great deal of enthusiastic comment. Hardly anyone there had seen anything like it. They admired its unusual pregnant form and the colours of the decoration. Almost everyone thought, like Charlotte, that it had been a good buy. But one of the guests, the painter Christoffel Bisschop, disagreed. He was an expert on fine Dutch china, so he said, and this was not fine Dutch china. It was German, cheap and ordinary. It was attractive, perhaps, but nothing more than a trinket and essentially worthless.

The Schreibers had made bad purchases before but Bisschop's verdict inevitably came as a disappointment. Something about the bottle still excited them, and when the guests had drifted away, and the tea things had been cleared, they talked for a long time about whether or not to keep the bottle, just in case. Pragmatism, in the end, prevailed. They could not afford to encumber themselves with second-rate pieces. They needed to save space, as well as money, for truly rare things – for the very best. So they agreed to resell the bottle, and on arriving in Utrecht a few days later, on 8 April, the matter was settled when a dealer there confidently announced that he knew an amateur collector who would give good money for it. The journal volumes record the Schreibers' relief: '"Then for goodness' sake let him have it," said C.S., who had been put thoroughly out of conceit with his purchase, and now only cared to be rid of it.'

The bottle was left behind, but as the Schreibers passed through Utrecht again six months later, in October 1873, the story begins once more. Relating the tale delightedly in his notes on his mother's collecting, Montague Guest recounts the dealer's verdict: '"I sold your bottle to the great amateur for 100 florins,"' the dealer explained. '"He took it home and was delighted with it, but in a few days he brought it back to me and would have nothing to say for it, for his friends had told him it was only a piece of German ware and of no value whatever."' History, it seemed, was repeating itself. The Schreibers had to take their bottle back, and forgo their hundred florins. Frustrated by the entire experience,

Charles was determined not to waste energy on carrying the disappointing bottle to England and a few days later he called at a sale in Antwerp to offload it: 'He got a letter to inform him that the troublesome bottle had been sold – this time sold outright, and had realized eighteen shillings.'

The sale represented a financial loss, but at least they were rid of the bottle, and as Charlotte noted stoically, 'These things will happen to the best regulated collectors.' Besides, they could be sure to recognize, and avoid, such inconsequential German pottery when they saw it in the future. This might have been some consolation, except that the next time they came across a piece exactly like their bottle was almost a year later, in August 1874, and it was not in a dingy junkshop backroom but in the elegant, beautifully lit cases of the Rouen Museum in Normandy, set on the most conspicuous shelf at the heart of the town's collection. There, carefully arranged 'in the very place of honour', was a group of bottles exactly like the one the Schreibers had dismissed, the same size and strange gourd shape, the same cheerful decoration. Aware that they had made a terrible mistake, they began to investigate further, and as they discovered more about the precious bottles they realized that 'nothing in Europe, or indeed in any other part of the world, [was] as rare as these productions. . . only about a dozen being hitherto known'.

In fact, the bottles were so rare that the experts could not agree as to exactly what they were: some claimed that they were the work of Denys Dorio, an obscure Italian who had once made a few such things at Rouen en route to setting up a studio in Holland; others claimed they were seventeenth-century Delft china from the renowned workshop of Aelbrecht de Keiser. Whatever they were, experts agreed that there were few known examples. Two were in a private collection; the rest were at the Rouen Museum. Except, of course, for the one that Charlotte and Charles Schreiber had once owned, that was now somewhere in

Holland, sold at an obscure sale for a song. It was infuriating: 'And now indeed there was wailing and gnashing of teeth! To have been unconsciously possessed of such a treasure, and to have been at such pains to have deprived oneself of it was almost more than amateur nature could endure.'

The Schreibers returned despondently to England. The thought of what they had lost preyed heavily on them. They did not have the heart to look over the things they had brought back, and they found no comfort in the familiarity of the collection waiting for them at home. All they could think about was what might have been. The weather in England now seemed chill and uninviting; the house seemed dull. They could not bear the thought of admitting their mistake to friends, and within the week they were back on the boat to Brussels, making the choppy Channel crossing and hoping that something would turn up to distract them from their disappointment.

The shops in the Belgian capital seemed intent on annoying them further; there was little to tempt them. Their latest journey had all the hallmarks of another wasted trip, but it was on this visit to Brussels, almost two years after Charles Schreiber had first spotted and bought the gourd-shaped bottle in Rotterdam, that something unexpected happened. They were about to leave a little-known dealers, Polonet's, in the newly built Rue Grétry by the covered market, a shop, according to Charlotte, 'of no great account'. Like the other dealers, Polonet had had nothing to interest them. But, just as they were leaving, Charlotte happened to cast her eyes 'to a topmost shelf' and there saw a bright and familiar object. By some extraordinary luck or accident, some tantalizing twist of fate, the Schreibers had a second chance: in a dark corner of the humble Brussels shop, explained Charlotte in triumph, 'I spied the lost and much-lamented Rouen gourd-shaped bottle, whose very history is a romance.'

Polonet had acquired the bottle at the Antwerp sale in the

spring and, like many people before him, he guessed that it was nothing more than simple German ware of more decorative than financial value. He had no hope of a great profit. But 'C.S... instantly paid whatever he was asked without demur.' The price was forty francs, quite a lot of money for a nondescript piece of German pottery. But next-to-nothing for the rare and beautiful work of art that the Schreibers had been tracking across Europe. With a nod of the head and a shake of the hand, the deal was done. The bottle was swiftly dusted and packed, and the Schreibers carried it 'triumphantly away'.[6]

The bottle did eventually turn out to be German. It was finally identified as a rare faience ceramic vase by one of a group of seventeenth-century studio painters known as the Nuremberg *Hausmaler*, artists who specialized in decorating ceramics or faience. The vase itself was probably made in Frankfurt, but it was the decoration which made it so eminently collectable, and it is believed it was painted by *Hausmaler* Abraham Helmback around 1700. The Schreibers treasured it, and, on Charlotte's death, it was inherited by her daughter Blanche, the Countess of Bessborough, who was herself a keen collector. It remained in the Bessborough family at their home, Stansted Park, on the Hampshire/West Sussex border, until October 1999, when it was sold by Sotheby's, attracting a guide price of £10,000–£15,000. Charlotte's investment, it seems, had ultimately been proved a good one.

For the Schreibers, the protracted story of the bottle ended in a sweet victory that bolstered their confidence in their own judgement. The confusing episode had shown how well-meaning friends and eager dealers could be wrong in their appraisals, and could not be relied upon to give the final word on an object, especially when so much collectors' pride was at stake. If the best pieces of European treasure were to be extracted from their hiding places, then Charlotte and her husband needed to trust to their own resources. But, for Charlotte, the open display of too much scholarship was not without its own problems. As we have seen, at a time when the intellectual and social activities of respectable women were constantly being scrutinized and judged, those who seemed too learned risked blurring the boundaries between an amateur hobby, which was acceptable, and a professional undertaking, which was not.

Charlotte was in the potentially awkward position of needing to acquire scholarly knowledge to make her collecting a success, and needing to obscure it to retain her social standing. Like collecting, art criticism remained a staunchly male domain, and there were few women willing to challenge this convention. Those who did had to be prepared to stand out from the crowd and have their names associated with a wide range of feminist causes. One of the best known of these was Emilia, Lady Dilke, who attended the South Kensington Art School in the 1850s before beginning to publish in a range of journals, becoming a contributor to the *Saturday Review* in 1864 and fine art critic for *Academy*. By the end of the century, she had published several major works of art history, including two volumes on *The Renaissance of Art in France* (1879), a critique of *Art in the Modern State* (1888) and a series of works exploring French architecture, sculpture, engraving and furniture.

But Emilia was a controversial woman, the subject of much discussion in polite Victorian society. During her unhappy first marriage to Mark Pattison, Rector of Lincoln College, Oxford, and a reputable scholar, she was publicly and frequently unfaithful, as a result of which several thinly veiled portrayals of adulterous wives and cuckolded husbands appeared in popular novels of the time. Her second marriage, to Charles Dilke, also carried a hint of scandal: they were married very shortly after Dilke was publicly named in a divorce case which ended his influential political career. In addition, Emilia's close association with the trades unions – in particular the Women's Trade Union League, of which she was president – and with feminist causes such as women's enfranchisement meant that she continually courted controversy. Certainly, her behaviour provided plenty of ammunition for those in the establishment who wanted to argue that female scholarship led to a breakdown of social order and the undermining of accepted values.

Another of the rare female art critics was Anna Jameson, who made her way from the twilight existence of a governess to become a woman of letters. In 1842, she wrote a *Handbook to the Public Galleries of Art in and near London*, and two years later she published *A Companion to the Most Celebrated Private Galleries of Art in London*. Between 1843 and 1845, she contributed over forty essays on Italian painters to journals. Her work was clever, analytical and original. She gained widespread respect for her knowledge and her ability to convey her ideas accessibly: 'her contemplation of the great works of the great schools was more intelligent than that of men in many ways more learned than she', observed one later commentator in 1879.[7] For her series on *Sacred and Legendary Art*, which appeared from 1848 until after her death in 1860, she had lengthy discussions with Charles Eastlake, who had been working on a similar theme. Eventually, in a rare act of scholarly magnanimity and as a clear indication of his respect for her work, Eastlake gave her all the material and references he had collected himself. Despite such achievements, however, Anna had to make her writing non-polemical and uncontroversial, weeding out phrases that seemed too explicitly feminist in an effort to get readers, both male and female, to take her views seriously. To sell her books to a wide public, it was critical that she seemed respectable, inoffensive and unchallenging. She had to consider what her writing might imply about other areas of her life, and was always conscious of her sensitive position as a woman in the masculine world of art scholarship.

Developing scholarship as an integral part of her collecting, Charlotte would certainly have been aware of the potential hazards of her situation. As far as we know, she was not particularly feminist in her views – her journals give little indication that she was interested in feminist issues – nor was she keen to disrupt her family life with controversy. But she was naturally intellectual and ambitious, and, while she may not have been willing to take up a wider feminist cause, her marriages, her close involvement with the Dowlais steel business and her Welsh studies all indicate that she was happy to challenge, on a personal level, Victorian preconceptions about what she could do as a woman. As her collecting developed, so too did this challenge to convention. Privately, without fuss, she was developing a level of erudition to rival any male collector's. Wide reading, learned discussion, an excellent visual memory and a talent for thinking on her feet got Charlotte the pieces she wanted. The history of the gourd-shaped bottle shows how her scholarship was constantly evolving and how important this was to her reputation as a collector.

Her knowledge paid dividends. In one 'very bad' shop in Genoa, 'a dilettante shoemakers', Charlotte was offered a set of cups decorated with red landscapes. They were fine and unexpected, and they immediately attracted her attention. When she turned one of them over to check the maker's mark, she found the name 'Jacques Boselly' painted crudely across the base, linking them to a small eighteenth-century ceramics factory in Savona, near Genoa in Italy. If they were genuinely Boselly cups, they were quite rare and desirable, a real find. But Charlotte continued turning them over. Three displayed the same scrawled signature. But fortunately Charlotte was not content until she had turned each one of the set and peered closely at every scratch and imprint, and that's when she saw something else: the name 'Wedgwood' impressed into the glaze: 'I confess the English name was rather faint so that the ingenious foreigner might be excused from expecting that it would escape ordinary attention,' she explained in her journal. At a time when Wedgwood was out of fashion and distinctly less collectable than Boselly, the dealer had tried to upgrade the English cups into something more sought after and valuable. But those with a good knowledge of the trade were not to be so easily fooled: 'the mark was quite strong enough to be quite clear to the initiated,' Charlotte noted.[8]

In the competitive world of European collecting, there was no substitute for acquiring better knowledge than other collectors, or acquiring it more quickly. Charlotte's scholarship gave her the opportunity to make profitable purchases and to speculate for the future. At the dealers in Genoa, Charlotte was quite as happy with Wedgwood cups as with Boselly. She had already decided that Wedgwood was quality china, worth collecting, and this was another opportunity to add the English ware to her collection at a time when ceramics from the factory were of little interest to the majority of European collectors and consequently relatively cheap to acquire. And as Charlotte's knowledge grew, so did the opportunities for such bargains. In March 1872, she was scouring the shops in Amsterdam when she noticed a china figure of a youth holding a comb. It was a fine piece, and in perfect condition. Charlotte at once recognized that it was scarce Bristol china, a hard, white eighteenth-century porcelain manufactured from Cornish china-clay and much sought after for the quality of its glaze. She was so astonished at the unexpected discovery 'that I put it down again, hardly believing my eyes at so great a find'. But looking around, she found that the dealer was paying little attention to her, and, when she tentatively asked him about the piece, she realized that he 'had no idea what it was'. Taking advantage of his ignorance, she struck a deal for the figure, along with two sauceboats which caught her eye, for £7. The shrewd speculation, Charlotte noted, 'amply repays the trouble of a seven hour drive'.[9]

A few years later, in early 1880, she instructed one of her French contacts, a dealer named Fournier (possibly the son of the Fournier who had disappeared during the violence of the Paris Commune) to buy on her behalf a small figurine. Charlotte had glimpsed the piece only once, briefly, as it lay unregarded in a display window, but she was immediately sure it was sixteenth-century Spanish. Fournier disagreed. Since he was being paid for his trouble, he continued to act on Charlotte's orders, but he maintained that the piece was nothing more than a modern reproduction. He wrote to her, warning her that she was likely to be disappointed, and finally he brought the figure to her rooms at the Hotel Drouot in Paris. The minute she saw it, Charlotte knew she was right. And her instincts were, once again, impeccable. After some straightforward research, she was able to show beyond doubt that the piece was special, and a bargain: 'It proved to be, as I anticipated, a very fine specimen of Spanish Cinquecento art, and we were wonderfully fortunate to obtain it for about £8. It was worth quite 3 times as much, but the ignorant French dealers did not know it.'[10]

Charlotte's journals are full of small incidents like these, where her scholarly approach to collecting bests even experienced dealers. And it was not just with ceramics that she could show off her skill. She was fascinated by the variety and history of board games and before long had acquired all kinds of counters and draughts and dice. Still cherishing the gift from her mother many years before, she also collected fans which had been a popular, and exclusive, fashion item across Europe since the sixteenth century, and which had the added advantage of folding easily for transport in the big red bag. Individual fan leaves in silk, linen or animal skin, supported on wooden, ivory or mother-of-pearl sticks, were printed with historical, political or social illustrations: Charlotte's collection included a scene from the coronation banquet of George II in 1727, maps, landscapes and pastorals, biblical stories such as

Moses in the wilderness and a spangled black gauze fan made to mourn the death of Louis XVI.

In September 1880, she was in Munich when something else caught her eye – her first set of playing cards. Hand-painted and early-printed playing cards featured all kinds of suits, from coins, cups and bells to acorns, sceptres and cudgels, as well as a variety of royal households that often extended beyond king, queen and knave to valets and maids. The Germans were the most imaginative and lively of early card-makers, and Charlotte was immediately captivated by the intricate designs. But the cards were expensive, even after some spirited negotiating, and Charlotte was strong enough to refuse them and return to her lodgings for dinner. Her resistance did not last, however. After desert had been served and eaten, she set off back through the quiet streets to the shop and bought three complete packs and two fragmented sets, 'for which I am ashamed to say we paid £10'.[11]

It seemed inexcusably extravagant. Charlotte was used to paying well for things that she knew were fine pieces and a sensible speculation, but with the cards she did not feel confident that her knowledge was strong enough to justify such expenditure. 'I am so inexperienced as yet in this branch of collecting, that I do not know if they are worth anything,' she admitted to her journal. Yet they were more than just a whim; she bought them because she liked them, but also as part of her ongoing collecting education, as an investment in her future as a collector as much as in the cards themselves. 'I must pay to learn,' she reminded herself.

This commitment to developing original areas of collecting, and backing it up with thorough scholarship, identified Charlotte with the increasing community of collectors who were moving away from the idea of simple connoisseurship (where collecting was largely a matter of personal taste) towards a more professional approach, based on wide learning. The work of men like J. C. Robinson and Augustus Franks in the public museums had set a standard of collecting – and an ambition for the collector – that began to be seen also among private collectors. Just ten years after its foundation, the more ambitious members of the Fine Arts Club, including Charles Schreiber, had become frustrated with its emphasis on socializing and dilettante connoisseurship. They felt its more serious aims were becoming lost, and set about founding a more scholarly offshoot which was established in 1866 as the Burlington Fine Arts Club and which operated alongside the original club as a refuge for the most committed collectors. By the 1880s, when Charlotte was beginning her research on playing cards, this impetus had grown. It was no longer enough simply to be enthusiastic. The influence of the museums and the increasing number of collectors in new fields meant that those who wished to distinguish themselves needed to demonstrate originality and a commitment to extending their knowledge. While Charlotte may have been excluded from professional collecting by her gender, she nonetheless developed a rigorous and independent approach that made her professional in everything except the fact that she was not usually paid for her work.

Before very long, Charlotte had begun to master her new field of study, and to collect playing cards feverishly. She admitted to her diary that, within days, the thought of finding new patterns and designs 'now occupies me very much' and she was tormented by the urgency of age and lost opportunity, afraid that 'I have begun too late to make my collection a very handsome one'.[12] But her fears were unfounded. With characteristic thoroughness, she soon added a detailed knowledge of playing cards to her lengthening list of specialities, and her international collection of over 1,000 packs, from Poland and Russia, Denmark, India, Java and Japan, as well as Italy, England, France, Germany and Spain – with designs featuring everything from seventeenth-century Latin grammar to the military science of fortification – proved good enough in the end for the British Museum.

Charlotte's purchases could be modest: £10 for the playing cards; £7 for the figurine and sauceboats; £8 for a piece of Spanish fifteenth-century art. In these cases at least, her bargains might have cost a lot more, but she could not always be trading on her knowledge to find things that had been overlooked, and most of Charlotte's transactions were at more or less market value. And even though she chose to collect in many areas that were unfashionable or relatively unknown, her collecting still cost her a great deal in comparison with everyday items. In the 1880s, when Charlotte was buying her first playing cards, the annual farm rent on an acre of decent land was between 15 shillings and £1, while, on the railways, excursion and season ticket fares around the home counties were set at under a penny a mile; a gross of quills, packed in a box, cost less than 2d; and a ton of large coal could be had for around 8 shillings.[13] While collecting was gradually becoming more accessible and widespread, it was still not within everyone's reach. Certainly, those hoping to buy as often as Charlotte did needed both a healthy income and an unshakeable commitment to building a collection.

By 1883, the bouts of illness that Charles had long been suffering had become more serious and protracted. Charlotte was alarmed, and, when a three-month trip to the south coast failed to have much effect, the doctor prescribed a bracing sea voyage. The Schreibers set off on their longest, and last, journey together, taking the slow ocean route to Cape Town where the climate was said to be good for ailing health. This time, there was no opportunity, or desire, to collect. There was not a bowl or fan or plate that could distract Charlotte from the aching fear of losing her husband; the showrooms of Paris and the bustle of Italian auctions seemed a world away. For eleven tense months, Charlotte was too busy acting as nurse to think of much else, but, despite her care, her husband's alarming symptoms refused to be assuaged by South Africa's warm air. And when it became clear that Charles's health was in fact getting worse, she took the decision to return to London, to the support of family and friends.

Charles never made it home. He became steadily weaker as the steamer travelled slowly up Africa's Atlantic coast. Confined to his cabin, he could not eat and hardly seemed to know that Charlotte was by his bed, holding his hand. He died finally at Lisbon on 29 March 1884. Charlotte could comfort herself only with the thought that it was 'within an appreciable distance of home'.[14] She was seventy-two years old, and her eyesight was failing fast. She felt more bewildered and alone than she had ever done in her life. Her second husband's illness and death seemed to drain her characteristic energy and optimism and on her return to England she went to live with her youngest daughter Blanche, in Cavendish Square, welcoming the comfort of family. Looking back wistfully on 'the days that were over; dreams that were done', she did not have the will to continue the European crusade alone: 'So ends my *life* on earth,' she wrote. 'It has been a very happy one, and I have much to be grateful for.' Even so, she did not neglect the collection. There was still much that could be done without the habitual travelling. After decades of actively pursuing objects across a continent, Charlotte set her mind now to the quieter tasks of sorting, cataloguing and arranging. She recognized that this was just as important as the work that had gone before and she welcomed the more contemplative aspects of life of a collector. Indeed, in her bereavement, her collection became more to her than ever: 'that is the only thing that gives any relief to my sadness,' she noted.[15]

It was shortly after Charles's death, in May 1884, that Charlotte had her first serious discussion with staff at South Kensington about giving the best part of the collection of English porcelain to the museum as a memorial to her husband. Over the years, she had loaned many pieces for exhibition and display, and had spent many hours in the galleries studying. Charles himself, possibly with an eye on posterity, had raised with his wife the idea that they might donate some of their collection to a public museum. The thought, noted Charlotte, 'was not a new one to me', and the museum, in its turn, was delighted at the prospect of acquiring such a unique collection of china.[16] In preparation, Charlotte cleared the two largest rooms in the house and arranged the pieces on seven long tables. Then staff from South Kensington arrived to take stock of what might be on offer and, with her husband no longer around to advise, Charlotte turned to Augustus Franks to help finalize the details of the bequest.

In the months that followed, Franks became an even more familiar face at Charlotte's home, calling on an almost daily basis to work with her on cataloguing the English ceramics and to help select the best pieces for South Kensington. When he could not spare the time, Charlotte went to him instead in the offices of the British Museum. It was clear evidence that, in her old age, Charlotte had become a respected collector, one of the most influential of her time. With Franks' help, a catalogue was written and printed, although not before Charlotte succumbed, even at such a late stage, to making the occasional extra purchase as a last-minute addition to the collection. She found it hard to break the habit of looking for treasure: 'Really I must stop these morning rambles into curiosity shops,' she chastised herself after a dark November day spent shopping. 'I shall be ruined – another £5 – but then it is all going to the South Kensington.'[17] There was satisfaction for Charlotte in securing her treasured pieces a good home, and there was a certain pleasure in seeing her lifetime's collecting honoured by such a robust institution, but all in all she found the process of transferring the collection unsettling and troublesome. She could not sleep. When the terms of the agreement were finally settled in October 1885, it was a relief:

'now that I have got the load of the settlement of the collection off my mind, all else seems trifling', she wrote, and promptly went to see a workman about dealing with her blocked drains.[18] A month later, on 19 November, the collection was finally packed and sent to its new home at South Kensington. It was a poignant parting. 'I close this sad volume with my adieux to the collection,' she wrote, perhaps even then unaware of what a singular slice of history she had just bequeathed to the nation.[19]

Over the next ten years, Charlotte campaigned vigorously for causes ranging from Turkish refugees to London cabbies, funding a Cabmen's shelter at Langham Place, off Oxford Circus. But her collecting years were behind her. Her journal entries finally stumbled to a halt and her days were filled with the comfortable, unremarkable routines of any wealthy Victorian matriarch. She died, almost totally blind, on 15 January 1895, at the age of eighty-two. Her more ephemeral and quirky pieces – the fans and the playing cards – she left to the British Museum. During the last years of her life, she worked with staff there on the fans in particular, publishing books on both English and European designs: the Worshipful Company of London Fan Makers awarded her the Freedom of the Company, one of only two Victorian women to be honoured in this way by livery companies.[20] One piece in particular was displayed as a highlight in the immense labyrinth of the British Museum's galleries: an eighteenth-century English fan, given to the museum by Charlotte in 1891 and celebrating the magnificent and chaotic firework display that marked the temporary end of the War of Austrian Succession in April 1749. With the design etched in paper, coloured by hand and mounted on ivory sticks, the fan showed rockets bursting over a huge makeshift palace erected in St James's Park. Meanwhile, across London, the English ceramics were installed at South Kensington. The rest of Charlotte's collection was handed down to her children, particularly her son Montague and daughter Blanche, who both inherited their mother's interest in collecting.

In some respects, Charlotte's collecting derived from the genteel habits of the past. Born into a wealthy, aristocratic family, she had the benefits of a decent education and she always mixed in elite circles. She was a rich woman with the time and money to indulge her hobbies. But her collecting could also have been restricted by such a background: she could have been a wealthy connoisseur with a fine aesthetic appreciation, or a fashionable society figure with a collection to catch the eye, or a woman at home, her collecting mediocre in scope and modest in ambition. Charlotte was much more than this. Using money from her marriage into the industrial, and industrious, middle classes, she helped show the way for new generations of collectors whose enthusiasm would be supported by erudition. She challenged the conventions about how female collectors could act and what they could achieve. She took collecting out of the drawing rooms of her aristocratic heritage and on to the streets of a changing Europe.

Pride, Passion and Loss: Collecting for Love

JOSEPH MAYER

CHAPTER ELEVEN

Waiting for the Rain to Stop

*J*oseph Mayer was having his portrait painted. It was around
1840 and he was in his late thirties, a successful silversmith
and Liverpool businessman, socially secure, reasonably wealthy,
a man of fashion – and an emerging collector.[1] This portrait, the
first Mayer had ever commissioned, was a way of marking how
far he had come, and where he was going. His business was
thriving: he was a partner in his brother-in-law's jewellers in Lord
Street, at the heart of the flourishing Victorian town. He lived in
considerable ease and some splendour in a townhouse on Clarence
Terrace, Everton Road (since demolished), establishing himself
as a member of Liverpool society. But this was not just another
standard Victorian portrait, reinforcing respectability and
professional success. It was a statement about Mayer's passions
and ambitions, a portrait of an aspiring connoisseur. Surrounded
by vases and busts, sculpture, classical marbles, Greek and
Etruscan antiquities, Mayer was showing off the part of him that
mattered – his collection.

When it came to choosing an artist for the commission, Mayer needed someone who would depict the story of his life in the objects around him, its bonds with the past and its potential for the future; someone who would pay as much attention to portraying the artefacts crowding the edges of the painting as to the man at its centre. He chose William Daniels. Daniels was ten years younger than Mayer, but was already becoming known in local circles. He was everything a painter should be: proud and eccentric, unreliable, passionate and poor. The town's middle classes delighted to hear how he had been discovered as a boy in a ditch in the brickfields, modelling figures from the clay; how he had been adopted out of the notorious Scotland Road district, Liverpool's poorest and roughest area, and introduced to the Liverpool Academy of Art by one of the masters, Alexander Mosses, and how he had learned so well and so quickly that he had won first prize for a drawing of a dying gladiator. Ashamed to clatter on to the wooden platform to receive his award in his clogs, Daniels had apparently borrowed a pair of boots from a gentleman's son. This poignant tale of talent in adversity further charmed Liverpool society when the penniless Daniels fell in love with a pretty girl called Mary Owen, who was also penniless and whom he painted as a rosy-cheeked gypsy pedlar in an attempt to raise money for a wedding. When the portrait was immediately bought by Sir Joshua Walmsley, MP and Mayor of Liverpool, Daniels had secured a future. He had a patron, and, better still, a romantic reputation.

It was not necessarily a straightforward commission. Daniels could be tetchy, puffed up by his sudden success and celebrity. He drank heavily, and, if he was in a sensitive mood, he would rage against the humiliation and sterility of being asked to paint to order; 'his inspiration was always fleeting,' explained one of his early Liverpool patrons, 'and when out of temper he would slash a partly completed canvas or daub it with aimless strokes'.[2] But for Mayer, Daniels seemed willing to cooperate. Perhaps

Mayer adopted a ruse that had helped some of Daniels' other customers manage the temperamental artist: one explained how he carefully displayed a 'few guineas on a convenient mantelshelf in the hope of attracting him, thus doling out the price as the picture went on'.[3]

However it was, the portrait was completed. Daniels painted the dim light idling through heavy curtains, throwing the room into shadow so that it seems something more than a study or even a museum, something like a great ancient tomb, newly opened and packed with objects. He lets the papers twist open under the table, a glove fall to the floor, and Mayer's spaniel peer, half-curious, from under his chair. The atmosphere is homely and relaxed, yet simultaneously strange and distant, as though Daniels is attempting to capture the sense of the past accumulating in the heavy quiet. And at the very centre is Mayer, contemplative and still; smaller than his sculptures and busts and the huge carved chair in which he sits, another piece in the collection, not separate from it but alive within it, a natural part of the things with which he is surrounded.

It was a portrait of its time, evoking the idea of the chaotic, romantic antiquarian study that had been made popular by writers like Walter Scott and which was the height of fashion when Daniels was completing the commission for Mayer in the early 1840s. In Scott's 1816 novel *The Antiquary*, he describes the 'sort of den' in which the collector might be found:

It was a lofty room of middling size, obscurely lighted by high narrow latticed windows. One end was entirely occupied by book-shelves, greatly too limited in space for the number of volumes placed upon them. . . while numberless others littered the floor and the tables amid a chaos of maps, engravings, scraps of parchment, bundles of papers, pieces of old armour, swords, dirks, helmets, and Highland targets. . . The top of this cabinet was covered with busts, and Roman lamps and paterae, intermingled with one or two bronze figures. . . A large old-fashioned oaken table was covered with a profusion of papers, parchments, books and nondescript trinkets and gewgaws, which seemed to have little to recommend them, besides rust and the antiquity which it indicates. . . The floor, as well as the table and chairs, was overflowed by the same *mare magnum* of miscellaneous trumpery, where it would have been as impossible to find any individual article wanted, as to put it to any use when discovered.

In Daniels' new portrait, Mayer's study fitted the model perfectly. It would have been immediately clear to anyone seeing the painting, just what kind of man Mayer was (or at least how he wished to present himself); the viewer would have understood that by surrounding himself with objects in this way he was displaying himself as both fashionable and apparently learned. Daniels painted Mayer to look exactly how most Victorians thought a collector should look.

In one hand Mayer holds a book. This is both serious and fitting, an indication of his connoisseurship. But when it came to selecting something particular for him to hold in his other hand, there was perhaps more of a problem. The random selection of objects in the painting aptly illustrates the haphazard and eclectic nature of Mayer's collecting, which was enthusiastic rather than particularly knowledgeable. Although he no doubt wished to appear studious and erudite in his portrait, he was in fact much more likely to be guided by his instincts than by learning. He was not, as he admitted himself, particularly scholarly. He was the product of an average education at a local grammar school and his classical, historical and scientific understanding was limited and uneven. He could show Daniels an intriguing jumble of things to be painted but not the ordered, comprehensive collection of an intellectual. Some of his pieces were significant and historic; others were merely curiosities, and a few were little more than household junk. Mayer liked all sorts: rare antique objects from the ancient civilizations of Rome, Greece and Egypt, and broken archaeological finds from Anglo-Saxon burial sites; arms and armour, swords, guns and all things military; manuscripts from Burma, scraps from German prayerbooks, illuminated medieval missals, books of hours and fine bindings; Napoleonic memorabilia; gems, ivories and enamels; engravings, cartoons, the occasional oil painting and examples of local Liverpool pottery. There were few things he could resist if they had the scent of history about them.

Mayer's table was littered with Roman and Etruscan antiquities, with candlesticks and antique figurines. But what he chose to hold in the portrait, in the end, was a miniature vase, shaped like an ancient Greek urn and set on a pedestal. It was small enough to fit comfortably in one hand, light enough for him to hold up through the long sittings, and pretty enough to hold Daniels' attention. But, in fact, it was a very ordinary piece, an example of English pottery from the Wedgwood works and unfashionable. It was not a status symbol; it did not testify to wealth or learning; it had not been unearthed during a risky foreign voyage. It was just something Mayer liked and apparently it did not disturb him that it was relatively new, or that in the 1840s no one else seemed to share his taste in china. Wedgwood pieces pleased him; he admired their colours and forms and their strong references to the ceramics of the past. It was, he thought, a fitting object to include in his portrait.

Within a few years, the room which Daniels had so carefully depicted had disappeared. By 1844, Mayer had given up the smart house in Clarence Terrace, and the gentleman's study, and had moved instead into modest and simple accommodation above his business on one of Liverpool's busy shopping streets. He had been apprenticed at the age of nineteen to his brother-in-law James

Wordley and had been a successful partner in the business since the early 1830s, but now he was looking for change and greater independence. In 1843, he broke the partnership with Wordley, acquired premises a few doors down, and set up alone. Without ties, he could do as he pleased. He could try his hand at designing and making his own silver, and he could begin to establish his own name in the trade.

Mayer's new workshop flourished. He became highly skilled in designing large, often ceremonial pieces of gold and silver plate, spectacular trophies and civic regalia, and he studied innovative techniques, exploring the commercial potential of affordable new processes like electroplating. The business became respected and thriving; the shop imposing and magnificent. Mayer presented himself within the tradition of Renaissance silversmithing, and he designed a new building to invoke a sense of monumental art and of continuum with an impressive past. Either side of the entrance door were two massive frescos, one of the Renaissance smith and sculptor Benvenuto Cellini, and one of the seventeenth-century goldsmith and royal jeweller George Heriot. Two huge busts, one male and one female, gazed down from the balustraded façade on to the shoppers below. Immense plate-glass windows were piled high with objects to the height of three or four men, and Mayer's name was emblazoned, twice, above the display. Inside, watches and clocks, cameos, precious stones, heraldic engravings and a glittering array of silver and gold were all carefully arranged in specially designed showcases.

With such a prosperous showroom, it was not enforced economies that persuaded Mayer to give up the ease of the Clarence Terrace house. It was the lure of collecting. All his energies and resources became focused on finding and buying objects: it became his obsession, his life's purpose. Unlike J. C. Robinson, he could not bear to have the distractions of fashionable living divert his attention, and his money. He was fascinated by the past, and the objects it had left behind, and he did not mind giving up the comforts of the present if it meant bringing him closer to history.

While Mayer contented himself with simple living in the rooms above his shop, he was anything but reclusive. He was naturally a sociable man, but, more than this, he understood that to be a successful collector he needed to explore new places and meet new people. He travelled whenever he could, sending frequent parcels and crates back to England. He made his first trip, at the age of twenty-five, in 1828, and he spent the next few decades exploring the archaeological sites of Italy and the ruins of the ancient world, steaming down the Rhône to the towns of Southern France, and uncovering objects in Bavaria, Austria, Bohemia and Prussia. Mayer was only nine years older than Charlotte Schreiber, but was setting out on his journeys when she was busy at Dowlais, long before she had begun to collect; twenty years the senior of J. C. Robinson, he was beginning to explore the treasures of the Continent at a time when popular Victorian collectors' routes were still being etched into the European map. In the 1820s and 1830s, collecting off the beaten track of the established Grand Tour had a sense of trailblazing; it seemed exciting, daring and new. Mayer travelled for business, to buy stock, make deals and keep abreast of fashionable trends. But his journeys soon became about much more than the demands of trade. His moment of conversion to collecting, he always maintained, came when he was convalescing from fever during a business trip to Dijon, and had time to wander around the town's museum and picture gallery. The antiquities he saw there captivated him, and suddenly turned his journey from business to pleasure; from commerce to collecting.[4]

At home, too, Mayer's urge to collect encouraged him to make contact with scholars, connoisseurs and other private collectors in an effort to improve his knowledge and expand his collection.

He was an enthusiastic member of the local Arts Association and a founder member of the Historical Society of Lancashire and Cheshire. He made regular visits to the library, meeting rooms and gallery of Liverpool's Royal Institution. Whereas the local clubs, like the Athenaeum and the Lyceum, were gentleman's clubs with restricted membership and predominantly daytime hours, the Royal Institution was open to everyone and was available for use during the evenings for those who, like Mayer, had to work during the day. Beyond the region, he also made an effort to know as many influential collectors as possible and as time went on his collection became a favourite stopping-off point for those travelling north from London: Charlotte Schreiber was among the visitors from the capital who made sure to see what Mayer was collecting. Making the journey in the opposite direction, Mayer frequently combined business in London with visits to museums, in particular the British Museum, and he became a member of a number of respected London organizations, including the British Archaeological Association, the Royal Society and the Royal Geographic Society. By 1850, he had also become a Fellow of the Society of Antiquaries, which put him in touch with some of the most knowledgeable and enthusiastic scholars of his day, including Augustus Franks at the British Museum.

Mayer's particular interest in antiquarian objects drew him into different circles of collectors from those of which Robinson and Charlotte Schreiber were a part. The term 'antiquarian' loosely – and usefully – covered a wide range of artefacts from the past, including archaeological finds, books, remains of the 'antique' classical civilizations and even scientific instruments, with a particular emphasis on objects as historical evidence of past lives. It had long been a popular area with collectors, not least on account of its variety, and a tradition of antiquarian writing went back as far as the Middle Ages. As early as 1572, a national society had been established to encourage the study and preservation of antiquarian remains and in 1717 this was officially constituted as the Society of Antiquaries, receiving a charter from George II in 1751.

In the nineteenth century, the enthusiasm flourished. The Victorians' adulation of progress and empire was accompanied by a reverence for history and an urge to preserve ideals, traditions and objects from the past. A taste for historical painting pointed to a nostalgic longing for an idealized lost age, while 'the antiquarian style' became a fashionable architectural genre during the mid-century. The antiquarian look brought together artefacts from a variety of historical styles and periods to create interiors full of everything from Greek sculpture to medieval tapestry and Elizabethan furniture. Robinson's Newton Manor owed much to this kind of eclectic decoration, but it was Sir Walter Scott's carefully designed home at Abbotsford in Melrose, created between 1812 and 1832, that was at the forefront of the trend. The fashion became associated with mystery and romance, and Scott's novel *The Antiquary* – featuring an historian, archaeologist and collector, family secrets, hidden treasure, a mysterious aristocrat, a ruined abbey and hopeless love – only added to a popular fascination with re-creating an imagined past. Even reasonably ordinary objects became increasingly entangled with the idea of memory and nostalgia: 'inanimate and senseless things' took on a new importance as the 'object of recollection', suggested Dickens in his 1841 novel *The Old Curiosity Shop*. 'Every household god becomes a monument.'

The popularity of all things antiquarian influenced what was being collected both by individuals and institutions. Since its foundation in 1753, the British Museum had largely turned its attention abroad, and had ignored British antiquities in favour of pieces from the Mediterranean and the Near East, such as the famous Elgin marbles or the Assyrian sculptures from Henry

Layard's excavations. The increasing expertise and enthusiasm of British collectors by the middle of the nineteenth century, however, brought growing calls to fill the gaps. In 1845, the British Archaeological Association, of which Mayer was a member, met at Winchester to express the hope that a museum of national antiquities would be formed, and three years later, when a hoard of Iron Age bronzes was found at Stanwick Park in Yorkshire on the land of Lord Prudhoe (later Duke of Northumberland), it was offered to the British Museum on the condition that a special room was set aside for these and other British antiquities. Although this was agreed, by 1850, nothing had happened. Politics, finance, the constraints of space and simple procrastination seemed to be in the way. It was not until the appointment of Franks, in March 1851, that any progress was made. His commitment to collecting British antiquities, and his links with collectors and collecting organizations, brought the issue to the forefront of the debate about what kind of role the British Museum should have. With the support of colleagues like Mayer at the British Archaeological Association and the Society of Antiquaries, Franks managed to persuade the museum's trustees and management that this popular area of interest deserved space and attention, and in 1866 he finally won approval for a new and distinct department devoted to British and Medieval Antiquities, with himself at its head.

Meanwhile, a new generation of private collectors began to move the study of the antiquarian on to a more professional footing. Dedicated and discriminating, they started to develop practices for fieldwork, and to create frameworks for shaping and preserving their collections. Some were members of the nobility. Lord Londesborough (1805–60) was an enthusiastic antiquary who published his collection of 'ancient, medieval and Renaissance remains' in an illustrated volume in 1857. The 3rd and 4th Dukes of Northumberland began to collect pieces found on their estates in the 1820s and went on to undertake their own excavations at home and abroad. Their collection included a number of objects from Pompeii; its museum in Alnwick Castle still survives today. Most of the enthusiasts, however, were of more modest means. Compared to art collecting, antiquarianism was a relatively cheap interest to indulge. The breadth of antiquarian interest meant there were always neglected objects to be had at a reasonable price: the medieval manuscripts, Anglo-Saxon finds and medieval ivories which Mayer collected were largely ignored at the time, unwanted by the national collections and passed over by wealthier collectors.

Antiquarianism brought collectors together without great emphasis on class, status or wealth, and, although most of the collectors were men, it was otherwise a relatively egalitarian activity. In Yorkshire, John Mortimer, a corn merchant, began a personal programme of research based around the Wolds. Inspired by a visit to the 1851 Great Exhibition, Mortimer collected stone implements, fossils and geological specimens before moving on to excavate prehistoric barrows and Anglo-Saxon cemeteries, eventually displaying his rapidly expanding collection in its own museum in Driffield and publishing his life's work in an illustrated volume. John Evans, a partner in a paper manufacturing firm, undertook scholarly work in periods from pre-history to the post-medieval, as well as in geology and numismatics. His publications, especially *Ancient Stone Implements* (1872) and *Ancient Bronze Implements, Weapons and Ornaments of Great Britain* (1881), marked an advance in antiquarian study. They shaped the way in which many antiquarian collectors worked, and are still important today. After Evans's death in 1908, his collection was presented by his son to the Ashmolean Museum in Oxford. A close friend of Franks, and President in turn of the Geological Society, the Numismatic Society, the Anthropological Institute, the Society of Chemical Industry and the Society of

Antiquaries, as well as a Trustee of the British Museum and a Fellow and Treasurer of the Royal Society, Evans was held in high regard across Europe and was knighted for his work in 1892. His visionary and committed collecting set the standard for many of those who shared his interests, raising the quality and profile of antiquarian study.

The status of antiquarianism, the role of antiquarian collectors and the importance of antiquarian objects were fashionable issues, and in the middle decades of the century Mayer was at the heart of these debates. As a member of the key societies, he was able to contribute both locally and nationally, and to meet his peers across the country. While this was important for all collectors, it was especially crucial for Mayer. Unlike Robinson, for example, Mayer had never acquired any particular assurance or expertise. He lacked confidence in his knowledge and scholarship, and much preferred learned company to having to display learning himself. Left to his own devices, he could be muddled and uncertain – an easy target for swindlers – and he looked to his more cultured colleagues for something more consequential than the usual social round. He needed them to help him make informed decisions about his collecting.

Among his many new acquaintances, Mayer came to rely in particular on two useful and loyal friends: Joseph Clarke, a natural historian, enthusiastic amateur archaeologist and Keeper of Saffron Walden Museum, and Charles Roach Smith, a pharmacist and Fellow of the Society of Antiquaries, as well as a leading light in the British Archaeological Association. Both men were collectors in their own right, and Roach Smith in particular was becoming an expert on objects that were exposed as London expanded and trenches were dug on new building sites throughout the city. Roach Smith's collection was accumulated over twenty years by bartering directly with labourers. He had no opportunity to study the building sites or to undertake any kind of contextual research, but he did what he could, rescuing objects from across London and relying on old texts and maps to piece together their history. By dint of his energetic legwork and extensive investigation, his collection eventually amounted to a coherent history of the capital, a 'Museum of London Antiquities', which included 'a very curious collection of swords and spear heads from the Thames' and 'an enamel buckle or brooch similar in workmanship to the Alfred Jewel. . . an object of great rarity'.[5] This is now recognized as an Anglo-Saxon treasure known as the Dowgate Hill brooch, a late-tenth- or early-eleventh-century gold disc brooch decorated with colourful cloisonné enamel and a filigree border set with four large pearls, found in 1831 at the foot of Dowgate Hill on Thames Street. By 1857, Roach Smith's collection was so extensive and so widely admired that it was given a home in the British Museum.

Roach Smith and Clarke appreciated the impulses driving Mayer and were conscientious on his behalf. They were his eyes and ears in London and for many years they were attentive to Mayer's needs, constantly on the lookout for objects he might like. 'If you set me to work I go to it in earnest,' declared Clarke enthusiastically,[6] and on one memorable occasion he discovered an entire shop full of pieces for Mayer: 'The owner told me he had not been in the rooms for seven years and only once for fourteen and if you had seen me when I came out you would have laughed, no chimney sweep would have been blacker, three washings, I am not clean yet.'[7] During the 1850s and 1860s, Clarke and Roach Smith acquired a variety of ancient artefacts to send back to Liverpool: 'I have received for you a fine British urn. . . found. . . at Felixstowe. . . I got it. . . for a little above £2,' enthused Roach Smith in a letter of December 1852. In April 1856, he wrote again, 'I yesterday secured a Roman vessel, from Blackfriars Bridge & two old English vessels from the Fleet Ditch for you.'[8]

More significantly, it was Roach Smith who was instrumental in helping Mayer acquire a number of complete collections that firmly established his reputation as one of the most influential collectors in the country. The first of these, the Faussett collection, had been assembled by Bryan Faussett of Heppington in Kent, an eighteenth-century churchman and amateur archae- ologist. Faussett collected thousands of Roman and English coins, and had so many duplicates that he was able to melt down 150lbs of bronze to be cast into a bell. His real interest, however, was graves, and he spent all his time between writing sermons and visiting parishioners excavating Anglo-Saxon barrows in the woods and downs across Kent. He opened up over 630 graves in an eight-year period during the 1760s and 1770s, amassing a collection of grave goods, from plain hammered-metal bowls to intricate brooches. Unlike many amateur archaeologists of the time, he kept painstaking journals of all his excavations, sketching the sites as he found them, and recording every detail of his discoveries in five substantial volumes which were kept with the objects at his house.[9]

By the middle of the nineteenth century, however, the collection had been forgotten. Faussett had died and the objects were simply gathering dust in the family home. Strolling in Kent in 1842, Roach Smith found himself close to Heppington and found the name half-familiar. Eventually, he managed to recall the details of an eighteenth-century work, *Nenia Britannica: or, a sepulchral history of Great Britain; from the earliest period to its general conversion to Christianity*. This was, as its title suggests, a wide-ranging survey published in 1793 by another Kent clergyman, James Douglas, who was also an officer in the Corps of Engineers. Douglas used his military expertise to survey barrows and other archaeological sites, and was one of the first antiquaries to meticulously record, draw and publish his findings to a high standard, laying the foundations for the work of the Victorians who followed. In *Nenia Britannica*, he recounted something of Faussett's collection, being the first to realize that the objects were Anglo-Saxon. Roach Smith recalled the description of Faussett's work, his archaeological explorations, and the diversity of his collection and he decided to pay a visit, unannounced, on whichever surviving relatives he could find.

Roach Smith was taking a chance. He had no idea whether the collection still existed, what state it might be in or what Faussett's descendants might make of his unsolicited inquiries. But he was fortunate enough to receive a warm welcome from Henry Godfrey Faussett, the collector's grandson, who was delighted that some-one was, at last, taking an interest in the family treasure. Henry spoke enthusiastically about his grandfather's achievements and spent hours showing Roach Smith boxes and drawers and shelves full of the antiquities that he had collected from local sites. The two men pored over slips of glass and pottery, over amber and amethyst beads, brooches, axes and spearheads, keys and daggers. Henry Faussett was eager that the collection should finally receive official recognition and urged Roach Smith to spread the word about what he had found. Roach Smith needed little encourage-ment. He was astounded by the quality and variety of the objects packed into the churchman's study and, when he finally left the Faussett house, as dusk closed in over the pale Kent hills, he promised to return with a delegation from the British Archae-ological Association.

Henry Godfrey Faussett was never to see the collection receive the attention it deserved, however. The British Archaeological Association did indeed inspect the finds and confirmed Roach Smith's evaluation of the objects as important and valuable, but no one in the Association could find the time or the money to publish the details of the collection and nothing more was done. Other collections became newsworthy instead, and when Henry Godfrey Faussett died, eleven years after Roach Smith had visited, interest in the Faussett finds had largely waned. It looked as though the collection might once more lapse into obscurity. Although the terms of Henry Faussett's will urged that it should be sold complete and intact, no public organization could be persuaded to find the £700 Faussett's heirs were requesting, despite the actual value of the collection being much greater. In 1853, Franks made four attempts to persuade the British Museum to make the purchase, but without success. The Department of Antiquities had an annual purchase grant of £3,000 but this was stretched by a previous liability of £550, and, without extra funds from the government, the museum was unwilling to commit to the Faussett sale. Even though the Society of Antiquaries sent a series of protests, and complained that 'there is a strong probability that it will be purchased in France; and that it will be a disgrace to England that English objects thought worthy of being purchased in France, should leave this country', the museum once again declined.[10] A trustees' meeting just a month later confirmed a request to the Treasury for a special grant of £86,000 to build and fit out the Round Reading Room in the Inner Courtyard. They perhaps thought better of asking for yet more money to acquire the Faussett collection, and were no doubt unwilling to jeopardize the ongoing programme of building work. The opportunity was lost.

Joseph Mayer, however, was much taken by the thought of the collection. As early as November 1853, when staff at the British Museum were still, in theory, negotiating for the pieces, he wrote a friendly and enthusiastic note to Franks, forewarning that he was in the market: 'Hurrah! For the Faussett Collection. I hope you will get them – not hearing from you I wrote to the Revd Faussett to ask about them if you refused them.' If he managed to make the acquisition, he knew he could claim to have saved the treasure for the nation: 'they ought to belong to the national collections and may yet when I have done with them,' he said.[11]

In the end, he moved quickly, and with a sensitivity to public relations' opportunities. Three days after the collection was finally and formally rejected by the British Museum, Mayer travelled to Kent to pay a first instalment and, with Roach Smith's help, he had the objects parcelled up and put on a train to Liverpool. He then approached Thomas Wright, an eminent historian, to give a lecture at the town's Philharmonic Hall to the British Archaeological Association about Anglo-Saxon antiquities in general, and the Faussett collection in particular. And he sponsored Roach Smith to begin work on publishing the Faussett archive – the journal notes, observations and sketches – in an illustrated volume that placed the collection in its historical context.

Mayer had always been competitive. As a youth, he had revelled in all kinds of sports, admitting a particular fondness for bear-baiting. The purchase of the Faussett collection was an opportunity to take on his rivals, and declare victory. Acquiring such a complete set of objects was a substantial triumph in itself, but it was all the more pleasing to Mayer because he had more or less trumped the British Museum, highlighting its deficiencies and putting himself forward in its place as the saviour of a national treasure. By afterwards supporting learned research about the collection, Mayer consolidated the impression of his success, and aligned himself with modern, forward-thinking antiquarian scholars such as John Evans. He emphasized the distance between himself and dilettante, amateur collectors whose studies and drawing rooms were cluttered with random historical objects. He was no longer confined to Walter Scott's model or Daniels' fashionable portrait, but was beginning to cut his own distinct path, creating a unique identity as a collector.

Mayer's purchase of the Faussett collection was a strong declaration of his intent to invest everything he had in collecting. The acquisition not only demanded the considerable financial outlay of £700, but more significantly it demanded that Mayer reveal his ambitions to his fellow, and rival, collectors. He seemed inspired and excited, more than daunted, by the prospect of such high-profile collecting, and for a while he seemed to relish the attention that came with the Faussett purchase. Many of his friends wrote to congratulate him on the success, and Roach Smith was particularly delighted, seeing more clearly than others how the acquisition might secure Mayer's place in history: 'the work will inevitably bring you GREAT returns in honourable fame. . . I am SURE of this:- many will envy you; and many will regret they are not in your position. There are chances, my dear Sir, which occur only once in an age, & the Faussett collection was a CHANCE OF CHANCES.'[12]

But Roach Smith was wrong. This was not a 'once in an age' opportunity, at least not for Mayer. Only a year after acquiring the Faussett finds, Mayer again swelled his collection by acquiring a large number of objects at once. In 1855, he bought the classical and medieval ivories, some Mexican pottery and a large amount of prehistoric metalwork from the Hungarian Fejérváry collection, which belonged to Franz Pulszky, an exile living in London. Again the British Museum declined to buy the pieces, reluctant to spend its limited budget on little-known medieval Byzantine ivories at the expense of such museum mainstays as classical sculpture. Its refusal to buy drew renewed and widespread criticism from antiquarians, archaeologists and the press: the *Art Journal* accused the trustees of 'incapacity of judgement' in failing to secure the ivories.[13] When Mayer stepped in to purchase everything for £1,500, he was able to present himself, once again, as some kind of national champion, at least to the scholarly community.

Within a few years, several other important collections came Mayer's way. In 1857, he acquired medieval antiquities and a range of objects from Anglo-Saxon cemeteries belonging to

W. H. Rolfe, a friend of Roach Smith's and an antiquarian from Sandwich. And, in 1868, he bought up the collection of his exhausted friend Joseph Clarke who had written plaintively to Mayer, explaining that 'I am utterly tired of collecting anything. . . if you but come and see me. . . and take the pick of my collections nothing would delight me more.'[14] Through such acquisitions, the range, variety and sheer size of Mayer's collection was growing at speed, filling his rooms and establishing him as a figure among the community of collectors.

By purchasing existing collections wholesale, Mayer was able to build on other collectors' work and expertise, and save on a great deal of bartering and research. He certainly had an eye to the future: his negotiations for both the Faussett and the Rolfe collections made much of his intentions to save them from obscurity and keep them intact, emphasizing the public-spirited nature of his motives. But there was also perhaps something obsessional about Mayer's bulk acquisitions. The cut-and-thrust of the hunt itself clearly excited Mayer as much as the final ownership of the objects; the overwhelming desire to possess was a driving force. Such intense collecting was later to be described – especially by Freud and other twentieth-century psychoanalysts – as 'fetishistic'. But it can also be seen as typically Victorian. At a time of imperial ambitions and unprecedented industrial expansion, Mayer's wholesale collecting could be viewed as part of a compulsive urge to do things bigger and better, to bring as many elements as possible under one protective umbrella, to control, to regulate and to extend. Those collecting on this scale shared many of the same motives and priorities as those championing rapid industrialization, competitive free trade and mass-production; Mayer's collection was as much an expression of the age as cotton mills or railways.

As with the Industrial Revolution, such progress was not without its pitfalls, however. Mayer was not an especially wealthy man; he had not inherited any fortune. None of his ledgers or account books survives, and there has been some speculation that he perhaps traded in diamonds, or was fortunate in some kind of financial speculation. But as far as we know he had to rely solely on the income from his jewellery business to fund his collecting. The scale and ambition of what he achieved convinced many that he must have had some other mysterious source of funds, but such wealth was an illusion created by the magnificence of the collection. Mayer lived simply, traded successfully – and invested everything he had in his objects. When he could not quite afford what he wanted, he turned once again to his friends for help. But large-scale collections necessarily require large-scale expenditure, and, in his overwhelming desire to acquire, Mayer sometimes underestimated the costs of his activity. His collecting had an element of brinkmanship about it and once or twice, perhaps inevitably, he came unstuck.

When the Bram Hertz collection of classical sculpture, cameos and over 1,700 gems came on to the market in 1856, priced at £12,000, Mayer put together a consortium of Liverpool businessmen to help him acquire it. He pressed and cajoled them into partnership, tantalizing them, so he thought, with the promise of rare and handsome objects which they could display in their home town. He presented the purchase as a civic duty, part of the growing movement to establish municipal collections. Here was the chance for private individuals to make an act of public generosity. But most Liverpool businessmen were not like Mayer. They were not particularly taken by the idea of collecting. Although the £12,000 was promised, and formal ownership of the collection was transferred into Mayer's hands, the consortium quickly crumbled, leaving him with a treasure trove he could not pay for.

Despite his profession as a jeweller, Mayer was no connoisseur of gems, and the Bram Hertz collection was probably overpriced: 'the British Museum people would have niggled about as many hundreds as he has given thousands for it!' confided a sceptical Joseph Clarke to Roach Smith.[15] Nonetheless, Mayer was devastated when the deal fell through: 'I cannot bear the idea of breaking up and scattering a collection,' he complained.[16] But he could not find the necessary funds to make the purchase alone and he had to part with things. Within a few months, some of the Bram Hertz collection was back on the market, followed a year or two later by a two-week auction at Sotheby's. For Mayer, the sale was heartbreaking. The collection was dispersed, just as he had feared and, to make matters worse, the £10,011. 2s. 6d. achieved by the sale left Mayer with substantial losses, after commission, of almost £3,000, which, as Clarke remarked, 'I am afraid prey on his spirits'.[17] Only the diligence and goodwill of Mayer's loyal friends, and of Roach Smith and Clarke in particular, managed to salvage anything at all from the disaster. When the collection came under the auctioneer's hammer, they bid for a number of gems which, before long, found their way back into Mayer's hands.

As the Bram Hertz affair made clear, relying on the support of other people to build a collection could be perilous. It was helpful to be able to draw on an extensive network of contacts and friends, but collecting could never just be about the large-scale public purchases, the notices in the press and the ambitious acquisitions. It was a personal and sometimes a painful quest; it demanded sacrifice, dedication and sensitive attention. Mayer was always destined to be a great collector. For all his high-profile purchases, and the gratification of buying intact existing collections, he also took his time over much smaller acquisitions, spending blustery evenings on site at archaeological excavations, waiting to barter for the smallest of Romano–British finds. He walked out on wet Sundays along the banks of the River Dee and across the Wirral, talking to villagers about whatever they might have turned up; he rescued dozens of Roman artefacts when the

London, Midland and Scottish railway cut a new line through to Lancaster. He was constantly and intensely on the lookout for objects. Better still, luck was clearly on his side, giving him the opportunity to make rare and inventive acquisitions, and taking his collection into the realms of the spectacular.

The first moment of luck came when Mayer was on a visit to London in 1845. He was invited to a tea party given by the wife of an old friend, and, as the slices of cake were passed around, he was introduced to a Mr and Mrs Wedderburne, an unexceptional elderly couple. There was no immediate reason for Mayer to find them of any interest, but the grapevine of collectors' gossip suggested that Wedderburne had once worked for Wedgwood, travelling for forty years to promote the company and sell their wares, overseeing their outlets and advising on the ceramic trade. When the opportunity arose, Mayer drew Wedderburne away from the company. Wedderburne was jovial and obliging. As we have seen, very few people at this time thought Wedgwood worthy of much attention and Wedderburne was unused to meeting anyone who cared for his stories. He was happy to entertain Mayer with anecdotes, but the more he went on, the more surprised he became at Mayer's attention. He ventured into increasing detail, emphasizing his technical knowledge of factories and sales figures, as far as he could remember them. He talked about the history of the works, expressing opinions as to which periods had seen the finest ceramics being produced at the Etruria factory in Stoke-on-Trent, and he described his day-to-day experience of selling, the accounting procedures, the tricks of getting Wedgwood into the big stores and to the front of the shelves. The more Wedderburne told, the more attentive and enthusiastic Mayer became. The more of the minutiae he remembered, the more delighted Mayer seemed to be.

Wedderburne could not help but be pleased and flattered by such attention, and after a long conversation he was lured into making an admission. He had been chief clerk and adviser to Wedgwood's London warehouse when it was shut down. Losing impetus after the death of its founder, Josiah, trade with Europe had slowed towards the end of the eighteenth century and the breaking up of the London premises had become inevitable. Wedderburne, who had spent so many years developing the business, had watched in dismay as pieces from the company's most successful and productive years were cast aside and sometimes smashed; great packages going to auction to be sold at bargain prices. And so, in a moment of sentimental folly, he had stepped in himself to buy up a vast quantity of the best and oldest examples, rescuing some of Wedgwood's most special objects, so that they could be safely stored and protected for the future. But the cost of his intervention had almost ruined him. He had not been a wealthy man, he explained, and his expenditure had made him considerably and uncomfortably poorer. His savings had dwindled, he was stretched by household expenses, and all he had to show was an attic packed full of old and unfashionable Wedgwood china.

Mayer became convinced that he had stumbled on to an undiscovered treasure trove. He asked Wedderburne to bring him a few specimens, to prove his story. He was not disappointed. 'When I saw them my heart beat as I asked him if he had any more, and how much he would want for them,' Mayer admitted. 'He suggested that I should visit him next day and see the remainder.'[18] And so, a day later, Mayer made his way through the quiet residential streets to see the rest of the china for himself. Soon he was surrounded by a vast and distinctive collection of Wedgwood – by plaques and vases, by jasper ware and basalt and pottery, representing every period and style of the company's history, as well as trial pieces from the factory, held back from normal sale, unique pieces, imperfect and blistered and misfired. Mayer bought everything. The terms of the sale were agreed there and then, the two men sitting in the dust of the garret, the sun filtering pale through the sky-light. The pieces were packed up and put on a train for Liverpool. Mayer's collection of Wedgwood had begun in earnest.

Mayer's meeting with Wedderburne had been a rewarding stroke of luck, the kind of once-in-a-lifetime opportunity of which myth is made. But better was yet to come. Within a short time, another fortunate encounter was to bolster Mayer's holdings yet further. He had, through Wedderburne, bought up the wealth of Wedgwood's past; now he was to discover the key to its history. It was a wet afternoon in Birmingham in 1848, three years after Mayer had done the deal with Wedderburne. He was in the Midlands on business, and found himself in Birmingham's back streets as a sudden thunderstorm broke over the low roofs of the workshops in the jewellery quarter. As the rain pummelled the pavements and the sky darkened, there was nothing for it but to take shelter and Mayer scrambled into the nearest shop. In his haste, he did not have time to notice anything about the place in which he was taking cover; he just pushed open the door and flung himself out of the rain.

The shop turned out to be a scrap dealer's, piled high with waste iron and copper and brass, broken furniture, pipes and cogs and wheels. It was dusty and slightly oily, and the floors were littered with slips of wood and paper, screws and bolts, oddments of cloth, bits of string and a good helping of grit. Everything was grimy. There should have been nothing at all to interest him. But he had to wait for the rain to stop. Looking out through a small window, he could see it still, battering hard on the street outside and throwing gobbets of mud against the close-packed brick buildings. He paced up and down, idling and looking around in the dim light. And in the midst of everything, what caught his eye were a number of heavy old ledgers, piled up at the end of the

A view of one half of the South Court at the South Kensington Museum, filled with the packed cases of the 1862 loan exhibition. This wood engraving appeared in the *Illustrated London News* on 6 December 1862, towards the end of the show.

John Charles Robinson in middle age, probably around the time he left the South Kensington Museum. The oil painting is by J. J. Napier and is in the collection of the National Portrait Gallery.

This photograph of a small corner of Newton Manor shows part of Robinson's extensive and varied collection in the domestic setting.

Charlotte Schreiber, around the time of her second marriage in 1855. The drawing is by George Frederic Watts, one of the most influential and renowned Victorian portrait painters.

Charles Schreiber possibly sat for this portrait on his election as MP for Cheltenham in 1865, ten years after his marriage to Charlotte. It is also by Watts.

The gourd-shaped bottle that tormented the Schreibers during 1873 and 1874.

Dante Gabriel Rossetti's collection in the sitting room of 16 Cheyne Walk in 1882. Rossetti is reading to the poet and critic Theodore Watts-Dunton.

The Peacock Room in the house of Frederick Richards Leyland, decorated by James Whistler in 1877. The photograph shows Whistler's portrait of 'La princesse du pays de la porcelaine' and some of the blue-and-white collection assembled by Murray Marks.

Murray Marks in his London home. The photograph shows Rossetti's characteristic portrait of Marks' wife, as well as some choice pieces from Marks' collection of blue-and-white on the mantlepiece.

Murray Marks' distinctive trade card, designed as a result of a collaboration between Whistler, Rossetti and William Morris.

MURRAY MARKS
395 Oxford St.W.

Joseph Mayer's first portrait, painted around 1840 by William Daniels, shows Mayer at the heart of his growing collection.

A view of the 'Mummy Room' in Mayer's Egyptian Museum in Liverpool, complete with stuffed crocodile.

Stephen Wootton Bushell's visiting card with a portrait photograph taken shortly after his arrival in China in 1868.

The semi-ruined Bronze Pavilion at the Imperial Summer Palace in Peking. This picture was taken by the pioneering Scottish photographer, John Thomson, on a trip to the city in 1871–2, during which he almost certainly worked with Stephen Wootton Bushell to document historical sites. Bushell owned an album of Thomson's photographs.

ACUTE CHINAMANIA.

Mon. "MAMMA! MAMMA! DON'T GO ON LIKE THIS, *PRAY!*"
Mamma (who has snatched a favourite pot). "WHAT HAVE I GOT LEFT TO LIVE FOR?"
May. "HAVEN'T YOU GOT ME, MAMMA?"
Mamma. "YOU, CHILD! YOU'RE NOT UNIQUE!! THERE ARE SIX OF YOU—A COMPLETE SET!!"

CHRONIC CHINAMANIA (INCURABLE).

Pale Enthusiast. "THIS IS THE CREAM OF MY COLLECTION, LADIES AND GENTLEMEN. IT IS QUITE UNIQUE. IT WAS MADE BY THE FALLOWBROOK POTTERY THAT WAS STARTED IN 1870. IT TOOK THEM THREE YEARS TO PRODUCE THIS PLATE, THIS ONLY ONE, AND THEN—AND THEN——"
Ruddy Philistine. "AND THEN THEY SHUT UP, I SUPPOSE?" *Pale Enthusiast.* "ER—YES!"
Ruddy Philistine. "AND I DON'T WONDER!!"

This pair of engravings by George du Maurier appeared in the *Punch Almanack* in December 1875. They present collectors as obsessive and strange, physically frail and emotionally incapable of interacting with family and friends around them.

9080. VICTORIA & ALBERT MUSEUM SOUTH KENSINGTON.   L.S.&.P.C?.

The architect Aston Webb was chosen to create a new complex of buildings on the South Kensington site in 1891; it finally opened in June 1909. The intervening years saw Webb modify many of his ideas, moving towards the finished buildings we recognize today as the Victoria and Albert Museum.

An exterior view of the domed glass palace at Old Trafford, Manchester, that housed the Art Treasures Exhibition in 1857. This picture appeared in an illustrated weekly periodical, the *Art-Treasures Examiner: A Pictorial, Critical and Historical Record of the Art-Treasures Exhibition*, which was published especially for the duration of the exhibition.

counter, leather-bound, scruffy, and instantly alluring to Mayer. They were not, he could be sure, scrap. He realized that they had to be a set, more or less complete, and, with the thunder still creaking overhead, he had nothing better to do than to sit down and take a look at them.

The scrap merchant thought Mayer was quite mad. They were just old papers, he explained, that he sold to butchers and greengrocers who used the broad thick sheets for wrapping bacon and butter. What on earth did Mayer want with them? But Mayer had begun to turn the close-written pages and was already absorbed. He could not be put off by the dealer. He was already experiencing the incomparable excitement of unearthing a find. What Mayer had discovered would have meant nothing to Birmingham's shopkeepers, had they even thought to look. The books were, in many ways, perfectly ordinary, even dull: they were filled with lists of names and calculations, business accounts and transactions, day-to-day dealings; they detailed workmen's wages. What made them special was that they had belonged to the two factories in Stoke-on-Trent, at Burslem and Etruria, that were the core of the Wedgwood operation. Pages that might have seemed tedious and commonplace to almost anyone else in Britain, books that would have been passed over without a second glance, had found their way to the notice of the one man who knew what he was looking at, and who could recognize them as valuable.

Mayer naturally asked about the history of the ledgers, and the dealer explained that he had bought them all, as a job lot, when Josiah Wedgwood's son had died five years earlier, in 1843, and the factories were being cleared out. He had got them for almost nothing, and had not thought much about them. There was, he guessed, a little profit to be made if he split them up and sold the paper. Now, however, seeing the gleam in Mayer's eye, he sensed the possibility of something greater than the small return he had envisaged. To Mayer's delight, he explained that there were more packets of papers and piles of documents stored in the loft above the shop, all from the same source, and all available for Mayer to see, should he care to.

The thunder had moved off and the rain was easing, but neither Mayer nor the scrap dealer noticed the change in the weather. They were now both absorbed by the promise of a deal. In the dingy loft, there were, as the merchant had promised, reams and reams of papers, far too many for Mayer to read there and then, stuffed in boxes, tied, folded and sometimes torn. Mayer needed only a brief glance to tell him that everything related to the Wedgwood factories, as he had hoped, and, crouched in the low loft space, he offered a price that satisfied both men.

Mayer spent long months back in Liverpool poring over the Wedgwood archives, deciphering, arranging and cataloguing them. He laboured long and studiously. He may have been lucky to have discovered the papers in an obscure scrap merchant's, but he was more than willing to make the luck work for him; to reinforce good fortune with industry. In the bundles of papers, his collection of ceramics came alive. He could show how each piece slotted into the history of ceramics; he could trace the evolution of the art of English pottery. To those doubters who questioned his taste for Wedgwood, he could better justify his choices. With the documents in front of him, it became clear how the leading factories were making progress in technical and stylistic developments, and he could trace more openly the manufacturing links with the craftsmen of the past.

By the time Mayer had finished his work on the documents, the reputation of Wedgwood was beginning to change. It was spoken of with growing respect and prices were rising: it was becoming recognized as one of the most desirable names in English ceramics. In the 1830s and 1840s, few other people were interested in Wedgwood and hardly any collectors were making any kind of systematic attempt to acquire the factory's china. But by the

1850s and 1860s, collectors like Charlotte Schreiber were beginning to look in new directions, while at the same time changes in fashion were making the wares once again desirable. During the second half of the nineteenth century, the early Wedgwood pieces that Mayer had found in Wedderburne's attic were to become the most sought-after examples of the company's output, and, by the end of the century, the demand for Wedgwood was so widespread and intense that one commentator noted that 'not only the shops but the private dwellings of France, Germany, Italy, Holland and Belgium have been ransacked by enthusiastic collectors'.[19] As Wedgwood china began to catch the eye of fashionable society, Mayer's collection was able to boast some of the most interesting and superior pieces in private hands, as well as the most comprehensive archives, testament to both his good fortune and his astute opportunism. Thanks to two strokes of luck, he stood at the vanguard of the rediscovery, accidentally leading the followers of fashion, and winning himself a reputation as a collector of exceptional shrewdness and guile.

CHAPTER TWELVE

Mummies, Crocodiles and Shoes for a Queen

*J*oseph Mayer presented all his friends with etchings of the Daniels portrait. In an age before the widespread use of photography, this was a standard way to prompt them to remember him. It was a means of keeping in touch and was not an uncommon thing to do: Augustus Franks gave his friends a specially made medallion struck with his name, degree and motto to help them remember him. This was made of gold, and was the mark of a gentleman, the forerunner of a bookplate which Franks later designed, giving his full title and dignities in Latin and displaying coats of arms that linked him to several ancient families. Mayer was not, yet, going this far. But the gift of the engravings seems to suggest that he was anxious not to lose ground to some of his wealthier and more well-connected colleagues; it was an indication of a certain vanity, and of his aspirations to be an important man.

Franks never had his portrait painted. It has been suggested that this was because it would have been in bad taste for a bachelor gentleman to 'advertise' himself so blatantly. Mayer, lacking

Franks' upper-class sensitivities, had no such reservations. In 1851, at the age of forty-eight, in his prime and unmarried, he commissioned another portrait, a bolder image, with the dignity of age and professional success. This time, he did not want a furnished study or a clutter of objects to distract and he opted for a simple image of his head and body against a featureless background – nothing but himself; no references to anything but his essential respectability. It is perhaps no coincidence that this was the year of the Great Exhibition. Mayer had been invited by the organizers to draw on his connections in the silversmithing world to exhibit 'works of ancient and medieval art'. Instead, he used the opportunity to show off his own work, displaying fifteen pieces of silver plate (then a new technique) and eighteen items of his jewellery. The display got him noticed, and several of his pieces were commended by the judges and rewarded with an 'honourable mention'.[1] It was in the light of this success that he commissioned another portrait to further consolidate his rising place in the world.

As an indication of this growing confidence, Mayer chose George Freizor (G.-A. Freezor), a London man of the art establishment. Freizor painted Mayer half turning to an imagined audience, and gave him weight across the chest, the decorum of middle age, the gravity of learning in his high forehead. In this second portrait, Mayer looks distinguished and active, a man pausing for a moment in the midst of important and pressing duties. It came at an apt moment. With the successful contribution to the Great Exhibition behind him and his collection growing, Mayer was embarking on his most ambitious project to date – his own museum.

It was on a visit to the British Museum that the idea came to him. Mayer was a frequent visitor to the huge dark galleries, packed with objects; he savoured the heavy scent of ancient lives, and the way the precious treasures stretched out into the shadows as if forever. And in particular he enjoyed the newly opened Egyptian galleries, pausing among the tombs of the Pharaohs, standing alone and quiet, without the press of the present in his head. It was an inspiration. It prompted him to think about his own collecting, and ways in which he could give it shape and authority and consequence. He decided he would open a museum, some-where with proper space for his best pieces, where they could be organized and catalogued and flaunted to the public. A museum of his own would be a brilliant triumph and, when the time came, the perfect memorial. It would allow him to share with the world the greatness of his collection.

Mayer had no doubt that the museum should be in Liverpool. He was proud of the town and his place within it and he wanted it to grow and prosper; he wanted its citizens to have all the advantages of those of the capital. Liverpool was thriving. It had everything to rival London: the magnificent stone buildings, the busy international port and packed docks, the shops and parks – as well as the slums and grime and starving poor. Moreover, it had a long tradition of successful private museums. As early as 1800, William Bullock, another jeweller and silversmith, had opened a popular museum of over 30,000 objects in Church Street, having tried out the idea for several years in his native Sheffield. The displays included works of art, armour, natural history specimens and ethnographic objects, many of which had been brought back from Captain Cook's expeditions abroad. The museum flourished, and by 1812 was such a success that it was deemed worthy of a London home and was transferred to its own 'Egyptian Temple' (later the Egyptian Hall), purpose-built in Piccadilly. Then, in 1851, just as Mayer was shaping his own plans, the 14th Earl of Derby opened a natural history museum in Liverpool's Duke Street, preserving some of the unrivalled collection of birds and mammals that his father had kept and bred in his zoo at Knowsley. Visitors flocked to see the stuffed, pinned and desiccated remains of colourful and bizarre animals, proof that the Liverpool public had an appetite for the attractions of museum visiting.

As yet, Liverpool had no permanent collection of antiquities or decorative art; this Mayer decided to change. In May 1852, he opened his new museum at Number VIII Colquitt Street, a few doors down from the Liverpool Royal Institution, at one of the town's most reputable addresses. Everything was done properly. He sought advice from many of his friends about what to display, and he drew on Franks' expertise to create a cataloguing system. He appointed a full-time curator who lived on the top floor of the building, charged a shilling entrance fee to contribute towards basic costs, and filled the rooms with the most precious and lovely things from his collection.

Perhaps because he could not shake off the memory of the moment in the British Museum galleries when the inspiration came to him, Mayer called his new project the 'Egyptian Museum'. The name usefully brought to mind not only the British Museum but also other successful private ventures, including Bullock's Egyptian Hall in London which had built on the original collection from Liverpool to put on a number of spectacular, and profitable, shows in the early years of the century, including a display in 1816 of Napoleonic relics which attracted over 200,000 visitors. The name also focused attention on at least some of the objects on display, which included ancient Egyptian inscribed tablets, carved figures and bronzes, as well as a designated 'mummy room' on the ground floor. More than anything, however, it was a way of enticing visitors. The name 'Egyptian' exuded mystery and romance; it was the buzzword of its day, a marketing phenomenon. By calling his new project the 'Egyptian Museum', Mayer was associating his collection with everything that was fashionable, stimulating and glamorous.

In the eighteenth century, and earlier, when travel in the Middle East was difficult and hazardous, only a trickle of Egyptian relics reached Europe, and there were consequently few collectors. In Britain, the Revd Robert Huntington, chaplain to the Levant Company in Aleppo for ten years from 1671 to 1681, had collected manuscripts and some antiquities. In the 1760s, Edmund Wortley Montagu (son of Lady Mary Wortley Montagu, the renowned eighteenth-century lady of letters) sent back a painted wooden coffin and mummy which became one of the earliest Egyptian exhibits at the newly opened British Museum. But, on the whole, few people were willing to brave the dangers of Middle Eastern travel in search of pieces to collect. It was after Napoleon unexpectedly occupied Egypt in 1798 that things changed. Suddenly the country was modernized and opened up to European travellers and entrepreneurs. Collectors poured into the ancient sites, flooding the markets with objects and sparking a fashion for things Egyptian.

The novelty of travelling in Egypt, and the promise of what could be collected there, drew men from a variety of backgrounds: George Annesley, Viscount Valentia, who amassed an enormous Egyptian collection at Arley Castle in Staffordshire in the early nineteenth century; Joseph Sams, a Darlington bookseller who visited Egypt and Palestine in the 1820s and brought back antiquities which he sold to the British Museum; and Henry Stobart, a clergyman who travelled extensively during the 1850s. The market in Egyptian objects boomed and private collections were soon appearing around the country. But the obsession was not confined to Britain. Expeditions to Egypt were funded by most European monarchs or governments. The most notable, led by Karl Richard Lepsius, was funded by the King of Prussia and sent back 15,000 antiquities and plaster casts for the Royal Museum in Berlin. Across the Continent, mummies were publicly unwrapped in staged spectacles that nodded only in passing to the interests of science, and publications proliferated, from the downright sensationalist to such scholarly works as the encyclopaedic, five-volume *Egypt's Place in Universal History*, written in German by Christian Bunsen but also translated into English and published between 1848 and 1857. The visit of the Prince of Wales (the future Edward VII) with his new bride, Princess Alexandra, to Egypt in 1868–9, and international politicking around the opening of the Suez Canal in November 1869, only consolidated the impression that an interest in Egyptian history and affairs was quite the right thing for a person of fashion, good standing and sound education.

Many of the archaeologists and antiquarians exploring Egypt were respectable men of the gentry, government and the church. But they often employed 'colourful' agents to rummage, cheat and steal on their behalf. One of the most active of these early collectors was the British Consul-General in Cairo, Henry Salt, himself a portrait painter, whose agents Giovanni d'Athanasi and Giovanni Belzoni ransacked ancient sites such as Thebes, the Pyramids and the Sphinx at Giza in a series of 'excavations'. Among the objects they removed was a colossal granite bust of Rameses II, and enough material to form three huge collections: one was acquired by the British Museum, another was sold to King Charles X of France for £10,000, and a third was auctioned at Sotheby's in over 1,000 lots (some of which Mayer later acquired) after Salt's death in 1827. The enormous popularity of Egyptian objects, and the prestige attached to discovering them, meant that many early collectors and their agents would stop at nothing to secure the pieces they wanted. Excavation methods were violently destructive, obliterating as much as they uncovered. Digs, explained Lepsius, often took place 'hurriedly and by night and with bribed assistance'.[2] There was ferocious rivalry, and the competitors could frequently be seen clambering over stones and broken sarcophagi, rooting through rubble and bartering with boys whose pockets were stuffed with ancient remains. There was little attempt at documentation and the contexts for the objects, as well as the opportunities for studying them on site, were almost always lost.

In his early travels, Mayer himself was not above such instant archaeology. There was undoubtedly a thrill to be had from hands-on intervention, and, at a time when European empires were expanding, there were few who would have questioned the right of British collectors to pieces from more 'primitive' cultures. What is now regarded as looting was seen by the Victorians as, at best, the rescue of historic objects for posterity and, at worst, little more than enthusiastic opportunism. In Britain, many expeditions were funded by the government, national and regional museums, or by respectable establishment organizations, and the pillaged artefacts were proudly displayed to an admiring public. Private and public collectors alike benefited from the free-for-all. As early as 1799, the Rosetta Stone was looted during Napoleon's Egypt campaign and eventually given over to the British, shown first at the Society of Antiquaries and then, from 1802, at the British Museum. Mayer's collection boasted numerous large pieces taken from Egypt, including the great granite sarcophagus of Bakenkhonsu, stolen from his tomb at Thebes, and thirty-three of the stone funerary tablets known as stelae.

But Egypt was not the only source of new objects. Lord Elgin's expeditions to Greece in the early nineteenth century famously resulted in the Parthenon Marbles finding a home in the British Museum; Austen Henry Layard sent the results of his excavations in Mesopotamia (now Iraq) to private enthusiasts like Charlotte Schreiber and also to the national collections. His looting was regarded as thoroughly respectable and his work was recognized with a trusteeship of the British Museum in 1866. In the 1860s, British troops sent to Abyssinia (now Ethiopia) took sacred wooden tablets, religious manuscripts, ceremonial crosses, a solid gold crown, chalices, textiles and jewellery from the imperial palaces in an operation that is said to have required 15 elephants and 200 mules as transport. Again, the British establishment openly condoned the thievery: the hoard, known as the Magdala Treasure, was largely divided between the Queen, the British Museum, the South Kensington Museum and the British Library. The remaining pieces were auctioned to private owners.

As the century moved on, however, there were signs that the consequences of such widespread looting were beginning to be acknowledged. In June 1871, less than four years after the arrival of the Magdala Treasure in Britain, Prime Minister William Gladstone conceded to the House of Commons that the whole affair had been 'unsatisfactory... from first to last' and that he 'deeply regretted that those articles were ever brought from Abyssinia and could not conceive why they were so brought'. Gladstone was, as we have seen, a collector himself, and his observation points towards a growing change of heart in some collecting circles. Clearly, there would remain unscrupulous and profiteering individuals, buying, selling and collecting objects thoughtlessly. The driving political imperatives of Empire still remained, but the increasing influence of scholarly curators such as Franks and Robinson, and of expert private collectors such as Charlotte Schreiber, meant that the emphasis was gradually shifting from acquiring objects at any cost and ripping them from their ancient sites to valuing and understanding them within their original contexts.

This was not, of course, as simple a matter as I might have made it sound. Attitudes were complex and progress was erratic. Some of the scholarship of the most learned of Victorian curators and collectors derived from studying looted objects; many early archaeologists like Layard combined a certain gung-ho acquisitiveness with a genuine spirit of inquiry; public and private collectors are, as we still see today, notoriously slow to agree to the repatriation of other people's treasures. Nevertheless, the nineteenth century saw a movement towards more structured, scholarly and responsible collecting, and this was reflected in the changing attitudes of collectors like Joseph Mayer. Through discussions with other, often more learned, collectors, Mayer came to appreciate the importance of documentation, research and publication. Though his own methods were not necessarily scholarly, he grew to appreciate – and support – scholarship in those around him. His friendship with Roach Smith in particular taught him to value objects as much for the light they shed on history as for their status as treasure. Roach Smith, Mayer admitted, gave him a 'valuable education', in which he learned how 'all kinds of antiquarian subjects. . . gave an impetus' to study and acted as 'corroborative help to written history'.[3] Over the fifty years that he was collecting, Mayer's attitudes changed. The instant gratification of on-site rummaging which had excited him in his youth gave way to a more considered and respectful approach to objects. This may have had something to do with simply growing up, and becoming older, wealthier and more reputable, but personal circumstances do not explain it all. Joseph Mayer was part of a collecting age when new and intriguing objects, like those from Egypt, created different collecting habits. He was part of a generation that was discovering largely uncharted territory and, in turn, developing new ways of doing things, influencing attitudes and forming opinion.

As with Wedgwood, Mayer was fortunate to be collecting Egyptian objects at the right time, when interest was at its height and when pieces of unique variety, character and quality were first becoming available on the open market. Such good timing, allied with unerring enthusiasm, meant his lack of expertise hardly mattered: he was still able to amass important Egyptian pieces that had both scholarly and aesthetic significance, and that would be valued in years to come. But callers at the Colquitt Street museum who came expecting no more than a display of Egyptian antiquities were both surprised and fascinated by what they found. There was a stuffed crocodile hung high over the ancient sarcophagi; there was Roman pottery; sculpture from Assyria and Babylonia; Anglo-Saxon metalwork; coins and commemorative medals; Burmese manuscripts; a range of fine Persian leather bindings; and examples of Chinese calligraphy. Visitors could browse an extensive reference library or study books in a dozen languages – none of which Mayer could read himself – before moving on to admire his collection of jewellery, or the artefacts of medieval life he had picked up while wandering the Wirral. The ground floor had a room set aside for the history of English pottery, especially local Liverpool ware and Wedgwood, and the first floor boasted a room devoted to Renaissance Italian majolica. On the stairs between the two floors hung a number of illustrations explaining the technical processes of engraving; a cartoon depicting a scene from Dante's *Divine Comedy*; and a painting of Noah's Ark breasting the rising waters of the biblical flood.

Most of all, though, Mayer valued objects that connected to famous lives of the past. Earlier generations would have dubbed him a 'curio': the type of collector who chose things not for their intrinsic aesthetic value but for their rarity, novelty or romantic associations. In many ways, he was part of the tradition of collecting for a 'cabinet of curiosities'; these cabinets of wealthy seventeenth- and early-eighteenth-century gentlemen embraced everything from geological specimens to coins. His museum owed much to eclectic forerunners such as John Tradescant, whose collection was described by a visitor in 1638 as including, among other things, 'two ribs of a whale, also a very ingenious little boat of bark. . . foreign plants. . . a salamander, a chameleon, a pelican. . . the hand of a mermaid, the hand of a mummy. . . all kinds of precious stones, coins, a picture wrought in feathers, a small piece of wood from the cross of Christ, pictures in perspective of Henry IV and Louis XIII of France... a scourge with which Charles V is said to have scourged himself and a hat band of snake bones'. Tradescant's collection was, according to another admirer, 'where a Man might in one daye behold and collecte into one place more curiosities than hee should see if hee spent all his life in Travell'. It was a marvel to his contemporaries, and an inspiration to those that followed, eventually becoming the core of the Ashmolean Museum in Oxford.[4]

In this tradition, Mayer's displays of genuinely significant objects at the Egyptian Museum were interspersed with a range of pieces of doubtful aesthetic value, but each of which came with a good story. There was a signet ring and a snuff box which Mayer claimed had belonged to Napoleon, as well as jewellery and another, gold-lined, snuff box which had apparently once been in the possession of the Empress Josephine. There was a 'large wheel-lock Gun' which, the label proudly proclaimed, had been 'used at the execution of Mary Queen of Scots', and, in the same room, 'The Armoury', there was 'a cocoa-nut Cup, set in silver, formerly belonging to Oliver Cromwell', as well as a pair of boots, also said to have been Cromwell's. Mayer also treated his visitors to the sight of a 'Pair of Shoes, worn by her present Majesty, on the night of her marriage to Prince Albert'.

Few of Liverpool's citizens had ever before seen this kind of display; they marvelled at the exotic, the far-away and the historic now all within reach. Mayer's idiosyncratic and unpredictable approach to collecting was amusing and spectacular, a stimulus to the imaginations of adults and children alike. Locals quickly added the museum to their list of entertainments, and many made return visits. Even in his own museum Mayer lacked the confidence to speak directly to visitors or answer queries about the collection, and the curator was kept busy explaining the displays and acting as tour guide for those unfamiliar with the town.

At a time when the distinctions between private and public collections could be hazy, Mayer's museum straddled the border between the two. Although there was an admission charge of one shilling for adults and sixpence for children (which Mayer regretted having to impose), the museum was genuinely accessible, useful and popular. It was created with the general visitor in mind, as much to entertain as to educate. While many museums – from the South Kensington Museum to Ruskin's educational experiment in Sheffield – were forthright in their didactic ambition, Mayer seems simply to have enjoyed the idea that people might like to come to see his things. Certainly, it seems clear that he regarded the Egyptian Museum as largely 'public', as an enterprise for the town of Liverpool that just happened to be funded by his personal wealth and made possible by his personal obsession.

With his museum open, Mayer felt an increased belief in himself as a collector. He commissioned a third portrait from John Harris, a competent local craftsman without pretensions. It is imposing and substantial. Mayer stands at the heart of his museum and replacing the eccentric clutter of his first portrait are a few choice objects: a colossal statue from the Abu Simbel temples, one of ancient Egypt's richest and most haunting sites; a rare thirteenth-century German prayerbook in an intricate medieval binding; and a beautiful ancient carved ivory, the Asclepius-Hygieia diptych, which had graced a Roman site of worship and been part of the Fejérváry collection. Behind him, retreating into the arcaded spaced beyond, can be seen the forms of his cases; under his hand the gilt-edged top of a heavily carved scholar's table and at the front of the picture, bold and large this time, both distinct from his objects and master of them, the figure of Mayer himself, half-smiling at his visitors, welcoming them to the museum he had created with an open, confident sweep of the hand.

CHAPTER THIRTEEN

The Treasures
of the North

𝓕ive years after opening his museum, Joseph Mayer found himself standing in a crowded field under a hot May sun, choking in the dust of passing horses and staring with slightly dismayed wonder at a vast vaulted iron and glass building whose low wings seemed to stretch far into the distance. He was with a group of his Liverpool friends. They had travelled together by train the few miles to Old Trafford, just outside Manchester, where, in the heart of the industrial grime and pragmatism of England's north-west, they were about to join the snaking queue to see an unprecedented event. Larger and more impressive even than the famous Great Exhibition, this was Manchester's Art Treasures Exhibition of 1857. Here, 16,000 works of art were collected under one roof: oils, watercolours, engravings and drawings; the controversial and avant-garde work of the Pre-Raphaelites; Michelangelo's unfinished 'Manchester Madonna'; photographs, textiles, sculpture, armour, furniture – and Joseph Mayer's choicest and most precious pieces.

Like Robinson's South Kensington exhibition a few years later, the 1857 Manchester display drew on the generosity of, and was an inspiration to, private collectors. 'Art in England may be said to have derived all its encouragement from private persons,' explained the organizers. Articulating the tension between private ownership and public display, they went on: 'The pictures of our leading artists, the work of our best Sculptors, as well as the most select of all other objects coming under the denomination of Fine Arts, are distributed in private houses throughout the kingdom, instead of being found as in Continental Countries in National Collections accessible to the public.' Like the 1862 show designed by Robinson and the Fine Arts Club, the purpose of the Art Treasures Exhibition was to display the finest of these works, to celebrate the achievements of private collectors, and to go some way towards redressing the balance from 'periodic gatherings of the production of industry' to exhibitions of more aesthetic interest: 'There appears no reason why an effort should not be made to collect together in one central locality, and in a suitable building, the Treasures of Art with which Great Britain abounds.'[1]

Everyone, it seemed, was eager to be involved. As for the later London show, the Queen and Prince Albert agreed to lend a number of pieces and, keen to be included in such exalted company, collectors from across the country hurried forward to make their possessions available. Members of the Fine Arts Club were asked to lend, and Charlotte Schreiber offered three paintings by the Welsh watercolourist Penry Williams to the section of 'Modern Masters'. But this was to be a regional showcase as much as a national event. It was a chance to polish provincial pride and highlight what could be done by the townsmen of the North; an opportunity for men like Mayer to prove that, even in the regions, there were collectors with taste and refinement whose objects rivalled the best in the world. Local collectors, in particular, readily committed their support and the organizers emphasized the choice of Manchester as a venue. 'Situated as it is, in the centre of the kingdom, in the midst of a dense surrounding population with railway facilities admirably adapted for bringing and returning visitors within one day', the city boasted both practical advantages 'calculated to ensure the financial success of the scheme' and, just as significantly, a tradition of active collecting and art appreciation: it was, pointed out proud local dignitaries, 'a district where individuals have done so much to encourage art'.[2]

In just fourteen months, the committee succeeded in building an enormous palace on land at Old Trafford leased from the Manchester Cricket Club and later converted into the city's botanical gardens. They filled the cavernous spaces, hanging paintings three or four high on the walls, installing cases with ceramics and glassware and creating corridors of sculpture in the airy nave. Over the entrance was a quotation from Keats – 'a thing of Beauty is a joy for ever' – and over the exit a line of Pope's, 'to wake the soul by tender strokes of art'. These set the tone for the exhibition. There were over 6,000 paintings, both by respected English artists such as Hogarth, Gainsborough and Constable and by the European Old Masters – Rubens, Raphael, Titian and Rembrandt. 'Modern' works by Turner and the Pre-Raphaelites were included, and the emerging art of photography was represented by evocative images of the Crimean War by James Robertson and an ambitious allegoric montage of *The Two Ways of Life* by the Swedish photographic pioneer Oscar Gustave Rejlander. The hall was subdivided by partitions, creating separate galleries, each shaded with calico to prevent damage to the artworks on sunny days. When things inside got too hot, firemen sprayed water on to the roof in a rudimentary form of air conditioning. Two public refreshment rooms also helped to reinvigorate visitors: in the convivial surroundings of the second-class restaurant, one reviewer noted that 'John Bull and his female may be seen in full gulp and guzzle, swallowing vast quantities of cold boiled beef, thoroughly moistened with porter or bitter'.[3]

Pride of place in the Old Trafford palace was given to the impressive collection of medieval and Renaissance decorative arts brought together in the 1830s and 1840s by the Toulouse lawyer Jules Soulages. It was a collection J. C. Robinson had already seen and admired. In 1855, when it had come on to the market after Soulages' death, a photographer had been sent by Henry Cole to France to record the objects, with a view to making a purchase. His photographs showed a Toulouse townhouse bursting with vases and platters, highly decorated chests, carved chairs, tables and mirrors, and elaborate fireplaces. It was clearly a unique and valuable collection, and, with the support of Prince Albert, Cole began arrangements to buy everything, in the meantime bringing the objects to England for temporary display in the Marlborough House galleries. There, Robinson began the meticulous task of cataloguing, producing an illustrated descriptive inventory for publication in December 1856, just as plans for the Art Treasures Exhibition were taking shape.

But the sale was not completed. The Prime Minister at the time, Viscount Palmerston, and the Treasury could not see what Cole and Robinson wanted with Soulages' rare and historic objects, nor how they could be used to educate designers and artisans. Once again, there was a debate about the purpose of the South Kensington Museum and the types of objects it should be collecting. Finally, emphasizing the principle of utility, the expenditure was vetoed. Instead, it was the organizers of the Manchester spectacle who audaciously agreed to pay the £13,500 needed to secure the collection for Britain. Robinson was forced to repack all the objects and the Soulages pieces left Marlborough House for Old Trafford, where they formed the core of the Art Treasures show. 'After repeated communications with the London managers which failed to secure its loan, the members of the Executive Committee, in their individual capacity and on their personal responsibility, agreed to purchase the Collection. . . and thus secured it,' explained the committee.[4] Manchester had scored a victory over the capital, and let it be fully known in the press. Numerous announcements and illustrations drew the northern crowds to see what it was that had been snatched from London's hands.

Lacking a formal organization like the Fine Arts Club to oversee the event, Manchester relied instead on bringing together an ad-hoc general council specifically for the duration of the project. This included the usual selection of gentry, MPs, wealthy merchants and municipal dignitaries. A few were also members of the London-based Fine Arts Club, such as Lord Overstone, but many more were attracted by the opportunity to make a local contribution. James Aspinall Turner, for example, was a Manchester cotton manufacturer, Whig MP and naturalist, who owned a scholarly collection of entomological specimens; Stockport-born Joseph Whitworth was a mechanical engineer who invented an hexagonal, high-performance rifle in 1859 and who left a number of bequests to the city of Manchester, including the core collection of the Whitworth Art Gallery; Thomas Goadsby, mayor of Manchester from 1861 to 1862, presented an imposing memorial of Prince Albert to the city in 'grateful acknowledgement of public and private virtues'; Sir Humphrey de Trafford held nearly 2,000 acres of land in Cheshire and was to become an implacable opponent of the building of the Manchester Ship Canal in the 1880s – it was his agreement to give over the lease of the Old Trafford land at favourable terms which made the exhibition possible.

While it was largely drawn from, and committed to, the area, the organizing committee was in no way parochial. It expressed ambitious hopes for the exhibition, setting it in a national context that went beyond 'the mere gratification of public curiosity, and the giving [of] an intellectual entertainment to the dense population of a particular locality'. As Prince Albert suggested in a letter lending his support to the project, such an intention might well be 'praiseworthy in itself' but the show could accomplish so much more: 'National usefulness', enthused the Prince, 'might be found in the educational direction which may be given to the whole scheme. . . If the collection you propose to form were made to illustrate the history of Art in a chronological and systematic arrangement, it would speak powerfully to the public mind, and enable, in a practical way, the most uneducated eye to gather the lessons which ages of thought and scientific research have attempted to abstract.' Such an achievement, Prince Albert went on, would have not just national, but also international impact, showing off Britain to the world and creating 'for the first time a gallery as no other country could produce'.[5]

The Manchester organizers decided to follow the Prince's advice, and the show was the first large-scale exhibition in Europe to present works chronologically in an attempt to reveal the historical development of art. More usually, art was displayed by theme, or by prominent schools. Here in Manchester, works from northern Europe, for example, were hung opposite artworks of the same period from southern Europe in order to highlight differences in style and technique. The conventional accepted hierarchies were set aside, so that equal emphasis was given to Italian, Spanish, Dutch and German painters. And, as the Prince had suggested, this approach was to prove influential beyond the immediate life of the exhibition. At a time when national museums were struggling to make their displays meaningful, the Art Treasures show became associated with some of the most forward-thinking curatorial practices in Europe. It came to be lauded as a model of 'teaching the mind as well as gratifying the senses', and discussions about the principles of display at the National Gallery, in particular, frequently referred to what was regarded as Manchester's great success.[6] 'Each work of Art appears as a link in a great chain, which receives an influence from the one preceding it, and imparts an influence to the one following,' explained Gustav Waagen admiringly in the exhibition catalogue. 'Each work is thus illustrated and made intelligible, while instruction is combined with enjoyment.'[7] Gradually, the example of the Art Treasures exhibition began to make itself felt in permanent displays across the country. When George Scharf was appointed Secretary of the newly founded National Portrait Gallery in London in the year of the Art Treasures Exhibition, he took with him the experience he had gained as art secretary of the Manchester show and the principles espoused there, and continued to uphold the value of chronological display and clear interpretation. In this way, he set in train the development, on a national scale, of new ways of displaying art inspired by the 1857 event.

Most visitors to the Art Treasures Exhibition, of course, were more concerned with enjoying themselves and seeing a fine spectacle than considering the event's effect on museum policy. And in this too it did not disappoint. On 5 May 1857, Prince Albert opened the show. Season tickets were sold in advance for one guinea; a two-guinea ticket included admission to both the opening and the official visit of Queen Victoria on 29 June. On most days, admission was charged at 1 shilling, although, on Thursdays and for the first ten days of the show, the price was set at half a crown. By the time the doors closed in the middle of October, over 1 million people had passed through the turnstiles. These visitors included European royalty, the politicians Disraeli, Gladstone, Lord Palmerston and the Duke of Wellington, the writers Charles Dickens, Alfred Lord Tennyson, Elizabeth Gaskell and Nathaniel Hawthorne, and critics such as Gustav Waagen and John Ruskin. The Schreibers visited the show on five consecutive days.

Many of the visitors had never before seen any works of art, and certainly had never seen so many gathered together in one place. This was a show to delight ordinary visitors as much as to impress eminent ones. As the organizers had predicted, railways were the key to getting masses of working people to the site: excursions by train were laid on not only from the north-west but from as far afield as Shrewsbury, Leeds, Grimsby and Lincoln. Titus Salt, the Bradford manufacturer and philanthropist, commissioned three trains to take nearly 3,000 of his factory workers to see the exhibition in September, while Thomas Cook, who had arranged trips to both the Great Exhibition in 1851 and the 1855 Paris Exhibition, this time advertised romantic 'moonlight' excursions that arrived in Manchester at dawn.

Such enthusiasm did not convince everyone that the exhibition was a worthwhile venture, however. For those who knew Manchester as a blackened industrial hub of factories and mills, it seemed an incongruous place to show art. Hawthorne, who visited the displays many times, commented that 'it is singular that the great Art-Exhibition should have come to pass in the rudest great town in England'.[8] More antagonistically, the Duke of Devonshire, whose Chatsworth estates lay on the other side of the Pennines and who refused to lend to the show, was sharply dismissive of Manchester's right to an event of any cultural significance: 'What in the world do you want with art in Manchester?' he demanded. 'Why can't you stick to your cotton spinning?'[9] The Duke was a collector himself, with a particular taste for illustrated botanical books, and he was not without philanthropic impulses: he donated land for public gardens in Buxton and endowed the Cavendish Laboratory at Cambridge, where he was Chancellor of the University for thirty years from 1861. But his apparent belief that art did not belong among the lower classes highlights the continuing reluctance of many of the country's wealthiest and most powerful men to countenance any change to the established systems for showing and viewing art. It reveals the lingering fear that accessible events like the Art

Treasures Exhibition, and the public museums they inspired, might in the end encourage unrest and distract workers from the essential business of their 'cotton spinning'. Cavendish recognized that, by taking works out of their more usual context of aristocratic privilege and placing them on open display, the Manchester spectacle was doing something potentially subversive. It was asking private collectors to share the treasures they and their families had amassed over the centuries with the rest of the nation – and not just the genteel part of it.

The Art Treasures Exhibition was a particular triumph for Joseph Mayer. His objects were a celebrated part of the display. He had already played a public role on other notable occasions: he designed the silver trowel with which Sir Philip Egerton, MP, laid the foundation stone for Birkenhead docks in October 1844 and the prize plate for the Royal Mersey Yacht Club. As we have seen, his pieces were well received at the Great Exhibition. Now, at this latest spectacle, he found his collection widely honoured and admired. Scholars asked for information and photographs, and even Gustav Waagen spoke 'of the importance of your great collection'.[10] The review volume that accompanied the exhibition carried illustrations of all of Mayer's pieces along with a description of one of his Wedgwood vases as 'an artistic treasure', an indication that Wedgwood was becoming noticed and valued. It also cited eleven of Mayer's pieces as among the finest examples of ceramic art.[11] In the galleries, a selection of his late antique and Byzantine ivories were laid out chronologically in two cabinets to display the history of European sculpture from the classical period through to the Renaissance, and his collection was praised for its exceptional quality: 'There is an excellent opportunity to make a perfect study of sculpture in monuments of small scale,' suggested Waagen, for example, in his commentary on the displays. 'To do so it is advisable to begin with the many fine antique sculptures in bronze and terracotta from the collection of Mr Hertz, now belonging to Mr Joseph Mayer in Liverpool.'[12]

One piece that attracted particular attention was an almost lifesize bronze statue of the Buddhist goddess of compassion, Guanyin. Another looted treasure, the statue had been taken from the pilgrimage island of Putuo, east of Ningbo near Shanghai in China, by Major William Edie, an officer in the British army during the First Opium War (1839–42). Made during the fifteenth century, it showed the contemplative goddess with twenty-two outstretched arms seated on a carved pedestal. Mayer had acquired it, along with four other devotional statues from Putuo, as part of the Bram Hertz collection. While he was waiting for the statues to be sold at Sotheby's, Mayer displayed the pieces in Manchester, no doubt aware that such publicity would do no harm in raising their profile and boosting his standing as a collector.

With such a showcase, Mayer's reputation continued to grow, within the region and beyond. The museum in Colquitt Street flourished. In 1862, it became a 'Museum of Antiquities', perhaps to emphasize the increasing range of the objects on display, and five years later it was renamed again as the 'Museum of National and Foreign Antiquities', leaving no doubt as to its breadth and ambition. The experiment of an accessible museum had clearly been proved a success, and in 1860, embracing the growing fashion for public museums, Liverpool Town Council opened a splendid purpose-built building with money and land provided by William Brown, a merchant, banker and politician. The neo-classical style of the new building was typical of the emerging Victorian museums. It was grand and imposing, a statement of municipal order, and it also recalled art of the classical period, still regarded as the standard by which all other art was judged. Just as the British Museum concentrated much of its energies and resources on collecting artefacts of the classical civilizations, so the architectural presence of these new museums suggested that they, too, would be displaying equally prestigious objects. Preston, Sheffield, Norwich, Cambridge and Manchester all raised new neo-classical buildings to house their municipal collections and act as temples to the arts. Elsewhere in Europe, neo-classicism was also the style of choice for new museums. In the 1780s, the Prado in Madrid was built to a neo-classical design by Juan de Villanueva; the Altes Museum in Berlin was designed in the same manner by Karl Friedrich Schinkel during the 1820s, using the Stoa in Athens as a model; and the New Hermitage in St Petersburg, designed by the German architect Leo von Klenze, combined elements of the classical, Renaissance and Baroque, all interpreted in a neo-classical style.

At first, the displays in the imposing new Liverpool building consisted almost entirely of natural history specimens, bequeathed from the collection of the 13th Earl of Derby, but, as elsewhere, private collectors soon began to make an increasing diversity of objects available through loans or legacies. In 1867, Mayer decided that the museum was the proper home for the 14,000 pieces of his collection. Roach Smith tried to persuade him that the town was unworthy of anything so splendid: 'There are certain classes to whom the gift of food is nothing, unless at the same time you chew it for them,' he fretted. 'You will find the Liverpool Citizens. . . of this class. Gratitude nor appreciation can never possibly spring from them. . . There are higher and better regions for you.'[13] But Mayer, for once, did not listen. He had made up his mind. Of course, he knew that the galleries of the British Museum were splendid; he had walked the corridors of South Kensington's Brompton Boilers and had admired the displays there. But he was closer to local collectors, curators and scholars and shared their regional pride. He had no desire for his collection to be scattered across the shelves of a large institution. And so Mayer wrote to the Liverpool authorities, offering his museum to the town, so long as they promised 'that the Collection shall be kept together and be known as and called "The Mayer Collection"'.[14]

When his offer was accepted, it seemed as though his future in Liverpool was secured, his reputation and his local roots honoured. 'Your museum has been nobly given and has most deservedly earned you a niche in the temple of Fame,' Joseph Clarke assured him. 'Your name will float down the stream of time.'[15] Some of the more idiosyncratic pieces were set aside by the municipal curators but much of Joseph Mayer's jumble of objects was duly catalogued and displayed, while the Egyptian pieces in particular formed the nucleus of the new, genuinely public, collection that made the Liverpool Museum known across the world, in Mayer's lifetime and today.

CHAPTER FOURTEEN

A Larger World

*J*oseph Mayer had decided it was time to move. With his ambitious collecting, the rooms above his shop were becoming increasingly cramped, overwhelmed by objects, books and papers. But there was also a new belief that he was worthy to take his place among the scholars he so admired. It was time for something grander than a shopkeeper's existence. So in the late 1850s Mayer took a proper house, one of substance and even grandeur, at Dacre Park on the Rock Ferry escarpment, looking across the Mersey from Cheshire to Liverpool. The guise of the country gentleman suited him – and his collecting – so well that just a couple of years later, in 1860, he moved a mile or so south to Bebington, where he established himself in a solid brick-built double-fronted farmhouse with gardens sweeping into open land, the potential for expansion and room for even the most vigorous of collectors and his possessions.

As with his museum, Mayer wanted a name for the house that would inspire, and he called it Pennant House after Thomas Pennant, the eighteenth-century traveller, antiquary, topographer and naturalist. Pennant was an amiable and progressive country squire, erudite, inquisitive, eloquent and fascinated by history.

Born in 1726 at Downing Hall in Flintshire, he wrote on subjects as diverse as earthquakes and the history of quadrupeds, but it was his remarkably popular series of travel books, beginning with *A Tour in Scotland* in 1769, and including accounts of Wales, Snowdon, and a *Journey from Chester to London*, which came to be seen as important records of antiquarian relics. His correspondence with Gilbert White formed the basis for White's *The Natural History and Antiquities of Selborne*. In taking his name for the Bebington farmhouse, Mayer was setting out a vision for his own future. Just as the 'Egyptian Museum' had captured the mystery and romance of the past, so Pennant House promised dignity, refinement and far-reaching scholarship.

In his new home, Mayer surrounded himself with light and bustle and company. He invited his unmarried sister Jane to move in with him as well as their niece Mary Wordley. Two of his nephews, Frederick and Henry Boyle, lived close by; Mayer opened his doors to them, enjoying the commotion of having young men in the house. He took to gardening, and his collecting instincts found a new outlet in rare plants, often fragile and fickle in the northern cold. He held dinners for his friends, entertaining with enthusiasm, and he talked earnestly to local residents, eager to find out what interested them. He was energetic and inventive, boyish even. He should have been happy, but there was something or, more properly, someone missing. There was a place in the house that could not be filled by nephews and nieces, or even by the most sympathetic of friends.

Mayer had never married. He had invested his time, energy and money in his business, and in his collection. But he enjoyed female company and, while he had resisted the best efforts of the Liverpool matrons to fix him up, he had been happy enough to chatter and flirt and dance with their daughters. He was approachable and friendly and he had an eye for the beautiful, the quirky and the rare. While he may have escaped the demands of marriage, however, he could not elude the complications of love. There had been Peggy Harrison. When Mayer came to commission from the Italian sculptor Giovanni Fontana a series of marble reliefs and busts of his friends, it was Peggy who was one of the first to sit for him. The sculpture, Mayer said, would stand as a lasting commemoration to the 'elegant manners, cultivated taste and affectionate friendship', which made Peggy 'a delightful companion in my pilgrimages to shrines of art and antiquities in many lands'.[1]

Very little is known about Peggy Harrison, or her exact relationship with Mayer. She certainly travelled abroad with him extensively, and the marble bust is a clear sign of his admiration and respect. Perhaps it was also a way of making amends. In an age with strict rules of propriety, Peggy may well have expected a proposal of marriage. A woman who travelled with a man to whom she was not married, who accompanied him to archaeological sites and along tangled streets of antique dealers, who studied sales catalogues in cold hotel rooms and who entertained, amused and comforted her companion on long journeys, risked a great deal – presumably for love. There is obvious intimacy in Mayer's evocation of 'a delightful companion' who had travelled so far and for so long with him, and there is clear admiration in his assessment of her manners and character. For a connoisseur like Mayer, too, his judgement of Peggy's 'cultivated taste' signals the highest praise. But perhaps she was too independent to submit to married life with a man like Mayer, or perhaps she was not quite what he was looking for. However it was, their relationship was never formalized, and eventually faltered. By the time Mayer had settled himself into Pennant House, their intimate companionship had somehow come to an end.

As Mayer's circle of friends grew, there were inevitably other women to whom he was attracted, and who understood his devotion to collecting. Not long after moving into Pennant House, he spent some weeks working with Elizabeth Meteyard, who was writing a biography of Josiah Wedgwood. Elizabeth was bright and appealing in her middle age. She was studious and she shared Mayer's taste in ceramics and his fascination with the past. Mayer was delighted to be in such company and gave Elizabeth free access to all his papers, helped fund her research and offered her the benefit of introductions to his long list of useful acquaintances, including members of the Wedgwood family. Elizabeth also noted demurely, that he 'permitted me to work for a fortnight under his personal guidance' and entertained her with stories.[2] There is no doubt that he found her a charming and knowledgeable companion. He may, for a moment, have thought of more. But Elizabeth had a career and was as committed to her work as Mayer was to his collection. Her biography was soon to be followed by five other books on Wedgwood. Making her way as a professional writer, she contributed articles and short stories to numerous periodicals under the pen-name 'Silverpen' and she also found success as a popular novelist. She could not spend too much time at Pennant House, no matter how pleasant it was, and she was unwilling to be distracted by Mayer. For each of her ceramics books, she drew on the resources of Mayer's collection, and over the years she became a familiar face in Bebington, attending the opening of an art exhibition there in September 1871 and visiting again to research Wedgwood books that were published in 1873 and 1875. Such visits seem to have been no more than an agreeable interlude for them both, and all too quickly she returned to London. Meteyard clearly retained a lifelong admiration for Mayer and his work, however, and at her death in 1879 her will bequeathed all her personal papers to Liverpool Museum; the wish was not respected by her executors.

In the summer of 1863, Mayer's sixtieth year, he finally became engaged. He wrote delightedly to all his closest friends, announcing his forthcoming marriage with pride, and they wrote back in turn, expressing their surprise and sharing in his pleasure. 'I am very happy to think that you have partially weaned yourself from things antique... that you have distracted your attention from coats of mail and bent it upon crinoline,' wrote Joseph Clarke, adding that he was 'in high glee at the pleasure of paying my most ardent but humble respects' to the new Mrs Mayer.[3] The wedding plans, it seems, were quickly set – there was little reason for delay. At Mayer's age, he could dispense with the reticence of youth.

We don't know who it was that Mayer was so close to marrying. All we know is that she lived in Kent, some 300 miles away. It is possible that Mayer had known her a long time and I believe he may have met her during the negotiations to buy the Faussett collection ten years earlier when he had spent time in and around Heppington. He may have been wooing her for a decade, or he may have had to shelve his advances until the way finally became clear on the death of a father or a husband. Nor do we know why the marriage never took place. There might have been last-minute nerves or a disagreement. The lady who Mayer had chosen for a wife may have faltered at the thought of uprooting herself and moving so far from familiar things. They may have been cheated, in the end, by death, leaving Mayer to mourn the woman he should have married. All we know for sure is that he was left alone.

The Victorians were inclined to think of avid collectors as life's losers. Although there was money to be made from collecting, and a certain prestige too for those who, like Mayer, managed to earn a prominent position within the community, it was difficult to resist the idea that a singular devotion to things was the mark of a man who had failed in other ways. Collecting was increasingly being seen as a means of expressing identity – or of compensating for personal shortfalls. In literature, the stereotype of the collector was associated with the withdrawn, the anti-social and the strange, like Wilkie Collins's Mr Fairlie in *The Woman in White*, a character portrayed as living in 'profound seclusion' and completely preoccupied with his possessions.[4] In popular journals like *Punch*, the collector was drawn as weak, obsessive and comical. A cartoon from the *Punch Almanack* of 1875 shows a 'pale enthusiast' in the grips of 'Chronic Chinamania (incurable)' and so absorbed by his collection that he is apparently oblivious to the charms of the young women encircling him. Similalry, a set of French caricatures features M. de Menussard, an imaginary collector who lives alone, never goes out, has no friends and is 'a little old man, dry, wrinkled, worn down, patched up'.[5] Even among collectors themselves, there could be ambiguity and embarrassment about their activity: *The Connoisseur: A Collector's Journal and Monthly Review* noted defensively that its readers might well display 'amiable weaknesses', and might even be in the grip of an 'unwise but never despicable passion'.[6]

The idea that collecting was somehow 'unwise' harked back to a more widespread discomfort with art, and how it might encourage potentially disruptive, or even immoral, pleasures. The behaviour of avant-garde artists such as the Pre-Raphaelites only reinforced this uneasiness. In 1850, John Everett Millais' work, *Christ in the House of His Parents*, was attacked as blasphemous, while the unconventional lives and loves of the painters attracted continual attention and at times caused outrage: John Millais' relationship with Effie, the wife of John Ruskin, her subsequent divorce and remarriage to Millais was the subject of a public scandal. Those of a religious turn of mind could be suspicious of art's appeal to the senses, and its portrayal of unpredictable emotional and psychological states. The emphasis on the utility of art objects – Henry Cole's commitment to proving their relevance to industry and manufacturing – was one way of divorcing them from desire or sensual pleasure, removing them from the domain of aesthetic pleasure to the less unsettling and more pragmatic structure of commerce.

The anxieties about such unhealthy passions were particularly evident when the Victorians thought about men collecting the decorative arts or antiquarians in their cluttered studies. Science collections were typically regarded as scholarly and progressive; paintings, sculpture and classical antiquities were respectable and had long been valued by the leisured and landed classes. Robinson's fondness for historical works, especially Renaissance masterpieces, was considered properly intellectual and cultured – but a preoccupation with what became known as the 'lesser' arts was more suspect. Modern manufactures carried the taint of the factory and warehouse; china, glass, silverware and textiles were a matter for household affairs and were associated with excess, decoration and femininity. As we have seen with the collecting of china, men who chose to collect these things risked being seen as odd, emotionally deficient or even effeminate.

For some Victorians – and for later psychoanalysts such as Sigmund Freud – there was something about collecting that suggested abnormality, sexual impotence and personal failure.[7] Writers like Henry James and George Meredith peopled their novels with collectors who turned to their objects as a substitute for love. In James' *The Portrait of a Lady*, the relationships of one of the central characters, Gilbert Osmond, are described in terms of collecting: 'We knew that he was fond of originals, of rarities, of the superior, the exquisite. . . he perceived a new attraction in the idea of taking to himself a young lady. . . in his collection of choice objects.' Osmond's emotional inadequacy and cold sexuality are directly linked to his collecting, which is seen as an impulse that disengages him from the more normal passions of those around him. During the collapse of his marriage, he turns to his objects, breaking off from an emotional scene with his wife to study some of his favourite pieces: 'He got up, as he spoke, and walked to the chimney, where he stood a moment bending his eye, as if he had seen them for the first time, on the delicate specimens of rare porcelain with which it was covered. He took up a small cup and held it in his hand. . .' Elsewhere in the same novel, another character, Ned Rosier, pursues love in a similarly frigid way, unable to dissociate his collecting from his emotional life: 'She was admirably finished,' he notes, on finding the woman of his dreams. 'She had had the last touch: she was really a consummate piece. He thought of her in amorous meditation a good deal as he might have thought of a Dresden-china shepherdess.' In *The Egoist*, Meredith explores similar ideas. The wealthy aristocrat at the heart of the novel, Sir Willoughby Patterne, is a collector. His overwhelming urge to collect people as well as things is presented not in terms of sexual desire but as a more insidious and general obsession with control. His collecting impulses become all-embracing – and dangerous – reducing him finally to 'a stone man'.[8] With such precedents all around in popular culture, it seems likely that knowing nods would have been exchanged in Liverpool drawing rooms when a man like Mayer, failing to marry, immersed himself instead in his collection.

With the knowledge that he would never now be a family man, Mayer threw himself so vigorously into collecting that, despite its size, Pennant House was soon full of objects, papers, letters and ledgers. Having already given his Egyptian Museum to the public, he now accumulated a second collection, one that was even more personal. In the quiet garden rooms that might in other circumstances have been used by his wife, he accumulated packets of autographs from famous people whom he admired. In cabinets and on tables were displayed over 200 engraved gems and rings. There were illuminated manuscripts, wood engravings, ivories, enamels and embroideries. There were calendars of plays performed at Covent Garden and the Theatre Royal, Drury Lane, during the early 1740s and the seventeenth-century manuscript

of John Crowne's play *Darius, King of Persia*. The greatest solace
was all kinds of papers and objects relating to pottery.

The house began to feel small under the pressure of the
expanding collection, and so Mayer was forced to extend. First a
two-storey bay was added, but it was almost immediately filled
and, just a few months later, in the autumn of 1873, Mayer added
a new wing on each side of the house, as well as a high tower. He
set himself the monumental task of writing a history of art
in England, drawing on his collection for material, and he
collaborated with his nephew Frederick Boyle on two books: *Early
Exhibitions of Art in Liverpool: With some Notes for a Memoir of
George Stubbs R.A.*, which he published in 1876, and *Memoirs of
Thomas Dodd, William Upcott and George Stubbs R.A.*, three years
later. The great art history was never completed and neither of
Mayer's published collaborations was particularly remarkable:
both were almost certainly ghosted by Boyle on his uncle's behalf.
It was a much less ambitious work, a paper on the 'History of the
art of pottery in Liverpool', first contributed to the *Transactions
of the Historic Society of Lancashire and Cheshire* in 1855, and revised
by Mayer in 1873 during this period of learned writing, that
proved that his lifelong lack of confidence in his own scholarly
credentials was misplaced. It became the definitive text on the
subject, and is still significant today.

As the years passed and he retired from his business, finally, at the
age of seventy-one, as his friends became too old to travel, too
tired to collect or too ill to spend time with him – and as loneliness
proved ever harder to keep at bay – Mayer must have seemed at
times like the archetypal collector, shuffling around rooms piled
high with the past, obsessed with the minutiae of history. But he
was not one to shut himself away. His collecting had always been
a sociable activity, a way to make friends and meet colleagues, and
even in old age he displayed no desire to become reclusive. His

nature was philanthropic and he spent his last years looking beyond the collection at Pennant House. When the evenings closed in, quiet and dark, he relished the hours reading his papers or writing notes, but he was proud, too, that his days were active and generous and useful. The village of Bebington was thriving, and Mayer was, by and large, responsible for its orderly growth.

With the construction of the railways and new roads, and the introduction of a ferry boat link with Liverpool, the population of Bebington more than trebled between 1841 and 1871. But whereas, in cities, the rapid mid-century rise in the number of inhabitants frequently resulted in overcrowded slums and desperate poverty, Bebington's growth saw an influx of professional people, rather than unskilled labourers, and, thanks to Mayer, there was a sustained programme of investment. 'Without losing its rustic air, the village has gained advantages such as many a town might envy,' boasted a local paper, *The Standard*, in 1878. 'A very few years since. . . it had neither gas nor pavements, its younger population went barefooted and women fetched water from two miles distance.' Now, however, the paper noted proudly, 'Bebington may be held up as a model village [and] the honour is chiefly due to Mr Joseph Mayer.'[9]

Mayer's involvement with the local people started simply enough, and had its roots in his collection. Arms, armour and things military had always fascinated him. At the age of twelve, he had a brief taste of army life, marching from his home in Newcastle-under-Lyme to Macclesfield as a drummer boy with the 34th Regiment of Foot in the weeks before Waterloo. As an adult, flintlocks, swords, daggers, axes, crossbows, suits of armour, powder flasks and spurs were prominent in his museum and he developed a particular interest in the history of local defence. In 1860, he was appointed Commanding Officer of the Liverpool volunteer borough guard. Four years later, he established a volunteer company of the 1st Cheshire Rifles: he became captain of the 4th Bebington Company, which he supported financially and presented with two challenge cups for shooting. Within six months, over a hundred men had enrolled to be part of Mayer's troop and he took satisfaction from serving as their commander. Mayer enjoyed the expeditions: the would-be soldiers camped together at Hooton, further along the Wirral, telling stories in the smoke of camp fires, testing themselves against the cold and trapping animals for food.

The 4th Bebington Company was one of many. The Victorian volunteer movement was a phenomenon which began in the 1860s, when fears of war with France were at their height. In 1858, reprisals were expected after a failed assassination attempt on Napoleon III was traced back to exiled French conspirators based in England. In March 1860, France annexed Nice and Savoy. Such territorial ambitions on the part of the French raised the spectre of invasion and were regarded as a threat to national security. A programme of coastal fortification led to the construction of defences such as Fort Nelson, near Portsmouth, and many towns began to establish local volunteer Rifle Corps.

The idea was an eighteenth-century one: volunteers were called upon between 1797 and 1805, before the Battle of Trafalgar brought to an end, for that period at least, the French naval threat. To a new generation, it proved a popular and sociable way to be seen to do one's duty. According to the report of a Royal Commission in 1862, the Volunteer Force consisted of 162,681 men including engineers, light horse and mounted rifles and, by the 1870s, one in twelve men throughout England had joined up.[10] Across the country, drill halls, training grounds and rifle ranges were quickly established. The attraction, as at Bebington, was not just military protection: musical, sporting and recreational activities were commonly organized for members, local teams travelled to take on rival corps, and men from all walks of life came together for target shooting, cricket and football. Each corps had its own character, depending on the area in which it was based and the type of men it attracted. One of the more well known was the 38th Middlesex (Artists') Rifle Volunteers, founded in 1860 by an art student called Edward Sterling. Consisting largely of painters, sculptors, engravers, musicians, architects and actors, the corps' first commanders were the painters Henry Wyndham Phillips and Frederic Leighton, and the regiment became celebrated in time as it attracted members such as William Morris, John Everett Millais, Edward Burne-Jones and Dante Gabriel Rossetti. The battalion was not finally disbanded until 1945: during the First World War, over 15,000 men fought under its banner, including the poets Wilfred Owen and Edward Thomas, the artist Paul Nash and the sculptor Frank Dobson.

As Mayer got to know his men, discovering how they lived and what it was they valued, he gradually immersed himself in their welfare. It was a small step from the needs of the volunteers of the 1st Cheshire Rifles to the needs of their families. Convinced that physical activity and fresh air were to everyone's benefit, Mayer founded bowling, cricket, quoits and football clubs, as well as starting a horticultural society and setting aside land for allotments. But he also heard from the men in his company how difficult and uncertain working life could be, and how everyday chores were unnecessarily exhausting and demoralizing. So he raised funds for a village hospital and campaigned for the introduction of gas and water. The obvious next move, in the tradition of the great Victorian patrons, was, of course, to open a school, but there was already a schoolmaster in the village doing an adequate, if modest, job, and, in any case, Mayer believed strongly in the value of informal, self-directed education, the kind of learning that had allowed him to take his place alongside scholars. He chose instead to invest in a public library. 'He who reads lives in a larger world, and has a knowledge and grasp of

251

possibilities far wider than he who is without the art, and even prospers when the latter would succumb,' he informed the village, and to make this larger world of literacy available to as many local people as possible, he rented a house, stocked it with 20,000 volumes on travel, poetry, history, natural sciences and art, as well as a good number of novels, appointed a librarian and a team of volunteers, established evening opening hours for study after work and set out the arrangements for borrowing books.[11]

The library was an instant success, and an extra room had to be provided almost immediately. Three years later, in 1869, Mayer had the opportunity to buy a farmhouse and barn alongside Pennant House and by January 1870 he had created a public garden, with walks of chestnut trees, a grand new reading room brightly lit with gas burners, and a public hall for art exhibitions and lectures. He was clearly joining the philanthropic trend of his age, aligning himself with wealthy industrialists and merchants across the country who were founding public facilities and open spaces. From the ambitious model villages at Saltaire, outside Bradford, and Bournville, near Birmingham, to smaller gifts like the Derby Arboretum, England's first public park, created for the people of the Derby in 1840 by textile manufacturer Joseph Strutt, philanthropic Victorians were reshaping the urban landscape. Mayer's projects were respectable and predictable outlets for his energies, positioning him at the heart of Victorian society. But his generosity was not simply a product of conformism. Mayer was a genuinely kind man; he was not interested in gestures. He envisaged sturdy and practical facilities for the young and the old, for learning and for entertainment, not an empty monument to his wealth.

All of this, he achieved. 'All classes meet at the library, farmer's boys in corduroy and heiresses in sable, clergy of the church and little girls of their Sunday School, servants and masters,' noted *The Standard*. Many villagers walked four or five miles or more with their families to use the library and 'each night a crowd assembles around the door as if it were a theatre, waiting with patience' until the readers could be admitted to browse the shelves.[12] Mayer was spoken of fondly and with respect. Far from shutting himself off with his things, he reached out energetically to the community, to the benefit of all in Bebington.

There was satisfaction in seeing the village thrive around him, and not a little pleasure in being greeted so warmly by local people. As the pains of age grew sharper and his breath came shorter, Mayer delighted in sitting by the counter at the library, helping the staff issue readers' tickets or watching from the terrace of Pennant House as local boys gathered up the chestnuts in the autumn. With his museum apparently in the safe hands of the Liverpool town council, Mayer made arrangements that, on his death, the objects in Pennant House should be sold to finance the public projects in Bebington. He left clear instructions detailing the sale, and he established a trust to manage the resulting funds and look after the necessary day-to-day administration. With one collection safely stowed for posterity, he could afford to use the other for more practical purposes: the sale of the Pennant House objects would, he knew, reach out into the future, imprinting his name on the village he had adopted as home. Everything was settled. He would leave the best of both worlds, the Liverpool Museum and the Bebington facilities, which, he believed, would last. His memorial would be secure. There would be no need of further portraits.

Fashion, Fine Dining and Forgeries: Dealing in Society

MURRAY MARKS

CHAPTER FIFTEEN

Rossetti's Peacock

The carriage pulled up quietly outside number 16 Cheyne Walk. Everything about this eighteenth-century Chelsea street was hushed and genteel. A light mist drifted up from the Thames and the bells from the medieval Old Church were subdued. Murray Marks paid the driver and stood for a moment on the wide stone pavement looking across the river. It was 1863, and Cheyne Walk was one of London's most desirable addresses. In 1810, Elizabeth Gaskell had been born at number 93 and in the early decades of the century, Isambard Kingdom Brunel had lived for nearly twenty years at number 98, a divided seventeenth-century townhouse. Admiral William Henry Smith, founder of the Royal Geographic Society and Vice-President of the Royal Society had lived at number 3 in the 1840s and 1850s, while next door to him, at number 4, was the Scottish painter William Dyce. Further along the street, J. M. W. Turner had lived quietly since the mid-1840s, before dying in 1851 at number 119. At 101, James McNeill Whistler had recently arrived. It was a street of celebrity, a place of invention, creativity and achievement, and Murray Marks had come to visit another of its famous inhabitants, the poet and artist Dante Gabriel Rossetti. He relit his cigar, settled his hat on his head after the ride and made his way through the high gate to the tall, flat-faced white house.

Marks became aware of a strange squawking, something like the shriek of a banshee. He stopped and looked around. But the citizens of Cheyne Walk, apparently unflustered, remained in their houses, and for a moment all was quiet again. Then the squawking continued; as Marks pulled the doorbell, it was louder and shriller than ever. It was coming from within the house, he could tell that, but he could not place the sound. He had not heard anything like it before; it was harsh and otherworldly; it did not belong. But when the door was opened to him, Marks saw nothing terrifying or supernatural. Nor did he notice, at first, the wide entrance hall with its stuccoed ceiling and sweeping stairway, because the source of the sound was showing off and Marks was confronted with the dazzling blue of a disgruntled peacock, in full display, flashing green and gold in the morning light from the street, and confronting a kangaroo.

Marks was not as surprised as he might have been. He had heard about the menagerie. In this most elegant of streets, Rossetti kept a zoo: among its inhabitants, described by his brother William, were: 'a Pomeranian puppy named Punch, a grand Irish deerhound named Wolf, a barn-owl named Jessie, another owl named Bobby. . . rabbits, dormice, hedgehogs, two successive wombats, a Canadian marmot or woodchuck, an ordinary marmot, armadillos, kangaroos, wallabies, a deer, a white mouse with her brood, a racoon, squirrels, a mole, peacocks, wood-owls, Virginian owls, Chinese horned owls, a jackdaw, laughing jackasses (Australian kingfishers), undulated grass-parakeets, a talking grey parrot, a raven, chameleons, green lizards, and Japanese salamanders'. It was a haphazard arrangement, and the collection of exotic creatures was not easy to control. The tent constructed in the garden to house the animals was by no means secure; William Rossetti wrote in his memoirs of how 'one or other bird would get drowned' or 'the dormice would fight and kill one another' or, worse still, the racoon 'followed his ordinary practice of burrowing, [and] turned up from under the hearthstone of a neighbour's kitchen, to the serious dismay of the cook, who opined that, if he was not the devil, there was no accounting for what he could possibly be'.[1]

Undaunted, Marks tried to take his unusual surroundings in his stride. The obvious eccentricity was unlike his own steady, respectable home, as though he had stepped over the threshold from the ordinary to the avant-garde. But there were also more familiar things to draw his eye; despite the shuffles and smells of strange animals, Marks admired the high ceilings, tall windows and elegant proportions of Rossetti's panelled rooms, strikingly painted in deep colours. Above all, he could not fail to notice Rossetti's idiosyncratic collecting. The house was full of bric-a-brac picked up at junkshops, an uncoordinated assemblage of brass and pewter, oriental rugs, velvets and chintzes; a jumble of musical instruments valued not for how they played, but for how they looked; Sheraton furniture and Spanish cabinets set alongside worthless junk; and banks upon banks of mirrors, reflecting the city light into the rooms.

Marks and Rossetti soon became friends. Rossetti had a collector's instincts. He liked to surround himself with the curious and the rare, and to talk excitably and at length about his finest objects. He could forget himself so absolutely in his curiosity that he was capable of ignoring the dictates of etiquette: upending a porcelain dish at a dinner party to check the maker's marks on the bottom, he promptly upset a salmon all over the tablecloth. But his fascination with collecting and display needed a reliable and respectable foil, and this is what drew him to Murray Marks. Marks was modest and quiet, reticent with strangers, and distinctly unflamboyant. He had a calming influence on the long-haired, ostentatious Rossetti. He was reliable and sympathetic, happy to help create the rooms the artist wanted with the minimum of fuss. Theirs was a marriage of opposites: Rossetti was excitable and unconventional; Marks was studious and proper. They were brought together by the desire to discover and acquire lovely objects, to dress Rossetti's home with the finest furniture and ornaments, to create a Pre-Raphaelite interior that would provide the perfect backdrop for the preening peacock.

It took a long time for the house at Cheyne Walk to be completed. Rossetti was strong-willed and unpredictable, and could be difficult to do business with. His life was full of distractions and often hectic and fractured. The Pre-Raphaelite brotherhood of painters that he had founded with John Everett Millais and Holman Hunt in the late 1840s was becoming increasingly popular for its aesthetic principles, and increasingly notorious for its extravagant lifestyles. By 1863, when Marks called on the Cheyne Walk house, Rossetti was working on a series of jewel-like watercolours and experimenting with the highly decorated, richly coloured oil paintings of beautiful, faintly exotic women that were to make him famous. His wife and muse Elizabeth had recently died after taking an overdose of laudanum, an opium-based, highly addictive painkiller that was commonly prescribed at the time for ailments ranging from headaches to tuberculosis. He was sharing his home, on and off, with his brother William, his mistress and model Fanny Cornforth, the controversial poet Algernon Swinburne, and the writer George Meredith, whose own wife had recently left him for another of Rossetti's artist friends. He was suffering from ever-lengthening bouts of depression, drank heavily and was addicted to chloral hydrate, a sedative and hypnotic drug, marketed for insomnia, that would eventually wreck his health.

Not surprisingly in the circumstances, Rossetti's collecting could be erratic. Marks might send notice of a striking table, or a pretty writing desk, only to have his note returned if his client were lost in a misanthropic haze of drugs and depression. For long weeks, Rossetti would refuse any guests, before a sudden obsession with a particular piece had him hounding Marks for information. His demands were exacting, and he expected his dealer to be thoroughly diligent on his behalf. He would think nothing of giving Marks apparently impossible commissions: 'get me two thimble-shaped lids for two little round pots I have', he demanded on one occasion, sending Murray to scour the length and breadth of Holland for just the right lids, of the exact shape and size he required.[2]

But Marks was patient and amenable, and prepared to ride the peaks and troughs of his client's moods. He found Rossetti 'the most amusing and at the same time the most intellectual man I ever met', and he was conscientious in his quests on Rossetti's behalf.[3] His friendship with the artist flourished. Marks commissioned portraits of his wife, her face blooming in Rossetti's characteristic red chalk, her long neck and full lips, her flowing hair, typical of Pre-Raphaelite models. Rossetti borrowed objects from Marks to use in his paintings: a mirror from the drawing-room fireplace, a blue jar. And as he mixed his paints, blending and reblending to capture a particular shade, he sent Marks on errands to the markets of Covent Garden to find iris or tulips of a particular colour or a lemon tree in a china pot. When Rossetti's funds dried up, as they were apt to do, Marks would pay some of his bills or negotiate discounts until the crisis passed. He could be found at auctions, bidding up the price of Rossetti's works so that his friend could be sure of a profit. In particularly hard times, he bought parts of Rossetti's collection, at a good price, and kept them safe. Years later, in 1882, Marks was one of the few mourners who made the journey to Rossetti's bleak funeral on the Kent coast, where he had gone to escape both his paralysing addiction and his creditors.

* * *

Despite the evident closeness between the two men, Marks never forgot that the relationship was primarily founded upon the business of collecting and dealing. It was this attention to commercial opportunity, partnered with a sensitivity to the nuances of fashion and the market – and hard-nosed ambition – which made Marks in time, perhaps inevitably, a successful man. He was part of a new generation of art dealers that was changing the collectors' world. Born in 1840, he was a near contemporary of both Joseph Joel Duveen, Charlotte Schreiber's rival, who was born just three years later, and of the prominent and respected art dealer Asher Wertheimer, born in 1844. Like many other London dealers, all three came from Jewish émigré families: Marks and Duveen had roots in Holland, Wertheimer's father was German. They fell outside the social circles that filled museum posts and gentlemen's clubs. They were born into an established community that stretched across all the major cities of Europe, one that viewed art as a business enterprise, that combined connoisseurship with commercialism, and was open about the fact that collecting was a market activity.

Marks, Duveen and Wertheimer were all socially accomplished, knowledgeable and astute. While they had been raised in business families, their love of art was both genuine and inquisitive. All three combined a life dealing in historic works with befriending and supporting emerging young artists. Duveen happily loaned pieces from his showroom to furnish the backdrops to paintings, providing Millais in particular with a number of valuable tapestries; John Singer Sargent dined weekly with the Wertheimers at their house in Connaught Place and painted twelve portraits of the family which were left to the National Gallery after Wertheimer's death in 1918. As social outsiders, they mixed not with the gentry and royalty of Robinson's acquaintance but more commonly with an avant-garde artistic circle that challenged the establishment. But they were also careful to maintain a precious air of respectability that attracted the wealthiest and most influential clients. By the 1860s and 1870s, when all three dealers were at their peak, they had become some of the most powerful men in the collecting world.

Marks had known connoisseurs and collectors since his earliest childhood, helping out in the shop which his father, Emanuel Marks, had opened around 1850 on London's Oxford Street, on the edge of the antiques heartland of Victorian Soho. He was a precocious child: by the age of ten, he was said to be fond of chattering happily to his father's customers, discussing fine points of art history, comparing the masterpieces of the past and arguing the case for forgotten painters. He developed an interest in Chinese art and pestered his father, unsuccessfully, to allow him to undertake a tour of the Far East. A few years later, he attended one of Europe's leading universities in Frankfurt, studying Spinoza and exploring the art of France, Italy, Austria and Germany as he holidayed with his friend, the philosopher Arthur Schopenhauer. He was unusually well educated for a dealer – erudite, articulate and cultured. As we have seen, Duveen's training in the docks of Hull was more practical, and Wertheimer learned his trade in his father's showroom. Marks, on the other hand, was an intellectual and a connoisseur; he could stand his own in society and, according to Rossetti, his 'taste amounted to genius'.[4]

After returning to London from Frankfurt, Marks settled to business, joining his father in the expanding Oxford Street shop that shared a building with Pickford & Co., then just starting out in the removals trade. In the early 1860s, he was conscientious and dutiful, but to a young man with ambition, Emanuel Marks' approach to trade seemed dull and lifeless. There was no sparkle to it. Marks, meanwhile, enjoyed nights at the theatre, spending hours at stage doors waiting for late-night actresses; talking politics and poetry and music with noisy young men; visiting artist's studios with the fashionable crowd for private views. He was warm and witty. He impressed with his learning, but wore his knowledge lightly. He was stylish and modern and smart. And so, despite his father's disapproval, Marks edged his way into the heart of society, to the dinners and dances and parties that mattered. He scoured his father's client list for the names he needed to know; he pressed for invitations; he was seen at all the right occasions. Before long, he had a bohemian circle of influential friends. As well as becoming part of the Pre-Raphaelite coterie, he was close to other men whose names dotted the fashionable journals and pages of *Punch*: the satirical artist and dandy George Cruikshank, who had once received a bribe of £100 from George III 'not to caricature His Majesty in any immoral situation'; the son of Charles Dickens, a lively, and often inebriated, socialite; and *The Times* journalist, and soon-to-be actor and entertainer, George Grossmith.

With this somewhat outré crowd, Marks kept late hours and attended all the new shows. But he did not forget himself, nor his profession. He was, even as a carousing young man, decorous and slightly reserved. He continued to work diligently, sensing that he was on the verge of making his business one of the most sought after and desirable in London. So, while he might on occasion be fashionable and frivolous, he was also comfortable assuming the character of scholar and intellectual on evenings spent with John Ruskin, or Charles Hercules Read, who worked with Augustus Franks at the British Museum. He took care of his credentials, continuing to read and study widely, and developing links with dealers abroad. And he discovered that even his more ostentatious friends and clients could be useful in sustaining a scholarly network: both Rossetti and James McNeill Whistler belonged to the Fine Arts Club, connecting Marks to the most prominent and active collectors of his day.

In a campaign to attract the kind of customers he wanted,

Marks sought to shed the stereotype of the grimy backstreet dive that Dickens had featured in *The Old Curiosity Shop*; the 'receptacles for old and curious things which seem to crouch in odd corners of this town and to hide their musty treasures from the public eye in jealousy and distrust'. He aimed instead for the bright and accessible, the professional but unstuffy, creating a business which would woo the fashionable without alienating serious collectors and the museums. He began by reinventing the Marks name, and with it the character of the art dealer. By 1862, the Marks entry in the London business directory, which for years had simply read 'curiosity dealer', was puffed and polished, and had become instead 'Importer of antique furniture, Sèvres, Dresden, oriental china and curiosities'. It was a statement of Marks' intent and ambition: the business was no longer just about unidentified 'curiosities' nor was he simply a 'dealer', tainted with overtones of the noisier, dirtier London trades. He was an 'Importer', a man who travelled, discerning and learned and slightly exotic; a man with contacts. The new entry associated him with the best and most desirable of European objects and, by association, the leading European dealers. And it kept him ahead of the competition. About the same time, Joseph Joel Duveen was similarly remarketing his own business, printing new stationery as 'Importer of Antique China, Silver and Works of Art' and looking to move to London from Hull, visiting premises on both Oxford Street and Bond Street. In the end, Duveen had to postpone the London move until 1876, but Marks was no doubt aware that other dealers were looking to expand and modernize, and that to succeed he had to find new ways of doing things.

While the description of the business was a good place to start, Marks was eager to go further. He tried talking to his father, making suggestions for ways in which they could improve and update the shop, but Emanuel Marks was suspicious of fashion and would not countenance change. So it was after his father set off to Europe for a long trip in 1864 that Marks took his next step, closing a deal on premises in stylish Sloane Street in south-west London, converting them into a showroom and, with a few selected objects carefully displayed, setting himself up alone, as 'Murray Marks, dealer in works of art'. The showroom at 21 Sloane Street was the epitome of fashionable chic: it was everything Emanuel's old shop was not. Its broad windows glistened in the evening gas lights; its heavy door was freshly painted and latticed in gold. The chattering window shoppers, parading between Chelsea and Knightsbridge, could not help but notice the new premises, while the artists and poets and collectors of Marks' crowd were delighted to have somewhere new to be seen. And Marks, sensing what might draw them in, chose for the focus of his display the intense colour and bold forms, the exotic oriental patterns, of blue-and-white china.

Rossetti's raucous bird, boldly displaying in the Cheyne Walk entrance hall, was a living, squawking testament to the popularity of the deep blues and glittering eye of the peacock feather. From curtains to carpets, from wallpapers to writing papers, the peacock motif became ubiquitous in fashionable homes as a symbol of the avant-garde and the daring, a motif for those wanting to throw off the mustiness of the mid-century and stand at the vanguard of a changing taste. It was an icon for the poets, writers, artists and designers clustering under the banners of the Pre-Raphaelites, the Aesthetes and the Art Nouveau that, by the end of the century, would be making claims for new ways of representing the world. It was beautiful and ephemeral, detached from establishment arguments about the importance of utility, and so the perfect symbol for those wanting to celebrate and collect art for its own sake. 'Remember that the most beautiful things in the world are the most useless; peacocks and lilies for example,' urged John Ruskin in *The Stones of Venice*.

Alongside the peacock feathers – on Whistler's mantelpiece and in Rossetti's parlour, in William Morris's country house at Kelmscott Manor and in Oscar Wilde's university rooms – stood the blue-and-white china that Marks' new shop was showcasing. In his premises on Sloane Street, he was pioneering a trend and promoting one of the biggest collecting crazes of the Victorian age. The fashion for pots and plates with willowy Japanese and Chinese designs would soon create an apparently insatiable market; the homes of the stylish rich and the aspirational middle classes would soon be full of themed rooms, extravagantly decorated in an oriental style with prints, fans, screens and matting and with the distinctive blue-and-white china taking pride of place.

The techniques of making a pure white ceramic with cobalt-blue decoration beneath the glaze had been introduced to China from the Middle East as early as the ninth century. By the fourteenth and fifteenth centuries, it was already being exported to Europe: during the Yuan dynasty (1271–1368) for example, China was part of the Mongol empire that controlled much of Asia, and blue-and-white travelled swiftly to the Mediterranean on its expanding maritime networks. By the end of the seventeenth century, sophisticated pieces from the K'ang-hsi period (1662–1722) were becoming available to the wealthiest collectors, and the Dutch East India Company was investing heavily in the profitable trading routes that supplied the growing demand in Europe. Blue-and-white became enormously desirable, a way for rich collectors to display their elegance and wealth. The royalty and nobility of Europe created a huge demand and fine examples became so highly prized that they appear in many seventeenth- and eighteenth-century paintings, either as the backdrop to portraits or extravagant allegories, or as subjects in their own right. As early as 1514, Giovanni Bellini's *Feast of the Gods* showed a satyr and nymph serving fruit to the gods from blue-and-white

Chinese bowls. A century later, blue-and-white was even more widely in evidence. The Dutch painter Jan Treck painted a still life in 1649 with two blue-and-white bowls (probably Ming), while in the 1650s Willam Claesz Heda, another Dutchman, evoked the luxury lifestyle of the seventeenth-century merchant with a still life of lobster, crafted gold goblets and blue-and-white; both works are now in the National Gallery in London.

With a guaranteed market, many pieces were designed and made specifically for export. Thousands of dinner services were ordered in China directly from Europe: drawings of a family's coat of arms would be sent out to China to be copied on to the porcelain which was then shipped back. Traditional oriental subjects were supplemented by those intended to appeal to European taste: Buddhist gods gave way to Tyrolean dancers and pictures of Adam and Eve; cranes and monkeys were replaced by pheasants and dogs. Taking account of the European fashion for tea-drinking, traditional Chinese patterns were used to decorate Western-style wares – European tea caddies, cups with handles and saucers, and matching milk jugs. European manufacturers, too, were keen to exploit the fashion, and worked hard to perfect techniques similar to those traditionally used in the Far East. By the middle of the eighteenth century, factories in England and the Netherlands were able to produce their own blue-and-white china. Delftware, from Holland, was particularly popular, and most of the major eighteenth-century collections included both imported Chinese ceramics and Delft. But, although the new sources made blue-and-white less exclusive, they did not dent the fashion for oriental-style china, and the demand fuelled some of the earliest mass-production techniques of the Industrial Revolution. By the nineteenth century, blue-and-white was no longer the preserve of the very rich. The more local supply, and the increasing wealth of the middle classes, meant that even relatively modest homes could boast at least a few pieces for display, while the effect of blue-and-white en masse delighted those with a taste for flamboyant decorative schemes.

Collections of blue-and-white varied enormously, from refined and extremely valuable collections of ancient Chinese pieces to mass-market versions produced to cash in on the trend. Some collectors, like Rossetti and Marks, were knowledgeable and scholarly but there were many others who cared less about the provenance of individual objects than about the lavishness of the display they could create at home. For these collectors, fashion was the driving force. The hierarchy of objects and collections tended, of course, to follow class lines: the wealthier, more aristocratic collectors set their sights on fine-quality Chinese and delftware; the enthusiastic collectors of the middle classes often settled for more ordinary, mass-produced examples.

Marks had fallen for the sinewy decoration and pure glazes of blue-and-white during his childhood studies of Chinese art. And with clients like Rossetti he could share his pleasure in ancient pieces, comparing the subtle developments between periods and dynasties, the evolution of forms and the effects of pigments and oxides. Serious collectors came to rely on his expertise and his skilful handling of the import market. But importing blue-and-white from the Far East remained hazardous, slow and expensive, and with his Dutch connections Marks was also well placed to exploit sources closer to hand. Many of his relatives, under the full family name of Marks van Galen, were based in Amsterdam, running shops and showrooms that drew enthusiastic collectors: Charlotte Schreiber was a regular visitor to what she called 'van Galen's'. As a young man, Marks had spent several useful weeks in his grandfather's Amsterdam shop, and as he grew older he used his contacts in Holland to create an unrivalled supply network. Holland was not only the source for delftware, but it also had large quantities of high-quality, original blue-and-white. This had been imported from China to furnish houses in the seventeenth century but had since become unfashionable. No one wanted it. This Chinese blue-and-white was cheap and plentiful and could be easily shipped back to London. Marks knew where to go, and who to talk to. His contacts kept an eye out at Dutch sales and clearances, buying up blue-and-white on his behalf. He had cousins who could stalk the dealers and search the dusty backroom shelves. And he could speak Dutch, so he could hire coaches to take him out into the countryside and knock on the doors of substantial, likely-looking homes himself.

Eventually, the Dutch caught on to the English mania and, inevitably, prices rose. In fact, they rose so quickly and so steeply that it actually became cheaper to import directly from the Far East. But for a few years in the 1860s, beautiful and ancient pieces were still to be found on farmhouse dressers in the flat lands along the Rhine or north into Friesland, or in everyday use on kitchen tables. That he was so well placed to manipulate the craze for blue-and-white, that he could respond so quickly and effectively to the booming English market, proved the making of Murray Marks. His artistic and bohemian friends applauded his success; collectors from across the country demanded his services and he expanded from Sloane Street to the bustle of High Holborn. In 1874, when Pickford's moved out of Oxford Street in search of larger premises, Marks seized the opportunity to expand yet again, and to create a showroom to match his crystallizing ambitions.

Marks asked the architect Richard Norman Shaw, one of the most influential of Victorian architects, to extend the Oxford Street premises and make it magnificent. Shaw had been a friend of Marks' for some years, and was a collector himself. In 1866, both men had been involved in creating Glen Aldred, the Surrey country house of the painter E. W. Cooke. Shaw had designed and built the house and helped choose the furnishings – by ransacking Marks' showroom for its finest pieces. In later years, Shaw would go on to design grand houses with a classical influence – Bryanston House in Dorset and Chesters in Northumberland in the 1890s, and London's huge Piccadilly Hotel in the early 1900s – but in the 1870s he was experimenting with a leaner domestic architecture that became known as the Queen Anne style. At 8 Melbury Road, 118 Campden Hill Road and 31 Melbury Road, all in North Kensington, he created three celebrated 'Artists' Houses', each including a light-filled studio space, for the artists Marcus Stone, George Henry Boughton and Luke Fildes. As estate architect at Bedford Park in London, he designed key elements in a pioneering model of suburban living which soon acquired a reputation for attracting 'a particular person, most likely artistic and bohemian': a survey of 168 early residents found that 40 were artists, 16 architects and 9 actors or musicians.[5]

All these projects were undertaken between 1875 and the early 1880s. Shaw worked with Marks on designs for the new show-room during November 1875. Once again, Marks was in at the beginning, creating rather than simply following fashion. Having seen what could be done at Cooke's house in Glen Aldred, he was convinced that a new kind of artistic architecture could prove popular. Even while Shaw was still experimenting with styles, Marks saw something in his work that fitted perfectly with his own aspirations for a striking aesthetic display space, and he was brave enough to back a new trend, while at the same time raising the profile of his friend's architecture within an influential artistic circle. A visitor to the shop in the 1870s noted admiringly that Marks had achieved 'the first artistic business elevation, in creamy coloured woodwork, which was erected in London in the style of Queen Anne'.[6]

Within months, nothing remained of Emanuel Marks' old shop. In its place was a ground-floor showroom thirty feet wide, fifty feet long and over twelve feet tall, a splendid airy space, with two more intimate showrooms upstairs. In defiance of the current fashion for blank plate-glass windows, there was a neo-Georgian bow window, with carved wooden frames, to lure customers off the street with a promise of old-fashioned courtesy and hand-picked treasures, and the huge doors were moulded with Renaissance ornament, the name Marks inscribed in large letters above them. And everything was painted in a single colour, a clean cream – the window frame, the walls, the showcases and doors, the display furniture. This might seem an obvious trick designed to show off the objects, especially the blue-and-white, to best effect, but this kind of attention to the interior of an art dealer's shop was completely new. Some manufacturers had had an eye on the marketing potential of glamorous display rooms since the end of the eighteenth century: the Wedgwood showrooms in London and Bath were carefully designed to appeal to the fashionable, and often female, shopper, and to show off a range of wares at their best. But the art dealers' premises that most collectors knew were cramped and chaotic in the spirit of the bazaar, the goods heaped up, the pictures double-hung, objects, styles and periods all jumbled, and nothing to be had without diligent rummaging. Marks was setting high new standards. He was trying something daring and innovative. And it caused an overnight sensation, attracting would-be buyers and winning Marks widespread publicity and instant celebrity.

Within two years, Marks' bright, clean, sophisticated method of display was being adopted by any dealer with ambition. In 1877, he was called in to advise on the decoration of the new Grosvenor Gallery, being set up in Bond Street, and the same year the art dealers Agnew's built a new and refined showroom at 43 Old Bond Street, very much with Marks' model in mind. These new shops saw themselves as private galleries. The attention to display was an indication that they were challenging established institutions like the Royal Academy and, perhaps more importantly, it signalled the respect being given to artists and their work. Where the Royal Academy tended to treat its artists as mere producers contributing to a crowded warehouse of paintings, the owners of these new gallery showrooms were developing courteous and creative friendships with their artists and collectors. The harmonious rooms where each piece was allowed generous space were designed to complement the objects, suggesting that works were valued and that those who spent their lives with these works should be valued too. It was a strategy that proved successful. The Grosvenor Gallery had 1,100 customer-visitors a day when it opened in its purpose-built temple to art, and Marks' equally popular showroom became a place to see and be seen.

Marks' new achievements took him back to the quiet pavements of Cheyne Walk, to Rossetti's drawing room and the magnificent peacock. Because he needed one more thing, and for this he called on his friends. And so, on a late spring afternoon, bright with sunshine, three of Europe's leading artists met together with Marks. They drank wine and smoked. There was the flamboyant and controversial James McNeill Whistler, a neighbour of Rossetti's, who was painting moody landscapes and severe and complex portraits. There was Rossetti, of course, in one of his better moods, and there was the rebellious William Morris, craftsman, designer and Socialist agitator. They were men who, between them, were to change the way people thought about art. But first, they had to design a business card for Marks. And what they came up with was gold and blue and maroon, with a heavily decorated border of the type for which Morris is still remembered, Chinese characters emphasizing Marks' connections across the world, and the inscribed names of all the fields in which he was now an expert: carvings, armour, leather, tapestry, furniture, bronzes, oriental and European ceramics and enamels. It was a card that swaggered with commercial confidence and poise, a statement of personal achievement and a flourishing display of Marks' influential friendships. At the centre, framed by the elaborate border and sitting on a highly polished surface, was a gorgeous blue-and-white ginger jar. Tucked inside the jar, and lying nonchalantly alongside, were the twinkling eyes of two large peacock feathers. Perhaps they were picked up from Rossetti's hallway, or out of his garden. Perhaps they came directly from the bird that had greeted Marks so boisterously on his first visit. With their luxuriance, their bold colours and their delicate fine forms, they were a perfect icon of everything Marks had so far accomplished.

CHAPTER SIXTEEN

A Notorious Squabble

*C*ollectors, artists, connoisseurs, other dealers – and simply the followers of fashion – flocked to see what Murray Marks was offering. Charlotte Schreiber called by at the showroom to see if there was anything to tempt her. Robinson was forced to take note of this energetic competitor. The shop buzzed with activity, commissions poured in and sales flourished. But it was a difficult time for most dealers. During the 1870s and 1880s, rural decline, a dip in world trade and a stuttering British economy led to a corresponding depression in the art market. The greatest success was to be had by those who, like Marks, were prepared to innovate, finding new ways to market their wares and services. As well as updating and improving their premises, many dealers began to specialize. Etching, oil painting and watercolour all began to find distinct homes in particular outlets, while smaller paintings and more portable works of decorative art continued to gain in popularity: 'The exhibition painting has had its day,' suggested Walter Sickert in a magazine article, adding that artists 'will have to learn to work on a small scale'.[1] Like Marks, many dealers were also forging links abroad, scouring Europe for works, bringing together an international client list of collectors and trying to offset a downturn in one nation's market with a potential boom in another. 'Art in England . . . is fast becoming cosmopolitan,' noted *The Times* in 1879. 'Our picture dealers and buyers lay under contribution the ateliers, not only of Paris, but of Vienna, Munich, and Dusseldorf, Brussels and Antwerp, the Hague and Amsterdam, modern Florence, Milan and Rome.'[2]

One of Marks' more original marketing ploys was his habit of holding exclusive dinners, with the showroom elaborately decorated and some of the best wares pressed into use on the table where collectors could handle them. The idea was instantly successful. Marks was a genial and accomplished host, and meals were presented with a wealth of exceptional silverware, china, glass and ornament. No hint of Marks' tradesman origins disrupted the carefully constructed atmosphere of refinement and style. He knew his wine, and served only the finest vintages to complement each course. He enjoyed his food, and treated his guests to complex dishes from around the world. For Marks the gourmet, dining was an experience, an adventure, and a chance to show how far he had come. These were dinners to dazzle even the wealthy; chic occasions to flatter the fashionable: like the visiting card, they presented London society with a well-worked image of Marks and his business. This was astute and effective salesmanship.

Encouraged by the success of his new showroom and with interest in blue-and-white china continuing to grow, Marks conceived his pièce de résistance, bigger, more elaborate and more expensive than he had ever before attempted. For this, he required a collaborator, and he turned to one of his best customers, Sir Henry Thompson. Sir Henry was a fashionable man, a member of the Fine Arts Club and the influential Athenaeum Club, founded in 1824 for leading figures in art, literature and science and their patrons. He was surgeon to Queen Victoria and his impressive patient list included several other monarchs: he successfully removed a bladder stone from the King of Belgium, Leopold I, when two other eminent surgeons had failed. He published respected medical works and had the wide-ranging interests of an educated and sociable gentleman: he was an enthusiastic astronomer, his paintings were exhibited twelve times at the Royal Academy, he wrote two successful novels, and he founded the Cremation Society, advocating cremation as an hygienic, convenient and modern alternative to burial. His celebrated 'Octave' dinners, when eight guests were served eight courses, were the talking point of London society. And when the fashion for collecting in general, and collecting blue-and-white in particular, gripped the city, Sir Henry inevitably wanted to be part of it.

Sir Henry first turned his attention to blue-and-white in 1870, and Marks soon persuaded the busy surgeon to allow him to act on his behalf. Combining his expertise with Sir Henry's apparently bottomless funds, he was convinced that they could together create the most impressive and important collection of oriental china that had ever been seen. He was under no illusions as to Sir Henry's long-term commitment to collecting china, and guessed that his enthusiasm for blue-and-white might be fleeting. But he recognized another opportunity to set himself apart from other dealers and consolidate his reputation among the most successful and wealthiest collectors. Bringing together the finest pieces was also an intellectual and aesthetic challenge, and Sir Henry's wealth gave him the chance to create a collection he could never afford for himself. He went to work and by 1878 had brought together a wealth of unique pieces on Sir Henry's behalf, sourced from his contacts in Paris, Holland and the Far East. No other man in London could have done so much so quickly. But this was not just a private arrangement with Sir Henry; it was a fashionable enterprise for them both, something of a publicity stunt. The next step was to show the world what they had achieved.

It was a dim city evening when the preparations were finished for the magnificent exhibition which was to display Sir Henry's collection to a discerning celebrity public. Marks' showroom glittered. Display plinths had been repainted, door handles polished, and extra gas chandeliers fitted down the length of the shop. Marks had gone back to Norman Shaw, now busy designing for his artist clients, and together they had thought through every detail of how the exhibition should look. A witty and elegant invitation was designed, showing many of Marks' friends, including a stern Whistler with his monocle. The window display gleamed, music was played by a liveried quartet and servants flitted to and fro. The immaculate display of blue-and-white was arranged in profusion in every part of the gallery.

Guests flocked out of the damp mist and soon the showroom was bustling with life. There was chatter and laughter, and animated admiration for the pieces on display. To guard against Sir Henry's fickleness, Marks had made sure there was a permanent record of the collection in an illustrated catalogue. It was in itself something to collect, elaborately bound in leather inlaid with a blue-and-white ceramic plaque and with artwork by Whistler; a polite scrum gathered around the table where it was displayed, as guests elbowed their way to the front to inspect it. But the best was yet to come. The highlight of the exhibition was a dinner, described by one of Marks' friends as 'a very recherché supper served. . . on wonderful Blue and White dishes, which formed extraordinary foils to the rich pastries, glowing lobsters and wonderful jellies'.[3] Even by the extravagant standards of wealthy Victorian society, it was a lavish meal: glittering with candles and dressed with flowers and feathers. Long tables ran the length of the gallery, piled high with intricate pastries, decorated sides of fish, piles of seafood, dripping joints of meat and platters of game, sweetmeats, fruits and elegant deserts – all carefully chosen to complement the shapes and patterns of Sir Henry's china.

Building on such landmark occasions, the Marks business continued to prosper, showing the way for a new type of art dealer. Old Emanuel, though impressed by his son's industry and ambition, was bewildered and dazzled. The hybrid of dealership and gallery which his son was inventing was very different to the dark, cramped premises of the original shop. It was a matter of style and celebrity and glamour as well as connoisseurship and collecting. As the last guests drifted away from the Thompson exhibition opening, clustering on the street to hail passing hansom cabs or hurrying through the mist to their clubs for a nightcap, they had been entertained and charmed. They had eaten and drunk well, had met their friends and had been close to the exquisite poise of a very special collection. It had been a memorable night on the fashionable circuit, with an underlying sense of scholarship and good taste lending a satisfying gravity. Marks had, as always, judged well. In the later decades of the nineteenth century, there were almost 500 dealers in London alone, offering collectors everything from prints and drawings to wood carving and fine furniture.[4] It was a cut-throat business – many dealers struggled, and many never made it from the backstreet premises and jumbled curiosity shops that had been the hallmark of the trade for years. But for those who, like Marks, were inventive in their marketing, knowledgeable and courageous, there were fortunes and reputations to be made.

What most clients prized in their dealers was not just the opportunity to socialize and dine well – although this was clearly a pleasant enough diversion – but expertise and unerring good judgement. Both Joseph Joel Duveen and his famous son were renowned for what was called 'the Duveen Eye' – a collector's instincts, a discriminating sagacity, a superb visual memory and the ability to spot hidden treasures. It was something that all successful dealers had to have, or claim to have, but there was no training for it. The only way to educate 'the eye' was through experience. It was, wrote the art critic Bernard Berenson at the end of the century, essential to acquire and understand visual language so that it became as instinctive as spoken language: 'Many see pictures without knowing what to look at. . . We must look and look till we live the painting and for a fleeting moment become identified with it.'[5]

It was, of course, a quality collectors also wanted for themselves. But even those who boasted an educated eye of their own were often still keen to employ dealers on their behalf. It was convenient to have someone to undertake the hard, often grubby, work – the travelling and research, the sourcing and bartering. The feeling remained that dealers were at the bottom of the collecting heap, there to do the tasks that collectors preferred not to tackle. In 1870, Charlotte Schreiber recorded a telling moment in her journal, betraying the entrenched attitudes of the elite collector. As she explored the Paris showrooms, she came upon 'a painful scene'. At 59 Rue Bourbon, she called upon Monsieur Bock, who told her his 'sad story': 'to the effect that he was a Russian of private means, had lived many years in England, and, in the course of his travels had made a fair collection; that he lost everything in the failure of a Bank and was obliged to sell it all; and then, having a wife and seven children, turned dealer. He told us of his struggles, but said he never lost courage. . . He had known Mayer, Franks, Panizzi, in fact all our finest collectors. If true, his tale was a very melancholy one,' marvelled Charlotte.[6] Her assumptions are clear: becoming a dealer was the last resort for a man of means and a collector, a source of some shame, requiring the utmost fortitude, a far cry from the honourable society of men like Joseph Mayer and Augustus Franks.

Marks was no doubt aware that he could only mix with the likes of Sir Henry Thompson – who was at the aristocratic apex of the collecting hierarchy – as a dealer, an odd hybrid of teacher, designer, banker and servant. But he was fortunate not to have to rely entirely on such high-profile society clients; there were other collectors less judgemental than Charlotte Schreiber. Rossetti and Whistler were both passionate about china, and genuinely fond of the man who supplied them. And alongside the extravagance of this artistic circle, there were also many more secluded collectors up and down the country who dealt with Marks on equal terms. In particular, in the increasingly international world of collecting, there was one set of wealthy clients conveniently detached from the English obsession with class: Marks was beginning to make himself indispensable to a number of Americans.

During the second half of the nineteenth century, wealthy travellers from the United States could regularly be seen around the great sites of European history – sitting in gondolas alongside the Doge's Palace in Venice, loitering in Florentine piazzas, climbing up to the Acropolis, ambling by the Seine and, of course, making their way around the National Gallery and through the museums and parks and squares of London. In a world of changing economic and social power, they were the new Grand Tourists, revisiting and reinventing the routes that had been trodden by eighteenth-century English aristocrats. Crossing the Atlantic was no longer the barrier it had been (although the voyage still took a good fifty days) and first-hand experience of ancient European culture was considered an indispensable way of improving one's education, cultural expertise and social standing (for those who could afford it). It was what Henry James called 'a mild adventure'; for those who preferred to stay at home, writers like James sent back long series of travel articles about Europe which were eagerly bought up by magazines.[7] To educated Americans, Europe appeared more civilized and sophisticated – though more stultified – than its transatlantic neighbour, not least because of its long legacy of cultural traditions and artefacts.

Among the American middle classes, there was a fashionable enthusiasm for old Europe, and for the objects that represented it. The Americans were becoming collectors.

The influx of Americans into English drawing rooms caused quite a stir. They tended to disrupt customary ways of doing things, and there was a widespread perception that they were modern and unconventional, less deferential to the rigorously enforced hierarchies of class and more relaxed in their standards of behaviour than the strict English Victorians. The contribution these outsiders made to society was greeted with considerable ambivalence – and the shrewd awareness that Americans had money to spend. The usual European visit lasted for months, and sometimes years, during which antiques and souvenirs were often required as mementos of place and time. In addition, a growing contingent of expatriate Americans were making their homes in London and other major cities. All in all, the new American collectors were a growing market, and for dealers like Marks it was important to claim a part of it. An outsider himself, he had no difficulty in accepting and working with Americans. His circle of friends included not only the witty and lively Whistler, born in Massachusetts in 1834, but also George Lucas, an American dealer who lived in Paris, and a number of prominent American collectors. The most significant of these was J. Pierpont Morgan, a Connecticut-born financier and philanthropist who was one of the world's richest men and one of its most influential collectors.[8]

Pierpont Morgan's taste was eclectic. He became particularly known for the collection of books, manuscripts and seals housed in his private New York library, and for his spectacular collection of gemstones.[9] He also appreciated painting and sculpture, as well as the decorative arts, and he had a prestigious collection of wrist and pocket watches. But his business concerns, in everything from steel and railways to the army, required most of his attention and he often preferred to rely on trusted dealers to put together his collections. His first jewellery collection was largely assembled by Tiffany & Co., and in particular by its chief gemologist George Frederick Kunz, while the New York editor, clergyman and collector William Hayes Ward had brought together the core of his collection of ancient engraved seals. To satisfy his desire for Renaissance treasures, Morgan was drawn to Europe and especially to England, which was the acknowledged centre for the market. In his house on London's Princes Gate, he consulted renowned experts like Robinson, who knew where the finest pieces were located and how to reach them. Before long, he had turned to Murray Marks, relying on him to undertake much of the research on his behalf and to navigate the London trade to arrange the best deals.

Working for Pierpont Morgan was high-profile and prestigious. It could do no harm to Marks' business to be seen dealing for the world's richest and most influential men. Better still, this kind of prominent collecting was often attended by lectures, articles, catalogues and books that acted as further promotional tools. When Marks helped construct Morgan's collection of Renaissance bronze sculptures and figurines, the result was immortalized in a three-volume publication by the German art historian Wilhelm von Bode, who could not help but mention Marks' contribution: 'I am especially indebted to Mr Murray Marks. . .', he wrote, 'through whose hands so many beautiful specimens have passed.'[10] When Marks undertook the research and investigation that enabled Pierpont Morgan to acquire a famous twelfth-century triptych from the Abbey of Stavelot in Belgium, he was rewarded with an evening at the Society of Antiquaries where the display of the spectacular gold and enamel medieval treasure caused a sensation. His shrewd scholarship and timely involvement were again applauded: 'We have here before us this evening a monument of medieval art workmanship of a kind and importance that is seldom found on the open market. . .' enthused the fellows, before noting that it was dealers like Marks who 'help to make London a market or exchange for works of art and the wealthy buyer is forced to come here to increase his collections'.[11]

Marks clearly had a taste for the sensational and the extravagant. Nowhere was this more evident than in his work to decorate one of Victorian London's most celebrated and controversial interiors, a statement of avant-garde Aesthetic taste which became known as the Peacock Room. Once the prosaic dining room of a house at 49 Princes Gate in Kensington, the Peacock Room belonged to Frederick Richards Leyland, a Liverpool shipping magnate and art collector. In 1867, Leyland took on the tenancy of the gracious timber-framed Speke Hall, on the north bank of the Mersey, but there was little that could be tastefully done to improve an Elizabethan mansion, and so he also bought less distinctive modern London townhouses, first at Queen Anne's Gate and then at Princes Gate – just a stone's throw from the South Kensington Museum – with the intention of creating a visually impressive status symbol at the heart of the capital. Leyland was a naturally conservative man and, when he first began collecting art for his homes, he bought traditional landscapes and watercolours. But then he commissioned pieces from the young Rossetti and began to appreciate the work of new, emerging, more innovative artists. He found that he liked being regarded as a trendsetter and, when it came to creating a new interior in the mid-1870s, he turned to two other members of London's thriving modern artistic scene – James McNeill Whistler and Murray Marks.

Whistler's contribution to the Peacock Room became famous, in no small part because a bitter row broke out between the artist and Leyland before it was even completed. The dining room had been designed by Thomas Jeckyll to showcase Leyland's collection of blue-and-white, and Whistler's initial commission was for a simple decorative piece. Leyland had recently acquired Whistler's painting *La Princesse du pays de la porcelaine*, but when Jeckyll hung it over the mantelpiece in the new dining room he found that some of the red tones in the antique Spanish leather wall hangings on either side clashed with the colours in the painting. So he asked Whistler to add a few decorative touches to the room to create a more balanced effect, to retouch the leather with traces of yellow and decorate the wainscoting and cornice with a simple wave pattern. And that is how Whistler started out. But he soon began to turn the dining room into a personal evocation of his aesthetic principles, a 'Harmony in Blue and Gold'.

While Leyland was in Liverpool, launching a shipping line, Whistler moved in, living on site for months so that he could commit himself entirely to the project. He undertook increasingly ambitious alterations, covering the ceiling with Dutch metal, an imitation gold leaf, over which he painted a vibrant series of lush peacock feathers. He gilded every inch of Jeckyll's walnut shelving and decorated the shutters with four magnificent golden peacocks. He wrote confidently to Leyland, delighted with the changes, explaining that the room was now 'really alive with beauty – brilliant and gorgeous while at the same time delicate and refined to the last degree... there is no room in London like it'.[12] He showed off his work to visitors and called in the press to admire what he had done. But when Leyland returned he was horrified, appalled by the liberties the artist was taking with his home and money. He refused to pay the 2,000 guineas which Whistler was demanding and, on Rossetti's advice, offered half the amount in settlement. But Whistler was a notoriously difficult and passionate man. He took the reduced payment as a personal slight, exacerbated when Leyland wrote out a cheque in pounds instead of guineas. A pound was worth twenty shillings, while a guinea was worth twenty-one, but worse still, while the pound was the currency of trade, the guinea was the currency of gentlemen and artists. Whistler was furious. In revenge, he painted over Leyland's antique leather with blue paint, creating a mural of two enormous gold peacocks, dominating the dining room, strutting and brash. The telling details were highlighted in silver: scattered at the feet of the squabbling birds were the silver coins Leyland refused to pay; the silver feathers on one of the peacock's throats recalled Leyland's taste for ruffled shirts while the silver crest feather on the other resembled Whistler's distinctive lock of white hair. He called the mural *Art and Money; or, The Story of the Room* and when it was finished, in March 1877, Whistler quit and never set foot in the dining room again.[13]

Behind the bluster and ranting and preening, Marks' contribution to Leyland's distinctive interiors has often been overlooked, but he was an integral part of the process of transforming the Peacock Room, and the rest of the house. He worked closely with Leyland's architect Thomas Jeckyll long before Whistler became involved, putting together the core of Leyland's distinctive collection and integrating it into a decorative scheme on his client's behalf. Marks provided a range of quality blue-and-white pieces that was displayed on the dining room's narrow carved shelves, rising in thin columns up the walls of the room. He was aiming to capture the spirit of the Renaissance, of the *Porzellankammer* or porcelain rooms which were statements of wealth at the heart of many seventeenth-century collections. But his contribution did not end with the fine china. As well as the blue-and-white, Marks supplied rugs, carvings and tapestries. He provided Botticelli drawings, paintings by his Pre-Raphaelite friends and heavily carved Italian chests. He found the highly coloured stamped leather wall-hangings that Whistler was to paint over in fury, and he set a striking female figure at the foot of Leyland's stairs, taken from the prow of a Renaissance galley.

After Whistler's extravagant intervention, much of Marks' work still remained. Despite the controversy, Leyland kept the

Peacock Room as Whistler had left it, and it still displayed the blue-and-white, even if the impact was muted in the new design scheme. As the room became famous, the subject of gossip and scandal, so visitors came to see what Whistler had done, and in turn were able to admire the beautiful pieces that Marks had assembled. In the other rooms of the house, Marks' original contribution remained untouched and the rest of the collection he had supplied to Leyland continued to provide a model for a fashionable townhouse. But Leyland's collecting was a fashion statement: he was interested in making a splash, not in making any kind of scholarly, long-term commitment. Twelve years after Whistler completed the Peacock Room, it was removed from Leyland's house in its entirety and exhibited in a London art gallery; the collection of blue-and-white was dispersed.[14]

Marks was accustomed to such dispersal. As he had suspected, Sir Henry Thompson's enthusiasm for china also proved short-lived, and in 1880, just two years after the exhibition opening, his pieces of blue-and-white were put into auction at Christie's (where Marks was well placed to buy back some of the most important lots) and he turned his attention to other fashionable pastimes. Marks was more aware than most that there was no single type of collector. Alongside those who entered into an intense, often obsessive, lifelong relationship with their collections, or collectors who combined fashion with scholarship, were men like Leyland and Thompson whose interest was fleeting and who wanted to buy fine things as status symbols rather than for intellectual pleasure.

Marks was unusual among the crowds of London dealers in advising on how to use collections to make a show, to define and create 'lifestyles' in the way we now expect from interior designers. His willingness to embrace this most ephemeral of collecting habits again set him apart. It was a shrewd way of doing business. Joseph Joel Duveen followed Marks' example and persuaded

Arthur Wilson, a Hull shipowner, to let him redesign his house in the early 1880s, noting that 'the decoration and furnishing of Mr Wilson's house was the finest advertisement I could have had, and his rich friends almost fell over each other to get beautiful objects, too'.[15] In the early years of the next century, Duveen's son Joseph went a step further, immersing his collectors in Old World luxury and frequently advising his wealthiest clients, especially Americans, on ways to make their homes impressive: 'This decoration always included enormous sales of precious things,' noted Duveen's nephew James.[16] In the late 1890s, in an echo of the Peacock Room, Joseph Duveen oversaw the decoration of the London house of J. P. Morgan, son of Pierpont Morgan, a few doors down from Leyland at 14 Princes Gate, creating a special room for a series of eighteenth-century painted panels by Jean-Honoré Fragonard. In 1915, after Morgan's death, he arranged for the sale of the 'Fragonard Room' to the industrialist Henry Clay Frick, reinstalling it at Frick's mansion in New York. At Whitemarsh Hall in Pennsylvania, he helped the banker Edward Stotesbury decorate his huge mansion with oriental rugs and French sculpture, while the American socialite Eleanor Elkins Widener Rice commissioned Duveen to decorate four houses, paying $2 million for her New York dining room in 1925.

For many years to come, the public face of such ostentatious international collecting owed much to the quiet industry of Marks' research and his early experiments with fashionable collaborations. In an age of conspicuous wealth, when the richest people in the world wanted to create glittering, gilded mansions to flaunt their success, collections were no longer confined to studies and parlour cabinets. They became an essential element of display; rooms, galleries and even entire houses were built to show them off. The luxurious interiors of seventeenth- and eighteenth-century European royalty and nobility were reinvented for a new generation of high-society aristocrats. And as Marks demonstrated, these new collecting showcases owed as much to the dealers who made them possible as to the owners who financed them.

CHAPTER SEVENTEEN

The Fake Flora

*T*he wax bust of Flora, Roman goddess of flowers and of Spring, was delicate and elegant. The close-coiled tresses of *Flora*'s hair were intertwined with roses, her smiling face was smooth and noble, the slip of material draped over her shoulders and breasts hardly imagined by the sculptor. It was a classic piece, a masterpiece, and it seemed to bear all the hallmarks of Leonardo da Vinci's distinctive style: the same alluring half-smile as the famous *Mona Lisa*, the expressive sculptural lines, the modest female form. Given that only a handful of Leonardo's works survived his experimentation with different materials and techniques, and the procrastination of a perfectionist, *Flora* was not just beautiful – she was also both important and rare.[1]

As a new century dawned, Murray Marks was seduced by *Flora*. It was 1909, and he was sixty-nine years old. In many ways, he had become a figure of the art establishment. He had worked closely with the giants of late-Victorian collecting from Pierpont Morgan to Wilhelm von Bode. Since the late 1870s, he had been in partnership with Durlacher Brothers, an old and established London dealer's, and in 1885 the new business moved into Bond Street, at the heart of the antique trade. His townhouse was replete with his collections: the dining room alone featured a helmeted head and a fine display of blue-and-white, glass showcases exhibiting jewellery, enamels and ceramics, and a French Renaissance cabinet and table. Another house, a seaside retreat at 75 Marine Parade, Brighton, was furnished with a Regency collection. He worked closely with several museums, especially South Kensington, attending auctions on the museum's behalf, and supplying eye-catching objects such as a marble and alabaster rood screen from the Cathedral of St John at Bois-le-Duc (or 's-Hertogenbosch), south of Amsterdam. This seventeenth-century masterpiece with statues of the saints, pillars and angels, delicate carvings, arches, balustrades and massive ornamental candlesticks, was a huge architectural gem 36 feet high and 32 feet long, and became a mainstay of the new Cast Courts (or Architectural Courts) when they were built at the museum in the early 1870s. To acquire *Flora* would be a crowning glory, an impressive finale to a great career.

Marks was offered the *Flora* bust by another dealer, and quickly agreed terms.[2] She promised to be one of his greatest finds, and as usual he made the most of her. He may not have been able to arrange a splendid dinner to show her off as he had his displays of china, but he ensured she was presented in the New Bond Street showroom he now shared with the Durlachers.[3] Raised on a high plinth, smiling provocatively at the customers, *Flora* charmed all who visited and news of her spread rapidly across Europe and the world, as the discovery of this new and lovely Leonardo da Vinci masterpiece became known. The art journal *Burlington Magazine* ran a feature extolling the virtues of the bust, and Marks' friends and customers travelled long distances to see the *Flora* he spoke of so enthusiastically.[4]

By the end of the year, the attention had attracted a number of high-profile buyers, and Marks agreed to sell *Flora* to Wilhelm von Bode for the Kaiser-Friedrich Museum in Berlin for around

£8,000. Bode was opinionated, politically astute and ambitious, in many ways a German counterpart of J. C. Robinson. Many of his contemporaries found him arrogant and egotistical with 'a tendency to lay down the law with more or less pontifical assurance' but he was devoted to his collecting and was one of the first museum directors to openly court private collectors in the hope of acquiring their objects.[5] He rejoiced in making prestigious purchases. He was also Marks' friend and had acquired a variety of pieces from him over the years; in addition, the two men had corresponded energetically as well as collaborating on scholarly publications.[6] They knew each other's tastes and respected each other's judgement. It was Bode who had authoritatively declared the bust to be fifteenth century, and unquestionably the work of da Vinci, when he had first seen it in Marks' showroom. So it seemed fitting that *Flora* should go to Berlin to begin a prominent new life. Only the British press objected, bemoaning the loss of such a treasure: 'Our own museum authorities might have bought it,' complained *The Times*, 'but nothing was done', adding that the inability of museums such as South Kensington to recognize the importance of *Flora* 'is humiliating to our national connoisseurship'.[7]

The bust had only been in Berlin a few weeks, however, when the press picked up on a more titillating element of the story: a letter to *The Times* from Charles Cooksey, a Southampton antiquary and auctioneer, claimed that the bust had nothing to do with da Vinci, and had never seen Italy at all, let alone the Renaissance. It was the work, Cooksey asserted, of Richard Cockle Lucas, a Victorian sculptor, who had been copying from a picture of a scantily clad woman draped in flowers. The picture had been shown to Lucas by an art dealer called Buchanan, and might well have had links to da Vinci, but the bust, Cooksey maintained, was nothing more than a second-rate copy that had spent almost forty years rotting in Lucas' garden. When it had

turned up in a Southampton junkshop a few years after Lucas'
death in 1883, Cooksey had been given the chance to buy it for
less than a sovereign, but did not think it worth the investment:
he knew its mundane history and, as he pointed out, 'it was in bad
condition owing to the long exposure'.[8]

Soon the story, which seemed to be confirmed by Lucas' son,
was in all the newspapers. Popular English dailies like the *Daily
Mail* carried opinions on what was dubbed 'the *Flora* affair', as did
the more serious *Times*. In Germany, too, the press published
pictures, claims and counter-claims, and the American papers kept
an amused eye on proceedings, noting that 'the man in the street
in both countries has become interested. . . if he is a German he is
very sure that the bust is a genuine Da Vinci, and if he is English
he is quite certain that Lucas made it'.[9] In an increasingly tense
Europe, such allegiances mattered. For several years, there had
been talk of the possibility of war between Britain and Germany,
while German naval expansion during 1908 and 1909 had
sounded alarm bells in Britain and prompted a nervy arms race:
'we should not complain of Germany's right to build as many
vessels as she pleased, she must not take it amiss if we built the
number of ships which we thought necessary for our own
protection,' explained Sir Edward Grey, British Foreign Secretary,
anxiously.[10] With national pride at stake, Kaiser Wilhelm II, son
of Princess Vicky, visited the Berlin Museum, examined the bust
for over half an hour, and proclaimed definitively that *Flora* was
indeed by da Vinci. He assumed that the weight of his opinion
would put any controversy to rest, and that he had saved German
blushes. But, as the *New York Times* pointed out, there was
considerable 'British joy over the discovery that the Germans have
been fooled' and, despite the Kaiser's intervention, impassioned
spats continued between London and Berlin, capturing the
popular imagination more thoroughly than any learned art
history discussion.[11]

As we have seen, Marks enjoyed publicity and even a little controversy, but the thought that he had publicly passed on a forgery to one of the world's leading museums horrified him. Collectors trusted him – and this trust was the foundation of profitable trading. As soon as the questions over provenance arose, he sent a banker's draft for the complete purchase price to Bode, begging him to send *Flora* back to London, hoping to clear his conscience and forget the entire matter. But the banker's draft remained uncashed. Unfortunately for Marks, Bode was not ready to accept defeat so easily. He had identified the bust as being by da Vinci, and he meant to stick by his opinion. He was not in the least worried by rumours in the press, and he suggested that *Flora* should be inspected scientifically, to prove to the world that he was right in his assessment.

Marks could do little but wait. But the reports, when they came, were not good. The chemists who examined the composition of the wax were far from convinced that it was fifteenth century. Worse still, it became clear that tucked inside *Flora* was a grey canvas of English origin (some newspaper reports claimed it was part of a Victorian bed quilt), while scraps of a modern newspaper were jammed into the pedestal. The evidence looked damning. Marks wanted nothing more than to be out of the limelight. He pleaded with Bode again to accept a refund and let the matter rest, and he dreamed of letting *Flora* slip quietly out of the international news.

But Bode himself was part of the problem. He had set himself up as an omniscient expert, 'a sort of Jove in art matters', and it was the appeal of deflating him that encouraged many of the attacks: 'He had exercised his authority in the world of art opinion in the most ruthless manner, bowling the little fellows over with a mere wave of the hand when they got in his way,' explained the *New York Times*, pointing out that it was therefore inevitable that people would welcome the chance to exact revenge, enjoying 'a keen delight over the fact that Dr Wilhelm Bode, curator of the museum, is the particular individual who has been victimized'.[12] What's more, Bode resolutely refused to change his opinion, or even to consider changing it: ignoring the apparent evidence from the investigation, he published a statement in *Die Woche*, maintaining his position that 'only Leonardo' could have been responsible for *Flora* and asserting that the modern material was the result of restoration work undertaken by Lucas.

The outcome was the worst possible for Marks. It was a deadlock, with the dealer stuck helplessly in the middle of the storm. Evidence and counter-evidence, rumour and counter-rumour, swirled around the art world and the whole '*Flora* affair' quickly became muddy and unsure. The debate was to drag on for years. Some art historians claimed that the bust was a product of Leonardo's workshop, though not made by the artist himself; others were of the view that the sculptor was one of Leonardo's contemporaries based elsewhere in Europe, perhaps in France. Well into the twentieth century, the belief that *Flora* was the work of Richard Cockle Lucas remained widespread. But Bode, too, had his supporters, who maintained that he was correct in his original assessment. As late as 1939, the art historian Kenneth Clark again raised the possibility that *Flora* might indeed have been a genuine work by Leonardo da Vinci: 'Nothing in Lucas's work suggests that he was capable of the noble movement of the *Flora*, and the evidence advanced of his authorship only proved that he had subjected the bust to a severe restoration,' Clark contended. 'Bode was right in seeing this piece as a clever indication of Leonardo's later sculpture... [she is] another of those mutilated documents through which, alas, so much of Leonardo's art must be reconstructed.'[13] In the mid-1980s, however, further chemical tests on the bust seemed conclusive. They revealed the presence of synthetic stearin, added to wax to help it harden, a substance that was not produced before the nineteenth century. It was finally concluded that *Flora* was a fake.

For Marks' contemporaries, without the benefit of any modern dating methods, the matter remained one of bitter dispute. Although Bode was the target of most of the criticism, Marks could not help but feel that his reputation had been damaged. With the limited techniques available, it was impossible to be certain what the truth behind the bust might be, but it was disappointing that the prospect of discovering a lost da Vinci masterpiece had embroiled him in such negative debate, perhaps undoing years of careful professional work.

The Victorian collecting boom and the irrepressible fashion for exotic objects from overseas, such as blue-and-white china, was a godsend for the unscrupulous, the profiteering and the criminal. Forgers flourished. While the *Flora* affair took place at the beginning of the twentieth century, it was over the previous fifty years or so – at the highpoint of Victorian collecting – that the threat from forgeries had really started to affect the market. For every knowledgeable collector, there were plenty of beginners and amateurs who could easily be seduced by a good story and some convincing brushstrokes, and there were many dealers who were more than happy to pass on dubious stock at a profit – but there were few cases as high-profile or controversial as *Flora*. Mostly it was a matter of an altered signature, a touch-up of paint, or an attempt to give modern objects the distinctive patina of age. Usually it was an inconspicuous sale in a backstreet dealer's or at a country auctioneer's, and in many cases the fact that the piece was not genuine did not emerge until the collection was sold on or broken up – if then. Without modern ultraviolet or X-rays, carbon-dating or chemical spectroscopy to test pigments, collectors had to trust to their eyes and their instincts. Many died unaware that some of their objects were products of a dubious trade.

The lucrative rewards of an increasingly international art market were too great a temptation for many forgers. Political uncertainty in Europe throughout the nineteenth century made it easier for unprincipled dealers to concoct convincing tales about a ransacked castle or an impoverished nobleman to explain the sudden appearance of a piece on the open market. And the apparently limitless demand for works from the Italian Renaissance in particular meant that, no matter how many objects appeared, there was always a ready buyer. Many forgers concentrated on perfecting the most profitable styles, such as those of fifteenth-century Florentine sculptors, so that they could produce a stream of credible copies. Under a carefully organized and structured system, the best forgers were contracted to international dealers, supplying them with imitation masterpieces in return for a comfortable salary. These artists were often highly skilled and the objects they created were beautiful in their own right, even if false. Some forgers even became briefly famous for the quality of their work: Giovanni Bastianini was an accomplished Italian sculptor who forged Renaissance busts and figures that thrilled nineteenth-century art historians. Several were acquired by the South Kensington Museum, and even when their actual provenance was revealed they were considered to be so fine that they were kept on display.

The growing taste for objects from beyond Europe also created new opportunities for deception. Oriental ceramics and Islamic art, for example, were relatively unstudied compared to the more familiar European genres, leaving the door open for the unscrupulous to dupe the ignorant. Victorian scholars struggled to keep pace with the fashion for foreign pottery, tiles, textiles, architectural and archaeological objects, and it became relatively easy to pass off modern copies as originals. A macabre fascination with quartz crystal skulls in the second half of the nineteenth century led to the sudden appearance of examples in both private and public collections, apparently from ancient sites in Mexico. Some were little over an inch high; a few were larger. Many dealers boasted a skull for sale, two were exhibited at the Exposition Universelle in Paris in 1867, and the life-size example in the British Museum was acquired at the end of the nineteenth century from the reputable New York jewellers Tiffany and Co. But no scientific archaeological excavations had yet been carried out in Mexico, and knowledge of pre-Columbian objects was scarce. This was a perfect environment for forgers. Scientists at the British Museum found that their skull had traces of tool marks which showed that it had been extensively worked with rotary cutting wheels, unknown in Mexico before the arrival of the Spanish in 1519, and analysis of the quartz was damning: it had come from a nineteenth-century mine in Brazil or Madagascar, far beyond ancient Mexican trade links.

Forgeries were so commonplace that everyone was deceived at some point, no matter how careful and scholarly they might have been, or might have liked to think themselves. Charlotte Schreiber became an expert on forgeries in order to be able to identify attempts to cheat her. Joseph Mayer's collection displayed a number of objects that turned out to be forged, from antique ivories and Babylonian onyx to French miniatures of Napoleon and Josephine. On one occasion, Mayer bought a large number of medieval pilgrim badges from a London dealer only to find that they had been manufactured by two Thames scavengers known as Billy and Charley, who had shrewdly created 11,000 pieces and sold them on with the tale that they were salvaged from a wrecked ship.

John Charles Robinson used the issue of forgeries to emphasize the distance between himself and Henry Cole, accusing Cole of being too easily duped into spurious deals which showed him up as an amateur. In 1864, Robinson was delighted to pronounce that Cole 'fell into every hotbed of falsification and fraud' while on a buying trip to Germany, handing over £260 to a dealer in Hanover for textiles of the most commonplace kind: 'they ought not to have imposed on anyone possessing even the most rudimentary acquaintance with art,' snorted Robinson dismissively.[14] A few years later, Robinson high-handedly ordered the return of some late-fifteenth-century French playing cards that Cole had bought in Paris and which Robinson believed to be forgeries, going on to discuss in a twenty-three-page letter to the board and colleagues at the British Museum why his own assessment was indubitably more accurate than the Director of South Kensington's.

After Cole's retirement, as Robinson made his case to be part of the new museum hierarchy, he was keen to emphasize his record on spotting fakes and forgeries. He felt he had strong justification, particularly when the press weighed in on his side, alleging that the loss of Robinson had opened the door to incompetent and costly mistakes. 'The authorities have been in the habit of buying spurious or counterfeit articles as originals, and. . . they have given a price considerably above what might be deemed the market value,' noted the *Daily Telegraph* in 1885, taking it for granted that the market was more or less flooded with forgeries.[15] There was a popular and lingering perception that the staff at South Kensington had been all too easily fooled, and Robinson was perfectly happy to encourage the idea that, without him, the museum was floundering. When he was invited to present the prizes at the Birmingham School of Art in 1888, he used the occasion to lambast the 'dull and comparatively stagnant regime' of 'mere administrators and inexperienced, irresponsible amateurs' who had attempted to run South Kensington in his absence, and pointed out their record of 'astonishing blunders' that, he claimed, had become 'notorious throughout Europe'.[16]

But matters were not quite as clear-cut as Robinson tried to make them appear. Like Murray Marks, he was involved in a complicated and frequently obscure trade. The market for forgeries was so rampant and sophisticated that it was almost impossible for collectors to avoid being taken in on occasion. Most famous of Robinson's errors was a large ornamental dish, which he believed was made by the sixteenth-century Parisian ceramicist Bernard Palissy. Palissy's works were enormously fashionable at the time. Consequently, there were plenty of craftsmen making a living by churning out pieces in the same style, and both Palissy originals and more modern copies had been shown at all the international exhibitions, including London's Great Exhibition. In 1887, on one of his trips to France, Robinson was delighted to be offered the chance to buy a genuine Palissy platter; on his return he sold it to the museum for £50. It was just the kind of prestigious, high-quality piece that he was known for supplying. It appeared to be another of his triumphs.

The platter looked as though it had been broken at some point and reassembled with strips of canvas cemented to the china, crossing each other on the reverse. At the South Kensington Museum, after a couple of months on display, staff noticed that the damp in the cases had made the canvas sag, and they took the dish to the workshops to be cemented more firmly. It was a job that had to be done delicately, and it took some time, but, as they reached the point where the canvas strips crossed, it became clear that a maker's mark was inscribed on the plate, hidden by the cloth. As the restorer eased away the last of the canvas, the letters PULL were revealed, the mark of Georges Pull, a German-born soldier and naturalist who took to making ceramics in Paris in the 1860s and 1870s. It was a modern mark, identifying the piece as no more than a copy worth around £10. Robinson had been cheated.

Pull was not a charlatan. He made precisely crafted ceramics inspired by the Palissy style, and often so closely modelled on the originals that it was difficult to tell the difference. But he signed his work, and did not try to pass it off as anything other than his own. It was unscrupulous dealers who, with a quick fix of sealing wax, tried to persuade unsuspecting buyers that they were holding original sixteenth-century ware in their eager hands. Robinson could not believe that he had fallen for such a simple trick. He was still convinced that the dish was genuine, and when he heard of the discovery at the museum he immediately sent a note arranging to call by and examine it himself. He presumed there was some mistake, that the staff were, once again, just being ignorant and crass. But when he arrived to inspect the platter, he could not ignore Pull's clearly marked signature. Robinson had to accept that he had been swindled, and had to begin the delicate task of vindicating himself to the museum.

Robinson wrote long and detailed notes of justification to Cunliffe-Owen, explaining that an extraordinarily astute French dealer 'with great ingenuity' had been so clever with the dish that it was 'practically indistinguishable from the ancient specimens of the same type'. He assured Cunliffe-Owen that it was no reflection on his competence as a dealer, nor on his ability to continue working for the museum. He offered to repay the £50; the offending dish was destroyed. And, in his own defence, Robinson emphasized the enormity of the forgery problem, and the constant battle collectors faced in their search for genuine pieces: 'It has become almost impossible even for the most learned and experienced connoisseurs and experts,' he pointed out unrepentantly, 'to avoid being from time to time deceived.'[17]

Among European experts, Augustus Franks at the British Museum became perhaps best known for his prowess in detecting forgeries. Despite acquiring objects at a rapid rate, across a variety of different fields and from a range of sources, Franks was rarely taken in. He, like Duveen, was famed for his 'good eye', 'a marvellously wide knowledge of every kind of antiquity... an almost uncanny faculty of recognizing forgeries whenever and wherever he saw them', in the words of a colleague.[18] In 1875, for example, he was granted a week's leave to travel to Switzerland to examine Palaeolithic remains excavated from a cave in Kesslerloch. His report to the museum trustees focused on several objects – a decorated bird bone, a perforated bone head, and engravings of a fox and a bear on bison bone fragments – that had been declared as genuine by numerous experts. Franks noted his 'grave doubts', however, as to the artefacts' authenticity. A few months later, Ludwig Lindenschmidt, founder of the Römisch-Germanisches Zentralmuseum in Mainz, published a paper proving beyond doubt that the pieces were forgeries and that the designs had been copied from the illustrations in a German children's book.[19]

Franks could count numerous such successes: there seemed to be something about the detective work involved with unmasking forgeries that he particularly enjoyed. An anecdote recounted by one of his colleagues at the Society of Antiquaries suggested that he relished the opportunity to expose cheats, and was able to appreciate the humour in what could be tense situations:

Dredging operations were going on at St Paul's wharf, and a large number of curious things were found. Medals of considerable size were among the finds. [Franks] drew an obverse and reverse of a medal, took it to the foreman of the dredging operations, and asked him if they had come across that medal. No, they had not, but of course they might come across one; if they did they would let him know. In three or four weeks' time they had the astonishing luck to come upon the very identical thing. The foreman himself brought it to Franks, so unfeignedly delighted was he to have found the desired medal. The thing was correct in every point. Franks asked the man if he knew the meaning of the inscription under the head of the obverse. No, he did not; he understood it was Latin. 'So it is; S. Fabricotus, the forged Saint.' The man fled.[20]

Yet, despite making himself an expert in forgeries, even Franks was by no means infallible. Several of the large collections he acquired for the British Museum contained one or two suspect pieces, and a German stoneware vase he accepted from his friend Charlotte Schreiber, moulded with the heads of European kings and dated 1587, is now known to be a forgery. A French porcelain vase painted with flowers and cupids, which he bequeathed to the British Museum from his own collection, is also fake. Even Franks could not afford to be complacent about the scale of the problem facing collectors. Indeed, like Robinson, he was keen to emphasize the pervasive threat of the forgery trade and the unscrupulous who profited from it: 'there is scarcely an object in the range of ancient or medieval art to which the attention of the forger has not been given,' he explained to the Society of Antiquaries. He went on to note that this was a problem not only for the individual, 'the hapless collector', but for collecting as a whole, since the market in general was inevitably distorted by the volume of forgeries being produced. The forger, Franks complained, tended 'to depreciate the value of even genuine remains of the past by his dishonest industry'.[21]

The ease of making forgeries, getting them into the shops and persuading collectors to buy them was driving prices down. With their livelihoods potentially at risk as a result of such widespread dishonesty, it would perhaps have made sense for dealers to be at the forefront of the battle to control the forgery rackets. But matters were not so simple. One or two Victorian dealers were notoriously crooked: in London, Louis Marcy, for example, was known to trade almost entirely in fakes and forgeries. A volatile character, his real name was Luigi Parmiggiani, and his motive was not so much personal gain as an attack on the capitalist art world and all it represented. He indulged an anarchistic streak by intentionally skewing the market with forgeries in an attempt to disrupt and embarrass those he considered pompous speculators living off an unfair system. His notable victims included J. C. Robinson, who bought a gold-mounted sword from the rogue dealer in the belief that it had belonged to Edward III, alongside two daggers, once allegedly in the possession of Edward III and Edward, the Black Prince. Few of those at the heart of the London collecting market were as blatant as Marcy, but equally few crusaded to shore up the value of genuine objects by stemming the influx of forgeries. It was too difficult a task. Many dealers acted honestly, but some of the forgeries were so skilfully made that even the most experienced and astute buyers were deceived. In addition, the existence of forgeries, while depressing the market as a whole, offered the individual the promise of riches. Many dealers could be tempted to turn a blind eye if there was enough profit to be made.

Often the circumstances in which a forgery came on to the market were so opaque that it was difficult to be sure just how much the dealer knew about the provenance of the object. Murray Marks appeared trustworthy, and his reaction to the *Flora* debacle emphasized his resolve to keep his good name unsullied. But there were murkier moments. In 1912, towards the end of his career, drawings of 980 designs by German goldsmith and jeweller Reinhold Vasters came – somehow – into his hands. Born in Aachen in 1827, Vasters was a consummate craftsman. Like Pull, he did not necessarily set out to make fraudulent sales, at least at first. His early work was clearly marked. But he also found that he was able to produce pieces convincingly like those of the Middle Ages and the Renaissance, and in time he began deliberately making forgeries. Between 1853 and 1890, he created a series of beautiful jewelled pendants, gold and enamel spoons, chalices, cups and bowls which were sold as genuine, with prices to match. When Marks acquired the Vasters drawings, he offered them to the Victoria and Albert Museum, but staff there turned them down and he took them back. They were sold at his death for £37.16s and then presented to the museum by the new owner. What became clear, almost immediately, was that the designs were the blueprints for Vasters' forgeries. They were clearly modern production drawings for pieces that had been sold during the last fifty years as genuine works from the Renaissance. Marks had owned the very documents that proved Vasters had duped the market, and its leading collectors.

It took time to prove exactly what Vasters had been up to, and it was a hundred years before further study revealed that many fine metalwork objects in collections across Europe and America, thought to be Renaissance, were actually examples of Vasters' work: refined, skilful, very beautiful – but false. The collections of the Rothschild banking dynasty and of William Waldorf Astor, the American financier and statesmen, both included Vasters' fakes; the Victoria and Albert Museum, the British Museum and New York's Metropolitan Museum are today among the public collections which own Vasters' work, often still on display because of the quality of its craftsmanship. But Marks, who was keenly interested in forged bronzes, was in a good position to identify what Vasters was doing. He had traded one or two of Vasters' pieces to clients; he now had in his hands almost 1,000 modern drawings that were identical to objects he must have seen coming into auction houses, showrooms and collections. He may not have had sophisticated dating techniques to help him, but he would surely have recognized some of the pieces in the Vasters portfolio. Was he suspicious? Did he turn a blind eye in the interests of business, or because he was daunted by the extent to which Vasters' forgeries had penetrated the market? Was there something about the audacity of Vasters' scheme that he admired? It remains a mystery. As with many of the numerous sales of forgeries during the nineteenth century, the exact role of the dealer is difficult to determine.

The waters were muddied even further by the fact that some Victorian collectors were not at all concerned by the idea that dealers might be supplying them with forgeries. To them, what mattered was the prestige or intrinsic beauty of the object, rather than its provenance. During the later nineteenth century, the Rothschild family employed a Parisian goldsmith and restorer, Alfred André. After his death in 1919, André's workshop was found to be full of plaster casts and wax models for making forgeries. Like Vasters, he had been producing pieces in the Renaissance style to satisfy the demand of Victorian collectors. Three of his pieces were found in the Rothschild collection, clearly marked, suggesting that the family was willing to buy beautiful work that looked genuine, even in the knowledge that it was forged.

Similarly, many of Vasters' forgeries were bought by Frédéric Spitzer, 'the greatest genius among nineteenth-century collectors', according to a German art historian in 1902, and also a dealer who made a substantial income from Vasters' work.[22] Spitzer seemed unconcerned by the fact that his renowned collection was based on a complex series of forgeries. Indeed, he sought out forgers other than Vasters who might supplement his collecting, including Alfred André. In 1910, the year after Vasters' death, another German art historian, Stephen Beissel, noted that 'as is well known', Spitzer happily 'employed for almost fifty years a series of first rate artists in Paris, Cologne and Aachen etc. who made old things'.[23] In some ways, Spitzer was simply defying the experts by filling his collection with forgeries. But his carefree attitude also raised a variety of complex questions that collectors had to address on a more or less daily basis: did authenticity matter? If the experts could not tell the difference between an original and a forgery, was the forgery not just as good? Which was the most important, an object's intrinsic value, based on its beauty, artistry or craftsmanship, or its monetary value, based on its provenance?

* * *

In January 2010, a painting called *La Belle Ferronnière* was sold at Sotheby's for $1.5 million. Thought to be of Lucrezia Crivelli, the mistress of an eighteenth-century Duke of Milan, the painting is the 'sister' to another version in the Louvre. For more than eighty years, the identity of the artists for both works has been a matter of bitter dispute. In 1920, when the owner of *La Belle Ferronnière*, Harry Hahn, tried to sell it as a work by da Vinci, authenticated by a French expert, a reporter from the *New York World* rang Joseph Duveen in the middle of the night to get an opinion. A sleepy Duveen instantly dismissed the work as a copy, even though he had never seen it. The only real da Vinci of Lucrezia Crivelli was the one in the Louvre, Duveen maintained. Many of the potential buyers took his word for it, and pulled out of the sale. A furious Hahn took Duveen to court, claiming half a million dollars of damages for the apparent slander, but the 1929 trial concentrated not so much on what Duveen had said, but why. The prosecution argued that Duveen wanted to control what was sold to whom, thus making sure that he remained the dominant force in the art market. Declaring an object to be a forgery was one sure way of deterring buyers and scuppering a deal in which he was not involved.

There is no evidence that Duveen was acting so manipulatively, but it is certainly true that expert connoisseurs were in a powerful position, with most of the market prepared to accept their judgement on key authentications. This was particularly the case for those like Franks, Robinson and Murray Marks, who were working before the widespread use of scientific techniques to identify forgeries. For most of the time, Victorian collectors had to rely on their 'eye' to decide what it was they were looking at. Only at the beginning of the twentieth century, and in high-profile cases like the *Flora* bust, did science begin to have much of a part to play. Even then, there was a lingering tendency to believe that such new-fangled techniques could not possibly add much to a connoisseur's verdict. During the last decades of the nineteenth century, art historians such as the Italian Giovanni Morelli and Bernard Berenson working in Europe and America developed a brand of connoisseurship which was identified as 'scientific' – and considered more than a match for emerging technology. Instead of relying on instinct and taste, vague spiritual qualities, Morelli and Berenson adopted a detective approach to small concrete clues. Their technique relied on the close scrutiny of tiny details that could be used to identify the style of a particular artist, often by looking at things that had been created almost unconsciously, like the folds of an ear, and which were unlikely to be closely imitated by a forger. 'Just as most men, both speakers and writers, make use of habitual modes of expression, favourite words and sayings, that they employ involuntarily, even inappropriately, so too every painter has his own particularities that escape him without his being aware of them,' wrote Morelli, and his books included images of disembodied hands and ears by famous Renaissance artists to make his point.[24]

Not everyone was convinced by these new methods: Wilhelm von Bode was particularly critical of such a schematic approach. But, in many ways, this kind of connoisseurship was a refinement of the expertise that collectors such as Schreiber, Robinson and Franks had been developing through the middle years of the century, continuing principles of detailed and informed observation. It also had the added advantage of retaining the air of gentlemanly scholarship that the Victorians valued. To many, this approach was the ideal 'scientific' compromise, and even well into the twentieth century there were art market stalwarts who did not want to sully their reputations with too great a reliance on less genteel techniques. As late as the 1920s, when Duveen was taken to court by Hahn over the *Belle Ferronnière* dispute, such Victorian sensitivities lingered. The American jury was distinctly unimpressed by Duveen's reliance on vague statements about the quality of his 'eye', and in the absence of factual evidence could not agree on a verdict, forcing Duveen to settle out of court to the tune of $60,000. In fact, Duveen had experts in modern X-ray techniques, as well as archival research, examine *La Belle Ferronnière*, but he never used their evidence, even though it supported his conclusions. He seems to have preferred to maintain his reputation as a connoisseur of impeccable instincts, and pay up, rather than be seen publicly to doubt his own connoisseurship or to relinquish the power of identifying forgeries to a new generation of scientists.

Victorian collectors were caught in this changing world, where untried science was beginning to encroach on long-trusted scholarship, and where the art market was continually confused by accusations of forgery. The more specialized and knowledgeable connoisseurs became, the more forgeries were discovered, and the more collections were undermined and the market disrupted. The thorny question of what was genuine had always mattered to serious collectors: in the seventeenth century, for example, Rubens' patron, Sir Dudley Carleton, quizzed the artist at length to find out which works were by Rubens himself and which were the product of studio collaboration. But it was during the nineteenth century that issues of authenticity became widely discussed, and collectors began to realize the extent of the forgery problem. In such an atmosphere of doubt, it is perhaps not surprising that many of them tried to shore up their authority and retain some control over the market.

In 1881, Murray Marks suddenly acquired a very beautiful twelfth-century enamelled gold reliquary cross. Like the Vasters drawings, the cross, which had originally belonged to Ludwig I, King of Hungary and Poland, appeared in Marks' showroom apparently from nowhere. It was spectacularly beautiful, and inevitably caused a stir. Marks, taken by the intricate workmanship of the piece, showed it off to customers with pride and eventually sealed a profitable deal. But the cross was never his to sell. It was not a forgery, but it was part of an ingenious plot to make money from forgeries. Twenty years earlier, a Hungarian dealer working in Vienna, Salomon Weininger, had been asked to do some restoration work on the cross and three other pieces which came from the city's Imperial Treasury. While the objects were in his workshop, he copied them, and then returned the forgeries in place of the originals. The genuine pieces he sold on secretly to collectors: one of them, the Holy Thorn Reliquary of Jean, Duc de Berry, eventually ended up in the British Museum.[25] So immaculate were the copies that the art world was confused for many years about which were the authentic objects and which were the forged ones. The case quickly became notorious, and Marks, who openly admitted that the cross came from Vienna, must have suspected that it was one of the pieces at the centre of the controversy. He may not have been sure whether it was an original or not, but that hardly makes his decision to act as dealer for the sale seem less dubious. It appears that he intentionally sold an object that was either a forgery or which he knew had been stolen from one of Europe's greatest treasure houses.

There was nothing secretive about the way Marks went about selling the cross. He openly invited clients to inspect it, and he used his contacts with other dealers to ensure everyone knew what a fine piece was in his possession. Robinson, in particular, was intimately involved. Like Marks, he was drawn to the quality of the reliquary's workmanship and, like Marks, it seems, he was willing to set aside any niggling doubts as to provenance. As far as we know, Robinson was not involved in the sale, but he was certainly part of the marketing drive to find the reliquary a new home: in March 1891, he borrowed it from Marks to display at the Society of Antiquaries in London where he wrote disingenuously that 'nothing is known of the history of this cross'.[26]

No doubt the two men shared quiet conversations, speculating over the origins of this most collectable of objects. Why did they choose not to make their suspicions public? We cannot, of course, be sure, but I doubt that it was simply a case of assuring Marks a profit. Robinson, after all, had no reason to have any interest in that. It is more likely that a complicated combination of factors kept them silent. The sale was prestigious, and turning a blind eye to the fact that the cross might be stolen or forged allowed Robinson and Marks to reflect the glory, asserting their positions at the top of their profession. Moreover, casting doubt on the piece's provenance would have destabilized the market yet again, and perhaps involved them both in an international scandal. In contrast, celebrating the cross as a legitimate masterpiece sustained the Victorian system of connoisseurship that they had both worked so hard to establish. It allowed them – like Duveen later – to stake a claim for saying what could and could not be sold. It put the power to decide in their hands.

While the *Flora* affair was to rumble on into the twentieth century, Marks found himself soon absolved for his part in it: 'there never was any ground for impugning in the slightest degree the good faith of the vendor,' reassured the *Times Literary Supplement*.[27] He also received a vote of confidence from staff at the South Kensington Museum, who were no doubt mindful of the number of loans and advantageous deals he was apt to make on their behalf. He provided 'much valuable information respecting the provenance and history of many. . . objects', asserted an official report.[28] With his name cleared and his reputation intact, Marks' association with South Kensington continued, and became one of the longest and most fruitful of the many enduring alliances he made over the course of his life. Having begun in the 1860s by luring Henry Cole with the splendour of the Dutch rood screen, he went on to work with five other Directors and generations of museum staff. His correspondence reflected the technological advances of a changing age: his handwritten letters gave way to typewritten notes and, finally, to telephone calls as he negotiated deals on the museum's behalf. His generosity filled the galleries with lovely things even as a new world order took shape: when he retired from business and moved permanently to Brighton in May 1916, during the darkest hours of the First World War, he offered all the objects from his London house on loan to the museum, brushing aside the staff's concern that the 'Zeppelin danger' was too great to risk such a display.[29]

In the five years before his death in 1918, at the age of seventy-seven, Marks gave numerous pieces to the collections. He marked his fifty-year friendship with South Kensington with photographs, carvings, portraits, ironwork, sculptures, an oak door and, inevitably, a lovely example of K'ang-hsi period blue-and-white china. In a final flourish of generosity, he also gave the museum a group of bronzes, showing Bacchus and his faun, which he believed to be a rare fifteenth-century work from Florence. It was finely modelled, elegant and yet substantial, and, since bronzes were something of a speciality for Marks, it was a fitting tribute to his lifetime's work. Yet there is now considerable doubt over the origins of the Bacchus bronze. Recently re-evaluated, there is something not entirely right about the modelling of the faun's 'knee', as well as evidence of later techniques in a cast screw; the work is now considered to be relatively modern. As it has not turned out to be as special a piece as Marks believed, it is not on display in the galleries. It seems that, in his final handsome gesture, Marks was himself undone by the rampant Victorian trade in forgeries.

Collecting the Empire: In Pursuit of the Exotic

Stephen Wootton Bushell

CHAPTER EIGHTEEN

The Route to Peking

*M*urray Marks' success with Chinese blue-and-white ceramics showed just how widely Victorian collectors were beginning to spread their net. The idea of collecting from remote and unfamiliar lands was taking hold, part of a fascination with voyage and adventure that characterized an age of discovery. In the early 1850s, the slightly scandalous Captain Richard F. Burton captivated audiences with accounts of how he undertook the haj pilgrimage to Mecca disguised as a Muslim. From 1852 to 1856, news of David Livingstone's conquest of the African wilderness was delighting the public. By the 1870s, the British Empire was at its peak, with Victoria declaring herself Empress of India in 1877 and extending her rule to huge swathes of the globe. The opportunities for travel had never been so great.

It was no longer only the rich, or the heroic, who had the chance to see new sights, and it was no longer only the familiar, traditional European destinations of the Grand Tour which drew the crowds. Taking the opportunities for employment that lay in building railways, roads, bridges and canals; in ministering to the sick and the religious; and in completing the reams of paperwork that kept the Empire working, the sons of the middle classes soon filled the berths on ships taking them to a new life overseas. The rising numbers of ordinary people who set sail from ports all over the country only added to the fascination with travel, bringing it ever closer to home, while a generation of writers brought tales of exploration into libraries, parlours and nurseries in articles, stories, poems and biographies. The flamboyant Henry Morton Stanley published journal pieces and reports of his African journey throughout the 1870s, including his famous meeting with Livingstone in 1871. In the 1880s and 1890s, Rudyard Kipling's exotic, romanticized tales of Indian life secured him a place as one of the most popular writers of his age. Victorian society relished the frisson of the foreign, and everywhere there were accounts of new lands, astonishing peoples and remarkable journeys.

The appetite for real-life stories about those who came and went across the Empire was accompanied by an equally voracious desire for the objects they carried with them. The world was brought into the Victorian home in the shape of silks and muslins; extraordinary plants, pinned insects and butterflies and stuffed birds; shells, furs and feathers; spices, teas and spirits – and in portable art objects. As today, few travelled to foreign lands without picking up something to remind them of their journey, and before long there was a booming international trade in souvenirs. Whereas in previous centuries souvenir-collecting had been largely the domain of aristocratic travellers on the Grand Tour, the Victorian middle classes were now adopting the same habits, in new contexts. The souvenir trade was by no means confined to exotic destinations. By the middle of the century, the main sites of Europe, such as the Alps and the great Italian cities, were swamped with low-grade memorabilia on sale to tourists. In Dickens' *Little Dorrit* (1855–7), Mr Meagles boasts a collection of 'model gondolas from Venice; model villages from Switzerland; morsels of tesselated pavement from Herculaneum and Pompeii. . . Roman cameos, Geneva jewellery, Arab lanterns, rosaries blest all round by the Pope himself, and an infinite variety of lumber'.[1] But this familiar trade in cheap collectables was also being reinvented in far-flung lands as new types of objects caught the traveller's eye.

On the whole, as in Europe, these foreign souvenirs were manufactured quickly and cheaply to supply the rapidly expanding market and to give even the poorest visitor the opportunity to purchase a memento. Modelled clay figures from India, known colloquially as Poona figures, for example, were shown at all the international exhibitions, including the Great Exhibition, and in turn became extremely popular with European travellers, so much so that the manufacture of affordable souvenir versions helped sustain the economy of Pune, the Indian city where they were produced. Visiting Mexico City in 1884, the American anthropologist and archaeologist William Henry Holmes was amazed to find 'relic shops' on every corner, selling ceramic vessels, whistles and figurines.[2]

Most of these souvenirs tended to be clumsy imitations of genuinely exotic objects, rapidly produced to cash in on current fashions. Quite often they were not even made abroad. While the people of Pune and Mexico City manufactured modern reproductions and fashionable cultural artefacts to sell to tourists, plenty of other objects were made in Europe, with European tastes firmly in mind. In Thomas Hardy's 1873 novel *A Pair of Blue Eyes*, naïve young architect Stephen Smith tries to impress Elfride Swancourt by sending her some glamorous souvenirs of his life in India, but he manages only to waste his money: 'One day I bought some small native idols to send home to you as curiosities, but afterwards finding they had been cast in England, made to look old, and shipped over, I threw them away in disgust,' he laments.[3] Hand-made objects crafted by local people were supplemented by mass-produced souvenirs churned out in enormous quantities in British manufacturing centres such as

Birmingham. With the Victorian commitment to exploration, and rapid improvements in shipping and rail, the volume of travellers across the world had become industrial and demanded souvenir production on an industrial scale. Little bits and pieces for tourists became another cog in the huge wheel of Empire.

Few of these objects were meant for serious collectors. They acted more as evidence of distances covered and lands visited than as objects of aesthetic pleasure or financial investment. Those with a more incisive eye were nonetheless aware that among all the false knick-knacks and tacky keepsakes there were important and handsome objects that encapsulated the mystery and glamour of the places they were made. But you had to know where to look. Just as in Europe, serious collectors had to be both wary and astute. They needed to be energetic enough with their research to keep one step ahead of the mass-market travellers and the traders who profited from them. And, just as in Europe, it was often a great advantage to be first on the scene. As Stephen Smith discovered in *A Pair of Blue Eyes*, by the middle of the nineteenth century, countries at the heart of the Empire, such as India, were enmeshed in a complicated and profitable souvenir trade: those who wanted to find the best objects had to be prepared to go to more remote, inaccessible, and often more risky, destinations.

On 29 February 1868, Stephen Wootton Bushell sailed from Southampton on a boat bound for Shanghai. He was twenty-three years old and had graduated as a doctor from Guy's Hospital in London less than two years previously. He was clever, likeable and mildly adventurous, but his experience of life so far had been sheltered and comfortable. He had grown up on his father's substantial farm in Kent, spent happy years at a minor public school and won easy success as a scholar. His natural talent for learning, an excellent memory, a personable manner and money in his pocket had allowed him to glide through childhood and adolescence and to emerge as a thriving and upright young man well equipped to begin a medical career. Now, however, his life was changing. For the first time, he was facing a challenge and striking out from the solid middle-class ways of his upbringing. As he joined the bustle in the Southampton docks, showed his papers and began the steep walk up the wooden gangplank, Bushell was setting foot firmly in the unknown.

It was a long journey. Back at his father's farm, the spring lambing was over and the summer crops ripening before Bushell reached his destination. At sea, there were wide, alien views and strange stories. There were long days of bright calm, and nervous stormy nights. There were dinners and concerts and games. And there was plenty of time to think. Bushell was not on a pleasure trip. He had his formal letter of appointment as Medical Attendant to the British Legation in Peking (now Beijing), a promise of £600 a year, and official approval 'to engage in private practice at Pekin' if he so wanted.[4] He was determined to use the months at sea to prepare himself properly for his new job. He began the task of learning Chinese and he brushed up on the medical conditions he might expect to encounter. He read and reread the scant official documentation he had been given. Yet he did not know what to expect. Very few European travellers had spent time in China, or travelled extensively there, and there was limited reference material for him to consult. He had little idea what his life was going to be like and he could not help but suspect that his preparations might all turn out to be useless. Huddled in his berth as he sailed across the world, Bushell had nothing in his experience to compare with where he was going. He would just have to wait and see.

Shanghai was noisy, crowded and prosperous. It was a city growing quickly and erratically, a newly affluent port on the mouth of the Yangtze river, ideally placed to trade with the West. It was a hub of commerce, a centre for travellers and a maze of narrow streets leading into still narrower alleys. From the moment he landed, Bushell was captivated by the colours, smells and sheer noise of such foreignness. He found himself welcomed into a thriving cosmopolitan community. But his journey was not over; he was hardly acclimatized to the light and the dust – or to the unfamiliar cadences of the Chinese language – before he was travelling onwards to Peking, around 1,300 kilometres to the north, away from the mercantile centre of China to a much more traditional heartland. As he left the modernity of Shanghai, Bushell became more and more a foreigner, a strange man with curious ways.

If Bushell had been hoping to find himself part of a community comparable to the one in Shanghai, then he was to be disappointed. When he finally arrived in Peking, tired and exhilarated by his journey, he discovered that there were fewer than fifty non-Chinese residents enclosed in a compound within the city, walled in with their families and servants, a fives court and bowling alley, a library, a billiard room and a stage for regular performances of amateur dramatics; an entrenched and unremarkable group of administrators and bureaucrats carefully recreating European society deep in the heart of China. There were luncheons and parties and evenings around the piano. There were lengthy discussions of British politics and imperial ambitions. The national anthem was sung, and the Queen toasted. But the restrictions of life within the legation did not dishearten Bushell. He enjoyed the security and comfort, and he became determined to use the legation as a springboard for exploration instead of a barrier to it, a safe retreat that would allow him to make forays into the bewildering city that lay all around him.

Bushell's fascination with China, inspired by his brief stopover in Shanghai, had become only more potent as he had moved north. His ten-day journey by boat up the Beihe river, and then overland on a mule cart, had given him the opportunity to begin a study of the country. Now he was eager to discover more. Not content to shut himself off in an expatriate enclosure, he wanted to learn more of the language, meet more of the people and explore more of the landscapes and the intriguing histories that China seemed to offer. Above all, he wanted to acquire some of the tempting things he had seen. China, he had already observed, was a country of extraordinary objects. On landing at Shanghai, Bushell wrote, 'one sees on the wharf a number of pedlars offering for sale teapots and cups of quaint form' fashioned like a dragon rising from the waves or a mythical phoenix, a gnarled tree trunk or an elaborate flower. In Peking, 'a garden of any pretension must have a large bowl and cistern for goldfish, and street hawkers may be seen with sweetmeats piled up on dishes a yard in diameter, or ladling syrup out of large bowls; and there is hardly a butcher's shop without a cracked Waul-li jar standing on the counter to hold scraps of meat'.[5] Although Bushell had not been a collector before, the extravagance and abundance of Chinese objects quickly seduced him.

Despite his enthusiasm, the contrast with the neatly kept fields of Kent was a culture shock, and settling in took time. Bushell knew he could not simply go out and start bartering for wares. First, he had to become familiar with the arcane workings of the British government abroad and the idiosyncrasies of his patients. He had to learn how to fit in with his colleagues and their families – and he had to improve his Chinese and begin to understand the habits of the Peking inhabitants, who were frequently hostile. Throughout the East, the British presence was often resented: in Japan, the legation's native interpreter was murdered at the compound gate in 1860, and the following year the building was stormed by angry locals. In China, the Second Opium War of 1855–60 pitted French and British troops against the Chinese in a series of bitter battles punctuated by incidents of kidnap, torture and looting. Unsurprisingly, when Bushell arrived in Peking in 1868, relations between the British and their hosts could be awkward, and the city could seem unwelcoming. Mary Crawford Fraser, the wife of the secretary to the legation, noted in her journal that the British 'were detested in the city and never passed outside the Compound without being made to feel it', and many preferred to spend as much time as possible in the Western Hills where they felt more welcome and secure.[6]

But Bushell was not intimidated. With the determination and optimism of youth, he knuckled down to establishing himself, and soon found that, with such a small British contingent to serve, his medical duties were reasonably light and relaxed. He had a great deal of spare time. So he set his mind to the community beyond the compound, studiously reading about Chinese history, improving his language skills and researching the country's ancient culture. He worked enthusiastically and conscientiously, and he made rapid progress. What might have begun as the naïve experiment of a young man soon developed into something more. His excursions from the compound became increasingly lengthy and ambitious; his conversations with the locals increasingly fluent. He grew in knowledge and confidence and within a couple of years he was moving boldly across the city, a familiar figure among its residents and an object of wonder to Mrs Fraser: 'our good Doctor Bushell,' she noted in amazement, 'could talk to the people of their ailments in excellent vernacular and gave them medicines free of charge. This fact alone set him quite apart from other human beings in their estimation.'[7]

The more Bushell saw and read of Chinese art, the more it fascinated him. He used his local contacts to find the best shops and market stalls in the Outer City, way beyond the compound, and he became familiar with the monthly markets in the temple courtyards and the lanes clustered around them, where all kinds of food, clothes and trinkets were on display. The market at Wu Men, the main gate into the walled Forbidden City, was, he discovered, a particularly rewarding source of objects from private houses, and he browsed the stalls there regularly. Sometimes, too, the objects came directly to him without his having to leave the compound: small-time dealers in curios would call daily at the legation and on its Western residents. 'The morning was spent in studying and cheapening the wares brought by native merchants and spread all over the floors,' explained an American visitor, apparently dazzled by the display, an alluring array of 'bronzes, porcelain, jasper, jade, amethysts and emeralds' as well as furs from 'sea otter, sable, Tibetan goat, Astrakhan, wolf, white fox, red fox, bear, panther and tiger skins'.[8]

Bushell was especially fortunate, however, in not having to rely only on curiosity dealers. 'I have obtained access, in the exercise of the duties of my profession,' he admitted gratefully, 'to several palaces and private houses, and have in this way had many opportunities of seeing the treasures of native collectors, which usually are so rigidly closed to foreigners.'[9] He began to acquire a variety of things: textiles and silks; enamels, ivories and jewellery; carved stone sculptures, bronzes, pictures and architectural specimens. He was increasingly impressed with the skills of both ancient and modern Chinese craftsmen. By 1873, just five years after his arrival in Peking, he felt confident enough to begin corresponding with Augustus Franks at the British Museum, alerting him to the treasures he was unearthing and sending one or two pieces to Franks for his personal collection. He also published his first scholarly article, a study of the 'mountain boulders roughly chiselled into the shape of drums' which stood in the city's Temple of Confucius.[10]

Bushell had settled quickly. The sheltered young man had grown into the role of pioneer and explorer. With archaeology yet to uncover the sites around Peking, he was becoming an expert in the ancient literary sources that made sense of Chinese history and its objects, and he was already on his way to becoming the first Westerner to undertake the serious study of Chinese art. In 1872, he set off for nearly 200 miles to the north with Thomas Grosvenor, a secretary at the legation, on a journey beyond the Great Wall, to Inner Mongolia, where he visited the ruins of Shangdu, the summer capital of Kublai Khan's Yuan dynasty. It was a fabled city, a byword for opulence, made famous in Britain as Xanadu in Coleridge's popular poem 'Kubla Khan' (1816). There was little left to see, but there were enough relics to captivate Bushell. The two men were the first Europeans to visit the site since Marco Polo in the thirteenth century, and the feeling of discovery was intense. Bushell used the journey to collect all kinds of pieces, and to begin to understand more fully the culture of ancient China. On his return, he took a period of leave in 1874 to return to Kent to marry, and persuaded his new wife Florence – herself the daughter of a doctor – to return with him to China the following year. The long voyage back was very different from the first. It was a journey home. The talk in the Bushells' cabin was about everything Florence could look forward to, the people she would meet, the places her new husband would show to her – and the abundance of things still waiting to be discovered.

The objects accumulating in Britain's museums provided tangible evidence of the Victorian fascination with their expanding world. The extension of the Empire, the growth of trade routes and the increasingly far-flung voyages of intrepid travellers such as Bushell were brought to life for museum visitors in the pieces beginning to appear in the display cases. At the South Kensington Museum, for example, alongside the Italian Renaissance sculptures and medieval French treasures that Robinson had tracked down, or the English manufactured wares championed by Henry Cole, there were now increasing numbers of objects from less familiar destinations: carpets, textiles and tiles from Persia and the Islamic world; models, busts, Buddhist reliefs and imperial treasures from India; Japanese porcelain and pottery; arms, ammunition and jewellery from Afghanistan; lace, costumes and embroidery from Mexico and South America. New forms, colours and ideas were beginning to appear in the museum, presenting visitors with alternative ways of looking at the world and its peoples. Collecting was making itself truly international.

These new kinds of objects required new methods of description. There was a long tradition of European anthropology that had often sat alongside abstract philosophical thought: the eighteenth-century German philosopher Immanuel Kant, for example, gave a series of lectures on anthropology for over twenty years from 1772. But such anthropology was not necessarily specifically concerned with foreign races and cultures (Kant mostly used examples from close around him to make his points) and there was no term at all for the tangible artefacts that collectors were now acquiring. In 1834, the term 'ethnography' was coined, and this was quickly adopted to cover anything that did not fit into the established hierarchies of works of art or that came from some distant, apparently primitive, possibly exotic, land.

Having a word for these things made it easier to define and categorize them, but it did nothing to make them more familiar. The arrival of objects from all over the Empire and beyond was creating a challenge for museum staff. Asian art, Japanese ceramics and Indian sculpture were not traditional subjects of study; they had not been considered important. A young gentleman's education in the Classics rooted him firmly in European culture; the Grand Tour and its Victorian hybrids prepared him for an appreciation of Western art. At small private endowed schools or grammar schools for the middle classes and respectable working classes, boys and girls had little chance of seeing any art, let alone works from distant cultures. These schools tended to be insular in their philosophies, with an emphasis on discipline and vocational skills, and even at progressive schools run by education reformers the aims were modest: 'to write a letter grammatically, to calculate rapidly without a slate and to keep accounts by single and double entry'.[11] Most ordinary people knew very little, if anything, about countries other than their own, while, even among dealers and connoisseurs, scholarship about non-Western objects was distinctly patchy. The world was simply growing too quickly.

There were exceptions. J. C. Robinson developed a love for Chinese ceramic art, which he regarded as 'the perfect consonance of material and decoration'.[12] And at the British Museum, Augustus Franks was making himself something of an expert in non-European works. Franks himself did not travel outside Europe. His contemporary and friend in Germany, Adolph Bastian, was a field collector, personally acquiring 2,000 artefacts from his travels to South Asia alone, and creating the Museum für Völkerkunde in Berlin in the 1880s with ethnographic collections six or seven times larger even than those at the British Museum. But Franks did not let his relative lack of field experience defeat him; he kept in close contact with numerous travellers, negotiated with a steady stream of collectors who brought objects to the museum on a more or less daily basis, and used his visits to Europe to acquire pieces by exchange, both with private collectors and museums.

When Franks joined the British Museum in 1851, there were around 3,700 ethnographic objects on show in a single gallery; by the end of his work there in 1896, the museum boasted an outstanding display of almost 40,000 pieces in a suite of rooms. As well as individual objects, Franks was instrumental in securing a number of substantial complete collections, such as the Christy Collection, which brought more than 1,000 items to the museum. A banker and textile manufacturer, Henry Christy had been a friend of Franks' and had spent much of the early 1860s undertaking excavations of cave sites in southwest France.

Alongside this archaeological material, however, he had collected almost 1,000 items from travels in Mexico, North America and Canada. After Christy's death in 1865, Franks worked on cataloguing the objects. He also purchased a further 20,000 pieces with £5,000 bequeathed to the museum by Christy, which Franks had invested into a fund specifically for making acquisitions. The museum's ethnographic collection grew quickly, and Franks' knowledge grew with it. He soon became an acknowledged expert on non-European objects, and was often called on to assist other institutions with their collecting; when the South Kensington Museum acquired a large consignment of Japanese ceramics from the International Exhibition in Philadelphia in 1876, Philip Cunliffe-Owen turned to Franks to research and catalogue it.

Nevertheless, there were few other scholars working in Britain on the new material from around the world, so the public collections were forced to look much further afield for help. Staff began to recruit collectors to work alongside their Western European specialists and provide a much-needed link with distant lands. They looked to the colonial service and the army, in particular, to start creating a collecting network that spanned the globe. In the first half of the nineteenth century, the British Museum acquired important objects from officers in the Royal Navy and the East India Company, and from public servants working in Africa, the Arctic and Australia. Captain Marryat, also known as a writer for children, gave a large lacquered Buddha and a colossal stone carving of Buddha's footprint in 1826, and the museum became the home for the stunning collection of Sir Stamford Raffles, Lieutenant-Governor of Java, who founded modern Singapore in 1819. By the mid-century, as the number of British territories grew and increasing numbers of people were involved in administering them, the quantity of objects arriving on ships from around the world rose steadily, and from the 1880s, collections made by professionals abroad were frequently arriving at the museum. Very few of these distant collectors were experts: most of them collected as a diversion from their day jobs and chose objects that caught their eyes as opposed to pursuing a disciplined programme of study. But they were enthusiastic and often acquired a sound knowledge of their local area and customs. And help was at hand to guide them, especially from Franks. He regularly briefed travellers in person about what to collect, and even handed out questionnaires for them to complete on his behalf, demanding details such as the kinds of clay employed in making pottery or the type of objects used for marriage and funeral customs.

Many of these overseas collections, rather like Franks' own, had an odd semi-official status. They were made during the course of official duties but they were usually privately owned. Once they were finished with – usually on the death of the collector, or on his return to Britain – they were commonly given, rather than sold, to public museums, as though it were understood that they had been borrowed by the individual for the duration of his time overseas. Collecting on this basis was clearly a popular distraction for those posted far from home, a way of understanding a new culture while marking public service with something tangible. The collecting network was expanding alongside the ambitions of Empire. In the early 1870s, the South Kensington Museum made contact with Major Robert Murdoch Smith, director of the British Telegraph Service in Persia, who agreed to source examples of historic and contemporary Persian art on the museum's behalf, and whose expertise enabled the museum to publish a guidebook to its Persian material. Then, in 1874, two cases of bronze vases, mirrors and bowls and twenty-three small spearheads, daggers and other weapons arrived in South Kensington. All the pieces were Chinese, and they were all on offer for exhibition. The consignment had come direct from China, via the Temple Club on the Strand, and the unfamiliar and occasionally bizarre objects were the property of Stephen Wootton Bushell.

Bushell's association with South Kensington was to be a long one, but it started humbly enough. When they were unpacked, the pieces turned out to be small and largely unspectacular. But they were a taste of things to come. And for Bushell, it was a means of establishing professional contact with the museum staff. When his marriage to Florence had been celebrated in 1874, he used his time back home to discuss his initial discoveries with the curators at South Kensington. He tried to describe the variety and wealth of objects waiting to be discovered in China, emphasizing how much more there was than the limited range of Chinese porcelain already familiar in fashionable circles. His enthusiasm was infectious, and the staff were delighted. Here was a learned man at the heart of one of the most mysterious countries on earth, with a collector's eye for the unique and historic, and with a willingness to ship his objects back to England and lend them for display.

Bushell turned out to be as good as his word. When he returned to China with his new wife, he found that his conversations at the museum had given him new impetus and direction, and immediately he began assembling a consignment to send back to South Kensington. Over the next few years, he began collecting with the museum in mind, acquiring an assortment of carefully chosen objects that would make a coherent display in the galleries. 'I have selected during my residence at Peking a few more typical specimens. . . to add to my small collection now being exhibited in the Loan Department,' he wrote modestly to Cunliffe-Owen in the summer of 1880.[13] The arrangement seemed to work perfectly. The museum had found a reliable source of expertise and a cost-free way of acquiring the best pieces, and Stephen Bushell could collect to his heart's content, knowing that his efforts were being appreciated back in England and that the South Kensington display cases would ease the pressure on the modest doctor's accommodation he was allocated in the Peking enclosure.

CHAPTER NINETEEN

The Promise
of the East

The objects Bushell was selecting for South Kensington and the British Museum, and the increasing number of pieces being sent to London by travellers from around the world, were creating something of a dilemma. With their odd symbolism, their unfamiliar materials and their sometimes naïve techniques, they were not easy to classify. Were they really art? Museum staff found it difficult to decide whether such things deserved to be displayed alongside European objects or whether their very difference marked them out as cultural curiosities, of social instead of artistic value, and inferior to the established displays. Bushell's Chinese objects were shown along with other foreign works, mainly on loan from private collectors, in the aptly named 'East Cloister' at South Kensington. It was here, at the edge of the museum, that visitors could see pieces from overseas, set out to dazzle and intrigue. The gallery was colourful and exotic, specially decorated in elaborate mock-oriental designs that emphasized its difference, and hung with objects that even the most dili-gent student of art would never have seen before. It was deliberately distinctive, distinguished by a kind of alluring otherness that set it apart from the rest of the museum. The damp grey of the London streets receded as visitors were invited to step into another world and to discover the strange skills and odd tastes of the people who lived there.

The gallery was far more than just a window on other cultures: it was at the same time a way of ordering and controlling the unfamiliar and unknown. Persia, China, India and Japan fascinated the nineteenth-century public. The apparently vast markets for British exports, as well as the promise of imported luxury goods such as teas and silks, excited merchants, shipowners and shop-keepers. Political uncertainty in many Eastern countries held out the prospect of the further expansion of British territory and fired imperial ambitions. But, above all, many Victorians were seduced by the idea of a glamorous Orient, a place of sultry nights, outland-ish wildlife and bizarre sensual rituals. They were intrigued by news of each new discovery and were anxious to see for themselves the unexpected and beautiful objects that emerged from the East.

The new wonders of Japan, for example, were a source of endless fascination to many ordinary Victorians. When Augustus Franks first joined the British Museum in 1851, Japan was still a closed country, governed by a policy called *sakoku* that had been in place since 1639 and which prevented the Japanese from travelling abroad and foreigners from entering the country. Little information about Japan leaked out, and few things: a small concession of the Dutch East India Company in Nagasaki supplied Europe's palaces with fine porcelain exports, known as 'Old Japan', from the 1660s onwards, but the only chance most people had had of seeing Japanese objects was the tiny handful of items included in the 1851 Great Exhibition, under the auspices of the Chinese display. In the 1850s, however, *sakoku* ended abruptly after the American naval commander Commodore Perry forced the Japanese to sign a 'Treaty of Peace and Amity' (or

Treaty of Kanagawa) in 1854. By the end of the decade, Japan had links with most Western nations, including a further treaty in 1858 which opened three of its ports to British traders.

Suddenly, Japanese art and antiquity were available to collectors – and they took full advantage. During the 1860s and 1870s, in Britain and France, the fashion for collecting Japanese artefacts was intense. A special term was coined in 1872 to describe enthusiasts – *Japonistes* – and netsuke (miniature sculptures) and tsuba (sword-guards), in particular, were enthusiastically acquired by Westerners. The influence of Japanese objects and aesthetics was felt across fashionable and artistic society: Degas, Renoir, Whistler, Monet and Gauguin were among the painters influenced by Japan, while, in the Victorian home, Japanese-inspired jewellery, ceramics, furnishings and wallpapers became hugely desirable. In 1875, Liberty's opened in London's Regent Street as a specialist supplier of Japanese goods, and in the popular theatre works such as Gilbert and Sullivan's comic opera *The Mikado* (1885) continued the craze for all things Japanese towards the end of the century.

But such widespread enthusiasm for new cultures and their objects was not without a darker dimension. There was also a sense of alarm, a niggling fear that disorder and disruption might creep into Britain from these mysterious lands with their weird customs. In many museums, the strange ethnographic objects from beyond the usual Western canon of art were shown together as evidence of the 'backwardness' of other cultures, rather than as beautiful and valuable objects in their own right. They were generally classed as wondrous oddities rather than being afforded the status of art, and were often displayed alongside natural history specimens to make a point about racial progress. African objects, in particular, seemed to emphasize to the Victorians the gulf of racial difference and these, of all pieces, were most commonly kept separate from more familiar works of art. When Henry Townsend, a young missionary, first travelled to Sierra

Leone in 1836, and then on to Abeokuta, a Egba kingdom inland from Lagos in 1843, he was bewildered and distinctly unnerved by the vastness of Africa, by the heat, the darkness, the wary tribespeople and the primitive transport arrangements, but as he settled into African life during the 1850s and 1860s it was the objects which occupied his attention. As well as converting suspicious worshippers to his God and energetically spreading the Christian message, Townsend took time to barter with the heathen villagers, and was frequently delighted with the unusual jewellery, sculptures and vessels he discovered. While fellow churchmen at home were collecting Anglo-Saxon archaeology or Greek antiquities to display in their parlours, Townsend demonstrated a more adventurous taste.

Regular shipments from Britain brought Townsend personal supplies and the kinds of things any active missionary might require: Bibles direct from Queen Victoria, money collected for the building of a church, and a steel corn-mill from Prince Albert for the practical improvement of African life. In return, he sent back colourful and curious things. Many of these objects simply confirmed to friends back in Britain just how much the Egba people needed European culture and values: an Eshu fetish figure, given to Townsend by Chief Ogubonna, for example, had been used at his door to protect against witchcraft before his conversion to Christianity. Back in Exeter, Townsend's home town, no one had ever seen anything quite like the strange African objects. Staff at the museum received Townsend's parcels with some consternation and in the end the decision was taken to keep all the African works physically separate from the main museum, carefully displaying them instead in a 'temporary depot' set apart from the displays of Western painting and sculpture.[1]

Even once it was agreed that ethnographic objects did not constitute art, however, it was still not easy to decide on an authoritative way of exhibiting them. During the eighteenth and early nineteenth centuries, collectors tended to adopt one of three different approaches to ethnographic display. There was the eclectic gentleman's cabinet of curiosities which could easily accommodate a random collection of objects of varying significance and needed little philosophical rationale beyond the driving passions of the individual collector. Then there was the model adopted by collectors like Walter Scott or Lieutenant-General Augustus Henry Pitt Rivers, who brought together 20,000 objects from across the world and gave them to the University of Oxford in 1884. This type of display often focused on arms and armour, and removed the works from any social or geographical context. Instead, it emphasized visual similarities and encouraged the visitor to follow the development of each type of object in a linear way, from the simplest to more complex forms: 'Specimens were arranged according to their affinities, the simpler on the left and the successive improvements in line to the right of them,' explained Pitt Rivers in 1874.[2] The displays positioned objects along these evolutionary timelines from primitive to modern, irrespective of the actual date they were made. They tended to enforce strict hierarchies and, in doing so, stressed racial differences. Taking up the work of anthropologists, the layout aimed to reveal the history of humanity and compare the cultures of different peoples. It was implicitly understood that the examples from distant countries were, even if modern, really only of value as evidence of the more primitive stages of Western development rather than as objects of a specific place and culture.

Finally, from the 1780s onwards, as explorers like Captain Cook brought ever more artefacts back to Britain, there was a growth in the third model of display: contextualized shows defined by geography. The enthusiasm for foreign objects by now could mean that sometimes over half the pieces on display in public museums had been shipped to Britain from far away, and plenty of galleries offered a 'South Sea Room', for example, or indeed an 'East

Cloister'.[3] Increasingly, merchants, diplomats, sailors, soldiers and churchmen were all taking time off from their trades to send things back to entertain and astound the public. A sledge rescued from William Parry's expedition to find the North-West Passage; a 'pair of garters worn by the Queen of Tahiti'; costume, ornaments, baskets and bowls from South America, Madagascar and the Philippines collected by plant-hunter John Gould Veitch; 'a valuable tortoiseshell comb, of immense size, as worn by the ladies of Mexico'; and a 'twentyfive Rupee note apparently Burmese, printed on native paper, taken from the body of a Rebel Sepoy shot by the donor at the recapture of Dharwalagiri in the Nepaul mountains' are just some of the objects I have seen noted in contemporary accessions registers.[4]

Following the third model of display, these various artefacts were sorted into orderly presentations defined by geography, and cases and printed guides were arranged to show material specific to one culture, such as the Canadian Inuit. Again, there was little sense of chronology. Objects were clearly linked to ideas of voyage and adventure rather than to historical scholarship, and were often shown to give visitors an idea of what travel might be like in strange and distant lands instead of examining cultural development in any detail. Over the course of the nineteenth century, this last approach to display became the most common – at the British Museum, the galleries were arranged geographically for over half a century, from 1808.

Yet the controversial question of how to classify and display such objects was far from resolved. In the 1860s, the unspoken principles behind these display choices were increasingly brought out into the open and discussed in public. During a decade of change, popular ideas about overseas cultures were challenged, and curators and collectors began to look again at the way their collections were presented. Previous work on evolution was transformed by the publication of Charles Darwin's *On the Origin of Species* in 1859, followed by Herbert Spencer's work on evolution and natural selection, *Principles of Biology*, in 1864 and, at the end of the decade, Francis Galton's experiments based on theories of biological inheritance. Traditional religious beliefs seemed to be under threat, scientific opinion was divided and often confusing, and the very nature of humankind was up for reconsideration. As debates raged, ethnographic collections in museums and in private hands were inevitably caught up in the fray. How and what people collected, and how these things might be displayed, became connected to controversies over race, religion, biology and 'the survival of the fittest'.

As Darwinian ideas spread, the evolution of human societies became the topic of urgent debate, as did the relationship between technologically advanced countries such as Britain and more apparently primitive cultures. Ethnographic collecting and display was at the heart of this discussion, providing for 'the scientific study of manners and customs of particular peoples' and showing, according to the British Museum, 'their development from savagery towards civilization'.[5] Displays of objects were an excellent way of presenting the complex intellectual ideas underpinning evolution. Visitors were encouraged to marvel at simple native objects, and draw comparisons with the 'better', more refined examples of pottery, clothing, jewellery, tools or artworks in their own homes. Foreign pieces were a source of entertainment, even laughter; the displays offered an experience comparable to travelling shows of living 'exotic' people that toured throughout Europe, becoming particularly popular during the 1870s and 1880s, and exhibiting novelties like Laplanders herding reindeer or African bushmen preparing meals. Closely linked to principles of social evolution, the display of ethnographic artefacts reinforced the Victorians' view of themselves as advanced, sophisticated and superior.

* * *

With the display of travellers' objects apparently fortifying Victorian notions of supremacy, collections became especially entangled with imperial ambitions. Empire building and collecting went hand in hand, and, by the 1870s and 1880s, public collecting could clearly be seen as a tool of state, an expression of how Britain saw itself on the world stage. In 1886, this was fully articulated in a Colonial and Indian Exhibition at South Kensington. Much more concerned with the display of imperial might than earlier extravaganzas like the Great Exhibition, this demonstrated how foreign objects could be used to illustrate and validate the glory of the Empire: 'It meant a proclamation to all and sundry that Victoria rules the Empire,' trumpeted the *Illustrated London News*, 'a just and equitable, but firm and fearless rule to the uttermost ends of the world, to the extremist limits of human civilization.'[6] It was not simply that Indian textiles were beautiful, for example: the display of such works in the exhibition also helped to highlight the dominance of the Raj in India and remind people of the extent of British power. One of the most popular pieces in South Kensington was the famous Tippoo's Tiger, an animated mechanical organ, made of painted wood and carved to look like a tiger mauling an Englishman. It had originally been commissioned by the Indian ruler Tipu, Sultan of Mysore, a symbol of his opposition to British authority, and in particular of his resistance to the British East India Company. Its presence in the museum not only recorded Britain's victory in India, but also reminded visitors of the need to take the cultivated ways of Empire to a place that was once governed by such a sadistic oriental despot.

Because of the long British involvement in India, the public collection and display of Indian objects was often more structured and considered than the presentation of art from other Eastern nations. The East India Company, trading since the days of Elizabeth I, had set up an Indian museum in London's Leadenhall Street as early as 1801. Despite being crowded, chaotic and squalid – it was described by one journal as 'practically inaccessible, and hid away out of sight. . . a bonded warehouse and not a museum' – it drew crowds of visitors, who were fascinated and horrified in equal measure by the eccentric hotchpotch of ancient tablets, religious sculptures and elephant heads.[7] There was soon a crisis of space and in 1858 a 'New Museum' was opened to the public, but the East India Company was already in decline. The Indian Rebellion of 1857, followed a year later by the Government of India Act, which set up a new government department for the subcontinent, unsettled old ways of doing things and reduced profit. The museum went through several decades of uncertainty and upheaval before finally being disbanded in 1879. The collection was then divided between the British Museum and South Kensington, where treasures like Tippoo's Tiger took pride of place in the Eastern Galleries. With the added attraction of more convenient and salubrious premises, the Indian material once again drew huge audiences: nine rooms and an adjoining landing were given over at South Kensington to the display of architectural fragments from Mughal palaces, models of Indian domestic scenes and religious festivals; fabrics, carpets and homewares. One of the most striking exhibits was a massive plaster cast of the Eastern Gateway from the domed Buddhist monument of the Great Stupa at Sanchi in India, a huge pillared entrance elaborately carved with elephants and scenes from the life of Buddha. So magnificent and popular were the displays that the travel publisher Baedeker even included a guide to the collections in its London itinerary.[8]

But interest was by no means confined to India, and, as British ambitions expanded, so too did collecting from the length and breadth of the world. In many cases, countries that were not yet under British rule were the priority, rather than potentially more reliable allies like India. Acquiring objects from intransigent states was one way, at least, of announcing supremacy. While the

Victorians were trying to gain control of Afghanistan, for example, the spoils of war helped to make British victories visible and tangible, both to those whose treasures were being removed and to an influential public back at home: a wooden panel from the gateway of Ghuzni, taken during the first Afghan war in 1842, and arms from the second Afghan war in 1878–80 all found their way into the galleries at South Kensington. Japan and China were similarly important. At a time of fierce rivalry for dominance in the region with other European and world powers, collecting acted to assert territorial claims ever more strongly. In a competitive world, acquiring objects from the Far East assumed unique symbolic and diplomatic value.

At South Kensington, an active programme of collecting from Japan began in the 1850s with the purchase of some modern Nagasaki lacquer work. It was soon boosted by Queen Victoria who added swords, armour, textiles and ceramics during the 1860s, while Britain's minister to Japan from 1865 to 1883, Sir Harry Parkes, also donated a fourteenth-century sword that he was given by the Meiji Emperor in 1872. At the British Museum, as well as decorative objects and sculpture, Franks persuaded the Trustees in 1881 to buy a collection of over 3,000 Japanese paintings put together by William Anderson, a doctor who lived in Tokyo from 1872 to 1880. In China, however, progress had been slower. The country was so huge, so apparently undeveloped and so completely unknown to all but a few Western travellers – and trade was so tightly controlled by the Chinese government – that the objects which emerged tended to be of limited variety, and sometimes low quality, often specifically designed for the Western markets. When Stephen Wootton Bushell sent his first consignment of boxes to South Kensington, there was little with which to compare it. The small bundles of objects surprised the Victorians with new ideas about Chinese art.

* * *

Bushell was delighted to be back in Peking. There was the pleasure of sharing everything with his new wife, and of being welcomed so enthusiastically to the compound. There was news to catch up on, patients and friends to visit. And there was the satisfaction of rediscovering his favourite places and immersing himself once again in the sights, sounds and smells of China that he had missed so much. Peking was not an obviously handsome place. It was one of the world's largest cities, a cramped collection of simple, low buildings, their roofs propped on poles, clustered around dusty, unmade streets, rutted by mule carts. The view was frequently monotonous: there was little vegetation, and the rocky ground was open and wind-blown. A huge blank wall, fourteen miles long, broken only by occasional gates and towers, loomed over the close-packed houses and divided the city in two, with a Tartar City to the North and a Chinese City to the south, the ancient and enclosed Forbidden City lying behind yet more walls of its own. There were no parks, and the only gardens were tucked out of sight in private homes. But the temples were beautiful, though often overgrown and weedy, with grass covering the roofs or pushing through the cracks in the stone paving. In the tranquillity of the Confucius temple, gnarled cypress trees sprawled among squat pavilions, and silk and paper prayer offerings fluttered in the breeze. Here Bushell could linger and plan for the future.

In his early thirties, with a settled family life and his medical career running smoothly, Bushell was in an enviable position. His visits to South Kensington had given him the support he needed to extend his collecting with confidence, and his conversations in London had convinced him that his scholarship would be valued. It was clear to Bushell from his early explorations that the understanding of Chinese art in Britain, even among collectors and so-called experts, was poor. The more he discovered, the more it seemed to him that the most important works were underrated and misunderstood. Even the study of Chinese ceramics, which had become so fashionable in Victorian London, was much more interesting and varied than he had imagined. There was just so much more to the craft than had so far been revealed.

There was, of course, the K'ang-hsi porcelain which changed hands in European showrooms for large sums of money and which, Bushell claimed, was 'the culminating epoch of the ceramic art in China by common consent of all connoisseurs, eastern and western'.[9] But this was just the beginning. What caught his eye as he sat in the quiet, darkened rooms of his wealthier Chinese patients, or followed a local guide along the narrow and steep paths to secluded shrines, was the fine form and lustre of much earlier Chinese ware, virtually unknown in the West, and certainly not yet at the forefront of fashion. This was historic work that was valued by the Chinese, and which they had kept safely out of the hands of traders and merchants; the ancient pieces of the Sung dynasty (960–1279) which Bushell could pick up surprisingly cheaply, and the refined work of the Ming dynasty, dating back to the 1360s. Here was a whole new perspective on the study of blue-and-white, a long and successful tradition waiting to be discovered by a pioneering collector, and a thrill for Bushell as he rummaged through the markets of Peking.

Bushell was keen to show what depth and quality there was to traditional Chinese blue-and-white, but it was the unusual, the quirky and the distinctly 'foreign' that really caught his eye. At heart he was an explorer, and simply re-evaluating the wares that could be found in London drawing rooms was not enough to satisfy him. What fascinated him were the pieces of art that helped define the people and explain the ways in which they lived. His acquisitions were more than just pieces for decoration: Bushell understood that they were cultural artefacts, historic markers which gave him an insight into a unique country. Every journey became an adventure, even if it was a brief trip into the markets of Peking to see what was on the stalls. Every conversation was a revelation of the links between the past and the present. Every object, however simple, began to fit into his growing understanding of the culture and its history, adding colour and diversity to the picture. Bushell was eager to find out everything he could about the pieces he saw: how and when they were made; where they came from; who had owned and used them; what they meant. He became a collector of stories.

One of the things he observed, particularly among his more respectable Chinese friends, was that it was common to wear a plain, flexible band of gold or silver around the neck or arm. At first he did not take much notice. He had never had much of a taste for jewellery, and there was always something else to interest him. Increasingly, he was able to leave his black leather doctor's bag tucked neatly away at home and venture out just for the pleasure of it. He was calling socially on old patients, and in the streets Chinese locals who had once welcomed him only for his medical skills were more than happy to talk about other matters. All the time, he was being shown new things and, with so much to attract his attention, the plain rings and bangles seemed insignificant.

But, as time went on and Bushell saw more and more people wearing the bands, he began to ask questions. Listening to the stories, he discovered that the necklaces and bracelets were much more interesting than they had first appeared. The bands were far more than simple ornament or fashion – they were portable property, the family wealth. But unlike the diamond necklaces and elaborate tiaras of the English upper classes, brought out with a flourish on important occasions to signal status and prosperity, this Chinese jewellery was practical and plain. What was important was its solidity: the weight and purity of the metal were far more significant than any craftsmanship or decoration. When times were hard, it was relatively easy to strip off pieces as required, sell them on and melt them down to provide funds. His appetite whetted, Bushell asked more questions and discovered that the custom of wearing bands was so ancient and widespread that it had become carefully organized and systematized: each piece was stamped by the original jeweller who, at any time in the future, was honour bound to buy back strips from his customer, by weight, without questioning the quality. Bushell was now alert to the bracelets: what had seemed insignificant and undistinguished became full of interest. He could not help noticing the bands everywhere he went, amazed at himself for not seeing much sooner that this was more than a random taste for body ornament. In a city full of beautiful and unfamiliar things, Bushell realized that even the smallest, plainest and most intimate objects were important. His European perspective was shifting, and he was beginning to see the details of Chinese life with new eyes.

Such small discoveries delighted Bushell, but he was not one for publicizing his breakthroughs. He kept his notes diligently but inconspicuously, and he treasured each advance that brought him a step closer to understanding China without feeling a need to broadcast his growing expertise. All over the world, royal, government and diplomatic representatives were making inroads into new lands, and Bushell knew that he was just a tiny part of a vast imperial network. He was, officially, nothing more than a respectable physician, helping the British machine to function and upholding its values. Many other expatriate administrators collected, and many local and national museums were grateful for the objects they sent back for display. Bushell was under no illusions as to his uniqueness or distinction. But even so, in his quiet way, through his systematic note-keeping, careful observation and scholarly collecting, Bushell was making himself special. He was doing more than simply picking up curiosities so that people back in Britain could wonder at the strangeness of the world – he was changing attitudes.

* * *

When it came to thinking about the East, the Victorians tended to view Japan as sophisticated and cultured, producing a range of objects which showcased the exquisite skills of Japanese craftsmen and were worthy of fashionable attention. Japanese objects were being imported in large quantities by the 1870s and popular shops like Liberty's set the tone for stylish middle-class homes. Japan was romantic. Yet, despite its appeal to the popular imagination, a patronizing mindset still lingered, a sense that beneath the refinement lurked a semi-barbarous 'foreignness'. Even Britain's first minister to Japan, Sir Rutherford Alcock, described the country as a place of primitive violence and natural disasters, noting that experiencing Japanese life was like taking a 'step backward some ten centuries to live again the feudal days'.[10]

But such condescension was nothing like the disdain and suspicion directed towards the Chinese. If the West was the source of rationality, order and progress, then China especially remained resolutely corrupt, chaotic and unsound. A taste for '*chinoiserie*' had been fashionable among the European elite since the eighteenth century, a special exhibition of 'Ten Thousand Chinese Things' had been shown in Hyde Park in 1841, and Chinese objects had been part of London's Great Exhibition, but these events had done little to change perceptions of the country, all too easily associated in Victorian minds with the seediness and corruption of the opium trade. The Chinese were typically viewed as childish and incapable, militarily weak and embroiled within a stagnant culture: 'toddling, little-eyed, little-footed, little-bearded, [and] little-minded', suggested the writer Leigh Hunt dismissively.[11] With the experimental new science of photography, travellers like John Thomson, an Edinburgh photographer, were able to document some of the most remote and spectacular areas of China, bringing to the English middle classes images of unfamiliar landscapes and communities, of pagodas, river villages and the Great Wall. But, even so, opinions remained entrenched:

what the British saw in the photographs simply reaffirmed the distinction between the barbarous East and their own more civilized way of life.

Such attitudes were fully on display in public museums. Most visitors expected the presentation of the collections to confirm the way in which they saw the world; in turn, the museum used the objects as a way of shaping opinion. The mechanics of this complicated mutual relationship were rarely explicit, but were clear enough in the arrangement of the exhibits and the language used to discuss them. The American *Harper's New Monthly Magazine* thought the displays of Chinese objects at South Kensington were important not only for bringing to light 'the romance of the East' but also, and more significantly, for their ability 'to revise, correct and estimate the traditions of the Oriental world'.[12] Only through the discipline imposed by the museum, it implied, might a respectable and acceptable impression of China emerge. The 1872 *Catalogue of Chinese Objects* at the South Kensington Museum was blunt about what it called 'the Chinese character', and was anxious to emphasize the distance between the middle-class visitor and the Chinese on display. 'It would hardly be supposed that an effeminate race like the Chinese should have a taste for working in metal,' it pronounced, 'but it must be remembered that they have not always been a degenerate race, softened by luxury and by too great a facility for enjoyment, but that on the contrary, they are still a hardy race.'[13]

Stephen Bushell, of course, had been brought up with such attitudes, and would have been familiar with the contempt which the British were apt to show to unfamiliar parts of the world. He worked for several years in Peking under Sir Rutherford Alcock, whose views of both the Chinese and Japanese were uncomplimentary, and life in a government enclosure would have given Bushell a daily dose of imperial pride and prejudice. But, from his own explorations of Peking and the land around, he knew that there was much more to China than most British people could ever imagine. The stories he listened to outside the compound revealed vibrant histories and contemporary achievements that confounded the common view of the Chinese as 'degenerate'. And he understood that perhaps the best way for the Victorian imagination to grasp the complexity, significance and beauty of Chinese culture was through the artefacts that he was able to collect and explain.

Bushell found an ally in Augustus Franks. Franks, too, was unwilling to be seduced by unthinking and damning caricatures. His wanted his ethnographic collection to speak for itself, to encourage intelligent minds into a new perspective on the world. He wanted more than just an attractive display of curious objects; he was determined to extend Western knowledge of distant countries and understanding of different cultures. His enthusiastic collecting of Indian pieces, for example, had little to do with asserting imperial supremacy or showing off the bizarre accomplishments of a heathen race. Instead, he wanted to raise understanding of Indian art until it was regarded as important and beautiful in its own right: 'I am ambitious to show the fanatics for Greek and Roman sculpture that the art of India is not to be despised,' he wrote in 1881.[14] Similarly, his energetic pursuit of Islamic pieces helped persuade museum staff and visitors that these objects were worthy of a place alongside the esteemed Western antiquities of the ancient world. Franks drew the line at costumes and examples of modern manufacturing from other countries, but otherwise he was quick to see the value of even the most ordinary objects, and their ability to change the way his fellow Victorians looked at cultures beyond their own: even 'the commonest things of the country', he maintained, had a place in explaining and understanding the world.[15]

Bushell soon recognized a kindred spirit in Franks, and, as well as working for the South Kensington Museum, he also joined the international network of collectors serving the British Museum curator. He was not content, however, with just sending back 'the commonest things' and worked hard to find objects that would intrigue, delight and inform back in Britain. He began to establish, and study, a considerable library of books to help him in his search, and he gradually extended his network of local contacts. As time went on, he developed an astounding breadth of knowledgeable interests in his curiosity about all things Chinese. Scrambling up trees, climbing rocky slopes and sliding down riverbanks, he collected plant specimens and seeds for the Royal Botanic Gardens at Kew, thinking nothing of wet feet, muddy knees and the bites of strange insects. He began to study a range of complex extinct Chinese scripts, coming to recognize the difficult characters and in some cases decipher them. He even led a small expedition to the sacred burial grounds of the Qing emperors in the mountains outside Peking so that he could capture rare monkeys that he had seen there, scampering around the ancient stonework. He successfully managed to lure a pair of young animals into his trap, before sending them back on the long journey to the Zoological Society in London.

His correspondence with Philip Cunliffe-Owen and the staff at South Kensington became increasingly enthusiastic. In 1880, he sent a consignment of bronzes for display, followed a couple of years later by four pieces of carved and perforated stone that were traditionally used as weapons and which were, Bushell added proudly, 'relatively rare in China'.[16] Soon, he was given permission to buy officially on the museum's behalf. Instead of financing everything personally, and loaning his own pieces back for display in London, Bushell was now given £250, with the understanding that he would act as an authorized agent and use his expertise to acquire 100 objects at around 50 shillings each. He was delighted. The arrangement gave him both extra funds to collect and the museum's formal sanction for his activities. 'The specimens will be collected gradually and sent to England when opportunities occur,' he wrote cautiously in February 1882 when the agreement was first made, but such was his eagerness – and the richness of what was available – that by November he had already sent a range of objects to the museum, hoping, modestly, that they 'may fill some gaps on the shelves'. By spring 1883, he had asked for, and was granted, another £250 to spend.[17] Jars, cups and dishes; figures, bottles, bowls and bronzes; a sacrificial wine vessel in the form of a rhinoceros and an ivory lion, as well as three glorious examples of early Ming porcelain, all found their way from Peking to South Kensington under Bushell's watchful connoisseurship. Perhaps more importantly, so too did at least some of his understanding of the culture from which they came. These were not objects from the dark, backward China of the Victorian imagination; they were the evidence of a precious past and of a country worthy of more positive attention. Bushell's collecting was beginning to reveal the East in a new light.

Despite what must have been frequent and lengthy absences from the compound, and a growing collection of lovely things adorning his home within it, Bushell's enthusiastic activity in Peking was rarely remarked upon by his British contemporaries. Caught up in the day-to-day responsibilities of government administration, it seems that they were unaware of the progress he was making in China, or of his contribution back in London. Quiet and unassuming, looking every inch the respectable and uncontroversial Victorian doctor, with a neatly trimmed beard, erect, even slightly stiff, stance and earnest demeanour, Bushell was content to keep his achievements to himself, perhaps unaware of quite how much he was accomplishing. When people asked him about his research into Chinese art, or about his collection of objects, he was modest and self-effacing, keen, he said, to 'disclaim any pretension to authority'.[18] He had no desire to get caught up in the academic debates that were starting to erupt as the study of China, or sinology, became more widespread in Europe, and he was acutely aware that, however much he learned, there was always more out there waiting for him in such a vast, ancient and varied nation.

Bushell also knew that he was not alone in his collecting. As Mary Crawford Fraser admitted, 'Of course everybody collected. Half the time there was nothing else to do.' Whiling away a long morning perusing the artefacts 'artistically spread out for inspection', or indulging in 'everlasting bargaining', was just part of the 'native' entertainment of living abroad.[19] During the Peking winter, from November to March, the British delegation was virtually cut off. All provisions had to be brought from Shanghai before the weather closed in and blocked trade routes, and the highlight of the year was provided by a delivery from London, from the Civil Service Stores or the Army and Navy store, once communications reopened. Collecting was a diversion from the enclosed monotony of life, a common talking point. Perhaps this explains why Bushell's activity went largely unnoticed by his colleagues. But, unlike the dilettante souvenir hunter, he was not simply killing time with a hobby. What set him apart was his knowledge and perseverance, his consistent attention to detail and his willingness to dedicate long hours to the study of the pieces he found. In many ways, he was the archetypal scholar, collecting for his own pleasure and to further his own knowledge, happy to share what he knew through the objects he sent back to London, and utterly devoted to his subject.

In time, Bushell collected his knowledge into an authoritative publication, *Chinese Art*, a pioneering study of oriental objects and the culture from which they emerged. He chose to end the first volume with a description of a white agate vase. It was elegant and graceful, a fine example of craftsmanship and a rare piece. And, like so many of Bushell's objects, it was intricately entwined with a story, the fable of the successful scholar. The vase, Bushell noted, was carved with three fishes, animated and lithe, captured in the act of springing into the air and becoming dragons. Only after a fish had managed to overcome the rapids and waterfalls of the Yellow River, after long perseverance and much noble effort, was it worthy of such a transformation. Bushell explained that the fish carved into the vase represented the triumphant scholar who, after arduous study, finally managed to have his name added to what the Chinese called the 'dragon list' – the first step on the ladder of official rank. Poring over the complexities of the Chinese script and overwhelmed by the variety of objects around him, Bushell may well have felt that he was still swimming hard in the river currents. But his collecting increasingly demonstrated an understanding of the combination of material, technique and symbolism, of tangible object and enigmatic myth; showing just how well he was coming to know China, and how close he was to taking the leap as a dragon.

CHAPTER TWENTY

Collecting
Without Boundaries

Magic Chinese bronze mirrors had first been seen in Europe in the early nineteenth century, when distinguished scientists had tried to explain how they worked. When Bushell saw one for the first time, with the sounds of Peking city life buzzing outside, he was enchanted and mystified. It did not seem possible. The front of the mirror was simply a highly polished bronze disc, slightly convex, its surface acting like an ordinary mirror and reflecting the image of anyone looking into it. The reverse was elaborately moulded with mythological figures, animals and birds, and floral scrolls in strong relief. The magic happened when the polished face of the mirror was held up to catch the sun streaming in through the window. Then, on the wall opposite, Bushell saw an exact image of the raised decoration on the back of the mirror. There was still nothing on the face except the glare of the sun, but it was as if the light was passing straight through, as though the mirror had become transparent, a thing no longer of solid metal but of air and light.

Bushell never tired of seeing the 'trick' repeated but it was not long before he found a logical explanation. It was, he concluded, 'an accidental effect', a dramatic but explicable phenomenon caused by 'irregularities on the reflecting surface as a result of uneven pressure in polishing'.[1] But this hardly seemed to spoil the spectacle. It remained special, made even more so by the rarity of the mirrors, and Bushell's knowledge that he was privileged to see in action objects that had been a source of pride to emperors as far back as the Han dynasty (206 BC–AD 24). Memories of the mirrors' translucence stayed with him, and, when he came to write up his experiences of Chinese art many years later, he relived the moment, bringing to life once again the mystery of the magic mirrors, not as a bizarre party trick for the Victorian parlour, but as evidence of Chinese tradition and ingenuity.

Bushell was always careful to see beyond the enigma of the mirrors, noting how beautifully they were designed and crafted, each a masterpiece of bronze metalworking and finishing, and evidence of the refinement of ancient techniques. With a collector's appreciation of fine workmanship, Bushell emphasized the skill of the decorative moulding and the quality of the materials, as much as the spectacle of illusion. This was what always drew him back to Chinese art: 'The connoisseur always looks at the intrinsic properties of the medium, and its effects in bringing out the skill of the craftsman which ennobles it.'[2]

Close inspection and detailed study became the hallmarks of Bushell's approach. Every style, skill and material came in for rigorous scrutiny. Ivory appealed to him, particularly Canton ivory, because 'there is no material more satisfying to a delicate and refined taste', and he spent long hours in the hot, close Peking summers learning the feel of the bone in his hand, studying the intricacies of the carving and examining the patina of the vessels in the dusty alleys along the city walls.[3] He became an expert in Chinese glazes, watching modern craftsmen at work as well as studying the techniques of the past, and he discovered that it was the addition of lime to the glaze that gave the familiar lustre to Chinese ceramics, creating 'a characteristic tinge of green or blue' as well as 'a brilliancy of surface and a pellucid depth'.[4] He investigated the methods for working jade, and he familiarized himself with the complex practice of lacquering, prizing in particular the elegance and delicacy of Foochow lacquer.[5] All around him was the evidence of unique and historic skills, luring him away from the aches and pains of the British officials and their wives, and into the bustle of the city markets.

Architectural detail, too, fascinated Bushell. He observed many of the same materials and techniques employed on a larger scale, to create ingenious buildings and stunning decorative effects. At the ChangLing Tomb, the best preserved of the thirteen Ming Tombs in Peking, he admired 'sunken panels worked in relief and lacquered with dragons' and in the Imperial Summer Palace, seven miles outside Peking, he loitered on the Pavilion Bridge, 'hung with bronze bells which tinkle softly in the breeze', and clambered over the steps of the Pavilion of Precious Clouds, 'piled with bricks and bushes to keep off pilferers', to get close to a building that was made entirely of cast bronze, shimmering blue in the light.[6] As with the smaller objects he took home to study, Bushell investigated details of construction and decoration techniques, exploring the intricacies of large-scale design with the same precision he applied to smaller pieces of art. Walking through the trees to discover the turreted pagoda in the Changchunyuan, or Garden of Everlasting Spring, in the Imperial Summer Palace, for example, he was struck by its distinctive colour and form, and went to great efforts to describe the ways in which these effects were achieved. 'The glazes used in the decoration of this pagoda are five in number; a deep purplish blue derived from a compound of cobalt and manganese silicates, a rich green from copper silicates, a yellow, approaching the tint of a yolk of an egg, from antimony, a *sang de boeuf* red from copper mixed with deoxidising flux, and a charming turquoise blue derived from copper combined with nitre,' he explained, with the scientific eye of a doctor, before adding a note with the enthusiasm of the collector: 'The fivefold combination is intended to suggest the five jewels of the Buddhist paradise.'[7]

But, even in the 1870s and 1880s, the objects of Bushell's admiration were not untouched. The ruins of the Imperial Summer Palace were not the result of centuries of natural decay and degradation, but of attack by British and French troops in 1860, after the end of the Second Opium War. In a retaliatory operation under the command of James Bruce, 8th Earl of Elgin, whose father had 'collected' the Elgin marbles, 3,500 British soldiers set the buildings alight in a fire that lasted three days. Only thirteen buildings in the enormous complex of palaces remained intact, mostly in remote areas, and the elaborate gardens were destroyed. There was widespread and chaotic looting. Over subsequent years, a variety of important pieces were sold to eager collectors by profiteering soldiers and local adventurers: embroidered robes, sculptures and carvings, furniture, paintings and porcelain. It is estimated that one and a half million relics eventually found their way into more than 2,000 museums in forty-seven countries, while many thousands more ended up in private collections.[8] At the British Museum, Augustus Franks negotiated directly with the military to acquire a pair of ancient vases and some glazed architectural roof tiles – similar to the ones Bushell so admired – which were taken as souvenirs by Captain de Negroni, a French officer. Plenty more ceramic pieces were donated by returning soldiers. All over Britain, the growing fashion for things Chinese was swelled by the looted treasures; collectors were anxious to profit from the sudden arrival of so many interesting objects and the market flourished. Back in Peking, amid the ruins of the Summer Palace, Bushell could only go so far with his studies. Ironically, many of the objects that would have most illuminated his work were now scattered across the world.

Looting was just one more way of getting objects on the move. In an age of international collecting, neither collectors nor objects seemed confined by national boundaries. The aristocratic atmosphere and dignified dining of the Fine Arts Club might have made it seem a quintessentially English organization, busying itself with London affairs and serving the needs of British collectors. In fact, it reflected the expanding world of collecting: truly international in scope and aspiration, it was in contact with collectors and connoisseurs from far and wide. It was not just that some members acquired a taste for things Chinese or Indian, for exotic objects from faraway nations. Nor was it that many members had trade interests that took them beyond Britain, making fortunes abroad that they could then spend at home on their collections. There was also a more far-reaching and fundamental internationalism, a growing recognition that collecting was a way of understanding, appreciating and managing the world, and that shrinking distances were allowing collectors from the furthest reaches of the Empire to meet together in London.

In 1840, the sickly Charles Fortnum, already bored at the age of twenty with his family's business interests, emigrated to Australia to develop land in New South Wales. He did not stay for long; five years later, he was back in London. But the trip had given him a taste for travel. He had discovered a new world whose natural history absorbed him, and a fascination with collecting that was to last a lifetime. Back in England, he married a wealthy cousin, who could fund his new enthusiasm, and immediately set off on buying trips; he began a long association with the Ashmolean Museum in Oxford, the British and South Kensington Museums, developed an expertise in Early German prints and became a member of the Burlington Fine Arts Club. There he met an Australian, George Salting, who had grown up in Sydney. They had plenty to discuss. They knew the same places in the growing Australian city, the bizarre flora and fauna of its bay, and they shared experiences of the protracted sea voyage. They became friends, and, when, at the age of thirty, Salting was left the fortune his father had made in Australia's sheep stations and sugar plantations, both men sat together exchanging collectors' anecdotes and scouring the catalogues and sales bulletins for the furniture, jewellery, bronzes, medals, enamels, ceramics, ivories, glass, textiles, leatherwork, manuscripts and paintings that were to become part of Salting's magnificent collection.[9] It was a long way from the harsh open terrain of New South Wales and the undiscovered wilderness of nineteenth-century Australia; the Fine Arts Club provided a retreat for collectors, no matter how far they had come.

Trends set by high-profile collectors like Salting were taken up all over the world, and particularly in America. Salting's enthusiasm for Chinese porcelain, for example, was shared by men such as William Thompson Walters, a Baltimore liquor merchant and collector who had opened his house to the public (for a visiting fee of 50 cents) in the mid-1870s. There was nothing limited or introspective about this type of collecting. There were no boundaries, and distance was not an obstacle. If an object had to be shipped around the world from its place of origin, sold in one continent and displayed in another, then there were increasing numbers of people with the resources and dedication to make this happen.

When William Thompson Walters developed an enthusiasm for Chinese porcelain and decided to assemble a significant collection, Stephen Wootton Bushell was by now the obvious man to guide such a project. By the 1880s, Walters' fortune was vast. What had begun as a relatively modest grain and then liquor business had expanded to take in banking and railways, from Washington DC to Florida and Missouri. He was a director of every line of steamers between Baltimore and the Southern states; he bred horses, patronized local Maryland artists and had amassed more than 3,000 pieces of Chinese porcelain in forty years.[10] All that remained was to record his achievements for posterity, and to find someone with the expertise to catalogue his pieces of oriental art. His first port of call was the British Museum, but staff there, aware of their own limitations, directed him instead to Peking where Bushell was continuing his studies. Without hesitation, Walters commissioned Bushell to write his catalogue, and in the late 1880s arranged for him to make the journey from China to see the pieces for himself.

After long years in the low-lying streets of Peking, arrival in Baltimore's busy port was something of a shock for Bushell. A smoggy industrial hub, the city echoed with the noise of shipbuilding and its skyline was already straining upwards, spiked with church spires and factory chimneys. Bushell was taken through the city to Walters' home in Mount Vernon Place, where the imposing townhouses with their European architecture and the neatly laid park around the Washington memorial column brought home to him again how far he had travelled. This bold American grandeur seemed like a different world. But, before too long, Bushell found himself surrounded by familiar objects, by forms and designs and colours that he had seen so many times before in Peking houses and market stalls, and the alarming size of the globe contracted to a room filled with China.

We don't know how long Bushell stayed in Baltimore to study Walters' collection. After such a journey, and with so much work to do, it seems safe to assume that he spent several weeks at least, and possibly several months, getting to know the collection, cross-referencing with the books he had brought with him from China and drawing on conversations he had had with Peking merchants and collectors. The two men had little in common beyond their collecting, but this proved more than enough to sustain them. Bushell had found a collector who was as passionate about Chinese culture and objects as he was, and in their spare moments there was also a variety of other distractions in Walters' vast collection: contemporary European paintings, sculptures, French landscapes and antique vases. With Walters' enthusiastic support, Bushell described not only the Chinese objects themselves, but also the intricacies of their construction and decoration techniques, their historical and social contexts, and their relationship to similar objects across the East. He translated ancient Chinese texts and consulted modern ones. The catalogue grew and grew, the pages of Bushell's manuscript mounted, his notes expanding into long and erudite descriptions. The time came for him to return to China, and still he wrote. As life settled back into a round of medical visits, the book continued to take shape, with the routine of writing punctuating the days.

Rooted in Walters' magnificent collection, the catalogue soon became much more than just a simple record. After returning from Baltimore as a young man in his late thirties, Bushell worked on the book for fifteen years, marking his forties with chapter after chapter of studious text. The result was to be a major work: the first comprehensive study of Chinese, Japanese and Korean art in the English language, a pioneering undertaking. Entering enthusiastically into its scale and ambition, Walters took on the task of commissioning illustrations, scouring America for someone whom he believed could provide accurate pictures to accompany Bushell's writing. He chose Louis Prang, from Massachusetts, to work on the lithographs, instructing him to supply the highest quality regardless of cost, and approving a final count of 2,000 printing stones to create 116 lithographic plates. He looked even further afield for an artist he thought capable of doing the water-colour illustrations, employing an Englishman, James Callowhill, along with his three sons, converting the second-floor north-facing library of his house into their studio and installing them in their own living quarters for the duration of the work.[11] Money was no object. Walters was reportedly willing to pay $250,000 to see the book produced to the highest standards and he was notoriously exacting in ensuring that everything was of the very best quality.

It was not until 1896 that the book was finally ready. It was entitled *Oriental Ceramic Art* and it ran to ten volumes, a monument to Bushell's scholarship and nineteenth-century American publishing. Each volume was lavishly bound in yellow cloth, backed with yellow silk, with silk bands to act as markers, each one tipped with a fine bone handle. Alongside the coloured plates, there were over 400 black and white illustrations, and each book in the limited edition of 500 was carefully numbered and recorded; subscribers' names were printed on the title page in return for their $500 investment. The finished article was exactly what Walters had hoped for. But, while Bushell now had this lavish achievement to his name, marking him out across the world as an intellectual heavyweight, his American employer did not live to see the project complete. Walters died two years before the catalogue's publication, in November 1894, with a reputation for 'judgement that was authoritative on all questions of art' and leaving behind him an incomplete masterpiece.[12]

Even before *Oriental Ceramic Art* was published, the book was attracting attention. Collectors all over the world became aware of Bushell's work, and watched with interest as the project evolved, not only intrigued to know what was in Walters' collection, but also interested to see what impact the catalogue would have. In America, particularly, others were eager to replicate Walters' ambitious venture and to have their own collections recorded in a similar way. The quiet scholar from

Peking was in demand, and it was another wealthy American businessman, Heber Reginald Bishop, who was next to employ Bushell's services for posterity.

Bishop, who had made a fortune first in exporting sugar from Cuba and later in gas, iron and the railways, had a taste for jade. He had known Bushell for some time – probably through his connections to Walters – when in 1889 he asked him to begin a catalogue of his jade collection. This was not a particular speciality of Bushell's, but he already knew something of the long and complex tradition of jade-working, and recognized that 'there is much to be gathered from Chinese sources' to illuminate Bishop's pieces.[13] He agreed to become involved and Bishop, inspired by *Oriental Ceramic Art*, made the long journey to China to see what they could unearth together. From his home in New York, he travelled overland to Vancouver, before setting sail for Yokohama in Japan and on to Hong Kong, continuing to Shanghai before finally arriving, many exhausting weeks later, in Peking.

Fortunately, the journey proved worthwhile. Bishop and Bushell purchased a wealth of spectacular jade objects, from practical but delicate vessels to pendants and ornaments designed for emperors; from flower holders and head rests to sceptres and screens, many with elaborate pierced and relief decoration. Traditionally, Chinese jade was a special material, invoked by poets to reflect the colours of nature and revered as a 'singing stone' because of its resonant qualities. It was reserved for imperial use. Workers laboured in a special compound of the palace enclosure, under close supervision from officials; the pieces they made were banned from sale to the outside world – so it was not an easy thing for an American visitor to collect. It took guile and bartering skills, Bishop's apparently bottomless purse and Bushell's long-standing network of loyal contacts to extract some of the pieces from their hiding places and amass a shipment to go back to New York.

In quieter moments, the two men also found time to agree a way of working on the catalogue and it was settled that Bushell would go to America for three months the following year to study the jade and help Bishop put together a publication. For Bushell, it was quite an undertaking. Still in the middle of writing his catalogue for Walters, it meant another long voyage overseas, new and demanding research and the challenges of working with another opinionated American tycoon. It was an intimidating prospect, and there were no doubt moments when Bushell felt he would have preferred things to have remained as they had been before Bishop's arrival – unhurried days of calm study in and around Peking's familiar monuments and undisturbed buying from trusted traders. Unfortunately, the process of publication turned out to be just as tortuous as Bushell feared: it was ten more years before he had amassed the information he needed about the collection, finished working with Bishop on the text, and completed 'procuring specimens of interesting ancient pieces' on the American's behalf.[14] The final two-volume catalogue was not published until 1906; in the Preface, Bishop praised his British colleague 'for the great assistance given to me, from first to last, in this work and all my studies of Oriental Art'.[15]

However daunting the task might have seemed, Bushell had little choice but to take it on: he needed the money. Bishop agreed to pay £300 for Bushell's work in New York writing the catalogue entries, an amount which was equivalent to half the doctor's annual salary. It was a financial lifeline. Beyond the day-to-day routine of medical consultations, government paperwork, the social life of the Peking compound and his reading and writing, a stalling world economy and general financial uncertainty had left Bushell broke. Just a few weeks after Bishop's visit to Peking, the collapse of the Oriental Bank took with it the family savings, and any kind of security Bushell and his wife might have hoped for. 'We are well-nigh ruined,' Bushell admitted plaintively to Bishop.[16]

But even the agreement with Bishop was not enough to do more than ease immediate financial worries. In the longer term, Bushell realized that he would have to find additional income to ensure some reserves for the future and funds for his collecting. He was forced to consider what he could sell: his knowledge and expertise. There was already the work for the extraordinarily wealthy like Bishop, acting as researcher and adviser, but he guessed there was also the possibility of acting as an agent for other, less wealthy, collectors who might be willing to pay him to buy in China on their behalf. With the resourcefulness of the impecunious, Bushell was soon contacting friends, colleagues and friends of friends to tender his services. He knew he had plenty to offer: there were still very few Europeans who had spent any length of time in China, or who knew as much as he did about its culture and there was hardly anyone who was as familiar with the markets, or as friendly with the traders. Indeed there were no other collectors in such a privileged position to acquire the finest Chinese objects.

Bushell's persistence paid off, and before long he was supplying a number of clients from a variety of backgrounds and with a range of interests: coins for Sir James Stewart Lockhart, Registrar General and Colonial Secretary in Hong Kong; archaeological specimens for Sir Aurel Stein, a British adventurer and explorer in Central Asia; and porcelain for Alfred Trapnell, a humble metal smelter from Clifton in Bristol. He kept his activities low-key, and was loath to advertise himself as any kind of established dealer, but nevertheless the business grew. As with his own collecting, Bushell was thorough in his research and wise in his buying, and no doubt his customers were delighted with the carefully chosen pieces he packaged up to send to them. But, even with a core of loyal paying clients, money was still tight and, having started to profit from his talents, Bushell began to see that with some astute buying and selling he could put an end to his financial woes for good. Perhaps inspired by the example of the American entrepreneurs with whom he was now working, Bushell abandoned the Victorian suspicion of 'trade' and decided to branch out into perhaps the most lucrative of his activities: playing the London art market.

The fashion for blue-and-white china, particularly pieces from the K'ang-hsi period, had not passed Bushell by. He may have been thousands of miles away in Peking, but he was aware that large amounts of money were changing hands in London showrooms for things he saw every day on local market stalls. The opportunity seemed too good to miss. Setting himself up to trade was not without awkwardness, however. Bushell collected antique and exclusive ceramics for himself and he selected similar pieces for his private clients, but the market in England for 'Old Nankin Porcelain' was apparently so voracious that just as much money was to be made from contemporary reproductions with none of the cultural history that Bushell so valued. There was nothing intrinsically wrong with such modern Chinese pieces, but, designed to look like antique K'ang-hsi wares and 'well calculated to deceive the unwary', they were part of a dubious trade designed to make quick profits out of enthusiastic but naïve collectors.[17]

It is clear that Bushell had reservations about what he was doing: during a series of sales at Christie's during the 1880s, he was careful to remain anonymous, appearing in the catalogues simply as 'A Gentleman in China', and never attending the sales himself. He was no doubt conscious of his dignity as a public servant, but the secrecy about his identity also suggests, I think, a certain embarrassment in exploiting a fashion purely for profit, even though there were plenty of other dealers doing just that. As a gentleman doctor and government representative, Bushell would have been wary of being seen as just another dealer, which could well have undermined his social standing. As a scholar and a collector, too, he might have wanted to keep this kind of business separate from his renowned work on high-quality pieces. However, as a financial experiment the venture was a success. One auction alone, in August 1888, brought Bushell over £600 (more than his annual salary), and it seems likely that over the decade he managed to earn as much as £10,000, a considerable supplement to his doctor's income.[18] But by continuing to feed a market that was already frequently unscrupulous, confused and opaque, the sales can also be seen as something of a lapse on Bushell's part, no doubt driven by necessity, but nonetheless threatening to undo the work of long years spent trying to dissociate the serious collecting of Chinese objects and the study of their contexts from the frivolous dictates of popular fashion.

From doctor to scholar to dealer, Bushell's life in Peking had taken a number of unexpected turns. He remained in post there for thirty years and never lost his affection for the city, his fascination with its buildings and delight in its objects. But what was a treasure trove for a learned collector was not always so ideal for family life, and Bushell's wife and children had to suffer the hardships of foreign living without the benefits of his diverting interests. Florence was resourceful, positive and loyal, and remained firmly by her husband's side throughout the three decades, but the infant mortality that was ever present in Victorian England was yet more of a fear in Peking. Even a doctor's family suffered, and in the winter of 1892, Sir Robert Hart, Inspector General of Customs in China, wrote: 'We are once more sorrowing for the Bushells who have just lost their little two-year-old daughter Dorothy, the fifth I think to die out of six charming children'.[19] Thankfully, the Bushell's youngest child, a boy, managed to survive into adulthood, but the years of sadness and loss in the Bushell household were long, and Bushell's exhilarating days in the grounds of ancient palaces were tempered by many agonizing nights at the bedside of a dying child. When his own ill-health finally forced him to retire from government service and return to Britain in November 1899, he knew the voyage home was a final one. He would not be returning to China again. As the ship pulled out of the harbour at Shanghai, there was the sorrow of parting and regret at the things that would remain undiscovered, but also a sense of relief at having come through something of a trial.

Bushell anticipated using his retirement to reinvigorate research on his personal collection and to begin work on what would become *Chinese Art*. In preparation, he wrote to South Kensington asking for the return of a group of Chinese bronzes which he had collected during the 1880s and loaned to the museum for display. He was formal and reserved, even curt. Since his early visits to the museum as a young man, the staff had changed and he now felt only a professional courtesy to those dealing with his request. Besides, he was eager to begin installing his collection in the house he had taken in Upper Norwood, south London. At the museum, the request was completely unexpected, and the staff were horrified. Accustomed to loans metamorphosing into donations, they had had no expectation that Bushell might actually want his objects back; it was noted with obvious dismay that 'the return of these bronzes will make a serious gap in our Chinese collection'.[20] George Salting advised the museum to try to buy the pieces instead, and, since this seemed the only option, hurried arrangements were made to organize a sale and thus preserve the displays.

Bushell, however, was 'not at all willing to part with the collection'.[21] He had plans for it. He entered into a tetchy correspondence with South Kensington, defending his right to the bronzes. In the end, he only agreed to consider the idea of a sale because it was 'put to him that if purchased by us, his name would be attached to the objects which would form an important collection'.[22] Like many collectors, the idea of having his name publicly linked, for posterity, to an assortment of beautiful pieces was too tempting for him to resist. There was fame in it, beyond the usual expectations of a government administrator, and there would be clear evidence for future generations of his pioneering role in understanding Chinese art. Bushell may have been unpretentious and modest, but he was not without enormous pride in his collections, and the museum's offer to publicly recognize his contribution turned out to be irresistible.

There were further negotiations. Bushell insisted on keeping some weapons and a large vase 'because it was a present to me', but he agreed to sell the rest of the objects for £400.[23] This in turn upset the museum, since George Salting had valued the collection at only £350 and budgets were, as ever, under pressure. It looked like a stalemate, but the museum was only impoverished, not foolishly stubborn. It was acknowledged that 'it is improbable that an equally favourable opportunity will occur of purchasing such a collection' and in the end the sale was agreed before Bushell's return to England; museum staff finally accepted his valuation on the grounds that, since he had not wanted to sell in the first place, 'we cannot well ask him to reduce his price'.[24] Florence, who had gone to London ahead of her husband to prepare their new home, accepted delivery of the vase and weapons as Bushell was leaving Peking; the remaining pieces were left, to the museum's relief, to form the core of the galleries' Chinese display.

After his retirement, Bushell spent his remaining years quietly, surrounded by the pieces that evoked for him the spirit of the China he had left. He continued to study and worked hard on *Chinese Art*, which was published in two volumes by the South Kensington Museum in 1904 and 1906. Although it professed to be simply a guide to the Chinese collection, it was of course much more. It was a unique and lasting achievement, a fine piece of scholarship in praise of the exquisite objects and fascinating traditions that had enthralled Bushell for so long. It is still valued today. Although Bushell remained characteristically modest about his achievements, he knew that the publication would identify him forever as a collector and connoisseur, and he was proud of this. There was also something reassuring and satisfying about seeing his contribution made tangible in museum displays, and when he died, two years after the second volume of *Chinese Art* appeared, Florence agreed to a series of loans and sales which further consolidated his presence at South Kensington. With prices for Chinese objects already rising sharply, the museum took advantage of a number of bargains. Thanks to Bushell's canny dealing in the ceramics markets, Florence was, staff noted, 'not by any means in straitened circumstances' and she seemed willing to preserve her husband's memory at the museum at the most reasonable of costs, agreeing to accept £700 in payment for vases valued at £1,054 and selling a number of small items for as little as £5 each.[25]

When Bushell sailed from Shanghai for the last time, just before the dawn of the twentieth century, China was changing fast. It was already more familiar to Europeans than it had been when he arrived during the 1860s, and was now a target for international territorial ambitions as well as an important trading partner. Peking, too, was becoming increasingly accessible and within a few years was linked by rail to strategic centres across China and so to the rest of the Continent. But it was also becoming a more turbulent and dangerous place for foreigners as locals rejected what they saw as the corruption of the West. Just a year after Bushell's departure, this spilled over into overt violence: during the Boxer Rebellion of 1900, the foreign legations in Peking were put under siege for several months, businesses that dealt with Western clients were attacked and there was fierce fighting between European and Chinese troops. The opportunities for collecting as Bushell had done – thoughtfully, sensitively and over long decades – were disappearing, and the contribution he had made to scholarship was increasingly recognized as bold and unique. Few collectors in the future would have such an opportunity to unravel the mysteries of an unknown nation through its objects, or would make so much of the chance when it came.

Epilogue

'To stay what is fleeting... to immortalize
things that have no duration.'

John Ruskin

W riting in *The Stones of Venice*, in the middle of the nineteenth
century (1851–3), John Ruskin urged his fellow Victorians
to look for something enduring and meaningful in art, a special
quality that would arrest the destructive forces of time and 'stay
what is fleeting'. It could have been the motto of the Victorian
collector. In an age of bewildering technological, scientific and
social change, the collection often appeared as a still point, a place
outside of time where all that mattered was the objects and where
the desire of the collector removed them from the chaos of the
world beyond. Then, as now, some collectors embraced the idea
of buying and selling, bartering and exchanging; they viewed
their custodianship as a temporary hiatus in the dynamic life of
the objects they collected. But many more had at least a core to
their collection that they wished to protect. Where they could,

they put in place mechanisms for ensuring that the collection would survive without them, defending it from the threat of an uncertain fate.

The collectors in this book were typical of many in imagining a durable future for their collections. They believed that they had created something lasting and self-contained, buffered from forces over which they had no control. Murray Marks and J. C. Robinson both celebrated a lifetime spent acquiring beautiful objects by donating to a range of public museums, making permanent in the galleries their expertise and achievements. Stephen Wootton Bushell arranged for his objects to become part of the collections at the Victoria and Albert Museum after his death, visibly marking decades of scholarly collecting. With her gift of English ceramics, enamels and glass to the same museum, Charlotte Schreiber hoped to preserve a memorial to her beloved husband, a sense of what they had enjoyed and achieved together. Joseph Mayer left both the collection at the Liverpool Museum and the thriving village of Bebington as a monument to his work, convinced he had secured their future by his lifetime's efforts.

All of these collectors tried to preserve the objects they thought best captured their dedication and expertise. They attempted to immortalize themselves in the continuing life of the collection. But they had all seen other collections come and go. Inevitably, if regretfully, they must have had a sense of collecting as an intrinsically ephemeral occupation. They had seen numerous collections sold and dismantled; they had indeed profited themselves from the ebb and flow of objects coming on to the market. What made them think, then, that this time it would be different?

The emergence of a network of public museums appears to have convinced many Victorian collectors that their collections would survive their deaths. Private collections, they had witnessed, were subject to death and war, bankruptcy and changes in taste and fashion. Public galleries, it seemed safe to assume, were immune from such vacillations. Once given over to the protection of the British Museum or the Victoria and Albert, it seemed, the fate of the individual was irrelevant to the survival of the collection. Original intentions – and the personality of the collector – would be preserved forever. By the end of the nineteenth century, almost every town in the country had a public museum asserting order and permanence, and many boasted impressive examples of philanthropy – parks and schools and libraries – that added to the impression that individual names could be saved from obscurity by being associated with lasting municipal projects. Collecting was perhaps not as fragile an occupation as it once had been. Instead, it seemed to be part of a wider public movement.

Of course, it was not always to turn out that way. It is true that public collections would have languished and faded without donations from private collectors. At the end of the nineteenth century, particularly in the uncertain economic climate of the 1880s and 1890s, the sums available for public purchases dwindled, and became increasingly difficult to tease out of government. By 1887, it was estimated that the value of gifts and bequests from individuals to the Victoria and Albert Museum, for example, had exceeded £1 million, at original prices – over three times as much as had been spent on acquisitions by the museum itself.[1] Nothing displayed the breadth of Victorian collecting so well as the range of objects bequeathed to the South Kensington galleries: books, Old Master drawings and prints in 1876 on the death of John Forster, the historian and critic who became famous for writing the biography of his friend Charles Dickens; six years later, a superb collection of French eighteenth-century furniture donated by John Jones, who had made his fortune in tailoring uniforms for the military; in 1888, hundreds of sketches from the studio of John Constable, given by Isabel, his last surviving daughter; and, at the turn of the century, the library of Emilia Strong, Lady Dilke, author and art historian. Victorian collections like these form the basis of most British museum displays today.

Yet these donations and bequests have largely become dissociated from the collectors who made them. Names have been lost; the objects have been re-presented and re-interpreted, often distancing them from their original contexts to emphasize their apparent relevance to modern visitors. In particular, the preoccupations and intentions of the original collectors have frequently been obscured, and very often collections that were meant to remain intact have become scattered. The objects themselves are no less important, rare or beautiful than they were a hundred and fifty years ago, but they have been pared of their personal associations. The ingenuity and pride of the people who acquired them has been dimmed, and the durability they envisaged has often proved fleeting. The safe haven that was imagined to exist in the galleries of public museums has proved precarious after all. As we have seen, even the most self-contained collection is subject to all kinds of social, economic and political forces. For a collection in a public gallery – rather than tucked away in a private study – these forces are, if anything, magnified; they are certainly inescapable. No matter how serene and timeless a public museum might at first seem, nothing about it is permanent.

While the publication of Charlotte Schreiber's journals gave readers a taste of her collecting adventures, it was not long before the redesign of the Victoria and Albert galleries broke up the collection itself. The pieces were exhibited alongside other similar objects, arranged by type, design or decoration, rather than as a discrete set, and the Schreiber name became a method of curatorial identification, printed in small type at the bottom of display labels, rather than the public celebration of an energetic collecting crusade.[2] The jewellery, plate, needlework and other items that Charlotte had been unable to resist on her travels were inevitably dispersed on her death. So, too, was the not inconsiderable collection of European ceramics and enamels. When Charlotte left Langham House to move in with her youngest daughter, Blanche, Countess of Bessborough in 1890, a sale at Christie's began the process of dispersal, and 217 lots found their way to new homes. The pieces that remained passed to Charlotte's family on her death, were divided among her children and divided again during later generations, until the original shape of the collection was distorted beyond easy recognition.

When Joseph Mayer died in 1886, at the age of eighty-three, his instructions to finance the Bebington projects by selling off the complete Pennant House collection – all the papers, documents and letters as well as the objects – were carried out promptly. Within weeks, his old home was cleared, the whole collection was put under the hammer, and the resulting funds went to the Mayer Trust to finance the village library, gardens and lecture hall. But Mayer's belief that he had created something permanent through his collecting was quickly shown to be misplaced. A growing village is not cheap to run, and the money raised by the sale was only sufficient to finance the Mayer facilities until 1894. After that, a crisis of funds forced the district council to step in, principally to maintain an efficient library service, and for a while things were run jointly between the council and the Mayer Trust. By 1930, however, the Mayer legacy had been exhausted, and the local authorities took over full responsibility: Mayer's involvement, already largely forgotten, officially came to an end. In 1971, traces of his name were further erased when a new civic complex replaced the original Mayer Library; during the subsequent decades Mayer Hall became neglected and shabby, its walls greying and its roof leaking. It can still be seen, at the heart of Bebington, offering a venue for local meetings and events, but rather unhappily awaiting repair.

Meanwhile, Mayer's injunction to the Liverpool Museum that 'the Collection shall be kept together' was, in time, ignored, or simply forgotten. Visitors lost any clear sense of what it was Mayer had collected, of the range and personality represented by his pieces – of who he was. The eccentricities disappeared; order was imposed. The Egyptian material was carefully displayed with other Egyptian pieces; the ceramics shown with decorative arts; many of the casts, cameos, prints and medals were lost or completely disassociated from the Mayer name. In May 1941, German bombing further added to the confusion: the Egyptian gallery was completely burnt out, the entire building was ravaged by fire, and it was not until fifteen years later that the museum could reopen. Although some of Mayer's objects had been moved out of the city for safety, many were destroyed. The Egyptian sarcophagus of Bakenkhonsu, for example, was smashed to pieces (although it has recently been restored in a major conservation project), and particularly hard hit was his collection of European pottery, which was almost completely wiped out.[3] The collection that Mayer believed would long outlive him had turned out to be fragile too; collecting proved a precarious way to arrest the uncertainties of time.

Murray Marks' conscientious support of the Pre-Raphaelite painters has largely been obscured by their subsequent popularity and success; the letters, notes and sketches which he kept as proof of his judgement and foresight have not been enough to prevent him from falling into the shadows. His friends found lasting fame; by contrast, Marks and his influential role in constructing Victorian aesthetics and taste have been more or less forgotten. He was not a diligent letter writer, and was apparently unwilling to enshrine his knowledge and experience in print: 'he does know a great deal but seems not to have the slightest faculty for writing it down,' remarked Rossetti.[4] The objects from his London house were dispersed after his death in several summer sales at Christie's in

1918, and have long since passed into the hands of other collectors. Very few of the pieces he bequeathed to the Victoria and Albert Museum are easy to locate today. A handful of blue-and-white vases displayed together in the British Galleries include two pieces which belonged to Rossetti and one which was part of Whistler's collection. They were quite likely to have passed through Marks' hands, and provide enduring evidence of the popular fashion he helped create. It is also possible to see Rossetti's pastel portrait of Marks' wife in the museum's Print Room. But, on the whole, Marks has simply disappeared. His collecting has been forgotten.

Similarly, few of Stephen Wootton Bushell's objects remain on public display to tell his story. Those pieces he sent back to London as an agent, working on behalf of the South Kensington Museum, are not at all easy to identify: his name is not attached to the labels, and only a prefix '1883' identifies things which Bushell collected. There are rarely more than a handful of objects on display. I would recommend that anyone wanting a real taste of Bushell's interests and wide-ranging research begins with a copy of *Chinese Art*, which offers a colourful and comprehensive insight into his activities.

Even John Charles Robinson, the most belligerent and ambitious of collectors, could not prevent a new generation from breaking up the collection he treasured. As we have seen, his pieces were quickly scattered after his death at home at Newton Manor on 10 April 1913. By September, many of the drawings were put up for sale, and, by February 1914, works from Robinson's collection were appearing regularly at Sotheby's.[5] Before long, the only reference to Robinson's passionate years of searching, haggling and manoeuvring was a short catalogue entry describing the provenance of an object, recording simply that he had once owned it but revealing nothing of the time and energy he had invested in acquiring it.

* * *

Despite the best efforts of so many of the leading Victorian collectors, the life of their collections proved uncertain. Some found lasting homes, and are still significant today: the Pitt Rivers collection remains a valued asset of the University of Oxford; the collections of Sir John Soane and Frederick John Horniman are both publicly displayed in London; over 4,000 objects, pictures and books belonging to Sir Thomas William Holburne continue to form the core of the Holburne Museum in Bath. But many more have been subjected to dispersal, disinterest and neglect. Each was the result of a particular preoccupation, a very personal adventure that proved not to long outlive the collector. Each was a moment in a specific time, a window on nineteenth-century concerns and attitudes, a quirky glimpse of a changing age. But, while the collections themselves may have been broken up, lost or discarded, their stories continue to offer snapshots of a Victorian legacy that has endured. In these collections, we see the evolution of scholarship, professionalism and expertise that informs today's collectors, curators and connoisseurs; we can understand the emerging possibilities for public collecting and accessible display which are the foundations of twenty-first-century museums; we sense a growing curiosity about other peoples and a respect for their objects which helped change entrenched colonial attitudes; we can trace a developing fascination with the ways in which we display and construct our identity through the things we own; and we witness the increasing sophistication and manipulation of a market which still drives much of the collecting world. The collections may not have lasted, but many of the cultural changes that they embodied still resonate today.

Acknowledgments

Some of the ideas for this book emerged during work on a Ph.D. thesis at the University of Sheffield, and I am indebted to Professor Sally Shuttleworth, now Head of Humanities at the University of Oxford, for the encouragement, guidance and perceptive criticism which set me on my way. As the book developed, however, it took on a character all of its own, and warm thanks is due to the archive staff and a number of specialist curators at the Victoria and Albert Museum who have helped inform and refine the project, especially Julius Bryant, Stephen Calloway, Peta Motture, Marjorie Trusted, Ming Wilson and Hilary Young. I would also like to thank those at the National Museums Liverpool who have given advice on Joseph Mayer, particularly Dr Ashley Cooke, Head of Antiquities, and David Moffat, assistant curator of Decorative Art. Professor Nick Pearce, Head of the School of Culture and Creative Arts at the University of Glasgow, kindly helped me on the trail of Stephen Wootton Bushell and generously shared some of his research.

Particular thanks is due to Tim Bates, for making *Magpies* happen, to Ravi Mirchandani for trusting that it would happen well, and to all the staff at Pollinger and Atlantic Books. It is always a pleasure working with them. I would also like to thank my parents for their continued encouragement and my lovely husband for everything, but in particular for sharing a moment of inspiration that created the book's title.

Notes

Chapter 1
1.   *The Building News.* (22 April 1864), pp. 297–8.
2.   J. C. Robinson (ed.), *The Catalogue of the Special Exhibition of Works of Art of the Medieval, Renaissance, and more Recent Periods, on loan at the South Kensington Museum*, revised edition (London: Eyre and Spottiswoode, 1863), p. 2.
3.   'The New Court, South Kensington Museum', *The Builder*, 3 May 1862, p. 305; 'The Loan Collection at South Kensington', *Fine Arts Quarterly Review* (1864), p. 20.
4.   'Art Treasures at South Kensington', *Bentley's Miscellany* (October 1862), p. 349.
5.   'The South Kensington Museum and Loan Exhibition', *Quarterly Review*, 225 (January 1863), pp. 176–207.
6.   'Les sculptures du musée du South Kensington', *Gazette des Beaux Arts* (14: 1863), p. 458.
7.   Ibid.

Chapter 2
1.   Report from the Select Committee on the South Kensington Museum (1860), National Art Library (NAL), pp. 10–11.
2.   'Obituary of Sir Henry Cole', *The Times*, 20 April 1882.
3.   Ibid.

4. Henry Cole, speech on 16 November 1867, published in H. Cole, *Fifty Years of Published Work* (London: George Bell, 1884), p. 293. A more detailed discussion of Henry Cole's vision for the museum can be found in Anthony Burton, 'The Uses of the South Kensington Art Collections', *The Journal of the History of Collections*, 14 (2002), pp. 79–95.

5. Quoted in Marjorie Caygill and John Cherry (eds), *A. W. Franks. Nineteenth-century Collecting and the British Museum* (London: British Museum Press, 1997), p. 18.

6. J. Ruskin, Evidence to the 1857 National Gallery Site Commission; M. Arnold, *Culture and Anarchy*, edited by Jane Garnett (Oxford: Oxford University Press, 2006), p. 32.

7. J. C. Robinson, *An Introductory Lecture on the Museum of Ornamental Art of the Department*, quoted in Anthony Burton, 'The Uses of the South Kensington Art Collections', p. 85.

Chapter 3

1. *The Times*, 14 August 1848.

2. G. Reitlinger, *The Economics of Taste: The Rise and Fall of Picture Prices, 1760–1960* (London: Barrie and Rockliffe, 1961), vol. I. p. 30.

3. *New York Times*, 21 August 1897, p. BR7.

4. Gustav Waagen, *Works of Art and Artists in England*, translated into English by H. E. Lloyd (London: John Murray, 1838), p. 98.

5. *Punch*, 28 (June 1855), p. 129.

6. *The Catalogue of the Soulages Collection*, compiled by J. C. Robinson, with contributions from Henry Cole (London, 1856). Archive of the Victoria and Albert Museum; *The Graphic*, 1:1 (4 December 1869), p. 2.

7. Mabel Tylecote, *The Mechanics' Institutes of Lancashire and Yorkshire before 1851* (Manchester: Manchester University Press, 1957), pp. 69–75.

8. Ibid., p. 221.

9. It is difficult to be sure of accurate figures since membership, and the number of Institutes, as well as their nomenclature, was constantly changing. In addition to Mechanics' Institutes, there were, for example, Mutual Improvement Societies, Institutes for the Advancement of Knowledge, People's Colleges and Artisans' Institutes. W. A. Munford gives a figure of 610 institutions of the type of Mechanics' Institutes in England as well as twelve

in Wales, fifty-five in Scotland and twenty-five in Ireland, and Jeffrey Auerbach suggests there were 600 Institutes with half a million members. See W. A. Munford, 'George Birbeck and the Mechanics' Institutes', in *English Libraries 1800–1850: Three Lectures delivered at University College, London* (London: Lewis, 1958) and J. Auerbach, *The Great Exhibition of 1851: A Nation on Display* (New Haven and London: Yale University Press, 1999).

10. Report from the Select Committee on Arts and Manufactures, 1835–6.

11. John Ruskin, *Fors Clavigera*, letter 59, and *The Crown of Wild Olive*, Lecture IV (14 December 1869).

12. L. Jessop and N. T. Sinclair, *The Sunderland Museum: The People's Palace in the Park* (Tyne and Wear Museums, 1996), p. 5.

13. *Magazine of Art*, 1 (1878), p. 154.

14. James J. Sheehan, *Museums in the German art world from the end of the old regime to the rise of Modernism* (Oxford: Oxford University Press, 2000), p. 115.

15. Ibid., p. 116.

16. *Chambers Journal of Popular Literature, Science and Arts*, 335 (2 June 1860), p. 342.

17. *The Builder*, 22 June 1872.

18. John Ruskin, letter to Henry Swan, 13 May 1885, from transcript at the Ruskin Gallery, Sheffield.

19. *Sheffield Independent*, 11 August 1887, p. 6; *Art Union*, 8 (January 1846), p. 17. The 1872 Nottingham exhibition featured objects on loan from South Kensington; the Halifax exhibition was organized by the town's Mechanics' Institute.

20. Royal Commission on Scientific Instruction and the Advancement of Science (Devonshire Commission), 4th Report, (1874), p. 14.

21. For an excellent discussion of the eighteenth-century world of the gentleman's art club, see Peter Clark, *British Clubs and Societies 1580–1800: The origins of an associational world* (Oxford: Oxford University Press, 2000). Walpole is quoted on p. 78.

22. C. E. Clement and L. Hutton, *Artists of the Nineteenth Century and Their Works* (Boston: Houghton Mifflin, 1897), quoted in C. Denney, *At the Temple of Art: the Grosvenor Gallery, 1877–1890* (London: Associated University Press, 2000), p. 54.

23. Evidence to the 1857 National Gallery Site Commission, in *Collected Works*, 12, pp. 412–13.

24. Charles Dickens, *Little Dorrit*, edited by Stephen Wall and Helen Small (Harmondsworth: Penguin, 2003), p. 67.

25. 'The Mausoleum Marbles', *Chambers Journal of Popular Literature, Science and Arts*, 317 (28 January 1860), pp. 49–52 (p. 52); 'The British Museum', *The London Review of Politics, Society, Literature, Art and Science*, 29 (March 1862), pp. 304–5 (p. 304).

26. Cutting annotated 'Some Manchester News (Times?) 1845', in scrapbook of George Wallis, vol. II, p. 81, the Library of the Victoria and Albert Museum.

Chapter 4

1. J. C. Robinson, letter to William Maw Egley, October 1845, copy of Robinson papers, NAL: copies of much of Robinson's correspondence as well as articles, memos, etc. are deposited at the National Art Library, Victoria and Albert Museum, and were consulted there unless otherwise stated. Egley, a painter of miniatures, was one of Robinson's closest friends.

2. Quoted in A. McClellan, *Inventing the Louvre: art, politics and the modern museum in eighteenth-century Paris* (Berkeley: University of California Press, 1994), p. 98, a book which also gives an excellent account of the impulses behind the development of the Louvre.

3. Dominique Vivant-Denon, diplomat, courtier and director of the Louvre from 1802 to 1814, quoted in McClellan, *Inventing the Louvre*, p. 140.

4. John Ruskin, *Letters on Architecture and Painting, delivered at Edinburgh, November 1853* (London: Smith Elder, 1854), vol. I. p. 50.

5. J. C. Robinson, 'Our Public Art Museums. A retrospect', *The Nineteenth Century*, 42 (1897), p. 941.

6. Jules Janin, 'A Summer and A Winter in Paris', in George Newenham Wright, *France Illustrated*, vol. 4 (London: Peter Jackson, 1845–7), p. 170.

7. Richard Redgrave, one of Henry Cole's closest friends and allies, visited the apartment with Cole in 1855: see F. M. Redgrave, *Richard Redgrave: A memoir compiled from his diary* (London: Cassell, 1892), pp. 147–8.

8. Quoted in H. E. Davies, *The Life and Works of Sir John Charles Robinson, 1824–1913*, p. 14.

9. J. C. Robinson, letter to William Egley, August 1851.

10. This was during a later trip to Italy, in 1859, on behalf of the South Kensington Museum, at a period when armed battles were increasingly common. J. C. Robinson, letter to Henry Cole, 25 April 1859.

Chapter 5

1. Henry Morley, 'A House Full of Horrors', *Household Words*, VI (4 December 1852), pp. 265–70.
2. *Art Journal* (1855), pp. 150–52; J. C. Robinson's introduction to the *Catalogue of Decorative Art* (1855).
3. Quoted in Anthony Burton, *Vision and Accident: The Story of the Victoria and Albert Museum* (London: Victoria and Albert Museum, 1999), p. 38.
4. J. C. Robinson, letter to Henry Cole, 7 November 1855, Cole correspondence, NAL; *Building News*, 6 March 1857, p. 225.
5. J. C. Robinson, 'Our Public Art Museums: A Retrospect', *Nineteenth Century* (December 1897), p. 955.
6. J. C. Robinson, *Introductory Addresses on the Science and Art Department and the South Kensington Museum*, 5 (London, 1858), p. 23.
7. J. C. Robinson, letter to Henry Cole, 25 October 1855, Cole correspondence, NAL.
8. J. C. Robinson, *Catalogue of the Museum of Ornamental Art (Part 1)* (London, 1855), Introduction.
9. Charles Dickens, *Our Mutual Friend*, edited by Michael Cotsell (Oxford: Oxford University Press, 1998), p. 245.
10. Ibid., p. 223.
11. *The Builder* (19 April 1856), p. 213.
12. General Post Office salary from Hansard, Income Tax Bill, third reading, 12 March 1857 (HC DEB, 12 March 1857, vol. 144, cc2272–5); others from R. V. Jackson, 'The Structure of Pay in Nineteenth-Century Britain', *Economic History Review* 4 (1987), pp. 561–70.
13. J. C. Robinson, 'On Our National Art Galleries and Museums', *Nineteenth Century* (December 1892), p. 1022; J. C. Robinson, *Italian Sculpture of the Middle Ages and Period of the Revival of Art* (London: Chapman and Hall, 1862); J. C. Robinson, letter to Henry Cole, 2 May 1858, Cole correspondence, NAL.
14. *Athenaeum*, 7 September 1878.

15. Interview with an unnamed artist by Moncure D. Conway, *Harper's New Monthly Magazine*, 51 (October 1875), pp. 486–503.
16. *New York Herald*, (11 February 1871), n.p.
17. 'National Gallery', *Quarterly Review* (1859), p. 375.
18. J. C. Robinson, letter to Henry Cole, 17 December 1858, Cole correspondence, NAL.
19. J. C. Robinson, 'Our Public Art Museums: A Retrospect', *Nineteenth Century* (December 1897).
20. Ibid., p. 942.
21. Hansard's Parliamentary Debates, 3rd series, vol. 160, p. 1308.
22. *Journal of the Society of Arts*, 16 (1868), p. 179.
23. *Art Journal* (1865), pp. 281–2.
24. See Geoffrey Swinney, 'Museums, Audiences and Display Technology', University Museums in Scotland Conference, 2002.
25. Précis of the Minutes of the Science and Art Department, South Kensington Museum, 1852–3, p. 425.
26. J. C. Robinson, letter, unknown recipient, 18 March 1863.
27. Diary entry, 3 February 1863; quoted in Burton, *Vision and Accident*, p. 70.
28. See Burton, *Vision and Accident*, pp. 70–71.
29. *Art Journal* (1863), p. 230.
30. Précis of the Board Minutes of the Science and Art Department, 1863–1869, pp. 242–5.
31. For further details of the Select Committee, see Elizabeth Bonython, *The Great Exhibitor: The Life and Work of Henry Cole*, p. 235.
32. Museum minute note, 23 December 1867, quoted in Burton, *Vision and Accident*, p. 71.
33. Letter to J. C. Robinson, 4 January 1868, quoting Board Minute of 30 December 1867.
34. Letter to J. C. Robinson, 20 January 1868.
35. A. W. Franks, letter, 8 May 1878, British Museum, Department of Medieval and Later Antiquities.
36. 'The Apology of my Life', in Caygill and Cherry (eds), *A. W. Franks*, p. 318.
37. Ibid., p. 320.

Chapter 6
1. Layard made his comments when Robinson was being considered for the vacant post of Director at the National Gallery in 1871.

NOTES

Quoted in Helen Davies, *The Life and Works of Sir John Charles Robinson, 1824–1913* (Ph.D., University of Oxford, 1992), p. 67.

2. A pamphlet on Newton Manor written by Robinson for the Dorset Field Club in September 1896. Robinson Papers, NAL.

3. Ibid.

4. Marian Robinson, letter to Henry Cole, no date.

5. William Gladstone, letter to J. C. Robinson, 8 November 1869.

6. Princess Vicky's visit to Newton Manor is recorded, briefly, in the lengthy *Times* obituary for Robinson (11 April 1913), but few details are known. (Copies of Robinson Papers, NAL.) The young princesses were Charlotte, Victoria, Sophie and Margaret. There were four other children: the family's eldest son, Wilhelm, born in 1859, succeeded his father as Emperor in 1888.

7. No. 4 Account Book, in copies of Robinson papers, NAL; also from Davies (see note 1). The account book was kept (as with much of Robinson's paperwork) irregularly during 1877 and concerns paintings only. The extent of Robinson's dealing in other media can only be guessed at, bearing in mind the high levels of activity noted.

8. The University of Glasgow runs a project looking at the culture of exhibitions and art dealing in London between 1878 and 1909. See www.exhibitionculture.arts.gla.ac.uk

9. Obituary, *The Times*, 24 March 1894.

10. Ibid.

11. Museum minutes, May 1879, Robinson archives, Victoria and Albert Museum.

12. J. C. Robinson, letter to Philip Cunliffe-Owen, 15 May 1879, Robinson archives.

13. Museum minutes, May 1879, Robinson archives.

14. Museum minutes, December 1881; January 1882, Robinson archives.

15. J. C. Robinson, letter to Philip Cunliffe-Owen, 20 January 1881, Robinson archives.

16. J. C. Robinson, letter to Philip Cunliffe-Owen, 6 January 1881, Robinson archives.

17. J. C. Robinson, letter to Earl Spenser, January 1882, Robinson archives.

18. Cole died suddenly on 18 April 1882.

19. J. C. Robinson, letter to Philip Cunliffe-Owen, 6 January 1881, Robinson archives.

20. J. C. Robinson, 'On Our National Museums and Galleries', *Nineteenth Century* (December 1892), p. 1022.

Chapter 7

1. A note from Robinson's bank manager on 23 October 1912, six months before he died, gave the balance of his account as £573 2s 7d. Copy of the Robinson Papers, NAL. It was quite possible, of course, that he operated several accounts.
2. Robinson 'inherited' the position from Richard Redgrave (1804–88), a painter. He was Surveyor from 1856 until his retirement in 1880. He and Robinson knew each other well: Redgrave held a number of posts at the South Kensington Museum and the Science and Art Department, and was a staunch ally of Henry Cole.
3. Notes for a speech made by J. C. Robinson at the inauguration of the Whitworth Institute, undated. Copy of Robinson papers, NAL.
4. Ibid.
5. The negotiations were completed in July 1891, almost two years after the Institute first opened. See Ann Sumner, 'Sir John Charles Robinson: Victorian Collector and Connoisseur', *Apollo* (October 1989), pp. 226–30.
6. Obituary, *The Times*, 30 March 1911.
7. Obituary, *The Times*, 9 March 1911.
8. Memo from A. B. Skinner to C. Purdon Clarke, 7 August 1901, Robinson archive. Skinner, who entered South Kensington as a Junior Assistant in 1879, went on to succeed Purdon Clarke as Art Director in 1905, when Purdon Clarke left to become Director of the Metropolitan Museum in New York. He remained at the museum until 1908.
9. G. F. Waagen, 'Thoughts on the New Building to be Erected for the National Gallery of England', *Art Journal* (1853), p. 102.
10. Details of Robinson's dismissal as Surveyor can be read in a series of letters in the archives, and in *The Times* obituary. The Queen died at Osborne House on 21 January 1901, and Robinson was told of his dismissal at the end of February.
11. *Catalogue of a valuable collection of Drawings by Old Masters formed by a well-known amateur over the last 40 years*, Christie, Manson and Woods, 12 May 1902.
12. Obituary, *The Times*, 11 April 1913.

13. *History of the Victoria and Albert,* <http:/www.vam.ac.uk/
collections/periods_styles/features/history/history_buildling>

Chapter 8

1. Quotations, as well as details of the Schreibers' journeys, are
taken from Charlotte's entertaining and comprehensive journals
of collecting, published in 1911 in a two-volume edited version
by her third son Montague Guest and covering the years
1869–85. A later edited version, by her grandson, the Earl of
Bessborough, was published in 1950, giving more details of her
early life and first marriage. The original journal manuscripts
are in the National Library of Wales. References given here are
to the 1911 published version, unless otherwise stated: Journal,
1 June 1871.
2. Journal, 9 March 1871.
3. Journal, 25 April and 12 April 1871.
4. Journal, 28 May 1871.
5. Journal, 11 April 1871.
6. Journal, 3 June 1871.
7. Journal, 19 May 1871.
8. Baroness Staffe, *The Lady's Dressing Room,* translated by Lady
Colin Campbell (London: Cassell's, 1892), p. 125.
9. For a more comprehensive narrative of Charlotte's youth, see
Revel Guest and Angela V. John, *Lady Charlotte: A Biography of
the Nineteenth Century* (London: Weidenfeld and Nicolson, 1989).
10. See Guest and John, *Lady Charlotte,* p. 10.
11. Ibid., p. 18.
12. Journal, 1 February 1834, Bessborough edition.
13. Journal, 15 August 1833, Bessborough edition.
14. Journal, 15–18 August 1833, Bessborough edition.
15. Quoted in the Introduction to the Bessborough edition.
16. Journal, 11 January and 10 September 1837, Bessborough
edition.
17. Journal, 3 July 1838, Bessborough edition.
18. Journal, 4 November 1839, Bessborough edition.
19. Journal, 18 January 1853, Bessborough edition.

Chapter 9

1. Schreiber, Journal, 8 April 1873.

2.   Figures taken from *International Historical Statistics, Europe 1750–1988* (London: Palgrave Macmillan), pp. 665–9.

3.   J. C. Robinson, 'Our Public Art Museums: A Retrospect', in *Nineteenth Century* (December 1897), p. 956; see also Burton, *Vision and Accident*, pp. 98–9.

4.   Journal, 23 March 1874.

5.   Editor's note to Charlotte's Journal, vol. II, p. 334. Details of Duveen's life and business can be found in the biography of his son, Meryle Secrest, *Duveen: A Life in Art* (New York: Knopf, 2005).

6.   Journal, Introduction.

7.   Ibid.

8.   Thomas Babington Macaulay, *History of England*, vol. 5 (London: Puttnam, 1898), p. 66.

9.   C. Lamb, 'Old China', *The Last Essays of Elia* (Pennsylvania: Carey and Lea, 1823), pp. 194–204.

10. Maurice Jonas, *Notes of an Art Collector* (London: Routledge, 1907).

11. *Punch*, 21 (July 1851), p. 10.

12. 'Acute Chinamania', *Punch*, 'Almanack' 1875, 68 (17 December 1874), n.p. This was part of a series of satires by George du Maurier, who waged a long-running crusade against what he saw as the affectations of the Aesthetic movement and its taste for collecting china.

13. Joseph Marryat, *A History of Pottery and Porcelain, Medieval and Modern* (London: Murray, 1857); see also Clarissa Orr (ed.), *Women in the Victorian Art World* (Manchester: Manchester University Press, 1995).

14. Journal, Introduction, 14 March 1870 and 3 November 1874.

15. Journal, Introduction, and see also, for example, 27 May 1876.

Chapter 10

1.   Schreiber, Journal, 23 August 1869 and 8 March 1872.

2.   Jules Janin, 'A Summer and A Winter in Paris', in George Newenham Wright, *France Illustrated*, vol. 4 (London: Peter Jackson, 1845–7), p. 112.

3.   Journal, 2 October 1869 and 22 March 1870.

4.   Journal, 10 May 1872 and 8 April 1874.

5.   Quoted in Orr (ed.), *Women in the Victorian Art World*, p. 130.

6. The story of the gourd-shaped bottle is related by Montague Guest in the concluding notes to Charlotte's journals: 'The Adventures of a Bottle', vol. II, pp. 484–8, with additional material taken from Charlotte's daily entries.

7. For an excellent discussion of female art critics, see Pamela Gerrish Nunn, 'Critically Speaking', in Orr (ed.), *Women in the Victorian Art World* (Manchester: Manchester University Press, 1995), pp. 107–25. This comment is from Alice Oldcastle, quoted on p. 114.

8. Journal, 22 May 1869.

9. Journal, 8 March 1872.

10. Journal, 19 and 20 March 1880.

11. Journal, 23 September 1880.

12. Journal, 28 September 1880.

13. 'Economic and Social History: Industry and Trade, 1500–1880', *A History of the County of Warwick: Volume 7: The City of Birmingham* (1964), pp. 81–139.

14. Journal, 29 March 1884.

15. Journal, 9 June 1884.

16. Journal, 3 May 1884.

17. Journal, 18 November 1884.

18. Journal, 17 October 1885.

19. Journal, 13 November 1885.

20. The book on English fans was finished in 1888, followed two years later by a publication on European fans. Neither is now in print. The other Freewoman was Baroness Coutts, a banker's daughter and philanthropist.

Chapter 11

1. The portrait, now in the Liverpool Museum, is dated 1843, but a letter from the Royal Academy concerning the work is dated 9 May 1840, suggesting it was already in existence then. Mayer was born on 23 February 1803.

2. Letter from H. T. Kemball Cook to G. J. Binns, 19 June 1828, archives of Liverpool Museums. For the biographical information on Joseph Mayer and his collecting, I am indebted to the work of the National Museums and Galleries on Merseyside, and in particular *Joseph Mayer of Liverpool 1803–1886*, edited by Margaret Gibson and Susan M. Wright (London: Society of Antiquaries/National Museums & Galleries on Merseyside, 1988).

The majority of Mayer's papers are deposited with Liverpool City Archives or at Bebington Library.

3. Ibid.

4. Obituary, *Liverpool Daily Post*, 20 January 1866.

5. A. W. Franks, quoted Caygill and Cherry (eds), *A. W. Franks*, p. 169. The brooch has the accession number MLA 1856.7–1, 1461.

6. Joseph Clarke, letter to Joseph Mayer, October 1852.

7. Joseph Clarke, letter to Joseph Mayer, 19 October 1854.

8. Roach Smith, letter to Joseph Mayer, 12 December 1852; letter to Mayer, 11 April 1856.

9. For details of the Faussett collection, see Roger H. White, 'Mayer and British Archaeology', *Joseph Mayer of Liverpool 1803–1886*, edited by Margaret Gibson and Susan M. Wright.

10. Officers' Reports, 15 November 1853, British Museum Central Archive.

11. Joseph Mayer, letter to A.W. Franks, 24 November 1853 and 26 February 1854, BM (MLA) papers.

12. Roach Smith, letter to Joseph Mayer, 20 February 1856.

13. 'Antique Ivory Carving', *Art Journal* (1 October 1855), p. 276.

14. Joseph Clarke, letter to Joseph Mayer, 28 March 1868.

15. Joseph Clarke, letter to Roach Smith, 22 November 1856.

16. Joseph Mayer, letter to W. H. Rolfe, 8 September 1857.

17. See *Joseph Mayer of Liverpool 1803–1886*, pp. 95–6 for further details of the sale. Joseph Clarke, letter to F. W. Fairholt, 14 April 1859.

18. C. T. Gatty, *The Mayer Collection in the Liverpool Museum considered as an Educational Possession* (Liverpool Art Club, 1878), pp. 20–21.

19. A. H. Church, 'Josiah Wedgwood, Master Potter', *The Portfolio*, 3 (March 1894), p. 100.

Chapter 12

1. Mayer's contribution to the Great Exhibition was first prompted by a letter from Edward Hawkins, Keeper of Antiquities at the British Museum, 11 February 1850 and the pieces were listed in the official catalogue, pp. 674–5 (*Jury Reports*, III.520, class xxiii).

2. R. Lepsius, *Letters from Egypt, Ethiopia and the Peninsula of Sinai*, translated by L. and J. B. Horner (London, 1853), p. 41.

3. Joseph Mayer, letter to Roach Smith, 27 January 1882.

4. For these quotations and further information on John Tradescant, see the Ashmolean Museum's extensive web pages at www.ashmolean.org.

Chapter 13

1. *Exhibition of Art Treasures of the United Kingdom Manchester 1857, Report of the Executive Committee* (London: Longman, 1859), p. 3.
2. Ibid., p. 4.
3. Nathaniel Hawthorne, *English Notebooks* (6 September 1857), p. 332.
4. *Exhibition of Art Treasures of the United Kingdom Manchester 1857, Report of the Executive Committee*, p. 17.
5. Ibid., p. 31.
6. Quoted in Charles Saumarez Smith, *The National Gallery: A Short History* (London: Lincoln, 2009), p. 74.
7. *Exhibition of Art Treasures of the United Kingdom Manchester 1857, Report of the Executive Committee*, p. 20.
8. Nathaniel Hawthorne, *English Notebooks* (6 September 1857), p. 332.
9. The Duke's criticism may be apocryphal, but it amused Manchester commentators and so was frequently repeated; see, for example, *A Handbook to the Gallery of British Paintings in the Art Treasures Exhibition* (London, 1857), p. 3, and the *Manchester Guardian*, 5 May 1857.
10. Gustav Waagen, letter to Joseph Mayer, 18 August 1856.
11. J. B. Waring, 'Ceramic Art', *Art Treasures of the United Kingdom from the Art Treasures Exhibition, Manchester* (London: Day & Son, 1858), p. 31.
12. Gustav Waagen, *A Walk through the Art Treasures exhibition at Manchester under the guidance of Dr Waagen, Companion to the Official Catalogue* (London: John Murray, 1857), p. 74.
13. Roach Smith, letter to Joseph Mayer, 11 April 1856.
14. Minutes of the Library, Museum and Education Committee, 14 February 1867; quoted in Gibson and Wright (eds), *Joseph Mayer of Liverpool*, p. 20.
15. Joseph Clarke, letter to Joseph Mayer, 28 March 1868.

Chapter 14

1. The inscription on the bust of Peggy (Margaret) Harrison, now in the Walker Art Gallery (7610, *Foreign Catalogue*). Very little is known of her, or of her exact relationship with Mayer.
2. Elizabeth Meteyard, *The Life of Josiah Wedgwood* (London: Hurst and Blackett, 1865), vol. I, p. xiv.
3. Joseph Clarke, letter to Joseph Mayer, 8 August 1863.
4. Wilkie Collins, *The Woman in White*, edited by John Sutherland (Oxford: Oxford University Press, 1998), p. 176.
5. 'Chronic Chinamania (Incurable)', *Punch*, 'Almanack' 1875, 68 (17 December 1874), n.p; *Les Français Peints par Eux-mêmes*, *Encyclopédie Morale du Dix-neuvième Siecle* (Paris: Curmer), vol. I, p. 277.
6. 'To our reader', *The Connoisseur: A Collector's Journal and Monthly Review*, 1:1 (January 1895), pp. 5–6.
7. Freud, writing mostly at the beginning of the twentieth century, identified, for example, a biological drive which directly links collecting to sexual drive, while also identifying a resemblance to hunting and the display of trophies from the aggressive drive. More recently, Jean Baudrillard described collecting as 'a powerful mechanism of compensation during critical phases in a person's sexual development'. (Jean Baudrillard, 'The System of Collecting', in *The Cultures of Collecting*, edited by John Elsner and Roger Cardinal (London: Reaktion, 1994), pp. 7–24 (p. 9).)
8. Henry James, *The Portrait of a Lady*, edited by Nicola Bradbury (Oxford: Oxford University Press, 1995), pp. 328, 558, 386; George Meredith, *The Egoist*, edited by George Woodcock (Harmondsworth: Penguin, 1968), p. 138.
9. 'A Free Village Library', *The Standard* (1878), pp. 11–12.
10. H. Cunningham, *The Volunteer Force: A Social and Political History, 1859–1908* (London: Croon Helm 1975), p. 2.
11. Mayer's speech at a celebratory dinner after the opening of the Free Library, reported in the *Staffordshire Weekly Times*, 5 March 1870.
12. 'A Free Village Library', *The Standard* (1878), pp. 18–19.

Chapter 15

1. See the reminiscences of Dante Gabriel Rossetti's brother William, in *Dante Gabriel Rossetti: His Family-Letters Edited with*

a Memoir by William Michael Rossetti, 2 vols (London: Ellis and Elvey, 1895), vol. I. p. 28.
2. For details of this and other of Rossetti's demands, see George Charles Williamson, *Murray Marks and His Friends* (London, 1919).
3. Quoted in Williamson, *Murray Marks and His Friends*, p. 52.
4. *Times Literary Supplement* (12 June 1919).
5. T. Affleck Greeves, *A Guide to Bedford Park: the first garden suburb* (1893) (London: The Bedford Park Society, 2010).
6. Williamson, *Murray Marks and His Friends*, p. 13.

Chapter 16
1. Walter Sickert, 'Small Pictures', *The Speaker*, 2 January 1897.
2. 'The French Gallery', *The Times*, 8 April 1879, p. 4.
3. Williamson, *Murray Marks and His Friends*, p. 38.
4. *Exhibition Culture in London 1878–1908*, database, University of Glasgow, 2006; <http://www.exhibitionculture.arts.gla.ac.uk/>
5. Bernard Berenson, Italian Painters of the Renaissance (London: Phaidon Press, 1956), pp. ix, xii.
6. Schreiber, Journal, 26 February 1870.
7. Henry James, Preface to *The Portrait of a Lady* (1881). The fascination was two-way: Charles Dickens, for example, found an eager audience for his *American Notes*, published shortly after his first visit to the United States in 1842.
8. J. P. Morgan appears less than sympathetically in Richard Armour's 1953 satire *It All Started with Columbus*: 'Morgan, who was a direct sort of person, made his money in money. . . He became immensely wealthy because of his financial interests, most of which were around eight or ten percent. . . This Morgan is usually spoken of as "J.P." to distinguish him from Henry Morgan the pirate.'
9. The Pierpont Morgan Library in New York was made a public institution in 1924 by his son, J. P. Morgan; many of the gems were donated to the American Museum of Natural History in New York. Pierpont Morgan also left works from his collection to the Metropolitan Museum of Art and founded the Yale Babylonian collection with over 3,000 cuneiform tablets.
10. William Bode, *Die italienische Bronzestatuetten der Renaissance*, 3 vols (Berlin: B. Cassirer, 1907–12), vol. I, p. 3; quoted in Clive Wainwright, 'A Gatherer and Disposer of other men's stuffe:

Murray Marks, connoisseur and curiosity dealer', *Journal of the History of Collections* (2002), p. 171.

11. Ibid.

12. James McNeill Whistler, letters to F. R. Leyland, 2 and 9 September 1876 (University of Glasgow Transcription 08796; Manuscript division, Pennel-Whistler Collection PWC 6B/22/1).

13. There has been much writing and discussion about Leyland's Peacock Room and Whistler's contribution. For a detailed and authoritative account, see Linda Merrill, *The Peacock Room: A Cultural Biography* (New Haven and London: Yale University Press, 1998). The room is now on show, complete, at the Freer Gallery of Art in Washington.

14. In 1904, twelve years after Leyland's death, the room was bought intact by the American collector Charles Land Freer, who later founded the Freer Gallery of Art in Washington, and it was taken apart, shipped across the Atlantic and reinstalled at Freer's house in Detroit, where it was used to display his own collection of ceramics.

15. Quoted in Meryle Secrest, *Duveen: A Life in Art* (New York: Knopf, 2005), p. 29.

16. James Henry Duveen, *The Rise of the House of Duveen* (London and New York: Longmans, Green, 1957), p. 84.

Chapter 17

1. There is still much discussion among art historians about the exact number of works that can be accurately ascribed, either in whole or in part, to Leonardo da Vinci, but there are around fifteen paintings on panels, murals and drawings on paper which form the core of the accepted body of his work. The two most famous examples are, of course, the *Mona Lisa*, displayed in the Louvre, and *The Last Supper*, in the Convent of Santa Maria della Grazia, Milan.

2. We know few details about exactly where or from whom Marks acquired the bust.

3. The new firm of Marks, Durlacher Brothers gave up the Oxford Street shop in 1885 and moved to 23A Bond Street. By 1887, they had moved again, to 142 New Bond Street, and the Marks name had been dropped, although he was still a partner in the business.

4. 'The Newly-Discovered Leonardo', *Burlington Magazine*, 15, number 74 (1909), pp. 108–13. There was also a follow-up article

in the same magazine: 'The wax bust attributed to Leonardo', *Burlington Magazine*, 16, number 81 (1909), p. 123.

5. *New York Times*, 5 December 1909.

6. There are 351 letters from Marks to Bode, just covering the period from 1890 to 1910, all of which are in the Zentralarchiv der Staatlichen Museen in Berlin. The first publication was the two-volume catalogue for the Pierpont Morgan bronzes, already mentioned in Chapter 11; the second was a three-volume book on bronzes in general which Bode published between 1907 and 1912.

7. Quoted in 'Did da Vinci or R. C. Lucas create *Flora*', *The Times*, 5 December 1909.

8. Ibid.

9. *New York Times*, 5 December 1909.

10. See Francis H. Hinsley, *British Foreign Policy under Sir Edward Grey* (Cambridge: Cambridge University Press, 1977), p. 556.

11. Ibid.

12. Ibid.

13. See Kenneth Clark, *Leonardo da Vinci: An Account of his Development as an Artist* (Cambridge: Cambridge University Press, 1939). The Kaiser-Friedrich Museum in Berlin reopened in 2007 as the Bode Museum, with *Flora* prominently displayed in the lecture hall (room 220). Museum guides still refer to the origins of the work as a mystery, and the label hedges its bets, describing the sculpture as 'both attributed to Leonardo da Vinci or one of his apprentices and viewed as a forgery of the 19th century'.

14. Art Referees Report, 6 April 1864, Robinson Papers, NAL.

15. *Daily Telegraph*, 2 January 1885; quoted in Burton, *Vision and Accident*, p. 132.

16. Speech at the Birmingham School of Art, 1888, Robinson Papers, NAL.

17. Museum minutes, 29 March 1887, Robinson archives.

18. Wallis Budge, Keeper of Egyptian and Assyrian Antiquities at the British Museum from 1892 to 1924, in *By Nile and Tigris: a Narrative of Journeys in Egypt and Mesopotamia*, 2 vols (London: John Murray, 1920), p. 73.

19. A. W. Franks, letter to the British Museum, 7 October 1879.

20. Right Revd G. F. Browne, *The Recollections of a Bishop* (London, 1915), p. 209; quoted in Caygill and Cherry (eds), *A. W. Franks*, p. 78.

21. A. W. Franks, *Proceedings of the Society of Antiquaries*, IV (1859), pp. 246–50.

22. E. Renard, 'Die Kunsthistorische Ausstellung, Dusseldorf, 1902', in *Rheinlande: Monatschrift für deutsche Kunst* (1902), pp. 41–2.

23. Christie's London, '19th Century "Renaissance" Works of Art: A Question of Supply and Demand', *The Collection of the Late Baroness Batscheva de Rothschild* (14 December 2000), pp. 102–106.

24. Giovanni Morelli, *Italian Painters: Critical Studies of their Works* (London: John Murray, 1892–3).

25. The Reliquary came to the British Museum as part of the Waddesdon Bequest, left to the museum in 1898 by Baron Ferdinand de Rothschild. It was only in 1959, when the fake reliquary was brought to London and compared with the original, that the truth was finally established.

26. *Proceedings of the Society of Antiquaries of London*, 42 (1891), p. 254.

27. *Times Literary Supplement*, 12 June 1919.

28. Official statement concerning the Salting Bequest; see Williamson, *Murray Marks and His Friends*, p. 198.

29. Murray Marks, letter to Cecil Harcourt-Smith, 12 June 1916, Murray Marks archives, Victoria and Albert Museum. Marks assured the museum that his insurance would cover any losses.

Chapter 18

1. Charles Dickens, *Little Dorrit*, edited by Stephen Wall and Helen Small (Harmondsworth: Penguin, 2003), pp. 236–7.

2. Jane MacLaren Walsh, 'Legend of the Crystal Skulls', *Archaeology*, 61.3 (June 2008).

3. Thomas Hardy, *A Pair of Blue Eyes*, edited by Tom Dolin and Alan Manford (Oxford: Oxford University Press, 2005), p. 186.

4. For the biographical information on Stephen Wootton Bushell, I am indebted to the work of Professor Nick Pearce, in particular his lecture 'Collecting, Connoisseurship and Commerce: An Examination of the Life and Career of Stephen Wootton Bushell (1844–1908)', *Transactions of the Oriental Ceramic Society*, vol. 70 (2005–2006), pp. 17–25. For details of Bushell's appointment, see p. 18. Bushell's archives of correspondence are held at the Victoria and Albert Museum where they were consulted, unless otherwise stated.

5. Details of Bushell's discoveries, his study of cultural meanings and his evaluation of technique and craftsmanship are taken from his masterly two-volume work *Chinese Art*, first published in 1904 and 1906 as a handbook to the Chinese collections at the Victoria and Albert. Despite being written in Bushell's old age, it retains the excitement of his early explorations and demonstrates the breadth and thoroughness of his understanding: S. W. Bushell, *Chinese Art*, 2 vols (London: Victoria and Albert Museum, 1904 & 1906), p. 10; pp. 240–1.

6. Mary Crawford Fraser, *A Diplomat's Wife in Many Lands* (New York: Dodd, Mead, 1910). See also Pearce, 'Collecting, Connoisseurship and Commerce', pp. 18–19.

7. Ibid., p. 19.

8. From an account by William Henry Seward, who went on to become US Secretary of State under Abraham Lincoln and Andrew Johnson. *William H. Seward's Travels Around the World* (New York, 1873), p. 135.

9. Bushell, *Chinese Art*, Introduction, p. 1.

10. Ibid., p. 22.

11. Shirley Gordon, 'Demands for the Education of Girls, 1790–1865' (MA, University of London, 1950), pp. 188–9.

12. H. E. Davies, *The Life and Works of John Charles Robinson* (Ph.D., University of Oxford, 1992), p. 46.

13. S. W. Bushell, letter to Philip Cunliffe-Owen, 20 August 1880, Bushell archives.

Chapter 19

1. For an account of Townsend's career, see G. Townsend, *Memoir of the Rev. Henry Townsend* (Exeter: James Townsend, 1887). Details of the early history of Exeter Museum are from G. T. Donisthorpe, *An Account of the Origin and Progress of the Devon and Exeter Albert Memorial Museum* (Exeter: Exeter and Plymouth Gazette, 1868), p. 24.

2. Quoted in George Robertson, *Traveller's Tales: narratives of home and displacement* (London: Routledge, 1994), p. 168.

3. See Kate Hill, *Culture and Class in English Public Museums 1850–1914* (Aldershot: Ashgate, 2005), p. 75.

4. Many acquisitions were noted with pride in local papers. See L. Jessop and N. T. Sinclair, *Sunderland Museum: The People's Palace in the Park* (Sunderland: Tyne and Wear Museums, 1996), p. 40;

The Exeter Flying Post, 6 April 1870. Details of other objects are taken from unpublished accession notes in local museums.

5.   *A Guide to the Exhibition Galleries of the British Museum* (London, 1899), pp. 98–101.

6.   *Illustrated London News*, 8 May 1886.

7.   *The Orientalist* (1869), quoted in J. Jones, 'Fugitive Pieces', *Guardian*, 25 September 2003.

8.   *Handbook for Travellers: Baedeker* (Leipzig: Baedeker 1885), pp. 278–80.

9.   Bushell, *Chinese Art*, vol. 2, p. 34.

10.   Sir Rutherford Alcock, *The Capital of the Tycoon: A Narrative of Three Years' Residence in Japan* (London: Longman Green, 1863), vol. I, p. xix. Alcock (1809–95) was, like Bushell, a physician by training. He had previously worked in China, having been appointed Consul at Foochow in 1844. During his ministry in Japan, he was reputedly the first foreigner to climb Mount Fuji in 1860. From 1865 to 1871, he returned to China, where he was British Minister in Peking, working of course with Bushell.

11.   Leigh Hunt, 'The Subject of Breakfast Continued.–Tea-drinking', *London Journal* (9 July 1834), p. 113.

12.   *Harper's New Monthly Magazine*, 51 (October 1875), p. 658.

13.   *Catalogue of Chinese Objects* (London, 1872), p. 57. See also the discussion of Eastern art in 'The Empire of Things: Engagement with the Orient', *A Grand Design: The Art of the Victoria and Albert Museum* (London: V&A Publications, 1997).

14.   A. W. Franks, letter to General Alexander Cunningham, 21 February 1881; quoted in Caygill and Cherry (eds), *A. W. Franks*, p. 259.

15.   A. W. Franks, letter to Colonel Sir C. Euan Smith, 26 May 1891.

16.   S. W. Bushell, letter to Philip Cunliffe-Owen, 9 February 1882, Bushell archives.

17.   S. W. Bushell, letters to Philip Cunliffe-Owen, 23 February 1882, 13 November 1882, Bushell archives.

18.   S. W. Bushell, *Chinese Art*, vol. 1, Preface.

19.   Fraser, *A Diplomat's Wife in Many Lands*, p. 111.

Chapter 20

1.   S. W. Bushell, *Chinese Art*, vol. 1, p. 94. There were all kinds of early-nineteenth-century explanations for 'magic' mirrors. Some investigators claimed a copy of the mirror's back design

was drawn on the face and then concealed by polishing; others that the phenomenon was caused by variations in the mirror's curvature. More recent research suggests that there may have been several methods of producing the mirrors, and that variations in the bronze caused by punching, stamping and polishing may all have produced an effect.

2. Bushell, *Chinese Art*, vol. 1, p. 115.
3. Ibid.
4. Bushell, *Chinese Art*, vol. 2, p. 17.
5. Lacquering is an ancient technique for laying down extremely thin layers of a natural varnish made from the sap of the lacquer tree.
6. Bushell, *Chinese Art*, vol. 1, pp. 39, 47, 49.
7. Bushell, *Chinese Art*, vol. 1, pp. 50–51.
8. Figures given by Chen Mingjie, Director of the Imperial Summer Palace, Bejing, in the state-run *China Daily* newspaper, 19 January 2010.
9. By 1874, Salting's collection had completely outgrown the space in his London home and he lent large numbers of pieces to South Kensington. When he died in 1909, he left a huge bequest to the museum which was displayed in separate Salting galleries.
10. Obituary, *New York Times* (23 November 1894), p. 9.
11. Born in Worcester, James Callowhill studied at the Worcester School of Art, before working at the Worcester Royal Porcelain Works from 1853. In New York, during the 1880s, he worked for the Faience Manufacturing Company at Greenport, Brooklyn.
12. Obituary, *New York Times* (23 November 1894), p. 9.
13. S. W. Bushell, letter to H. R. Bishop, 23 April 1889. On his death, Bishop left his collection to the Metropolitan Museum of Art in New York, and the letters with Bushell are held there as part of the Jade Correspondence.
14. H. R. Bishop, letter to S. W. Bushell, 27 February 1891.
15. Preface, *The Bishop Collection: Investigations and Studies in Jade* (New York: privately printed, 1906).
16. S. W. Bushell, letter to H. R. Bishop, 24 July 1892.
17. W. G. Gulland, an art historian, observed in 1898 that the Chinese interest in porcelain stemmed largely from 'the object of making large profits' from the fashionable market. See Nick Pearce, *Photographs of Peking, China 1861–1908* (New York: Edwin Mellen, 2005), p. 61.

18. See Pearce, *Photographs of Peking*, pp. 60–61.
19. *The I.G. in Peking: Letters of Robert Hart, Chinese Maritime Customs, 1868–1907* (Cambridge, Mass., 1975), vol. 2, p. 877, letter 827.
20. Note in the file, November 1898, Bushell archives.
21. Museum minute, 16 January 1899, Bushell archives.
22. Ibid.
23. S. W. Bushell, letter to Purdon Clarke, 25 November 1898.
24. Minute note, 18 February 1899, Bushell archives.
25. Minute note, 8 April 1909, Bushell archives.

Epilogue

1. See Burton, *Vision and Accident*, p. 122.
2. Some of Charlotte's pieces remain on display, however, at the heart of the V&A's Ceramics Galleries, and modern technology has even made it possible to glimpse a shadow of the past by virtually re-creating the original collection. Although the pieces on exhibition are still integrated with objects from all kinds of other sources, the Schreiber name is resolutely attached to everything from the original bequest, both on display and in store, and from online records it is possible to bring them together again. Those who want to see exactly what it was that Charlotte sought out so energetically can use searches and keywords to dip back into the past and assemble details and images of her bequest. Although it is unlikely that we will ever again be able to view all the objects together in a real space, breathing their collective connection to history, this virtual exercise can at least give a glimpse of the original magnificence of the Schreiber collection.
3. The fully restored sarcophagus is on display in the World Museum, Liverpool, alongside other of Mayer's pieces, identifiable from the letter M prefixing the acquisition number.
4. D. B. Elliott, *Charles Fairfax Murray: The Unknown Pre-Raphaelite* (London: Book Guild, 2000), p. 89.
5. See Ann Sumner, 'Sir John Charles Robinson: Victorian Collector and Connoisseur', *Apollo* (October 1989), pp. 226–30.

Select Bibliography

Alcock, Rutherford, *The Capital of the Tycoon: A Narrative of Three Years' Residence in Japan* (London: Longman Green, 1863)

Altick, Richard, *The Shows of London* (Cambridge, Mass. and London: Harvard University Press, 1978)

Appadurai, Arjun, *The Social Life of Things: Commodities in Cultural Perspective* (Cambridge: Cambridge University Press, 1986)

Auerbach, Jeffrey A., *The Great Exhibition of 1851: A Nation on Display* (New Haven and London: Yale University Press, 1999)

Baker, Malcolm, and Brenda Richardson (eds), *A Grand Design: the Art of the Victoria and Albert Museum* (London: V&A Publications, 1997)

Barlow, Paul (ed.), *Governing Cultures: Art Institutions in Victorian London* (Aldershot: Ashgate, 2000)

Bennett, Tony, *The Birth of the Museum: History, Theory, Politics* (London and New York: Routledge, 1995)

Belk, Russell W., *Collecting in a Consumer Society* (London and New York: Routledge, 2001)

Belk, Russell W., and Melanie Wallendorf, 'Of Mice and Men: Gender, Identity and Collecting', in *The Material Culture of Gender; the Gender of Material Culture*, edited by Katherine Martinez and Kenneth L. Ames (Hanover and London: University Press of New England, 1997), pp.7–27

Black, Barbara J., *On Exhibit: Victorians and their Museums* (Charlottesville and London: University Press of Virginia, 2000)

Bonython, Elizabeth, *The Great Exhibitor: The Life and Work of Henry Cole* (London: Victoria and Albert Museum, 2003)

Bowlby, Rachel, *Just Looking: Consumer Culture in Dreiser, Gissing and Zola* (New York: Methuen, 1985)

Briggs, Asa, *Victorian Things* (London: Batsford, 1988)

Burton, Anthony, *Vision and Accident. The Story of the Victoria and Albert Museum* (London: Victoria and Albert Museum, 1999)

Burton, Anthony, 'The Uses of the South Kensington Art Collections', *Journal of the History of Collections*, 14 (2002), pp. 79–95

Bushell, Stephen Wootton, *Chinese Art*, 2 vols (London, 1904 & 1906)

Caygill, Marjorie, 'Rare Birds: Female Collectors and the British Museum', *Creating a Great Museum: Early Collectors and the British Museum*, Columbia University, The Fathom Archive

Caygill, Marjorie, and John Cherry (eds), *A. W. Franks. Nineteenth-century collecting and the British Museum* (London: British Museum Press, 1997)

Clifford, James, *The Predicament of Culture: Twentieth-century Ethnography, Literature and Art* (Cambridge Mass. and London, Harvard University Press, 1988)

Cole, Henry, *Fifty Years of Published Work* (London: George Bell, 1884)

Colley, Linda, *Britons. Forging the Nation 1707–1837* (New Haven and London: Yale University Press, 1992)

Crary, Jonathan, *Techniques of the Observer: On Vision and Modernity in the Nineteenth Century* (Cambridge Mass. and London: MIT Press, 1990)

Cumming, Elizabeth, and Wendy Kaplan, *The Arts and Crafts Movement* (London: Thames and Hudson, 1991)

Davies, H. E., *The Life and Works of Sir John Charles Robinson, 1824–1913* (Ph.D. diss., University of Oxford, 1992)

Donisthorpe, G. T., *An Account of the Origin and Progress of the Devon and Exeter Albert Memorial Museum* (Exeter: Exeter and Plymouth Gazette, 1868)

Eastlake, Charles, *Hints on Household Taste in Furniture, Upholstery and Other Details* (London: Longmans, 1868)

Eatwell, Ann, 'Borrowing from Collectors: the role of the Loan Formation of the Victoria and Albert Museum and its Collection (1852–1932)', *Journal of the Decorative Arts Society*, 24 (2000)

Elsner, John, and Roger Cardinal (eds), *The Cultures of Collecting* (London: Reaktion, 1994)

Flint, Kate, *The Victorians and the Visual Imagination* (Cambridge: Cambridge University Press, 2000)

Forgan, Sophie, 'The Architecture of Display: Museums, Universities and Objects in Nineteenth-century Britain', *History of Science 32* (1994), pp. 139–62

Fraser, Mary Crawford, *A Diplomat's Wife in Many Lands* (New York: Dodd, Mead, 1910)

Gibson, Margaret, and Susan M. Wright (eds), *Joseph Mayer of Liverpool 1803–1886* (London: Society of Antiquaries and National Museums and Galleries on Merseyside, 1988)

Gloag, John, *Victorian Taste: Some Social Aspects of Architecture and Industrial Design, from 1820–1900* (London: A & C Black, 1962)

Greenhalgh, Paul, *Ephemeral Vistas: The Expositions Universelles, Great Exhibitions and World's Fairs, 1851–1939* (Manchester: Manchester University Press, 1988)

Greenwood, Thomas, *Museums and Art Galleries* (London: Simpkin and Marshall, 1888)

Guest, Revel, and Angela V. John, *Lady Charlotte: A Biography of the Nineteenth Century* (London: Weidenfeld and Nicolson, 1989)

Gunn, Simon, *The Public Culture of the Victorian Middle Class, Ritual and Authority and the English Industrial City, 1840–1914* (Manchester: Manchester University Press, 2000)

Harrison, J. F. C., *A History of the Working Men's College 1854–1904* (London: Routledge & Kegan Paul, 1954)

Haywood, Ian, *The Revolution in Popular Literature: Print, Politics and the People 1790–1860* (Cambridge: Cambridge University Press, 2004)

Herrmann, Frank, *The English as Collectors. A Documentary Chrestomathy* (London: Chatto and Windus, 1972)

Hill, Kate, *Culture and Class in English Public Museums 1850–1914* (Aldershot: Ashgate, 2005)

Hilton, Tim, *The Pre-Raphaelites* (London: Thames and Hudson, 1970)

Impey, Oliver, and Arthur MacGregor (eds), *The Origins of Museums: The Cabinet of Curiosities in Sixteenth- and Seventeenth-Century Europe* (Oxford: Clarendon, 1985)

Inkster, Ian, 'The Social Context of an Educational Movement: A Revisionist Approach to the English Mechanics' Institutes, 1820–1850', *Oxford Review of Education*, 2 (1976), pp. 277–307

Jessop, L., and N. T. Sinclair, *Sunderland Museum: The People's Palace in the Park* (Sunderland: Tyne and Wear Museums, 1996)

Jones, Mark (ed.), *Why Fakes Matter: Essays on Problems of Authenticity* (London: British Museum Press, 1993)

Jones, Maurice, *Notes of an Art Collector* (London: Routledge, 1907)

Jones, Robert W., *Gender and the Formation of Taste in Eighteenth-Century Britain. The Analysis of Beauty* (Cambridge: Cambridge University Press, 1998)

Karp, Ivan, and Steven Levine (eds), *Exhibiting Cultures: The Poetics and Politics of Museum Display* (Washington and London: The Smithsonian Institution Press, 1991)

Kidd, Alan, and David Nicholls (eds), *Gender, Civic Culture and Consumerism: Middle-class Identity in Britain 1800–1940* (Manchester: Manchester University Press, 1999)

Kowaleski-Wallace, Elizabeth, *Consuming Subjects: Women, Shopping and Business in the Eighteenth Century* (New York: Columbia University Press, 1997)

Leapman, Michael, *The World for a Shilling: How the Great Exhibition Shaped a Nation* (London: Headline, 2001)

Levine, Philippa, *The Amateur and the Professional: Antiquarians, Historians and Archaeologists in Victorian England 1838–1886* (Cambridge: Cambridge University Press, 1986)

Logan, Thad, *The Victorian Parlour* (Cambridge: Cambridge University Press, 2001)

MacCarthy, Fiona, *William Morris: A Life for our Time* (London: Faber, 1994)

McClellan, Andrew, *Inventing the Louvre: Art, politics and the modern museum in eighteenth-century Paris* (Berkeley and Los Angeles: University of California Press, 1994)

MacDonald, Sharon (ed.), *The Politics of Display: Museums, Science, Culture* (London and New York: Routledge, 1998)

Macleod, D. Sachko, *Art and the Victorian Middle Class* (Cambridge: Cambridge University Press, 1996)

Merrill, Linda, *The Peacock Room: A Cultural Biography* (New Haven and London: Yale University Press, 1998)

Meteyard, Elizabeth, *The Life of Josiah Wedgwood* (London: Hurst and Blackett, 1865)

Miller, Andrew, *Novels behind Glass: Commodity Culture and Victorian Narrative* (Cambridge: Cambridge University Press, 1995)

Munford, W. A., 'George Birbeck and the Mechanics' Institutes', in *English Libraries 1800–1850, Three Lectures delivered at University College London* (London: Lewis, 1958), pp. 33–58

Orr, Clarissa, *Women in the Victorian Art World* (Manchester: Manchester University Press, 1995)

Pearce, Nick, 'Collecting, Connoisseurship and Commerce: An Examination of the Life and Career of Stephen Wootton Bushell (1844–1908)', *Transactions of the Oriental Ceramic Society*, vol. 70 (2005–2006), pp. 17–25

Pearce, Nick, *Photographs of Peking, China 1861–1908: Through Peking with a Camera* (New York: Edwin Mellen, 2005)

Pearce, Susan M., *Interpreting Objects and Collections* (London and New York: Routledge, 1994)

Pearce, Susan M., *On Collecting: An Investigation into Collecting in the European Tradition* (London and New York: Routledge, 1995)

Pomian, Krzystof, *Collectors and Curiosities: Paris and Venice 1500–1800* (Cambridge: Polity Press, 1990)

Richards, Thomas, *The Commodity Culture of Victorian England: Advertising and Spectacle 1851–1914* (London and New York: Verso, 1991)

Robertson, George, *Travellers' Tales: Narratives of home and displacement* (London: Routledge, 1994)

Robinson, John Charles, *The Catalogue of the Soulages Collection, compiled by J. C. Robinson, with contributions from Henry Cole* (London: South Kensington Museum, 1856)

Robinson, John Charles, *Italian Sculpture of the Middle Ages and Period of the Revival of Art* (London: Chapman and Hall, 1862)

Robinson, John Charles, 'Introductory Address on the Science and Art Department and the South Kensington Museum', *On the Museum of Art* (London: South Kensington Museum, 1858)

Ruskin, John, *The Works of John Ruskin*, edited by E. T. Cook and Alexander Wedderburn, Library edition, 39 volumes (London: George Allen, 1903–12)

Schreiber, Charlotte, *Journals of Lady Charlotte Schreiber by Mr Montague Guest* (London and New York: John Lane, 1911)

Secrest, Meryle, *Duveen: A Life in Art* (New York: Knopf, 2005)

Steegman, John, *Victorian Taste: A Study of the Arts and Architecture from 1830–1870* (Cambridge, Mass.: MIT Press, 1970)

Stewart, Susan, *On Longing: Narratives of the Miniature, the Gigantic, the Souvenir, the Collection* (Baltimore: The Johns Hopkins University Press, 1984)

Sumner, Ann, 'Sir John Charles Robinson: Victorian Collector and Connoisseur', *Apollo* (October 1989), pp. 226–30

Townsend, G., *Memoir of the Rev. Henry Townsend* (Exeter: James Townsend, 1887)

Tylecote, Mabel, *The Mechanics' Institutes of Lancashire and Yorkshire before 1851* (Manchester: Manchester University Press, 1957)

Vergo, Peter, *New Museology* (New York: Routledge, 1992)

Vincentelli, Moira, *Women and Ceramics: Gendered Vessels* (Manchester: Manchester University Press, 2000)

Wainwright, Clive, *The Romantic Interior: The British Collector at Home 1750–1850* (New Haven and London: Yale University Press, 1989)

Wainwright, Clive, 'A Gatherer and Disposer of other men's stuffe: Murray Marks, connoisseur and curiosity dealer', *Journal of the History of Collections*, 14, 1 (May 2002)

Waring, J. B., 'Ceramic Art', *Art Treasures of the United Kingdom from the Art Treasures Exhibition, Manchester* (London: Day & Son, 1858)

Waterfield, Giles, *Palaces of Art: Art Galleries in Britain 1790–1990* (London: Lavenham Press, 1991)

Whitehead, Christopher, *The Public Art Museum in Nineteenth-Century Britain* (Aldershot: Ashgate, 2005)

Williamson, G. C., *Murray Marks and His Friends* (London: John Lane, 1919)

Wright, Susan M., *The Decorative Arts of the Victorian Period* (Avon: Bath Press; The Society of Antiquaries, 1989)

Yanni, Carla, *Nature's Museums: Victorian Science and the Architecture of Display* (Baltimore: The Johns Hopkins University Press, 1999)

Index